Yemen

a Lonely Planet travel survival kit

Pertti Hämäläinen

Yemen

3rd edition

Published by
Lonely Planet Publications
Head Office: PO Box 617, Hawthorn, Vic 3122, Australia
Branches: 155 Filbert St, Suite 251, Oakland, CA 94607, USA
10 Barley Mow Passage, Chiswick, London W4 4PH, UK
71 bis rue du Cardinal Lemoine, 75005 Paris, France

Printed by
Colorcraft Ltd, Hong Kong

Photographs by
Bethune Carmichael
Pertti Hämäläinen

Front cover: Shihara (Bethune Carmichael)
Spine: Minaret in San'a (Bethune Carmichael)

First Published
January 1988

This Edition
January 1996

Although the authors and publisher have tried to make the information as accurate as possible, they accept no responsibility for any loss, injury or inconvenience sustained by any person using this book.

National Library of Australia Cataloguing in Publication Data

Hämäläinen, Pertti
Yemen – a travel survival kit

3rd ed.
Includes index.
ISBN 0 86442 319 5.

1. Yemen – Guidebooks. I. Title. (Series: Lonely
Planet travel survival kit)

915.3304

text © Kwayyis International Oy 1996
maps © Lonely Planet 1996
photos © photographers as indicated 1996
climate charts compiled from information supplied by Patrick J Tyson, © Patrick J Tyson, 1996

Pertti Hämäläinen

Pertti Hämäläinen was born in Turku, Finland, and lives in the capital of the country, Helsinki. Pertti has an MSc in Applied Mathematics from the University of Turku and runs a consulting company of his own, specialising in local area networks and data communications.

He was introduced to travelling by his first wife Tuula, in the late '70s. Her great interest in Islamic architecture led them to southern Arabia in 1984 and many times since. Pertti is a member of die Deutsch-Jemenitische Getsellschaft eV and the American Institute for Yemeni Studies.

From the Author

Updating this edition was postponed by more than a year because of the unfortunate civil war of 1994.

Increasingly unnerving reports emerged from the country for almost a year prior to the war, including stories of hijacked foreign oil workers and armed highway robberies. Consequently, we were somewhat concerned about what was awaiting us.

However, the tragic war had apparently been necessary to seal the unification of the country. We found a relaxed people busy trying to put their former divisions behind. Not that their problems were all solved – far from it – but the admirable optimistic Yemeni nature was certainly visible again. Paradoxically, Yemen is still one of the most enjoyable destinations on the Arabian Peninsula.

A year's break from the flow of Western tourists has also had positive effects. While Yemenis warmly welcome foreign travellers, misbehaved crowds can drastically alter local attitudes. A Western man drinking whisky or a woman showing her bare arms is deeply offensive to the Yemenis. When visiting Yemen, please go out of your way to respect the values of your hosts.

We've received lots of readers' letters: from travellers rushing through the country in a couple of weeks to those who have lived and worked in Yemen for several years. Thanks to everyone who took the time to write with information, comments and sug-gestions (your names are listed below), and apologies to those we've left out.

More than to any single individual, thanks should go to the friendly people of Yemen, especially the Yemeni children whose assistance and friendliness provided much inspiration for the writing of this book.

Florence Akst (UK), Jürgen Ammann (B), Patrick Boman (F), Paul Bowater (NZ), Tim Brice (UK), Michael Crouch (US), Franco Furlan (I), Massimo Furnari (I), Mark A. Griffin (UK), Antonella Guanziroli (I), Eddy Hefford (UK), Baldur Hoffmann (G), Steffen Kiel (D), Patrice Legeay (F), Marco Livadiotti (Y), Stephen Manser (Y), Maik Marahrens (D), Giuseppe Mazzocchi (I), Barrie McCormick (UK), Irene Metrat (F), Paolo Milani (I) Mrs Robert Ian Mill (UK), W Nabers (NI), Tim Payne (UK), Stephen Porter (UK), Piero & Josiane Rovinelli, Jeff Rowell (C), Yvonne Saardson, Amy Sandridge (SA), Martin Svmok (CZ), Paulo Torrelli (I), Doug Traverso (UK), Marianne Tudor-Craig (UK), F Vanderhof (NI), Ruud Verkerk (NI), Peter Verlinden (B), Dr Luigi Vigliotti (I), Laura Wedeen (USA), Prof. Brian Windley (UK) and Dr Andy Yelland (UK).

A – Australia, B – Belgium, C – Canada, CZ – Czech Repubic, E – Egypt, F – France, G – Germany, I – Italy, NI – Netherlands, NZ – New Zealand, S – Switzerland, SA – South Africa, UK – United Kingdom, US – United States of America, Y – Yemen

Dedication This book is dedicated to the memory of my mother.

From the Publisher

This 3rd edition of *Yemen* was edited at Lonely Planet's Melbourne office by Rachel Scully with assistance from Bethune Carmichael. It was proofed by Samantha Carew, Paul Smitz and Susan Noonan. Samantha took the book through production. Sally Jacka was responsible for the mapping, assisted by Greg Herriman, Chris Klep, Louise Keppie and Paul Clifton. Sally also handled the design and layout. Simon Bracken designed the cover with assistance from Adam McCrow and Paul. Thanks to Greg Herriman and Tuula-Maria Merivuori for the illustrations; to Diana Saad for invaluable editorial guidance; and to Kerrie Williams for compiling the index.

Warning & Request

Things change – prices go up, schedules change, good places go bad and bad places go bankrupt – nothing stays the same. So if you find things better, worse, cheaper, more expensive, recently opened or long since closed please write and tell us and help make the next edition better.

Your letters will be used to help update future editions and, where possible, important changes will also be included in a Stop Press section in reprints.

We greatly appreciate all information that is sent to us by travellers. Back at Lonely Planet we employ a hard-working readers' letters team to sort through the many letters we receive. The best ones will be rewarded with a free copy of the next edition or another Lonely Planet guide if you prefer. We give away lots of books, but, unfortunately, not every letter/postcard receives one.

Contents

Map Legend

BOUNDARIES

.... International Boundary
.... Disputed Boundary
.... Regional Boundary

ROUTES

.... Freeway
.... Highway
.... Major Road
.... Unsealed Road or Track
.... City Road
.... City Street
.... Minor Street
.... Railway
.... Walking Track
.... Walking Tour
.... Ferry Route
.... Cable Car or Chairlift

AREA FEATURES

.... Parks
.... Built-Up Area
.... Old Town Area
.... Market
.... Cemetery
.... Reef
.... Beach or Desert
.... Rocks

HYDROGRAPHIC FEATURES

.... Coastline
.... River, Creek
.... Intermittent River or Wadi
.... Rapids, Waterfalls
.... Lake, Intermittent Lake
.... Canal
.... Swamp

SYMBOLS

✪ CAPITAL	.... National Capital	
◉ Capital	.... Regional Capital	
🕸 CITY	.... Major City	
● City	.... City	
● Town	.... Town	
● Village	.... Village	
■ ▼	.... Place to Stay, Place to Eat	
☎ ⚑	.... Cafe, Pub or Bar	
✉ ☎	.... Post Office, Telephone	
❶ ❸	.... Tourist Information, Bank	
◕ 🅿	.... Transport, Parking	
🏛 ⛺	.... Museum, Youth Hostel	
⌖ ⚐	Caravan Park, Camping Ground	
✚ ✚	.... Church, Cathedral	
☾ ✡	.... Mosque, Synagogue	
卍 卐	Buddhist Temple, Hindu Temple	
✛ ★	.... Hospital, Police Station	

○ ⚑	.... Embassy, Petrol Station	
✈ ✝	.... Airport, Airfield	
⌷ ✿	.... Swimming Pool, Gardens	
❖ 🐘	.... Shopping Centre, Zoo	
← A25	One Way Street, Route Number	
⛩ ⚓	.... Palace, Monument	
⛩ ▣	.... Castle, Tomb	
⌒ ⌂	.... Cave, Hut or Chalet	
▲ ※	.... Mountain or Hill, Lookout	
⛭ ☡	.... Lighthouse, Shipwreck	
)(◎	.... Pass, Spring	
🐚 ⚑	.... Beach, Surf Beach	
∴	...... Archaeological Site or Ruins	
	.... Existing Ancient or City Wall	
	.... Site of Ancient or City Wall	
	...... Cliff or Escarpment, Tunnel	
	.... Railway Station	

Note: not all symbols displayed above appear in this book

Introduction

Yemen made a brief appearance in the Western media from May to July 1994, when a two-month civil war raged in this south Arabian country. For most of the audience this was another easily forgotten episode starring another Third World country hardly ever heard of.

This was history repeating itself. During the past decades, Yemen has often made negative headlines in the Western press: revolutions and civil wars in the 1960s; border clashes, assassinations of presidents and the hosting of Palestinian and Western terrorists in the 1970s; and economic catastrophes and riots in South Yemen in the 1980s.

Only recently, at the turn of the decade, a remarkable piece of positive news went largely unnoticed. The Republic of Yemen was formed on 22 May 1990 by the spectac-ular merger of North Yemen (the Western-oriented Yemen Arab Republic, or YAR) and South Yemen (the People's Democratic Republic of Yemen, or PDRY, 'the first and only Marxist Arab state in the world'). The event peacefully ended a bitter separation that had lasted for hundreds of years. The unification, which preceded that of Germany by more than four months, became possible when the PDRY modified its leftist doctrines following the global demise of Soviet influ-ence and financial support in the late 1980s.

However, the world took hardly any notice, even though the country was a member of the United Nations Security Council at that time. In the ensuing months, during the crisis leading up to the Gulf War, Yemen attracted a lot more attention because of its awkward attempts to strike a balance

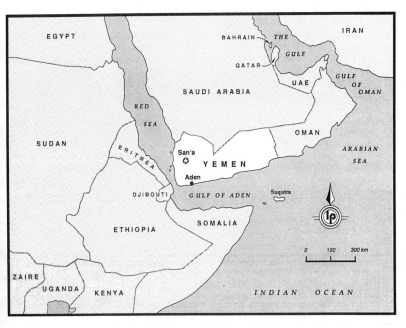

between the UN resolutions against Iraq and the powerful notion of the all-embracing Arab Nation. After the defeat of Iraq, Yemenis were left to struggle through their national unification on their own, without sympathy or aid from outside.

Indeed, good news about the country has been rare: a few cultural and historical TV documentaries and books produced by people who had visited the and fallen in love with the country, presented an unlikely wonderland of biblical-oriental flavour. It has been aptly said that only a few explorers, dreamers and scientists visited the region before the 1980s, with the dreamer's viewpoint most apparent in works describing Yemen.

However, this image of Yemen conveys only a tiny fraction of the truth. For most visitors, Yemen is a very positive experience – even seasoned travellers are impressed by the country's beauty and friendliness.

The separation that preceded unity was nothing new: the historical Yemen was never a single state. The region inhabited by people who today regard themselves as Yemenis ranges from the Najran oasis and 'Asir area in south-western Saudi Arabia to the Mahra region in easternmost Yemen. In ancient times, around 1000 BC, this part of southern Arabia was divided into warring kingdoms and, later, into rival Islamic imamates. Moreover, the region fell frequently (though always temporarily) under foreign occupation. The last colonists withdrew only in the 20th century – Turkey from the north in 1918 and Britain from the south in 1967.

While foreign powers left their mark on Yemeni society, they were unable to uproot the original culture – a culture that had survived intact under the rule of local sheikhs

and imams for more than a thousand years. Although this policy had the positive effect of reinforcing national identity during and after occupation, it also isolated the Yemeni people from the outside world. Today, Yemenis uphold their cultural heritage with pride while striving furiously to modernise their society. It is the privilege of today's traveller to witness the endurance of the world of 'a thousand and one nights' in the grip of the abrupt modernisation that began barely a generation ago.

Yemen is more accessible today than it has ever been. Modern air traffic has put this remote area within everybody's reach and recent developments have removed most of the barriers erected by local rulers to keep outsiders away. Military clashes have only caused temporary setbacks, and reconciliation has put an end to crises which in other countries, would be likely to drag on for years. After the revolutions, the two Yemens started to welcome tourists in the late 1970s. While the flow is not yet a flood – a few tens of thousands visitors each year – it has grown steadily.

The Yemenis have even tried to develop a flourishing tourist industry but their attempts have largely failed, at least when compared to countries such as Morocco, Tunisia and Egypt. There are no holiday resorts in Yemen, Western-style hotels are rare and many attractions are inaccessible. If you're an individual traveller looking for adventure, you'll enjoy Yemen as it is today. If, however, you're after an inexpensive tour within a comfortable framework, you should look elsewhere. Don't expect to make your way through Yemen without some difficulties – but, then, it certainly is worth the effort.

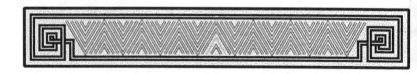

Facts about the Country

HISTORY

Yemen is one of the oldest inhabited regions in the world. According to tradition, Shem, the son of Noah, founded the city of San'a (hence the improbable name 'Sam City'). Whether this is folklore or historical truth, we do know that Yemen's history dates from the very dawn of humankind. In the 1970s and 80s Soviet archaeological teams found similar Palaeolithic flint stone tools on both sides of the Bab al-Mandab Strait, suggesting that the first human migrations reached Yemen from the Olduvai culture in East Africa about 40,000 years ago.

Pre-Islamic Kingdoms

The earliest known civilisations in southern Arabia existed more than a thousand years before Christ. The kingdoms around the region occupied by today's Yemen sometimes existed side by side, sometimes one after another.

Very different information can be gathered on when these kingdoms were founded or destroyed, their inhabitants, their means of livelihood and the faiths they professed. Modern Western research has concentrated on cultures closer to European ancestry, and much of Arabia's prehistory has remained obscure despite the many ruins, inscriptions and other information about them. And although the Yemenis are proud of their ancient origins, local research concentrates on Yemen's Islamic period because research into pre-Islamic history is discouraged.

The Frankincense Trade The ancient kingdoms based their existence first on agriculture in the valleys and deltas of the greater wadis and, second, on trade. The trading communities were able to accumulate greater wealth than those communities engaged only in agricultural activities; the settlements along the main trade routes became mightier than the others – or perhaps it was the mighty kingdoms that dictated the course of the trade routes.

In ancient times, the most important commodities produced in southern Arabia were myrrh and frankincense, the resins of trees of the Commiphora and Boswellia genera growing only on the southern coastlands of Arabia and on the northern coast of the Horn of Africa. (Frankincense is produced today in western Oman, Yemen and, to a lesser extent, northern Somalia.) These aromatics were highly valued everywhere in the civilised world for the pleasant odours they release when burned as incense. They had great ritual value in many different cultures – from the Egyptian to the Greek and Roman. The oldest Egyptian scriptures describing frankincense date from the 15th century BC; myrrh oil was also used to perfume royal mummies. As the Christmas gospel shows, the Jews, too, valued myrrh and frankincense as highly as gold.

These commodities were carried by sea or by land; and the land routes through Arabia were the first ones to be used on a large scale. Originally, donkeys and mules predominated but, around the 11th century BC, the introduction of camels made transport much more effective. Camels can walk much longer distances without rest or water than donkeys and this meant that the routes could be plotted through dry lands, with only a few stopping places needed for food, water and lodging along the way. From the important port of Qana on the shore of the Arabian Sea, in the midst of the frankincense production area, it became possible to reach Ghaza, Egypt, in a matter of two months.

The caravans were huge and a single convoy could involve thousands of camels. In addition to fragrances, they carried commodities, such as gold and precious items, that came to Qana by sea from India. As demand for myrrh and frankincense increased around the Mediterranean, all kinds of trade flourished.

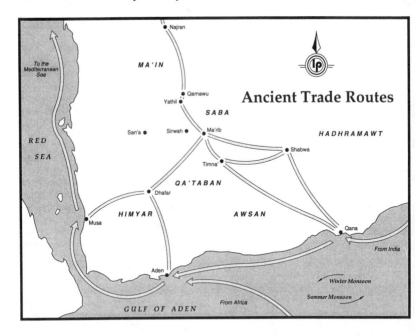

Saba & Its Rivals In southern Arabia, several mighty kingdoms along the trade route rose and fell within a period of 1500 years. The most important of these was Saba, which existed for at least 14 centuries from about 1000 BC. Sometimes it was conquered but, most of the time it was the strongest power in the region.

Saba had been a flourishing kingdom long before written history began. It is first mentioned in the Old Testament description of the visit of the Sabaean queen Bilqis to King Solomon. Obviously, it had became necessary to cement friendly relations between the two powerful rulers, one of whom controlled the southern end of the frankincense road while the other held sway at the northern end. The mission was successful and precious presents were exchanged in an abundance that aroused great admiration among the Biblical chroniclers. Arabian tradition has it that Menelik, the son of King Solomon and Queen Bilqis, became the ruler of Aksum,

today's Ethiopia. His ancestry was then claimed by all Ethiopian leaders up to Haile Selassie.

Saba was initially founded in Sirwah but the capital was eventually moved to Maryab, later to be known as Ma'rib. Both towns still exist in present-day Yemen as small villages. The location was strategic, since the natural land route from Qana to the north through the Hadhramawt valley eventually crossed this region. The agricultural wealth of Saba was based on the famous dam in Ma'rib, which was built in the 8th century BC and stood for well over a thousand years.

However, Saba had powerful rivals along the trade route: Najran (in what is now southern Saudi Arabia), Ma'in, with its capitals Qarnawu and Yathil (in today's al-Jawf Province), Awsan, with its capital Miswar (suspected to have been in the Shabwa Governorate of today, although the location of site is disputed), Qa'taban, with its capital Timna' (near present-day Bayhan in the

Shabwa Governorate), and Hadhramawt, with its capital Shabwa (in the Hadhramawt and Shabwa governorates). Between the 7th century BC and 2nd century AD, these states alternately fell under Sabaean rule and freed themselves from it.

In the 2nd century BC, still another rival kingdom emerged: Himyar, with its capital Dhafar (now a small village in the Ibb Province). The Himyarites lived a little way off the traditional incense route but were closer to the Bab al-Mandab Strait. By 50 AD, Himyar controlled the south-westernmost part of the peninsula and was established as an important regional power.

What helped the rise of Himyar over Saba was the progress of science in the Mediterranean area. In the 1st century AD, a seafarer called Hippalus (some sources cite him as a Greek, others as a Roman) not only discovered the secrets of monsoon winds but developed a practical application for them. 'Let the summer monsoon blow the ships south of the Red Sea and all the way east to India, and the winter monsoon bring them back', he said. According to the nature of each ship's business, it could stop in the port of al-Muza north of Bab al-Mandab (probably near present-day al-Makha) or in the port of Aden a little further off. The Himyarites, who controlled the ports in south-western Arabia, benefited from this development while the Sabaeans were faced with a decline in land-based trade.

External threats were not uncommon either. The Romans tried to conquer Arabia Felix between 25 BC and 24 BC, sending an expedition led by Aelius Gallus, but were forced to retreat after reaching the walls of Ma'rib. In the 2nd century AD came the Ethiopians, who managed to occupy the region for a few decades. Meanwhile, the old Sabaean dynasty had been replaced by new rulers from the Yemeni highlands and, around 190 AD, the new Sabaean rulers were able to throw out the Ethiopians.

By the end of the 3rd century AD, Himyar had again risen to power and this situation lasted until the Ethiopians returned in 525 AD. Many important developments occurred in the region during this second period of Himyarite rule: the old gods of Saba were forgotten with the conversion of the Himyar kings to Christianity and Judaism. These religions had greatly intensified their missionary activities in southern Arabia with the weakening of the once mighty Kingdom of Saba. The Ethiopians were Christian too, and many Christian churches were built in the 4th to 6th centuries AD.

The rise of Christianity on the shores of the Mediterranean also had a remarkable impact on life in southern Arabia. Christians did not want to use 'pagan' ritual fragrances, so the importance of the frankincense trade gradually diminished. This trend culminated in 395 AD when Theodosius ruled that Christianity was to be the state religion of the Roman Empire, thus completely halting the flow of frankincense to what had been its main area of consumption.

The Sabaean Kingdom thus faced a decline in the foundations of its wealth and the deterioration of its traditional social base. Under these circumstances, maintenance of the great Ma'rib dam was neglected and it broke several times during the first few centuries AD. In 570 AD, the year Muhammad was born, the dam broke for the last time and the inhabitants abandoned Ma'rib, and settled in new locations across the Arabian Peninsula.

The year 570 AD is called 'the year of the elephant' because of a third important event: the Ethiopians, whose warring troops had based their superiority on elephants, were at last defeated. But the Himyarites did not benefit from the victory, since they had achieved it by allying themselves with the Persians; by 575 AD, the Persians had managed to subdue this region, as they had already done across the rest of the peninsula.

Medieval Islamic Yemen
In 628 AD, Badhan, the Persian governor of Yemen, converted to Islam and the whole of Yemen soon followed. The expansion of Islam in Yemen, as elsewhere in the Arabian Peninsula, was rapid because the local strongmen – the sheikhs – always had their

whole tribes converted with them; the new religion thus quickly spread from the top of society to the very bottom. Prominent Yemenis visited the Prophet Muhammad, and the newly established Islamic centre was quick to send preachers and missionaries to guide the new converts along the righteous path. It was during the Prophet's lifetime, in the early 630s, that the first Yemeni mosques were built in San'a, in al-Janad and near Wadi Zabid. The first two still stand today and the third later served to mark the site of the city of Zabid.

At the southern edge of the Islamic Empire, Yemen was soon divided into provinces that actively participated in spreading the Islamic revolution. In 632 AD, the year that the Prophet died and the rule of the first orthodox caliphs began, the Yemenis sent more than 20,000 troops to serve in the army of Caliph Abu Bakr and to bring Islam into the area now occupied by Syria and Iraq. That same year, Yemen was divided into three provinces: San'a, al-Janad and Hadhramawt.

Further developments within the Islamic Empire caused Yemen's importance to wane, especially when the empire's capital was moved away from the Arabian Peninsula. Soon after the Umayyad Caliphate was founded in 661 AD, the capital was moved to Damascus, leading to the definition of Yemen as one province of the empire. When the Abbasid caliphs seized power in 750 AD, they moved the capital to Baghdad and in 812 AD made Yemen one of their provinces. As a result of these developments, Yemen saw numerous small, short-lived, semi-independent states and kingdoms – a situation that makes a condensed account of Yemen's medieval history seem very fragmented.

The Ziyadids In 819 AD, the tribes in southern Tihama revolted against the Abbasid governor in San'a. The governor appointed an able man, Muhammad ibn Ziyad, to settle the dispute and become the new governor. In 820, ibn Ziyad founded the town of Zabid near the famous Mosque of Abu Musa bin Asha'ir and, eventually, he made his realm virtually independent. The dynasty founded by Muhammad ibn Ziyad lasted for approximately two hundred years but gradually declined under his successors.

Ibn Ziyad turned the al-Asha'ir Mosque into a 'university', which was to be one of the most important centres of Sunni teaching in the Islamic world for hundreds of years. The Zabid university was reportedly in operation as late as the 18th century but, today, only the al-Asha'ir Mosque remains.

The Zaydis In 897 AD, a descendant of the Prophet, Yahya bin Husayn bin Qasim ar-Rassi, was called from Madina to mediate a war between the Hashid and Bakil tribes in northern Yemen. He founded the dynasty that was to last longest in Yemen – the Zaydi dynasty of Sa'da.

Yahya bin Husayn preached the Shi'a teachings of Islam, claiming that the Muslims should be ruled only by men from an unbreakable line of infallible imams descended from the Prophet's cousin and son-in-law, 'Ali. The teachings of Yahya made a clear distinction between what belonged to the state and what was private, both materially and spiritually, and placed great emphasis on the art of war. These principles greatly contributed to the formation of an exceptionally stable state and sustained the Zaydi dynasty which, during the centuries, controlled various regions around Sa'da and was only temporarily conquered by foreigners.

The Zaydi state was at its largest from 1918 to 1962, when it was simply called Yemen. The 1962 revolution replaced imamic rule with a secular government, ending a 1000-year era in Yemeni history.

The Najahids & Sulayhids In 1012, the Ziyadid dynasty of Zabid ended when its last ruler, ibn Salama, died and left an infant successor. After the ensuing power struggle, an Ethiopian slave called Najah rose to power in Zabid. He ruled for 40 years and founded a dynasty carrying his name.

Meanwhile, in the mountainous Haraz district, a devout Muslim by the name of 'Ali as-Sulayhi slowly gathered followers and, in

1046, founded the Sulayhid state on Jabal Masar. Over the next 17 years, this state extended its influence across Yemen. 'Ali as-Sulayhi belonged to the Fatimid faction of the Ismaili group, part of the Shi'a sect of Islam (see Population & People, later). Today, the remaining Yemeni Ismailis live near Manakha, close to the original birth-place of the Sulayhid state.

The Najahids and the Sulayhids struggled for control of the southern part of Yemen for the next 100 years. Often, the Najahids ruled the Tihama in summer, while the Sulayhids descended from the mountains during the cool winters to tax the Tihamese. In the mountains, Sulayhid rule remained largely undisputed.

In 1067, an exceptional thing happened in the history of Islamic Yemen: a woman became the head of the Sulayhid state when King Mukarram's widow, Queen Arwa bint Ahmad, succeeded her husband to the throne. Queen Arwa, an extraordinarily wise and well-educated woman, ruled the Sulayhid state until her death in 1138. She moved the capital south from San'a to the town of Jibla (near Ibb), where the Mosque of Queen Arwa still stands in honour of her memory.

The Ayyubids & Rasulids After the demise of the Najahid and Sulayhid dynasties, there was a brief era of disorder in Yemen. For about 50 years (from 1173) most of the country, excluding the Zaydi state in the north, was ruled by the Egyptian Ayyubids. The Egyptians were not particularly successful in controlling such a remote area and, finally, in 1229, the country was left to the rule of one al-Mansur 'Umar ibn 'Ali ibn Rasul, a man of Turkoman origin. The Rasulid dynasty had its capital in Ta'izz and remained in power for more than two centuries, until the year 1454. At times, the dynasty ruled most of Yemen, from Hadhramawt to Mecca.

These times were beneficial for the university of Zabid, which was at its most active during the Ayyubid and Rasulid

eras. Thousands of Yemeni and foreign students attended the more than 200 schools of the town.

The Tahirids & Kathiris The Rasulids were followed briefly by the house of at-Tahir from Lahej, who ruled the south-western part of the country from 1454 to 1526. In the Hadhramawt area, a new dynasty, the Kathiris, rose to power in the 15th century. They managed to stabilise the region and it remained under their rule for centuries. The Kathiri state still existed at the time of the 1967 revolution, though much weakened by then.

With the Zaydis, these dynasties were the last Yemeni houses to rule the country. From about 1500, Yemen was confronted by a totally new phenomenon: European colonialism.

Modern Yemen

In 1507, the Portuguese annexed the island of Suqutra in the Arabian Sea. This event was not only important for the island (the population of which still is predominantly Christian), but it was also the start of an ever-increasing European presence in southern Arabia. This development was made possible partly by the general rise of Europe and partly by the gradual degradation of local Yemeni powers, who had exhausted themselves over centuries of hostilities. While there were still important centres of Islamic learning in Yemen, the region as a whole had already ceased to play a major role in world history. The emerging colonial powers of Europe soon recognised the strategic importance of this slowly developed vacuum and were eager to take advantage of the opportunity.

The First Ottoman Occupation The Portuguese tried to extend their presence to mainland Yemen in 1513, when Affenso d'Albuquerque, who had led the invasion of Suqutra, attacked Aden. His attempt failed, however.

The Portuguese operations prompted the Mameluke rulers of Egypt to protect their interests in the southern Red Sea. They sent a large fleet to Yemen and succeeded in taking control of most of the Tihama and large portions of the highlands. However, they too were unable to conquer Aden. The Mamelukes were supported by Ottoman Turks, who equipped them with modern firearms.

In 1517, the Mamelukes in Egypt were themselves dethroned by the Ottomans. The Ottomans, too, soon managed to conquer most of Yemen: Ta'izz in 1545, Aden in 1547 and San'a in 1548. This was the beginning of the first period of Ottoman rule in Yemen – an era that lasted for a century.

Although the Ottoman occupation was a difficult time for Yemen, the period also saw important economic developments. The coffee trade, which had started in the late 1400s, greatly expanded under Turkish rule. The town of al-Makha on the southernmost shore of the Red Sea became the most important coffee port in the world and, in 1618, English and Dutch traders opened coffee factories in al-Makha to refine coffee grown in the Yemeni highlands.

The Ottoman occupation ended in 1636 when the Zaydi imams finally fulfilled their dream of freeing all of Yemen from Turkish oppression.

Zaydi Rule (1636-1849) The prospects for the newly expanded Zaydi state seemed glorious indeed in the 17th and early 18th centuries. The realm extended from Hadhramawt in the east to 'Asir in the north and the coffee trade boomed in an unprecedented way. Belgian, French and Danish merchants were actively trading in al-Makha and, by around 1720, Yemen virtually had a monopoly on the world coffee market – merchants found it hard to meet the demand for coffee.

The situation changed rapidly, however, when the coffee plant was smuggled out of Yemen and replanted in Brazil and Indonesia. Demand for Yemeni coffee soon vanished after 1740. In addition, the Zaydis faced growing internal and external threats to their authority. The Saudi sheikhs invaded

the northern Tihama several times during this period; the most serious assault occurred between 1805 and 1809 when the Wahhabis (from what is now central Saudi Arabia) looted the Tihama down to al-Hudayda, leaving hardly a house standing.

In the south, the Shafa'i sultan of Lahej, who belonged to the Abdali tribe, put an end to Zaydi domination in 1728. The Zaydi imams lost control of Aden and the coasts of the Arabian Sea. This event can be seen as the beginning of a process that culminated in the eventual formation of the two independent Yemeni states in the 20th century.

British Occupation of Southern Yemen In the 19th century, the British expressed growing interest in the region. Already in 1799, they had annexed the island of Perim near Bab al-Mandab and, in 1839, they conquered Aden. By 1843, Aden had become a fortress belonging to the British Raj in India. It was not only seen as an important port on a major sea route but was also highly valued for the artesian wells in Sheikh Othman, which provided plentiful supplies of drinkable water. The Kuria Muria islands were occupied in 1854.

A friendship treaty between Britain and the Sultan of Lahej was signed in 1857. Moves towards further colonisation of southern Yemen continued in the 1870s when Britain, worried by the Turkish advance in the north, signed more and more 'protection' treaties with local sheikhs. In addition to the sultanate of Lahej, 20 small states or sheikhdoms in the Adeni hinterlands and on the island of Suqutra signed 'peace and friendship' treaties with Great Britain between 1880 and 1914, thus gradually forming what was to be known as the South Arabian Protectorate of Great Britain. The line between Turkish Arabia and British Arabia was drawn in 1905 and, with minor modifications, this so-called 'Violet Line' was to mark the boundary between the North and South Yemeni states of the 20th century.

Up to the 1950s, areas around Aden continued to be added to those under British control, with the eastern parts of the region

BETHUNE CARMICHAEL

BETHUNE CARMICHAEL

BETHUNE CARMICHAEL

BETHUNE CARMICHAEL

Faces of Yemen

Goat herder on Jabal Sabir, Ta'izz

BETHUNE CARMICHAEL

SAUDI ARABIA

Khamis Musayt

Abha

Narjan

Umm Layla

Jizan

Suq at-Talh

Sa'da

Suq al-'Inan

Midi

Harad

Al-Hazm al-Jawf

Shihara

Huth

Dhi Bin

Baraqish

Suq al-Khamis

Khamir

Rayda

Az-Zuhra

Kuhlan

Hajja

'Amran

Ma'rib

Al-Luhayya

Al-Qanawis

Kawkaban

Sirwah

Kamatan As-Salif

Al-Marwit

At-Tawila

Thilla

Shibam

SAN'A

Hajar Kuhlan (Timna')

Shabwa

Az-Zaidiya

An-Nabi Shu'ayb (3660m)

Hadda

Eastern Desert

Bajil

Manakha

Nuqub

Al-Marawi'a

As-Sukhna

Dhawran

Ma'bar

Harib

Bayhan

Hajar bin Hamid

Al-Hudayda

Al-Mansuriya

Hammam 'Ali

Baynun

Dhamar

'Ataq

RED SEA

Bayt al-Faqih

Zabid

Yarim

Rada'

Habban

'Aza

Mayfa

Hanish Islands

Hays

Al-'Udayn

Dnafar

Ibb

Hammam Damt

Al-Baydha

Lawdar

Mukayras

Al-Khawkha

Mudhaykhira

Jibla

Al-Janad

Qa'taba

Adh-Dhala'

Suq adh-Dhabab

TA'IZZ

Jabal Sabir (3006 m)

Al-Habilayn

Al-Makha

Yifrus

Ar-Rahidah

Kirsh

Shuqra

At-Turba

Lahej (Al-Hawta)

Zinjibar (Abyan)

Aseb

Shaykh Uthman

ADEN

ERITREA

Perim

Al-Burayqah (Little Aden)

DJIBOUTI

Bab al-Mandab

GULF OF ADEN

DJIBOUTI

44° E

46° E

ELEVATION	
	2500 m
	2000 m
	1000 m
	500 m
	0

SAUDI ARABIA

OMAN

The Empty Quarter)

• Thamud

Ghubbat al-Qamar

• Al-Ghayda

16° N

Qabr Nabi Allah Hud •

Tarim •

Wadi *Hadramaut*

Say'un •

Shibam •

Al-Qatn •

Al-Huraydha •

Al-Hajjarayn •

Qishn •

Sayhut •

Ghayl Ba' Wazir •

Al-Hami •

Ash-Shihr •

Riyan •

Al-Mukalla •

Burum •

Bir 'Ali •

14° N

YEMEN

0   50   100 km

ARABIAN SEA

SUQUTRA

Qalansiya •   Hadibu •

12°30 N

54° E

Same scale as main map

12° N

48° E   50° E   52° E

Say'un, Wadi Hadhramawt   BETHUNE CARMICHAEL

People of Yemen

the last to join. In the end, British South Arabia consisted of the Aden Colony, the Western Protectorate and the Eastern Protectorate.

The Second Ottoman Occupation The Turks returned to Yemen in 1849, first occupying the Tihama as a result of skirmishes with the British and the Egyptians. After the opening of the Suez Canal in 1869, the Turks were able to greatly strengthen their presence in the region. In 1871, they occupied Ta'izz, in 1872 San'a and finally, in 1882, even Sa'da, the Zaydi capital. From 1901 to 1905, the borders between Turkish and British spheres of influence were defined and the 1905 border agreement between the colonial powers drew the line that was later established as the boundary between the two Yemens.

Although the second Turkish occupation involved all of Yemen not under British rule, the power of the Turks was certainly not undisputed. The Turkish administration was notorious for mismanagement and oppression; local sheikhs frequently rebelled against the foreign authorities and several mountain fortresses were never conquered by the Turks. Constant resistance effectively prevented Turkey from founding a stable province in Yemen.

In 1904, the leadership of the Zaydis passed to Yahya ibn Muhammad, the son of Imam Muhammad ibn Yahya, from the highly respected Zaydi family of Hamid ad-Din. Imam Yahya quickly established himself as the undisputed leader of the Yemenis, organised a most efficient insurrection against the Turks and, by 1905, had succeeded in conquering almost all the Turkish garrisons. The Turks quickly deployed over 40,000 men to recapture the country and fighting continued until a peace treaty was signed in 1907. In the treaty, Turkey agreed to begin fundamental administrative reform in Yemen.

Although a framework for peaceful coexistence had been agreed between Imam Yahya and the Turks, another source of rebellion arose – the 1909 uprising of several

North Tihama tribes under the leadership of Sayyid Muhammad al-Idrisi, who was to play an important part in the subsequent developments. In 1910, Imam Yahya's troops in the highlands also took up arms after finding out that the Turks were unwilling to meet their treaty obligations.

In 1911, however, the Turks succeeded in reoccupying the garrisons seized by Imam Yahya. Negotiations between the warring parties produced the Treaty of Da''an, which gave Imam Yahya and his Zaydi rule certain autonomy in the Yemeni highlands. This treaty was observed until the end of the second Ottoman occupation.

Meanwhile, hostilities between the Turks and the Idrisi forces continued in the Tihama, with an increasing number of players becoming involved before and during WW I. During the Turko-Italian War (1911-1912), all the Tihama ports were bombed by the Italians, who dreamed of making the Red Sea an Italian lake. In 1915, the Anglo-Idrisi Treaty guaranteed the Idrisi forces some support from the British in Aden. Imam Yahya remained neutral in the Turko-British conflict.

By the time the Turks finally retreated from Yemen in 1919, WW I had stripped the Ottoman state of its imperial status. The country was left to Imam Yahya, who became king of Yemen and, in the Lausanne Treaty of 1923, Turkey officially relinquished all territories in the Arabian Peninsula.

The Imamate of Yemen The problems of the newly established Yemeni state, the Kingdom of Yemen, were still not over. Idrisi forces continued to occupy much of the Tihama and it was not until 1925 that Imam Yahya was able to seize al-Hudayda. From there, the imam's troops rapidly advanced north of Midi, very near the present border between Yemen and Saudi Arabia.

The declining Idrisi state had to ally itself with the head of the evolving Saudi state, ibn Sa'ud, whose goal was to annex the former Idrisi state (that is, all of the Tihama to the north of al-Hudayda). To the north, Imam

Yahya had similar plans, claiming the 'Asir region. The conflict culminated in the Saudi-Yemeni war of 1934. The Saudi forces rapidly advanced to al-Hudayda, forcing the imam to accept peace on Saudi terms. The Ta'if Treaty left 'Asir and Najran temporarily under Saudi rule for 40 years – still the status quo.

After the Turkish retreat, the British did not lose interest in the northern part of Yemen. The forces opposing Imam Yahya could freely use Aden as their stronghold and, in 1948, a group led by Sayyid Abdullah al-Wazzir succeeded in killing Imam Yahya. However, the imam's eldest son, Ahmad, was able to throw the insurgents out of the country.

Imam Ahmad moved the Yemeni capital from San'a to Ta'izz and cautiously began to open the country. Imam Yahya had secured his power by keeping Yemen in a state of extreme isolation and backwardness; Imam Ahmad used foreign aid to start some development programmes and also established Yemen's first diplomatic relations with countries such as Britain, the USA and Egypt in 1951 and the Soviet Union in 1956.

The Imamate of Yemen remained, however, an underdeveloped country. By the end of Imam Ahmad's rule, there were still no paved roads, no Yemeni doctors (and only a handful of foreign ones), no schools other than Koran schools (which were attended by only one child in 20), no legislation except the Koranic Shari'a law, and no factories. Disease abounded, with around 50% of the population suffering from some kind of venereal disease and 80% from trachoma. In 1962, Yemen was probably the most medieval country in the world.

The 1950s saw frequent border disputes between Yemen and the Aden Protectorate. In 1958, Imam Ahmad sought protection from Cairo. These negotiations led to the foundation of the United Arab States, a union of Yemen and the United Arab Republic (Egypt and Syria). The pact had little practical significance and was formally dissolved in 1961 by the United Arab Republic (UAR). Nevertheless, it certainly served to promote Egyptian interests when revolution broke out in Yemen one year later.

Birth of the Yemen Arab Republic (YAR)

Although Imam Ahmad had faced considerable resistance, including an assassination attempt in 1961 in which he was wounded in the shoulder, he stayed in power until his death in September 1962. He was briefly succeeded by his son, Crown Prince Muhammad al-Badr, but a group of army officers led by Colonel Abdullah Sallal started a revolution after only a week, actively backed by troops from the UAR. Many of the officers had studied abroad and were influenced by Nasserite Arab Nationalism. The new regime founded the Yemen Arab Republic (YAR). The YAR was soon recognised by the USA and the USSR and, early in 1963, became a member of the United Nations.

Despite this, Muhammad al-Badr was not defeated. He fled to the northern mountains and began a bitter, eight-year civil war backed by Britain and Saudi Arabia. The Republicans, supported by Egypt and the Soviet Union, were able to hold their position against the Royalists but could not achieve a final victory. The battles were often fierce, with heavy casualties on both sides; it has been estimated that up to 4% of the North Yemeni population was killed in the hostilities and Egypt lost almost 20,000 troops – more than in the 1967 war against Israel!

The prolonged war did not yield any positive results for the Nasserites and, by 1967, competing views had evolved within the Republican party about the course the revolution should take. The faction that emerged as the winner held that the existence of the new republic could only be guaranteed by establishing a friendly relationship with the Saudis. This view was considerably at odds with the ideology that had spawned the revolution five years earlier and, indeed, in late 1967, President Sallal was exiled to Iraq. He was replaced by Qadi Abdul Rahman al-Iryani, with General Hassan al-Amri as the head of the Republican army.

At the same time, the Egyptians left

Yemen, defeated in June 1967 by Israel and disillusioned by the ideological unreliability of the illiterate Yemeni tribespeople, who tended to be 'Royalists by day and Republicans by night'. The situation was perhaps best reflected by the emergence of two new verbs in the Arabic language: *tamallaka*, 'to go Royalist', and *tajamhara*, 'to go Republican'.

The scene was thus left to the Yemenis. To the surprise of almost everybody, the Royalists were not able to defeat the Republicans after the Egyptians' departure, although they laid siege to San'a from December 1967 to February 1968. After this unsuccessful siege, the Royalist side seemed to run out of steam and the final battles were fought between different Republican factions.

Victory was won by General al-Amri, who allied himself with the tribal sheikhs to uproot the leftist elements from the army – the very same elements most responsible for starting the revolution in 1962. He simultaneously sought peace with the remaining Royalist forces, tribe by tribe and, backed by the Saudis, was finally able to end the war in 1970. Imam al-Badr was exiled to Britain and, in July 1970, the Yemen Arab Republic was recognised by Saudi Arabia.

Birth of the People's Democratic Republic of Yemen (PDRY)

Developments in the southern part of the country were also extremely violent during the 1960s.

Britain had certainly done little to develop its protectorate states in southern Arabia during its 100-year presence. The area had been ruled from Bombay until, in 1927, the hinterlands and, in 1937, the Aden Colony were officially proclaimed British colonies. The 31 small sultanates that formed the South Arabian Protectorate served as little more than a buffer against possible threats from the north – Britain had opted for 'indirect rule' through the Western and Eastern Arabian protectorates. This meant that Britain maintained a minimal presence outside Aden itself, intervening only when local power struggles and the frequent border disputes with the Kingdom of Yemen required it.

In the early 1960s, the British still saw Aden as one of their most important permanent bases and planned to unite it with the hinterlands via the newly established Federation of the Emirates of the South (renamed the Federation of South Arabia in 1962). However, nationalist spirit in the region had already awakened – frequent strikes in opposition to British rule occurred in the colony as early as the late 1950s – and Britain faced mounting difficulties in controlling developments.

The final boost for the nationalist movement came from the 1962 revolution in the north. The British decision to back the Royalists there certainly helped spread Republican ideas to the south, particularly when a third of the Adeni population were migrant workers of North Yemeni origin. In 1963 and 1964, full-scale guerrilla warfare was in progress in the Radfan mountains. The strife spread to the city of Aden in the following years as the nationalists gained increasing support among the Yemeni population.

The principal force on the Yemeni side was the National Liberation Front (NLF), formed by Marxist and nationalistic militants who had gone north after the 1962 revolution. In contrast to what had occurred in the north, the Nasserite wing of the liberation fighters (FLOSY – Front for the Liberation of Occupied South Yemen) did not gain a strong foothold in South Yemen. The NLF was a far more left-wing organisation than any that could have developed in the imamate of the north – Aden's status as a major port with trade unions and contacts with the outside world had created a group of freedom fighters with much more radical ideas.

By late 1966 and early 1967, the British finally began to make preparations for the independence of South Yemen, promising to withdraw from Aden in November the same year. However, in June, after Egypt's defeat by Israel, the date of withdrawal was pushed back to 9 January 1968. The Yemenis refused to wait that long. Intense fighting late in 1967 forced Britain to announce that British South

Arabia would become independent on 30 November 1967. The NLF forced the last Britons to leave Aden by midnight on 29 November. The People's Republic of South Yemen was born.

The new republic, under the leadership of President Qahtan ash-Shaabi, found itself in a most difficult situation. External relations were in a very sensitive state, with Saudi Arabia naturally suspicious of a Marxist country on their southern border, open hostilities at the Omani border (where the NLF supported the guerrilla movement in the Dhofar region) and the YAR supporting a right-wing opposition. Internally, the final power struggles lay ahead. The economy was on the verge of collapse following the departure of the British and this situation was exacerbated by the closure of the Suez Canal that same year, which greatly diminished Aden's importance as a port. The country was able to survive only with economic support from Communist countries, especially the Soviet Union, China and East Germany.

The internal power struggle was resolved in June 1969 when the government moved even further to the left in the so-called Corrective Movement. Qahtan ash-Shaabi resigned, Salem Rubaya 'Ali was appointed president and a new constitution was drafted. In 1969, a major nationalisation of the economy left only the oil refinery of British Petroleum untouched and, in 1970, the name of the country was changed to the People's Democratic Republic of Yemen (PDRY).

The Two Yemens

At the beginning of the 1970s, there existed two independent Yemeni states. Both had emerged from very difficult conditions and faced the task of building modern states from scratch. Both had to rely on foreign aid; funds came to the PDRY almost exclusively from the Eastern Bloc, while the YAR received developmental aid from Saudi Arabia, Western countries and the Soviet Union.

As if to emphasise the enormous problems faced by the two Yemens, the 1970s saw two

short border wars between them. The first, in September 1972, was mediated by the Arab League. In the resulting Cairo Treaty, the two Yemens agreed to merge within 12 months to form the Yemeni Republic – a surprise announcement confirmed in November 1972 by presidents al-Iryani of North Yemen and Salem Rubaya 'Ali of South Yemen.

The unification was postponed, however, and relations between the countries gradually became more remote. In 1974, a bloodless coup in the YAR replaced President al-Iryani with Colonel Ibrahim al-Hamdi. This development steered the country further to the right and improved North Yemen's relations with Saudi Arabia and the USA. The PDRY continued to follow a leftist path and, although relations with its neighbours gradually improved (in 1976, Saudi Arabia finally recognised the country, and hostilities with Oman ended), the unification of the two Yemens still seemed improbable.

The late 1970s were a difficult time for the government of the YAR. In 1977, President al-Hamdi was assassinated, possibly by northern supporters of the former imamate, and his successor Colonel Ahmad ibn Husayn al-Ghasmi ruled for less than a year before also being assassinated. Al-Ghasmi was killed by a bomb carried in a suitcase from Aden and, although there was no conclusive evidence on who had planned the operation, South Yemeni President Salem Rubaya 'Ali was ousted and executed in July 1978. Armed clashes between the two Yemens occurred immediately and were renewed for the last time in 1979.

The battles were to no avail – the largely undemarcated border between the two countries did not move a single cm.

YAR: Towards Stability The first 15 years or so after the revolution were tumultuous ones for the YAR, which faced both internal and external security problems during this period. When friendly relations with Saudi Arabia, the YAR's big neighbour, were finally secured by the pro-Saudi military government of 1974, the basic conditions for improved stability were created.

In 1978, Lieutenant Colonel 'Ali Abdullah Salah became president of the republic. Whether because of his personal capabilities as a leader or because of the weariness of opposing forces, the country enjoyed a period of increasing stability under his rule in the 1980s. The last serious unrest occurred in the Ta'izz, Ibb and Dhamar provinces in 1981 and 1982 when dissidents from the PDRY, in coalition with fundamentalist Islamic forces, urged rebellion against the central government.

The cabinet consisted of some 20 ministers and, in 1979, the Constitutional People's Assembly was expanded to 159 members, with the president as chair. It was this body that, in 1983 and 1988, elected Colonel Salah to his second and third five-year terms as president. No political parties were allowed in the YAR and all important positions were held by the army.

Conflicts between competing interest groups were increasingly contained within the army and cabinet stability was guaranteed by carefully choosing the ministers so that different tribes were equitably represented. President Salah himself belongs to the Hashid tribe, who saved him in the 1979 confrontation with the PDRY by quickly mobilising some 50,000 troops.

Under its constitution, the YAR was an Arab, Islamic and independent state which derived all its laws from the Shari'a, the Islamic law. Nevertheless, personal freedom, private property, freedom of speech, and the inviolability of homes, places of worship and centres of learning warranted special attention in the wording of the constitution. Indeed, life in the YAR was apparently based on a largely Western set of values in spite of the deep religiosity of the people. Some Western visitors have found this mix of modern Western and traditional Arabic attitudes disappointing and criticised the Yemenis for having blindly adopted 'Western-style consumerism'.

While it may be true that the government catapulted the YAR from the medieval system of the imamate to the 20th century in less than 20 years, this was clearly the will of the Yemeni people. In the days of the civil war, the last tribes of the north only dropped their weapons to give the new central government a chance to fulfil its promise to turn Yemen into a state as advanced as those developed by oil-rich Saudi Arabia. It may be said that the vision of the welfare state earned the government the necessary support from the people.

PDRY: Continuing the Struggle From the very beginning, the development path chosen by the PDRY was diametrically opposed to that of its northern neighbour. Because the forces that expelled the British in the late 1960s were extreme leftist, the revolution in the south led eventually to the birth of the first and only Marxist Arab state. The ruling Yemen Socialist Party was seeking to steer a path between Chinese and Soviet influences, and its declarations on world affairs during the 1970s were further to the left than those of the leading countries in the Communist world, peaking in such publicity-seeking acts as offering political asylum not only to Palestinian hijackers but also to West European Marxist terrorists using similar methods.

The developments of the early 1980s had a somewhat moderating influence, while the government moved closer to the Soviet camp. The PDRY was one of the very few countries in the world with which the USA did not establish diplomatic relations throughout the 1980s. This may have been more the result of impassivity on the part of the South Yemeni side than a sign of active decision-making in Washington, but the effect was that the PDRY was generally regarded as ruled by an extremist, leftist government.

While the YAR was becoming a more stable and controlled society, the PDRY continued to be beset by internal and external conflicts. During the first years of independence, the young republic was engaged in exporting its revolution to neighbouring countries, leading to serious conflictswith Oman and Saudi Arabia. Once these problems were resolved in 1976, skirmishes with the YAR continued, culminating in the 1979 war.

During the 1980s, there were only minor clashes on the country's borders but internal problems were far from being resolved. Most of the conflicts were personified in two men, Abdul Fattah Ismail and 'Ali Nasr Muhammad, who competed for power during the late 1970s and alternately held the post of president after the execution of former president, Salem Rubaya 'Ali. In April 1980, following the 1979 YAR-PDRY war, 'Ali Nasr Muhammad was finally nominated as president and Abdul Fattah Ismail flew to exile in Moscow.

Under the rule of 'Ali Nasr Muhammad the country appeared to steer a less isolated course and very gradually opened its doors to the outside world, especially to other Arab countries, while strictly maintaining its socialist doctrine. Although the country seemed to have entered an era of relatively stable development in the first half of the 1980s, tensions again surfaced after the return of Abdul Fattah Ismail in late 1985. In January 1986, fierce civil war broke out in Aden, destroying many buildings and killing thousands of people in just a couple of weeks (the official figure was 3000 while unofficial estimates claimed up to 42,000 people were killed).

As a result of this catastrophe, 'Ali Nasr Muhammad fled to Ethiopia and Abdul Fattah Ismail was killed. The new president of the republic was chosen from those who had watched the crisis from a safe distance: in February 1986, Haidar Abu Bakr al-Attash flew to Aden from Moscow to become head of state. The new leadership continued pursuing the same leftist policy as the deposed one. Apparently, the key questions in all these disputes may have been more tribal than political in nature: Abdul Fattah Ismail was born in a village that belonged to the YAR, while 'Ali Nasr Muhammad's birthplace was inside the borders of the PDRY.

One Yemen

Global politics changed a lot in the last years of the 1980s. The Gorbachev era and the imminent collapse of the Soviet economy dried up the flow of both ideological and financial aid to Moscow's Third World allies, forcing them to re-evaluate their situation. The government of the bankrupt PDRY had few friends to turn to: they chose the brothers next door, the YAR.

In fact, the quest for the unification of Yemen had continued since the birth of the two states. It had already become a tradition that, after any armed conflict, the countries publish a declaration and sign an agreement of eventual unification. However, the practical questions were always left unresolved. For example, the 1986 agreement, signed in Libya, stated that one of its goals was a 'unified political organisation'. Whether this meant a no-party, one-party or multiparty system was not specified.

Apart from the economic disaster status of the PDRY and the deep wish of the Yemeni people, there was another pressing reason for unification: in the mid-1980s, significant oil fields were discovered in the desert area between the countries, on both sides of the undemarcated border. The governments faced the choice of defining the boundary or forming a neutral zone to be used cooperatively. Sensibly, in May 1988, they chose the latter option, accelerating the progress towards unity.

On 30 November 1989, the leaders of the two countries agreed on a concrete, 14-month plan to complete the process of unification. According to the plan, the legislative bodies of the two countries were to complete a proposal for the constitution of the Unified Republic of Yemen within one year, to be approved through a referendum within two months after that. Thus, the new state should have been born on 30 January 1991.

There was both internal and external opposition, though. The religious elite of the north, centred in Sa'da, used the mosques to spread terror propaganda about the secular south, where 'women go unveiled and men go drunk in the streets'. They received considerable support from the Saudis, who had watched nervously as the YAR gradually drifted out of the Saudi sphere of influence. With oil wells of its own now in production, the YAR had succeeded in diminishing its economic dependence on Saudi Arabia. In 1989, the YAR, together with Egypt, Iraq and Jordan, founded the short-lived Arab Cooperation Council, a move that was certain to make the Saudis worry about losing their dominance on the peninsula. A unified Yemen, with a population surpassing that of their own, and strategically located by the shores of the Red and Arabian seas in control of the Bab al-Mandab Strait, was a nightmare to Saudi security analysts.

Opposition to the unification backfired, however. Facing the possibility of failure at the critical moment, the Yemeni governments decided to wait no longer. During the spring of 1990, several preparatory steps were taken in rapid succession: the border was demilitarised and opened, state security forces were dissolved, currencies were made valid in both countries. Free enterprise was legalised in the PDRY and political parties were legalised in the YAR.

Then on 22 May 1990, several months ahead of schedule, the Republic of Yemen was declared, under a provisional constitution, 'with San'a as the political capital and Aden as the economic capital'. The president of the YAR, 'Ali Abdullah Salah, continued as the president of the whole country, while the vice president 'Ali Salim al-Baydh came from the

south. The southern president Haidar Abu Bakr al-Attash became prime minister.

Towards Democracy The unification was followed by an exceptional experiment in the Arabian Peninsula: democracy. All of a sudden, some 40 political parties were founded in anticipation of the first free elections in the Arabian Peninsula, and freedom of the press was granted.

In a referendum held on 15 and 16 May 1991, the Yemenis voted for the new constitution, sealing the unification. The main opposition came from the religious parties who in vain demanded that the constitution declare Islamic Shari'a as the 'sole' rather than the 'main' source of legislation. The first parliamentary elections were held on 27 April 1993, six months behind the schedule. The elections were generally regarded as free and fair, save some local exceptions.

The first few years of the new Republic of Yemen were, however, marred by troubles both from within the country and outside of it. During the 1990-91 Gulf crisis, Yemen adopted a moderate stand towards the Iraqi occupation of Kuwait. It favoured an 'Arab solution' and demanded the withdrawal of Iraqi troops from Kuwait and of Western forces from Saudi Arabia. This was badly viewed by the Saudis (and Kuwaitis), who soon expelled all Yemeni citizens and cut off all economic aid to Yemen. The Western press also criticised the Yemeni position, which was interpreted as support for Iraq and even alliance with Baghdad. The benefits of the unification were thus quickly

Provinces & Governorates
The former YAR was divided into 11 administrative regions, usually called provinces in English, while the six regions of the former PDRY were called governorates. After the unification both of these terms were in use for a while, but it seems that the word 'governorate' has gained wider acceptance for the northern regions and also among Yemenis producing English-language documents.

However, not only the names but the whole issue of local government in Yemen has been under intense debate since unification. The southerners have promoted decentralisation and local autonomy to ensure, among other things, the continuity of the ruling structures inherited from the PDRY. For the opposite reasons, the northerners advocate strong central government and, in their most extreme views, would like to see the role of administrative regions restricted as a tool for electoral procedures only. Several proposals have been made for administrative redivision of the unified country, and this might well happen during the lifetime of this book. ∎

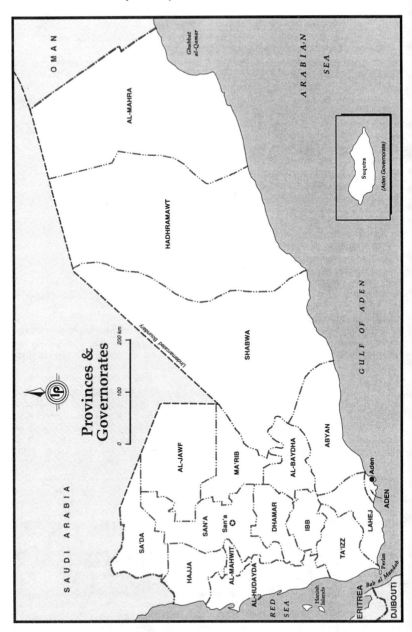

Provinces & Governorates

negated by developments Yemen had had no part in.

Mounting economic problems soon caused friction between the ruling parties. According to the provisional constitution, power was shared between the president's People's General Congress (PGC) and the Yemen Socialist Party (YSP) of the south. After the elections they were joined by a newcomer on the political scene, the Yemeni Congregation for Reform (Islah), which represented tribal and religious sentiments. However, the positions gained turned out hard to abandon for the old parties, especially for the YSP. The conflict was personified in President 'Ali Abdullah Salah and vice-president 'Ali Salim al-Baydh.

Prior to the elections the general security situation worsened gradually, with Bedouins and tribespeople robbing 4WD vehicles and hijacking oil workers, demanding ransom from the government. The elections were followed by a calm period, but disappointment at the new PGC-led government soon gave rise to similar incidents, generally regarded more politically than economically motivated. High-ranking YSP officials were assassinated in the streets of San'a but no attempts were made to prosecute the assassins.

After the summer of 1993 'Ali Salim al-Baydh decided to stay in Aden instead of returning to San'a, refusing to participate in government meetings unless the differences were solved and the security of himself and other YSP members was guaranteed, citing 150 as the number of slain YSP members. With talks leading nowhere, southerners started arguing for a federation in order to preserve their local power structure. While the Yemeni people had welcomed democracy, their leaders were apparently not ready for a new system.

As the situation worsened, the general sentiment anticipated war. Affluent Yemenis were sending their families abroad, and those who had taken to work in other parts of the country moved back to their home towns or villages.

Civil War of 1994 Unfortunately, the unification of Yemen had been carried out only partially, and the crucial element not unified was the armies of the former states. The border between the Yemens no longer existed, and army units were relocated around the country, but the command chains leading to the president and the vice president remained untouched. In every major Yemeni town there were two separate army camps. These army units were on constant alert, and suspicious of each other.

In early 1994 violence erupted at several camps all around the country, both in the former YAR and PDRY. Although several hundred lives were lost, the incidents were contained at first. Finally, fierce battles in Dhamar on 4 May 1994 marked the beginning of civil war.

The following morning, emergency was declared in San'a while Aden's Mig fighters appeared above the city. They were the first in a series of bombing raids and Scud missile attacks against strategic targets in the northern part of the country. Northern troops started their march towards Aden from the former border.

The war went badly for the southerners from the very beginning. President Salah's campaign against the 'secessionists' proved popular in the north, and recruiting tens of thousands of volunteers from the tribes was easy – the villagers even raised the funds to provide their sons with weapons bought from local arms bazaars.

In the south, defending the power structure inherited from the days of the PDRY didn't prove to be a sufficient cause for most of the residents of the Lahej and Abyan governorates to risk their lives. Defections were common, and money bought many of the southern defenders. President Salah's government used some 500 million riyals to bribe the commanders of the YSP forces, tribal sheikhs and community elders on their march towards Aden.

Yemen & Saudi Arabia: Volatile Neighbours

Throughout most of this century, Yemen has been haunted by its powerful neighbour. Saudi Arabia, wealthier and more advanced, represents the big brother Yemenis have loved to hate, while the Saudis have regarded Yemenis as a particularly low-class people. They know each other well – hundreds of thousands of Yemenis have flocked to Saudi Arabia to work when the relationship between the two countries has been prosperous, and the Saudis have not been able to resist the temptation to mingle in Yemeni politics.

During the Gulf crisis of 1990-91 a so-called 'Riyadh Highway Code' which circulated among Western troops stationed in Saudi Arabia stated things bluntly: 'If you hit a Saudi, it's your fault. If you hit a Korean, it's his fault. If you hit a Yemeni, go to the nearest police station to claim your prize.' During the Yemeni civil war of 1994, the general feeling among many Yemenis was that Saudi Arabia was somehow behind it all, encouraging the southern secessionists and providing them with arms. However, these concerns were based on little proof.

Border disputes have contributed much to the troubled relationship between Saudi Arabia and Yemen. After the Saudi-Yemeni war in 1934 Yemen had lost the 'Asir and Najran provinces, which were left under Saudi Arabian rule for 40 years. In 1974 the YAR was still recovering from the civil war of the 1960s and didn't want to touch the issue. On the pretext that since Yemen was still a divided country and the government of the YAR could not speak for the entire Yemeni people, the Ta'if Treaty was prolonged for another 20 years.

In 1994 there were again no negotiations since Yemen was suffering from another civil war. After this war, however, the Yemeni government was eager to normalise relations with Saudi Arabia. There were two border issues to address: the fate of the two lost provinces, and the desert border that went undemarcated all the way from Najran to the Omani border (the latter had been fully defined by a border pact finally signed in 1992).

The border disputes were certainly intensified by the Saudis. After the Yemen civil war of 1994, Saudi Arabia issued ultimatums to Western oil companies exploring Yemeni deserts in some disputed areas, demanding them to leave Saudi territory immediately. Tensions rose rapidly, leading to border clashes in January 1995.

The Saudis, however, didn't want war. Instead, negotiations were carried through in rapid progression, leading to a memorandum of understanding, signed on 26 February 1995. The Saudis had succeeded in linking the border issue with the return to pre-1990 economic relations between the countries, while Yemenis had failed to link the 'Asir-Najran question with the demarcation of the desert boundaries. The final pact is subject to further negotiations, but it seems that the provinces the Kingdom of Yemen lost in 1934 will remain under Saudi rule despite considerable grass-roots level resentment in the Republic of Yemen. However, relations between these historically troubled neighbours appear to be improving. In early June 1995 President Salah completed his landmark visit to Saudi Arabia, and relations between the countries were at their warmest since the Gulf War. ∎

On 21 May 1994 'Ali Salim al-Baydh proclaimed the independent Democratic Republic of Yemen in an effort to win support from the Peninsular Arab countries more or less openly hostile towards Salah's government. The outcome of the war was, however, sealed: Aden was already surrounded by the advancing northern troops and al-Baydh himself had fled to al-Mukalla, 600 km to the east, where he kept his headquarters until the end of the war. Whatever support the secessionists may have been promised before the war, no country ever recognised the Democratic Republic of Yemen.

Finally, on 7 July 1995, Aden fell completely in the hands of northern troops after a devastating siege, marking the end of the two-month war. Al-Mukalla had been captured earlier. 'Ali Salim al-Baydh fled to Oman, which granted him asylum on the condition that he withdraw from politics for the rest of his life. The conflict had claimed 7000 lives and left 15,000 wounded. The operational cost of the war was estimated at US$3000 million and the overall damage to the economy estimated at US$5500 million.

Contrary to what most observers had feared, the war succeeded in reinforcing Yemeni unity instead of tearing the country apart. President Salah declared a general amnesty to all secessionists dropping their arms, excluding only a 16-strong clique of leaders. The gamble seemingly paid off; all parties now support national unity even if they disagree on other issues.

GEOGRAPHY

Yemen's Arabic name, al-Yaman, suggests its geographic location at the southernmost tip of the Arabian Peninsula. The early Muslims living around Mecca divided their lands into those lying northward, or *sha:man*, and those lying to the south, or *yamanan*. Even today, Syrians informally refer to their country, and especially its capital, as *ash-Sha:m*; while *al-yaman* became the official name of Yemen. (Yemenis are eager to point out other derivatives of the root verbs in question, relating the name to prosperity, but this is not fair to the Syrians, whose country's name would then foretell calamity.)

Yemen lies between latitudes 12°40'N and 19°N and between longitudes 42°30'E and 53°E on the shores of the southern Red Sea and the western part of the Arabian Sea, the Gulf of Aden. The seas are joined by the narrow strait of Bab al-Mandab ('gate of lament'), which separates the peninsula from the African continent.

Yemen shares borders with Saudi Arabia to the north and Oman to the east. The Saudi border is a largely undemarcated desert boundary and you may find it drawn quite differently on maps; the countries were involved in negotiations aimed at fully defining the border in 1995.

Some islands also belong to Yemen. Kamaran and the Hanish Islands in the Red Sea and Perim in the Bab al-Mandab Strait are relatively small, while Suqutra, off the tip of the African Horn, is the largest and most important. The extremely poor island of Kamaran has some symbolic value for the Yemenis: in the early days of its independence, the PDRY claimed this island (together with the Kuria Muria Islands off the Omani coast), hundreds of km out of its reach but only a few km off the coast of the

YAR. Today, the most popular cigarette brand in the country is Kamaran.

Across the narrow seas are Black African neighbours: Ethiopia to the west, Somalia to the south and tiny Djibouti between them, just across the Bab al-Mandab Strait. Cultural exchange in the region has always been significant and the coastal areas of Yemen possess a distinctively 'African' flavour. The inland areas, on the other hand, have remained purely 'Arabic'.

Yemen's location by a major waterway has exposed the country to more remote influences, peaking with the colonisation of the northern parts by Ottoman Turks and of the southern parts by the English. Despite this history, Yemen has remained remote and isolated from the West and its extraordinary geography has greatly contributed to this. Indeed, understanding the landscape of the region is the key to understanding Yemen in other respects as well.

The Arabian Peninsula is an immense plate of granite, partly covered by shallow layers of younger sedimentary rocks. The plate is tilted, with the south-western edge (Yemen) elevated and the north-eastern parts warped down. Accordingly, Yemen is sometimes referred to as the roof of Arabia or even the Tibet or Switzerland of Arabia, though the latter nicknames are misleading.

When looked at from west to east at the latitude of San'a, the topography of Yemen offers remarkable variety. The coastal strip (known as the Tihama) extends along the Red Sea from the southernmost tip of Yemen north into Saudi Arabia. This sandy plain, some 20 km to 50 km wide, is absolutely flat and has a tropical character. It ends abruptly at a steep, mountainous ridge known as the western mountains. Several of the peaks are well over 3000 metres and the highest point on the Arabian Peninsula, Jabal an-Nabi Shu'ayb, rises about 3660 metres above sea level.

Further to the east lie the fertile high plateaus for which Yemen is famous. The Yemeni capital, San'a, is in the centre of the San'a basin at an altitude of 2250 metres. Mountains completely surround the plateaus. The eastern mountain ridge is somewhat less dramatic than the western, with fewer and lower peaks and a more gently sloping appearance. Several parts of the highlands are still volcanically active; hot springs can be found here and the area is prone to earthquakes. The Dhamar quake of 1982 killed 2500 people, the highest casualty figure recorded in Yemen.

The eastern mountains slowly descend from above 2000 metres to about 1000 metres. At this altitude, the rocky landscape is transformed into the great sands of the vast Arabian desert, ar-Ruba' al-Khali, which extends its southernmost tip into the middle of Yemen. The name means 'the empty quarter' and it is this quarter of the peninsula that dominates the Western impression of Arabia. You *can* find camels in Yemen, however, only an estimated 1% of Yemenis are nomadic – most of the population practise agriculture on the coastal plains, along the wadis of the mountain foothills or in the central highlands.

In the southern part of Yemen, a narrow coastal plain is occasionally broken by volcanic rocks extending right to the seashore. In western Yemen, the land rises rapidly inland in enormous fractures to the highlands of northern Yemen. Further to the east, the steepness of the terrain gradually eases and, at the Omani frontier, the highest point in the north-south cross section of the country, it is less than 1000 metres above sea level.

The vast mountain ridge that runs between the southern coast and ar-Ruba' al-Khali offers, for the most part, a very nondramatic landscape of arid tableland. Eastern Yemen does, however, have an important topographic feature – the valley of Wadi Hadhramawt. The valley is some 150 to 200 km inland and runs parallel to the coast (west to east) for half the width of the country before suddenly turning south-east to reach the sea. This fertile valley is an important part of Yemen and its inhabitants live in relative isolation from the rest of the country.

All this geographic variety is crammed into a country of only 532,000 sq km – smaller than France. At least two-thirds of this area is uninhabited; most of Yemen's important centres are in the western coastlands and mountains.

CLIMATE & VEGETATION

Climatically, Yemen lies in the Sahel belt and shares many features with African countries at around the same latitude. However, because of its topographic characteristics, Yemen has never been a country haunted by famine. While some years bring less water than others, the high mountain ridges trap moisture from the winds blowing in off nearby seas and, as a result, Yemen is the most arable spot on the Arabian Peninsula. Indeed, it is known as 'the green land of Arabia'.

Because of the extensive variations in its topography, Yemen has several distinct climatic regions.

The Tihama & Southern Coast

Despite the proximity of the sea, the Tihama 'hot lands' and the southern coast form an arid zone. Rainfall is scanty – in most parts, between 100 mm and 200 mm annually. Most of the rain falls between late July and September, with only occasional showers during the rest of the year. Temperatures are high year round. Night-time temperatures fall to between 18˚C and 20˚C from December to February and to about 27˚C to 35˚C in June and July. Maximum daytime temperatures range from 32˚C in winter to 40˚C or close to 50˚C in summer. Humidity is always extremely high and hot winds blow fine sand inland from the seashore. Indeed, the name Tihama means 'hot lands'.

Life throughout Yemen, even in the Tihama, relies on the monsoon winds to bring ample summer rains from the south and south-west. (Winters are dry; the winter monsoon winds blow from the north and north-east, carrying cool, dry air from central Asia.) When the moist summer winds reach the western mountains, the air mass rises rapidly, cools suddenly and frees moisture in the form of torrential showers.

The rains are irregular and do not compare

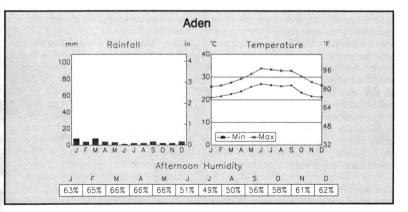

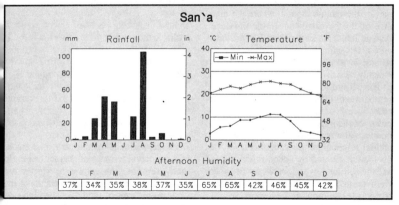

with the monsoon rains of, say, eastern India. In different years, the rains may come in different months and, some years, there may be no rain at all. The showers are very localised and often violent, causing extensive erosion. If you're travelling along mountain roads during the rainy season, you may be forced to stop because of heavy streams flowing down the steep slopes, carrying huge rocks and sometimes destroying mountain roads altogether. In contrast, neighbouring villages only one km away may receive no rain at all.

The mountain rains give birth to perennial rivers flowing west towards the Tihama and the southern coast. Because of the extremely high evaporation rates in the coastal areas, these rivers die in the sands and never reach the sea. Agriculture along these foothill wadis is intense, yielding up to four harvests a year. Ground water is also efficiently pumped in most parts of the Tihama. Some people say that the pumping rate already exceeds the replenishing water flow from the mountains, which causes sea water to flow in and endangers the agricultural potential of the plains.

The Tihama's vegetation varies from the mangroves and salt-resistant plants of the seashore to the sparse grasses and shrubs of inner Tihama's dune valleys. Further inland, the wadi shores and mountain foothills are moist enough to sustain evergreen plants such as palms and acacias. (The level of human interference here is high, however; most areas suitable for cultivation are used so intensely that there are few remaining examples of the natural vegetation.)

The southern coast has a more varied topography. Volcanic rocks extend right down to the ocean at several sites, including Aden and Bir 'Ali. Cultivated areas are scarcer here due to infertile or scanty soils.

The Western Mountains

Rainfall is highest on the western slopes of the western mountains and in the southern part of the mountain area, where the Province of Ibb is called 'the fertile province'. Around Ibb, it rains every month of the year – only a few mm in January but, in July and August (when there may be daily rain), a monthly rainfall of almost 500 mm is common.

The natural vegetation of the western and southern mountain slopes is tropical – evergreen forests of acacia, ficus and tamarisk – however, the impact of thousands of years of human settlement has left very little of the natural vegetation. Instead, there are vast open areas created by uncontrolled grazing and the cutting down of forests for firewood. Cultivation of dates, mangoes, bananas and papayas is common on the lower slopes. At higher altitudes (up to 1500 metres), wheat, maize, lucerne, and especially sorghum crops are typical.

Higher in the mountains (on terraced slopes between 1500 and 2500 metres) are qat crops (see Qat under Society & Customs, later). They have largely replaced Yemen's former cash crop, coffee. It is hard to tell which plants would constitute the natural cover of the land here, since every possible spot is under cultivation and only the steepest, rockiest slopes with their few small shrubs have escaped human interference.

The Central Highlands

Towards the north, the rains gradually diminish. In the central highlands, the summer is dry, with only a couple of showers a month. Most rain occurs in these regions in two distinct rainy seasons, the lighter in March and April and the heavier around August. In San'a, April may bring about 100 mm of rain and August usually sees almost 200 mm.

Temperatures in the highlands are mild and San'a's maximum daily temperatures range from 25°C to 30°C throughout the year. Minimum nightly temperatures are around 0°C in January and 10°C in July. In large areas of the Yemeni highlands, nightly frost is possible during winter but, because that happens to be the dry season, the Yemenis see no snow.

On the central highland plateaus, sorghum is widely cultivated at about 2300 metres above sea level. All kinds of vegetables abound, including potatoes, carrots, onions, garlic, lettuce and cabbage, as well as various spice plants. Even vineyards are a common sight; wine is a forbidden drink in this Islamic country but raisins are popular.

The wadis and springs of the highlands provide a suitable environment for various fruit trees. Almonds, walnuts, peaches, apricots, pears, lemons, pomegranates and many others grow readily here.

In the highlands, there are elaborately built irrigation terraces of ancient origin. In many regions, the mountain slopes are covered by terraces, from the strands of the wadis to the tops of the hills. The high plateaus have also been converted to huge terraces. 'Rainwater harvesting' in Yemen takes two main forms. In *sawaqi* irrigation, farmers collect rainwater from areas not used for agriculture and channel it to their fields. In *sayl* irrigation, it is the run-off water from floods that is collected. Sawaqi irrigation is used on mountain slopes as well as on the plains while sayl irrigation is most frequently seen around the wadi villages. Rainwater harvesting is not limited to field irrigation – household water is also collected by these methods.

The Outskirts of ar-Ruba' al-Khali

To the east and north, the rains become scantier and less frequent, ceasing altogether in the northern central parts of the country, where the stony semideserts gradually turn into sandy deserts. Here, only a few shrubs and grasses survive. In the past, large wadis carried enough water from the eastern mountains to the desert to sustain entire civilisations. The famous Kingdom of Saba owed its prosperity to a dam that collected water from the vast Wadi as-Sudd flowing north-easterly.

In the eastern part of the country, the huge Wadi Hadhramawt gathers the scanty rains that fall on the rocky area between the Arabian Sea and the central deserts of the Arabian Peninsula. This wadi, though sufficiently fertile to allow a sizeable population to derive a living from agriculture, never yields its waters anywhere near the sea. Date palm is the most notably cultivated tree here; the Hadhramis grow enough dates for export to other countries.

FAUNA

Yemen has little in the way of wildlife. Most sizeable animals have long since been hunted into extinction in this country where firearms abound and natural forests have been cut down. If you're lucky you may spot a leopard or hyena, or the *Hamadryas baboon*, a species found only in the mountains of Yemen and 'Asir in south-west Saudi Arabia. Some are kept as pets, and some can be found clowning at suqs; these animals are often miserably undernourished and badly kept.

For ornithologists, Yemen is well worth a field trip. In addition to 13 indigenous species, a large variety of migratory birds from Europe or Northern Asia either spend their winter here or traverse the country on their route to East Africa. The island of Suqutra has its own special fauna, however, it is difficult for travellers to visit the island (see Suqutra in the Aden chapter).

GOVERNMENT

Military governments were the rule since the revolution days of the 1960s – the governments of both Yemens based their power on the army. In the hasty unification of 1990, the two cabinets were combined to form a new cabinet of 39 ministers. The parliaments – the north's 159-seat People's Consultative Assembly and the south's 111-seat Supreme Consultative Council – were strengthened by the addition of 31 members from the hitherto illegal opposition and became the new 301-seat Council of Deputies. Also important was the five-member Presidential Council, made up of the topmost officials and headed by President 'Ali Abdullah Salah.

The stated political direction of the new republic largely followed that of the YAR, both in internal and external affairs. Gone were the secular and Marxist ideologies of the former PDRY; Islam and free enterprise are the basis of the new state structure. The new Yemen also automatically became a member of those Arab state councils to which the YAR had belonged. What was new was the embracing of democracy: close to 40 parties were quickly formed, making Yemen the first multiparty state in the Arabian Peninsula, to the horror of the conservative Arab Gulf states.

The first parliamentary elections were held on 27 April 1993. Of the 301 seats, 179 went to the former ruling parties – the People's General Congress, or PGC, of the north (122) and the Yemen Socialist Party, or YSP, of the south (57). Islah, the biggest religious party, won 62 seats; the rest of seats went to independents and small parties. The new government was formed between the big three, with all but eight of the 29 portfolios going to former ministers.

However, the civil war of 1994 left the YSP in shambles, leaving the PGC and Islah ruling the country with no meaningful opposition. It remains to be seen whether the YSP will ever recover; with its former leaders running a National Opposition Front in exile, the party has an uphill battle in reorganising itself into a convincing force within the country. Islah is the rising force in the country, and its leader and the paramount sheikh of the Hashid tribes, Abdullah Bin Husayn al-Ahmar, is the man to watch in Yemeni politics.

However, the undisputed leader of the country is currently President 'Ali Abdullah

Salah, supported by the army. He faces no serious competition: when he was re-elected for another five-year term on 1 October 1994, only six votes in the parliament didn't support him. In the same occasion the Presidential Council was abolished, leaving all power in the hands of the president. Recent months have seen the ousting of sympathisers of the separatists from the ranks of the PGC.

ECONOMY

By Western standards, Yemen is among the very poorest of the world's nations. The United Nations Conference on Trade and Development (UNCTAD) classification places Yemen in the group of the 40 least developed countries in the world, with an estimated per capita gross national product (GNP) of slightly over US$500 (1990). However, visitors to Yemen may get the impression that there is plenty of economic activity, especially in the northern part of the country. (This region does not get included in official figures.)

The unified Yemen inherited two totally different economies: the bustling Western-style economy of the YAR, where the annual growth rate of the per capita GNP had averaged 6% during the 1980s; and the stagnating centrally planned economy of the PDRY, where the per capita GNP had been declining by 2% per annum over the same period.

The economies had evolved in isolation after the 1962 and 1967 revolutions. Earlier, the British port of Aden had been central to the industrial and commercial development of the region. The British developed the port town from a mere fortification with little more than 1000 inhabitants to a bustling city of 150,000 people. Thousands migrated from all over lower Yemen to take part in Aden's labour-intensive activities. One of the goals of the unification was to re-establish the port's status as Yemen's economic capital, and to this end Aden was declared a free trade zone on 29 May 1991.

However, with the unification proving more difficult than envisaged, the economy

has suffered badly: the yearly inflation rate exceeded 100% in the early 1990s, the budget deficit for 1992 was US$1700 million and that same year the country's accumulated debt was US$6500 million. The unemployment rate continues to hover somewhere around 30% among men – for women no such statistics exist.

Little economic development has taken place since the unification. Up to the civil war of 1994 the economies of the former YAR and PDRY developed more or less separately, with the latter's currency retaining legal status in wait for a pending monetary union. Six months after the war there was very little progress in the government's willingness to solve the problems of the economy.

Agriculture

The backbone of the former YAR was agriculture, with industry accounting for less than 10% of the GNP. In the former PDRY, agriculture was also the main economic activity, employing some 75% of the population, but it provided only 25% of the GNP.

Only 2% of the area of the former PDRY is arable and even this limited potential has not been fully exploited; the southern governorates are self-sufficient only in vegetables and dates. In contrast, climatic conditions in the northern provinces are extremely favourable and the country should be able to grow all the food its people need. This has been the case for 3000 years, since the early days of the Sabaeans, but the oppression of the second Ottoman occupation and the subsequent Imamate ended this kind of economic prosperity.

Restoring self-sufficiency in agricultural production has been the stated goal of the governments but, so far, the trend has been to increase food imports. Glorious plans to develop Yemen into the granary of the Arabic world have been confined to the level of political eloquence.

Today, most agriculture is small-scale and intended for the sustenance of the family. In the former PDRY, the estates of sultans and other feudal landowners that had been

Top: Market scene at Bab al-Yaman
ottom: Women shopping at a market in San'a

Top: A view over Old San'a
Bottom: Creek in Bayt Baws

transformed into state-run farms are now being privatised again.

The main output of Yemeni agriculture is cereals – sorghum, millet, wheat and barley, typically species that are resistant to drought. Bananas, grapes and dates are grown as cash crops along the wadis where the climate is warm enough, while qat, a mild narcotic, is common in the highlands. Once the country was famous for its coffee, but today the yearly output is only a fraction of its former extent at 5000 tonnes.

The Yemenis also breed livestock; cattle, sheep and chickens are a common sight. Honey is a highly valued commodity in Yemen, so with any luck, you'll come across migratory beekeepers hunting for flowering plants with their transportable beehives – honey is a highly valued commodity in Yemen.

The waters of the Red and Arabian seas are rich in fish; the Yemeni fishing industry has great but largely untapped potential.

Development Aid

Both Yemens depended heavily on foreign development aid and the Republic of Yemen continues to do so.

In the YAR, all of the basic infrastructure built after the 1962 revolution was the result of development projects with industrialised states – for example, the asphalted roads were built with Chinese, West German, US and Russian aid, while East Germany helped build the telephone connections between San'a, al-Hudayda and Ta'izz.

Many projects were financed by oil-rich Arab countries, where several rich emirs trace their lineage to Yemeni tribes; the new US$90-million Ma'rib dam, constructed in the late 1980s, was personally financed by United Arab Emirates President Sheikh Zaid ibn Sultan al-Nahyan.

The YAR lacked not only industrial expertise but educated workers of all kinds. There are still very few Yemeni doctors and 90% of the country's teachers have come from abroad, most from Arab countries such as Egypt and the Sudan.

In the PDRY, the whole economy was in

ruins after the 1967 revolution. The closure of the Suez Canal had already cut off 75% of Aden's trade, the PDRY's main source of foreign currency. The British evacuation left 20,000 labourers without work and the complete withdrawal of British aid reduced the state's total budgeted income by 60%. With no agricultural or mineral exports, the country had to make do in conditions of extreme austerity.

With development aid from communist countries, the PDRY did survive and, with Arab countries later joining the ranks, the economy was gaining some balance towards the 1980s. In the late 1970s, the economy grew a massive 8% per annum and the main goal of the government – self-sufficiency – seemed closer than ever. However, internal political problems and the dwindling of Soviet aid in the *perestroika* years of the late 1980s had disastrous consequences. The economy was actually shrinking at an average of 2% annually during that decade and, on the eve of unification, the state was practically bankrupt, with hordes of people in the cities queuing up for government-subsidised food.

After the unification of Yemen, the Gulf crisis of 1990/91 caused many donor countries, both Arab and Western, to suspend their aid. In 1992 and 1993, total external assistance climbed back to about US$250 million yearly, far surpassing the domestic development budget, which was about US$150 million by official estimate, US$12 million by parallel market exchange rates. However, the civil war of 1994 again effectively stopped all foreign projects, most of which are recovering only slowly.

Oil

Until the early 1980s, the Yemens were considered an oddity because they were on the Arabian Peninsula but had no oil. The oil industry was restricted to the formerly British Petroleum-owned oil refinery in Aden, nationalised in 1977. The shortage of crude oil plagued the plant, which was already making losses before the revolution. However, the refinery, operating with

Labour Export

The most important export commodity of both Yemens in the 1970s and 1980s was raw, unskilled labour. The early 1970s oil boom in Saudi Arabia and the Gulf States created an unprecedented demand for manual labour. The newly opened YAR was especially eager to satisfy this demand. It has been estimated that in 1975, at least 350,000 North Yemenis were working abroad; by the end of the decade, there were an estimated 500,000 to 1.5 million, most of them working in Saudi Arabia. Formidable figures have also been quoted for the PDRY, with even less precision. For the unified Yemen of 1990, the estimate was 2.5 million.

The significance of this labour migration lies in the fact that the workers sent the greater part of their earnings back home. In 1978, the peak year, some US$900 to US$1500 million flowed to the YAR in worker remittances, the latter sum being almost as great as the country's entire trade deficit. For the PDRY, it has been estimated that, between 1975 and 1987, about 70% of the GNP came from worker remittances, the highest percentage of all Arab countries.

This enormous influx of cash changed the YAR more profoundly than any revolution, and gave the people a chance to buy imported commodities previously unimagined. Portable TV sets and stereos became a must. Donkeys and camels were carried to the market in Toyota jeeps instead of walking. The imported money greatly diversified the economy; returning workers invested their savings in small shops, handled the trade or maintenance of imported technological wonders or started working as taxi or truck drivers. The construction industry also boomed and, in turn, utilised more and more imported new materials. In other words, small-scale capitalism flourished in the YAR.

In the centrally planned PDRY economy, the flow of incoming money was more tightly controlled and the impact was less visible. Moreover, commodity goods were harder to obtain than in the YAR, where anything from radios to Toyota jeeps was smuggled in from Saudi Arabia with the silent approval of both governments. The economies of the YAR and Saudi Arabia grew so close in the late 1970s and early 1980s that the YAR can be said to have been a Saudi satellite. It was only in the late 1980s that the YAR began to distance itself from the Saudis. The governments also made an effort to end the smuggling.

During the 1980s, the demand for Yemeni labour in the Gulf States greatly diminished, partly because of the cheaper labour that began to flow into these countries from other parts of Asia and partly because falling oil prices forced the revision of construction plans. The worker remittances of both Yemens combined diminished to about US$300 million by the end of the decade.

Nevertheless, many Yemenis chose not to return home. Their previous abundant remittances caused severe inflation in the former YAR – almost 17% in 1988 – and have all but crushed the agricultural sector in many regions. There is also little demand for their labour at home. As a result, many continue living in foreign countries, starting small businesses after accumulating enough money.

The biggest problem with the migrant workforce is that they leaked abroad gradually but returned home in one huge wave: in October 1990 Saudi Arabia expelled all Yemenis because of San'a's lack of support for UN resolutions against Iraq during the Gulf crisis. Within a month or so, 600,000 Yemenis returned to their newly unified homeland. By the 1991 Gulf War other Arab countries opposing Iraq had followed the example, and the figure rose close to one million. The direct costs of the repatriation, combined with the lost remittances in the future, were estimated by the Yemeni government to cost the country the equivalent of 15 Yemeni annual budgets. ■

imported oil, accounted for 80% of the PDRY's industrial output.

In the mid-1980s, before the unification of the two Yemens, oil was finally found in the desert area between them. Commercial exploitation of the fields first began in 1986 in the YAR, in an area east of Ma'rib, with the expertise of the Hunt Oil Company. Five oil wells were opened in the Ma'rib/al-Jawf region and a pipeline was built from the fields to the Red Sea coast. By 1989, output reached 200,000 barrels per day and the YAR became an oil-exporting country. Plans for developing the huge reserves of natural gas were also finalised.

In the PDRY, oil was first found near

Shabwa in 1987 but the development of the fields was slow because the Russian partner company, Technoexport, had great domestic difficulties with the effects of *perestroika* and Soviet economic hardships. Oil was transported to Aden by road and output was limited to 6000 barrels per day in 1989. However, a pipeline to Bir 'Ali was completed in 1990.

The unification of the two Yemens has facilitated the exploration and exploitation of oil and gas reserves in the former border region. While Shabwa has been somewhat of a disappointment, the most promising new oil fields have been found in the Masila region east of Wadi Hadhramawt, with a pipeline to ash-Shihr completed in 1993.

Fortunately, the oil producing infrastructure survived the 1994 civil war largely undamaged – even the Aden refineries resumed soon after the war. Three international oil companies pump oil in Yemen today (Hunt in Ma'rib, NIMR in Shabwa and CanOxy in Masila) but no less than 29 companies have been engaged in exploration projects.

Even so, Yemen remains a minor player, with its daily production of 350,000 barrels or so accounting for only three per mille of the total oil output of the world and one third of it going for local consumption. The unstable price of oil in the world market will remain an incalculable factor but domestic oil will at least keep the Toyotas climbing the Yemeni mountains, even if the rest of the economy founders.

POPULATION & PEOPLE

In general, statistics on Yemen are unreliable. Population censuses have been carried out once every decade, with increasing accuracy. The 1994 census showed the population of Yemen to be about 15.8 million. In 1975 the population of the YAR had been five million, while the 1986 census gave a figure as high as 9.3 million. The PDRY population was considerably smaller; figures ranged from 1.8 to two million. The population of the united Yemen was estimated at 12 to 13 million in May 1990,

however, this figure excludes the number of Yemenis working abroad.

Yemen is still a very rural country; most of the population is scattered across the countryside in small villages or even smaller groups of houses. The biggest province is that of Ta'izz with 2.2 million inhabitants, followed by the provinces of Ibb, San'a (excluding San'a city) and Al-Hudayda (Tihama), with almost two million inhabitants each. The biggest cities are San'a with its population of 970,000 and Aden with 560,000 inhabitants, followed by Ta'izz and al-Hudayda. In 1986, other towns had a few tens of thousand inhabitants at most but they are growing fast, with several towns over 100,000 in 1994.

Life expectancy was 43.8 years in the YAR and 46.5 years in the PDRY, and medical care remains very rudimentary. According to UNICEF statistics released in 1990, 192 out of each 1000 Yemeni children fail to reach age five – the 21st worst figure in the world. This, however, is a significant progress from 1960, when the Yemen's under-five mortality rate of 378 per 1000 was the third worst in the world.

On average, a Yemeni woman gives birth to 7.7 children during her lifetime. Each working person supports 4.6 persons on average, and 52% of the population is under 15 years of age – a fact vividly illustrated by the hordes of curious children that surround you wherever you go. Regional variations are huge: while the average size of the nuclear family is 7.5 persons in Ma'rib, it is less than four in the Abyan Governorate. The annual population growth rate is 3.7%, doubling the population in 20 years.

In the late 1980s, the average age at first marriage in the YAR was 18 years for women and 22 years for men. It is not uncommon for girls under 14 years of age to marry. Surprisingly, divorce is also common; according to some studies, as many as 15% to 20% of women in some rural regions are divorced at some time of their life, and many remarry. In this respect, Yemen differs distinctly from most Arabic countries, where divorce is a social catastrophe for a woman.

Religious Groups

Islam, like any major religion, is divided into different sects, or schools of thinking. The two main divisions, Sunnism and Shi'ism, are both represented in Yemen. Most people in the former PDRY, the Tihama and the southern part of the highlands as far north as Dhamar belong to a Sunni sect called the Shafa'i, while the northernmost provinces are inhabited mainly by Zaydis, a Shi'a minority sect. The Zaydis make up one-third to one-half of the Yemeni population. The division is by no means strictly geographical; rather, you will find a gradual transition from the dominance of one group to that of the other as you travel from south to north or vice versa. Still another Shi'a sect, the Ismailis, constitute barely 1% of the population.

Shafa'is Sunnism is, in general, what might be called 'orthodox' Islam. There are four main schools within Sunnism: Hanafi, Maliki, Shafa'i and Hanbali. All derive their names from their founders, who lived during the first 200 years of Islam. Imam Muhammad ibn Idris Ash-Shafa'i, the founder of the Shafa'i school, died in 820 AD. The differences between the four schools lie not so much in questions of faith as in the interpretation of the Shari'a, the Islamic law, and all but the Hanbali school regard each other as equally orthodox.

Shafa'i teaching spread through most of the Arabian Peninsula and the eastern coast of Africa. Ash-Shafa'i himself travelled extensively and visited even Yemen, but his teachings were ultimately implanted in Hadhramawt by his disciple, Sayyid Ahmad ibn 'Isa al-Muhajir, 100 years after his death. The learned Shafa'is in the Hadhramawt area still trace their origins to Ahmad ibn 'Isa. From Hadhramawt, Shafa'ism rapidly spread across the southern parts of the country, while Tarim and Zabid have been important centres of Shafa'i teaching.

Zaydis The other main sect of Islam, Shi'ism, developed during the very first decades of the new religion. Its founder, the Prophet's cousin and son-in-law 'Ali, was the head of his own party – *Shi'a* in Arabic. It was a doctrine of the party that leadership of the Muslim community rightfully belonged to the descendants of the Prophet. This view was not taken for granted by all believers and, during the first turbulent 120 years of Islam, the Muslims suffered three bloody and devastating civil wars. 'Ali became the fourth caliph but was assassinated in 661 AD; other direct relatives of the Prophet were killed in 680 by the Umayyad Caliphate, which thus secured power for a few decades.

However, Shi'a opposition was not crushed and, in 750, they succeeded in destroying the Umayyads and enthroning descendants of the Prophet's uncle, al-Abbas. This was the beginning of the Abbasid dynasty on the Arabian Peninsula.

Gradually, Shi'ism also split into different sects. Major sects can be distinguished from each other on the basis of the number of imams they recognise. According to Shi'a belief, a secret interpretation of the Koran was transmitted from one successor of 'Ali to another; they thus became imams, considered some kind of superhuman beings. According to the biggest Shi'a sect, the Twelvers, the last imam was Muhammad al-Muntazar. He died in 873 but later returned to earth.

The Zaydis of Yemen recognise only four of the imams, all descendants of Zayd ibn 'Ali, in turn a direct descendant of Caliph 'Ali. Zayd ibn 'Ali was killed in Kufa in 740 while rebelling against the Umayyads. His followers founded the Zaydi branch of Shi'ism. Zaydism reached Yemen in the late 9th century and, in 901, a wise man named Yahya bin Husayn bin Qasim ar-Rassi became the first Zaydi imam after successfully mediating between warring Hashid and Bakil tribes.

Sa'da became the capital of Zaydi rule and teaching which spread over a territory that varied in size over the centuries. Zaydi rule continued uninterrupted in the northern part of Yemen and was at its zenith in the era of independent Yemen (from 1918) when the Zaydis ruled the whole country. Finally, the revolution of 1962 replaced the imam with secular rulers.

Although the Zaydi state no longer exists, people continue to call themselves Zaydis. There is no visible friction between Zaydis and Shafa'is in Yemen today, though you might expect it to exist when you remember the Iran-Iraq war, or the continuing confrontations between Shi'a and Sunni factions in Lebanon and in other parts of the modern Arabic world. Instead, these groups largely inhabit overlapping areas and use the same mosques for prayer.

There are certain differences between the religious practices of the two groups but these are relatively minor, like the wording of the prayer calls. Other features are more prominent, such as the adherence to the traditional tribal structure, always much stronger among the Zaydis of the north than with the Shafa'is in the south. The social occupations of members of these groups also differ; the Zaydis have mainly distinguished themselves as fearless soldiers, while the Shafa'is have always been merchants and tradespeople and control most of the country's trade.

Ismailis The third religious group in Yemen is another Shi'a sect, the Ismailis. They differ from the Twelver Shi'as in that their sequence of imams diverges already on the seventh imam Ismail, who died in 760 AD. The Ismaili movement flourished in eastern Arabia under the Qarmatians in the 10th century. It also thrived in Egypt during the rule of the Fatimid caliphs between 969 AD and 1171 AD, and there are several Ismaili groups living around the world in relative separation from each other.

In Yemen, the first successful Ismaili expansion took place in 1061 AD in the form of the Sulayhi state, founded by 'Ali ibn Muhammad ibn 'Ali as-Sulayhi. The Ismaili Kingdom lasted 79 years and had its capital in Jibla. Later, the Ismailis were oppressed by the Zaydis and many fled to India, where the community of Buhras still exists. Presently, the Ismailis make up less than 1% of the population of Yemen. Most live in or around the town of Manakha. The grave of an Ismaili saint, Hatim bin Ibrahim, in al-Khutayb in the Haraz mountains, is an important place of pilgrimage.

Tribal Groups

Next to religion, the most important factor dividing the Yemeni population into smaller units is the traditional tribal structure.

The basic building block of Yemeni society is the nuclear family, *'ayla* in Arabic. The family tends to be quite large by Western standards and averages 5.6 persons. Many women bear 10 or more children and some men have more than one wife. According to the Koran, men can have four wives and, while this is in accordance with the legislation of Yemen, polygamy was banned by law in the former PDRY.

The nuclear family never exists in isolation but is contained within the extended family. This is called *bayt*, meaning 'house'. The term can be taken literally; usually, each Yemeni house is inhabited by several generations of the same extended family. The archetypal bayt houses a man, his wives, his sons and unmarried daughters, and his sons' wives and children.

The extended families form larger units by genealogy, *fakhdh* and *bayn* being the next groups in the hierarchy. The largest unit is called *qabila*, or 'tribe'. On a Yemeni map, you may find areas with names such as 'Bani Matar' or 'Bani Husayn'. The word *bani* literally means 'the sons of', so it is clear that all members of these units trace their origin to a common forefather.

Finding names of this kind on the map also suggests that, in traditional Yemeni society, the tribes and subtribes have always occupied a more or less strictly defined territory. This reflects Yemen's dependence on agriculture, with economically independent tribes growing crops sufficient to feed their community. The static pattern of residence is very much true even today, since the buying and selling of land always takes place between members of the same tribe. An exception to this rule is the Bedouin tribes of the east; these nomads do not settle in a certain area but keep wandering along the outskirts of the big Arabian desert, forming a vast qabila of their own.

Belonging to a unit confers both rights and obligations. Conflicts are resolved within the smallest unit to which both participants belong and, the closer the opponents are to each other within the tribal structure, the smaller the number of people involved. If a *qabili*, or 'tribesman', kills a member of another tribe, everybody in his tribe is responsible for paying the compensation.

Over the centuries, many customs and external signs have evolved to distinguish members of different tribes from each other. An experienced observer can easily deduce the tribe to which a qabili belongs from the design of his *jambiya* (a ceremonial dagger worn by men at their waist), the way his *futa* (men's skirt) is made or the way he winds his headcloth. Women's clothing also varies considerably from tribe to tribe. Various ceremonies are held to mark events such as marriage, childbearing and so on. Some tribes in the Tihama practise the circumcision of women. Each tribe has a its own folklore, music and dances.

Every tribe elects a sheikh *(shaykh,* or 'the eldest one'), a respected and supposedly wise man who will resolve conflicts arising within the tribe according to Shari'a, the Islamic law. In the case of an unresolvable conflict with another tribe, it is the sheikh who is responsible for recruiting an army and leading the battle against the aggressor. His power is not absolute, however, and a new election may be held if he fails to live up to expectations.

The tribes form even bigger units that could be called tribal federations. Three such units exist in the northern part of Yemen today: the very strong Hashids and Bakils of the mountains and the Zaraniqs of Tihama, whose power was crushed after the 1934 Saudi-Yemeni war. Land in the San'a basin for example, is divided between seven tribes. Five of these tribes (Arhab, Bani Bahlul, Bani al-Harith, Bani Hushayh and Bani Matar) belong to the Bakils and two (Hamdan and Sanhan) are Hashid tribes. These tribal units still have such influence in Yemen that no cabinet can be formed without balancing tribal representation.

While the tribal structure is strong in the northern parts of the Yemen, the role of tribes gradually diminishes as you move southwards. In the Hujjariya area south of Ta'izz, where most of the population are Shafa'is, tribal ties are very weak and mobility is high; many people have moved to other parts of the country to become merchants or professionals. In the former PDRY, where the stated goal of the government was to diminish the power of local sheikhs, tribes are smaller and even more fragmented.

Social Classes

In traditional Yemeni society, the religious elite has formed the highest social classes. The *sayyid* class (plural in Arabic: *sada),* direct descendants of the Prophet Muhammad, were at the top of Zaydi society and are highly respected to this day. The *qadhi* group (plural: *qudha),* legal specialists who inherited their position without being sada, form

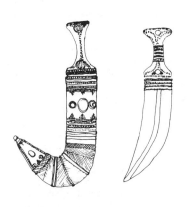

Jambiyas

another elite group and are respected for their literacy.

At the lowest level of Yemeni society are those people called *akhdam* (singular: *khadim*). They can be seen in the cities sweeping streets, cleaning public baths and performing other jobs regarded as menial. A little higher up the social ladder have been the slaves (brought from Ethiopia to the Tihama) and their descendants, called *abid*. These dark-skinned people were often treated as family members, despite the low status of the work they performed.

Most Yemenis fall somewhere between these two extremes – *qabili* (tribespeople) in northern Zaydi terminology, or *'arab* or *ra'aya* in the southern Shafa'i parts of the country. These people, mostly farmers or landowners, take pride in their family connections.

Below this class but above the akhdam are those people of uncertain genealogy and those who perform odd jobs, such as barbers or artisans. They go by many names, such as *nuqqas, bani khums* or *jazr* (butcher), which describe their suspect origins or low-status occupations.

In recent years, this traditional structure has started to break down. As money became a central part of Yemeni daily life during the 1970s, occupations once seen as lowly came to command more respect and, today, Yemenis are more willing to break the social barriers. Although it is still rare for a sayyid to open a restaurant, this is no longer impossible in bigger towns. The rising educational level of the population is also likely to contribute to these changes, since literacy is no longer restricted to the sayyid and qadhi classes. However, marital restrictions still prevail.

EDUCATION

During the imamic rule, education was limited to Koran schools which had the somewhat limited goal of teaching children to memorise the Koran by heart.

After the revolutions of the 1960s, new schools were built throughout the country, giving every child the chance to learn to read and write Arabic. English is taught as the foreign language. School attendancy is low, however, in the remote mountains of the northern part of the country. Before the unification, the PDRY had the more efficient schooling system.

Yemen suffers from a lack of teachers, aggravated by troubled relations with other Arabic countries. In the YAR nine teachers out of ten used to be foreigners, usually Egyptians. During the Gulf crisis of 1990, however, some 30,000 teachers were forced to leave the country after their salaries, which had been paid by the states of Kuwait and Saudi Arabia, were cut off, leaving the Yemeni education sector in chaos. Since then, replacements have arrived from the more fundamentalist Muslim countries such as the Sudan and Iran, and consequently religion has again been emphasised in the curricula.

ARCHITECTURE

Yemeni architecture is unique. Houses are built from local materials: mud, brick and reed on the plains, stone in the mountains. Human settlement here always displays a fantastic harmony with the natural surroundings. Buildings from the mightiest tower houses to the tiniest shacks seem to form part of a great unified plan, as if the Yemenis had an instinctive understanding of the art of building.

Tihama

In the Tihama, houses are low; the only structures of considerable height are the minarets of mosques. Building materials and styles vary from region to region. The most common type of house in the countryside is the reed hut – a round or rectangular house with one room and a sharply topped roof. The appearance of a village of round reed huts is astonishingly African, suggesting links across the Red Sea.

The reed huts are built of reeds, sticks and palm woods, the walls are often covered with a smooth layer of mud and reeds are left visible on the roof. The housing compound of a single family may consist of several one-room huts. Despite the primitive appearance of such dwellings, their interiors are decorated imaginatively and treated with great care.

The larger villages and towns have houses built of brick. The buildings are still low – one or two storeys – and, in larger towns, may extend into many rooms and courtyards. Decorations on the outer walls include unfinished patterns of protruding bricks or elaborate plastered ornaments. Often, the most beautiful decorations face the inner court, with the view from the streets revealing little of the owner's wealth. The most beautiful examples of such houses can be found in the region of Zabid. Brick houses can also be found further to the north, in the town of al-Qanawis.

A third type of Tihami house is the so-called Red Sea house, a townhouse-style building that reflects foreign influence. These multistoreyed houses can be found in al-Hudayda and, to a lesser extent, in al-Makha in the south and al-Luhayya in the north. Turkish windows and balconies are characteristic of Red Sea houses.

Highlands
In the highlands, the most commonly seen dwelling is the tower house. These buildings are made of stone, brick or mud, depending on which material is locally available, and embody the architectural style that most foreign visitors to Yemen remember for the rest of their lives. It has been said that Yemen was where skyscrapers were invented and that all Yemenis are architects. There is certainly something very special in the way mountain Yemenis build their houses. The four to six-storey towers are imposing, even more so when you realise that houses here have been built this way since time immemorial.

Each tower house is home to one family, with several generations living under the same roof. Various storeys are reserved for different purposes; the bottom floor is for animals and bulk storage while the top floor, often a small attic in the roof of the house, is the most highly valued in the whole house –

called the *mafraj*, it is where the owner meets guests. The intermediate storeys contain the living rooms, the women's room, kitchens, bathrooms and the *diwan* (a large room reserved for celebrations).

Mountains
In the western and southern mountains, stone is the main building material. Building facades are differently decorated in each region; an expert in Yemeni architecture can identify the village from a house's facade.

Although the outer walls may show mere stone to the streets, the inner walls are often plastered with mud and finished with white gypsum, giving the rooms a pleasant appearance. Often, the plaster is extended outside from the window openings; the windows are generally the most decorative detail of the house, with an elaborate plaster-and-glass fretwork called *takhrim* giving them an air of prestige. The window panes have traditionally been constructed from pieces of alabaster; today, glass of different colours is used.

High Plateaus & Valleys
On the central plateaus and by the wadis in the Shabwa and Hadhramawt governorates, houses are built of mud or brick, often used with stone. San'a is a brilliant example of a town in which various techniques have been combined to achieve a most pleasing result: the first couple of storeys are laid in stone and the upper storeys are built of brick, with elaborate decorations.

In Rada' and Sa'da, you will see mud houses built using the *zabur* technique. The walls are made of layers of mud, each layer carefully laid on top of the last and left to dry for a few days before the next layer is added. The building's stability is ensured by letting the walls lean against each other at the corners, giving the structure its characteristic conical shape. The walls are then carefully finished to give the house a very smooth appearance.

In the wadis of the southern governorates, mud-plastered brick architecture dominates. There are whole villages and towns built exclusively of sun-dried mud bricks: tower houses, palaces, tombs, mosques with their minarets and public wells. In al-Mukalla and the Hadhramawt valley, the decoration of many houses shows Indian and Indonesian (especially Javanese) influence because, according to local tradition, emigrant business people eventually come home to Yemen, building mosques and houses there.

Imported Styles

Unfortunately, all imported architecture is not to be celebrated. Modern or post-revolutionary architecture in Yemen incorporates imported materials and techniques such as reinforced concrete and cement bricks. Worst of all are the port cities of al-Hudayda and Aden and the new part of al-Mukalla, with the Egyptian block style dominating in the north and the Soviet style in the south. Examples also abound in other big cities like Ta'izz and San'a, and even in Hajja and Sa'da.

Yet in most parts of Yemen, few new houses look wholly 'imported' in style. Even walls built with cement blocks usually have a facing made of local stone.

How long traditional building styles will survive is hard to tell. A trend not to be celebrated may, however, be emerging in the form of the worst examples of modern architecture: the schools of Yemen. Unvarying in style, these stone buildings dot the towns and countryside of the northern provinces in their hundreds as if destined to influence the buildings of the future by shaping the architectural vision of today's young Yemenis.

MUSIC

Yemeni music culture is rich and has long-standing traditions. Traditional music styles vary greatly from region to region, and the San'ani, Tihami, Adeni, Laheji and Hadhrami styles are clearly distinguishable. The feverish rhythms of the Tihama hardly appeal to the dignified oud player from San'a.

The most celebrated instrument in Yemen is the oud, or *'ud*, from which the name of the Western lute is said to derive. Variations of this instrument are widely used in various Arab cultures. While the oud is popular in the mountains and highlands, the *simsimiya*, like a five-string lyre with a small resonator box, is the most common instrument along the Yemeni coast. This instrument is popular throughout the Red Sea area and in the Arabian Gulf, where it is called a *tumbara*. Reed pipes known as *mizmar* are an important part of Yemeni music, forming the basis of a large variety of rhythmical instruments including the *madiff*, the *mafra'*, the *qulqula* and the *tabla*. Many variants of instruments are only used in certain religious ceremonies, such as the Tihami madiff, which is only used in the zar ceremony of exorcism.

Some Yemeni artists, like the Hadhrami singer Badwi Zubayr, are popular all over the Peninsula. You can also hear a lot of Yemeni songs in the Gulf countries, where local stars perform them without ever giving credit to the composers. Among the Adeni musicians is the legendary Iskandar Thabit born in 1924. His popular songs served the Yemeni revolutions of the '60s.

The best way to obtain popular Yemeni music while in Yemen is to hang around the small cassette stands that abound in the suqs, keep your ears open while the local folks do their business and purchase those recordings you like. A week or two of travelling in Yemen should be enough to distinguish the most popular hits of the day (even though the rhythmic and melodic conventions differ considerably from those in the West), since radios and cassette recorders generally blare at full volume in taxis and buses. Besides domestic productions, Egyptian, Lebanese and Sudanese music are also quite popular in Yemen.

Although she's never performed in Yemen, Ofra Haza (an Israeli of Yemeni origin) has

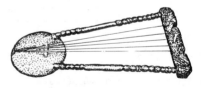

Simsimiya

made the songs of Yemeni Jews available worldwide.

Some recordings of Yemeni folk music are available in the West. Try, for example, *Music from Yemen Arabia* (Lyrichord LLST series records 7283 and 7284), *Music of the Tihama in North Yemen* (Lyrichord LLST series records 7384) or *Music of South Arabia* (Ethnic Folkways Library P 421). The *UNESCO Collection 'Zaidi & Shafii'* (Philips 6586040) is a collection of religious songs from San'a, while *Musical Atlas* (EMI 3 C-064-18352) includes folk music from the Tihama, Sa'da, Hajja, Manakha, San'a, Zabid and Bayt al-Faqih. Also available is the French *Anthologie Phonographique du Récital Oriental* (Arabesque 6).

SOCIETY & CUSTOMS

Don't expect to be a quiet spectator of the daily show of local life. Most of the time, you will be the protagonist in that show and the focus of attention. Wherever you go, the Yemenis will show their interest in you by cheering and smiling, greeting you, talking to you and gathering around you. The interest is genuine and friendly, so don't make the error of thinking they are only interested in getting something from you. Generally, this is not the case and, even in the suqs, most traders are not as overly eager to sell their products to you as experience in other Arab countries would suggest.

The Tihami people are accustomed to seeing strangers, being a mix of different races themselves. In fact, in the course of history, they have developed some indifference towards other people when compared to the mountain Yemenis. In the lower Yemen (that is, the southern highlands), you can easily gather a crowd of exhilarated Yemenis around you; all you need to do is ask for a taxi to an unusual destination and, all of a sudden, drivers and passengers will be offering their help.

If you happen to walk near a village school at noon, when the students get out, every child will try to catch a glimpse of you. You soon feel like the queen in a swarm of bees, surrounded by hundreds of small and very active creatures. Everybody is eager to try out the English they have learnt in school (not much) and each expects to be addressed individually. If you have some Arabic greetings at your command, you can easily give them a surprise. Never make the mistake of getting angry with them or they might start throwing stones at you – a common way of treating despised people (like the Yemeni Jews in the past).

As you move further north, people become less open and, in the higher Yemen, they are particularly reserved. Around Sa'da you will still meet many very friendly people but they won't gather around you in such numbers. In the northern highlands, you may even find villages where a stranger is frowned upon and you could have some difficulty finding a place to stay if night falls upon you in a village without an inn. Normally, however, this is not the case and you will find that the legendary Arab hospitality is alive and well.

Dress Code

Yemen is a strict Muslim society, which means that you don't come here for a suntan.

Western women are seen as a 'third sex' and, consequently, are not required to wear veils as Yemeni women do. Nevertheless, it is wise to dress appropriately; you should not make an insult of your appearance or give an improper impression of your sexual availability. Wear loose clothes that reveal nothing above the ankles: long skirts, pants or dresses and tops, preferably with long sleeves. Tops should be long and worn outside pants. Covering your hair might make you feel more comfortable.

Men wearing shorts are not offensive to the Yemenis – merely ridiculous. Long pants and a shirt are recommended. For both sexes, loose clothing and protective headgear also make sense for reasons of climate.

Visiting Mosques

There are over 40,000 mosques in Yemen, not counting small one-room prayer houses. This includes many gorgeous historical buildings, a couple of them dating from the days of the Prophet. When the YAR was opened to foreign tourism, the mosques were seen as a major attraction. The imams were told to treat tourists well and, in the late 1970s, it was possible to visit many mosques, as long as you took off your shoes. Similar arrangements applied to tour groups in the former PDRY.

Unfortunately, this is no longer the case. The foreigners, with their strange behaviour, disturbed those praying in the mosque and the imams soon began to restrict the flow of non-Muslims into the sacred buildings. Today, most Yemeni mosques don't allow non-Muslims to enter at all and, according to Muslim purists, a non-Muslim should not be allowed to visit even the graveyards outside the mosques. Still, a few mosques allow visitors outside prayer times and some historical mosques that are not in active ritual use can also be entered.

If you belong to a tourist group, your entry to a specific mosque may be arranged. A Yemeni friend may also help you get into a mosque. If you show interest in taking a look inside one, you may be able to make friends with somebody if you loiter around the entrance long enough – sometimes they even fetch a younger man working in the mosque to serve as your guide. On the other hand, your mere presence at the outer door of a mosque may cause such a stir among the believers that you would be wise to leave the scene quietly.

Never rush into a mosque without asking permission. If you are granted entry, take off your shoes. For females, proper dress is crucial: you should not expose your hair or any skin other than your face, hands and ankles. Don't make a fuss in your picture-taking and do not insist on aiming your camera towards those deep in prayer. You may not be allowed into all parts of the mosque, so accept these restrictions. If the imam asks for *baksheesh* or alms, it is a good idea to oblige.

Qat

Yemen's most popular drug, qat, enjoys quasiofficial status as the national narcotic – the qat plant was even depicted on the one-riyal note. This mild stimulant is used weekly, even daily, by almost every adult Yemeni in the mountainous northern provinces and, according to some sources, trade in qat made up one-third of the economic activity of the YAR in the late 1980s.

The unification of Yemen in 1990 spread qat to the southern provinces, where previously it was not as common because low altitudes made that part of the country unsuitable for qat cultivation. In the days of the PDRY, consumption of the drug was only allowed on Thursdays and Fridays.

The qat plant, *Catha edulis*, is a small, evergreen tree or bush and is three to seven metres high when cultivated. It is a hardy plant that needs little care, the main requirement being an adequate supply of water. In favourable circumstances, a qat tree may reach 10 metres; such giants can be seen near Ta'izz on the slopes of Jabal Sabir, which gets heavy monsoon rainfall.

Qat prospers only at relatively high altitudes (1500 to 2500 metres). Like coffee, it originated in the mountains of eastern Africa. Nowadays, it occurs naturally in a vast geographical area from South Africa and Madagascar to Afghanistan. It is also cultivated in Kenya, Somalia and Ethiopia but nowhere is it as ubiquitous as in Yemen.

Yemenis use qat by chewing the fresh leaves. It can also be consumed in other ways – in parts of East Africa, qat is used in tea. Qat is harvested by picking the ends of the branches. These are bound into small bundles to be sold at the market. Only the youngest and freshest leaves are suitable for chewing and, as the leaves wilt within a couple of days of picking, they lose their value very quickly. Qat cannot be dried or otherwise preserved, which means that it must be sold and used by the day after harvesting.

Since qat grows only in the highlands, where communication has traditionally been poor, its use has mainly been restricted to the areas where it is grown. Its cultivation has spread throughout the Yemeni highlands and you can hardly find a village without qat

Chewing Qat

The most important feature of qat is that it is a social drug – you rarely chew it alone. Most qat is chewed at qat parties. These take place in the afternoons in the mafraj of Yemeni houses. The fact that the streets of a Yemeni town are almost deserted in the afternoons does not mean that the locals are having a siesta; rather, it reflects the widespread popularity of qat parties. Every male Yemeni has to attend such parties at least once a week; those who can afford it attend daily. A man who avoids these parties will soon be regarded as some kind of freak, a voluntary social outcast.

Qat parties are not planned days ahead; like everything in Yemen, they happen spontaneously. In the morning, men meet each other in the suqs, mosques and elsewhere, exchange news and find out where each one is going to chew qat that day. Everyone offers their house for this purpose in turn and each man attends the qat parties of those social circles with which he wishes to be associated.

Although most talk in the qat chews is just everyday chattering, many important decisions are actually made in the qat parties preceding the formal occasion. This extends from marriage contracts to politics at its highest levels: nobody has a say at the government level if he's not invited to President Salah's qat parties.

You will frequently be asked whether or not you have chewed qat. Your answer will reveal more about you than you might think. If you haven't chewed qat, you haven't been in the country for long or, if you have stayed for a while, you are willing to maintain your foreigner's status and are not prepared to mingle with the Yemenis. If you have chewed qat, you obviously have some Yemeni friends with whom you have been chewing and you will be given much more respect.

You will often be offered qat. The Yemenis consider it courteous to offer a branch of qat to the stranger next to them in a taxi, for example. If you accept it, you will be at the very centre of exhilarated attention. Don't be embarrassed; they are not making a fool of you. The bulging cheek of a Yemeni arouses similar admiring reactions. You are not likely to be offered a whole cheek-full of qat. If you are invited to chew with somebody and you accept the invitation, it's wise to buy your own qat preceding the gathering. ■

growing nearby. It is reported that qat has replaced coffee in large areas of Yemen because the farmers derive greater profits from it. You can find both growing side by side on the terraces.

Chewing qat is an acquired skill. The leaves themselves are not swallowed; instead, they are pushed against one cheek, where the chewed paste forms a slimy ball that grows steadily as new leaves are added. Maintaining that lump between your teeth and cheek is a complicated trick, as you will find if you try chewing qat. Some kind of anatomical adaptation obviously occurs over many years of chewing: old men's cheeks

often appear extraordinarily wrinkled when empty but are capable of holding a wad of qat the size of a tennis ball. Those with the most bulging cheeks are admired most.

The physiological effects of qat have been much studied but, so far, no satisfactory understanding of the drug has been reached. The World Health Organisation (WHO) has divided the world's drugs into seven categories; qat forms one of these by itself. Chemical analysis has revealed a plethora of effective compounds in the leaves but it is not clear which of these are the most effective. All that can be said with certainty is that qat is a mild stimulant, it does not have any proven side effects that are hazardous to the health of even a heavy user (though it does cause some constipation) and it is obviously not physically addictive. It *appears* to be at least psychologically addictive when observed by a foreigner conditioned to think that all drugs are addictive but research does not confirm this.

Yemenis attribute all kinds of positive effects to qat. Because it is said to increase endurance, qat is often chewed when people are engaged in heavy or monotonous labour, especially when travelling. It is said to help you do without food, drink or sexual relations; on the other hand, it is customary to eat well before chewing qat because it is supposed to enhance the pleasure of drinking and smoking. It is also said to strengthen potency. It certainly helps you stay awake.

Qat is said to stimulate the intellect, raise the spirits and increase mutual understanding and communication. Based on direct observation, I can confirm that it enhances the talkativeness of Yemenis although, after chewing qat for a few hours, the user ends up in an introverted, meditative, almost depressive state of mind. Mystics tend to believe that qat intensifies their communication with God.

You will have ample opportunities to observe qat chewing. Almost any gathering of Yemenis between 2 and 6 pm tends to become an occasion for chewing qat, be it a bus trip or a football match. Taxi drivers chew qat while driving, shopkeepers have bulging cheeks in the early evenings, men walking in the streets chew it – you can't avoid encountering qat in Yemen. Women also chew qat, though not as visibly.

Qat is not cheap. A *rubta*, or small bundle of six or 10 qat branches containing enough leaves for a typical three to four-hour chewing session, may cost anything from YR 150 to YR 1500 (typically YR 250 to YR 700) depending on supply and demand, the season, the quality of the qat and the general income level of customers in that particular suq. This is expensive in a country where an unskilled labourer may earn YR 150 to YR

350 a day and a skilled worker may earn only double that.

Yemenis tend to chew one rubta once a week or two rubtas every day; heavy users who chew qat in the mornings while working and in the evenings after qat parties may chew as much as four or six rubtas a day. When asked how much they chew, a Yemeni often tells you how much they spend on qat in a week. Surveys show that most Yemenis chewing qat regularly spend between one-quarter and one-half of their total income on it. Those on meagre incomes buy cheaper qat in order to chew more often, while those enjoying large incomes display their wealth by buying the most expensive qat. It is absolutely essential that a person buy their own daily qat supply – this is a kind of basic status symbol in Yemen and continuously measures the income standard in a very public way.

Sport

Soccer is the national pastime in Yemen, evident upon visiting any village: children play soccer in the streets and alleys everywhere, often with fancy rag-balls. However, it's unlikely you will spot Yemen in the world cup charts in the near future. Organised sport is, in general, very rare in Yemen, and the country has very few international-level athletes. In San'a and a few other cities you can watch an occasional national league game at a football stadium. A recent addition to organised sport in Yemen is the Yemeni Cricket League, completing their first season in early 1995.

To date, Yemen has participated in three Olympic Games, sending as many as 120 athletes to the Barcelona Games in 1992. However, Yemen has yet to win an Olympic medal, the athletes having usually been eliminated in the first round of each game. Yemenis brought up abroad make up the few exceptions, such as the European lightweight boxing champion Nasim Salim Kashmim, whose father had emigrated from the Rada' region to the UK 30 years before his son achieved champion status at the age of 20 in 1994. Despite his British citizenship, his achievements warranted him a Yemeni national award, offered personally by President 'Ali Abdullah Salah.

Yemen abounds with fantastic mountains and wadis for hang-gliding, but since the sport is an expensive one, it is not common. If you want to bring your own equipment, contact the Yemen Hang Gliding & Para Gliding Club (fax 967-1-204999), PO Box 1946, San'a.

RELIGION

The state religion of Yemen is Islam. Yemen was one of the very first regions to join the Islamic revolution, with the local Persian rulers converting to the new religion as early as the year 6 AH (Anno Hijra) – that is, 628 AD. According to official sources, all Yemenis today profess the religion of Islam, and it certainly appears this way.

A small but important Jewish minority existed in the country through the first 14 Islamic centuries. During the years 1948 to 1950, the newly established state of Israel organised operation 'Magic Carpet', a major airlift from Aden through which some 50,000 Yemeni Jews emigrated to Israel, leaving only a few hundred – maybe up to one thousand – behind. Most of them are today scattered around Yemen, with the biggest concentration in a village near Sa'da. They are visited time and again by Israeli interest groups trying to persuade them to emigrate, which would put an end to an era of cultural interaction that has lasted for thousands of years.

There are also small Christian and Hindu communities in Aden.

Islam

The Islamic faith is based on the believer's total submission to God and this principle is a very visible part of the daily life of every Muslim. In fact, in Arabic *islam* means 'submitting' and a *muslim* is a 'submitter' to God. The faithful observe the five so-called pillars of Islam: the creed, performance of prayer, giving of alms, observance of fasting and performance of pilgrimage.

There is almost a sixth pillar: *jihad*, which means both 'holy war' and 'striving in the way of God'. The concept of jihad has been much disputed and misunderstood by Muslims and non-Muslims alike. It may just as easily be interpreted as meaning a holy war against the godless, the unbelievers, as meaning an internal struggle against man's basic unholy instincts. While the latter interpretation is much preferred today, there will always be those who use the word to encourage war and disorder. It is for this reason that Islam has gained a reputation, in the eyes of many Westerners, as a dangerous religion with fanatical followers. However, in its essence Islam is as peaceful a religion as any.

The Creed The core of Islamic belief is expressed in beautiful calligraphy on the flag of Saudi Arabia: 'There is no God but God and Muhammad is the Prophet of God.' Anybody who utters this phrase in the presence of two reliable witnesses may be regarded as a Muslim. We have heard men walking the streets of small Yemeni villages recite this testimony to no-one in particular.

Muslims also believe in the angels who brought God's messages to humans (it was the archangel Gabriel who communicated the Koran to Muhammad), in the prophets who received these messages, in the books in which the prophets expressed these revelations, and in the last day of judgment. The Koran mentions 28 prophets, of whom Muhammad was the last and the one who received the final revelation from God – there will be no more prophets. This makes the Koran the last of the books, towards which the revelations of earlier prophets progress. The day of judgment will be announced by the archangel Asrafil blowing a trumpet and, at that time, all people will be summoned to either paradise or hell, according to whether they have struggled along God's path or abandoned it.

Islam shares many holy men and scriptures with Judaism and Christianity. Twenty-one of the 28 Islamic prophets are also mentioned in the Bible, and Adam, Noah, Abraham, David, Jacob, Joseph, Job,

Fundamentalism in Yemen

Media in the West has recently linked Islam with religious extremism and fundamentalism. This regrettable development has evolved largely because of the politicisation of Islam – religion has increasingly been used as a tool and a weapon for political ends.

Yemenis have traditionally been very tolerant towards differing views and different lifestyles. In previous years political parties were banned in the YAR while the PDRY was strictly a one-party country, so there were no politics where religion could have played a role. Upon the unification of the country the formation of new political parties was legalised, and religion predictably became a force in politics. In the southern governorates, adhering to northern symbolic practises became very important after the civil war of 1994, and today in Aden, for example, you can't find a woman not wearing a veil.

The heat is felt by the religious minorities such as the Ismailis and many Shafa'i groups of the south. Zaydi fundamentalist groups have attacked quite a few shrines and tombs on the pretext that the Koran prohibits erecting a mosque on top of a grave. Since the civil war, shrines have been pillaged and destroyed all over the country, from the Ismaili villages in the Haraz mountains to Jibla, Aden and Hadhramawt. In particular, the right wing of the Islah party reportedly has connections to extremist groups.

Fortunately, Yemen has not joined the Islamic countries such as Iran or Algeria whose domestic politics has bred attacks against Western influences and, in extreme cases (so over-publicised in the Western media), Western individuals. The danger is there, however, kept alive inadvertently by the actions of moderate Arabs and Western countries, for example, stopping development aid in response to Yemen's unwillingness to support their actions against Iraq during the 1990/91 Gulf crisis.

When Egypt called their school teachers back from Yemen in 1990 after a political row, they were replaced by teachers from Sudan, just when Sudan was suffering from an image problem created by US allegations that it supported Islamic fundamentalists who planned terror acts against the West. This, of course, only served to radicalise Sudanese intellectuals, teachers in Yemen included. ■

Moses and Jesus are particularly honoured, although the divinity of Jesus is strictly denied. The Koran also recognises the scriptures of Abraham, the Torah of Moses, the Psalms of David and the Gospel of Jesus as God's revelation.

Prayer The ritual of prayer is an essential part of a believer's daily life. Every Muslim should pray at least five times a day: at sunrise, noon, late afternoon, sunset and night. Five times a day, the muezzin (from Arabic *muwadhdhin)* calls believers to the mosque for prayer. It is perfectly permissible to pray at home or elsewhere; only the Friday noon prayer should be conducted in the mosque. It is preferred that women pray at home. (Only a few mosques are designated for women.)

The act of praying involves a series of predefined movements of the body and the recital of prayers and passages of the Koran, all designed to express the believer's abso-

lute humility and God's sovereignty. First, believers wash themselves to show their will to purify themselves – there are fountains or ablution pools in mosques for this purpose. Then, they go to the place of prayer, face Mecca (the proper orientation is indicated by the alignment of the mosque) and perform one or more *rakats* (cycles of prayer), during which they read certain passages of the Koran, pray, bow and prostrate themselves. There is a different series for each of the day's five prayer times.

Alms A Muslim should pay one-fortieth of their annual income to the poor as *zakat*, or alms. To the believer, this institution is as essential as prayer. The practice of giving alms reflects both the need to 'purify' earthly wealth and the individual's willingness to demonstrate social responsibility.

The giving of alms may once have been an act of a more individual nature than it is today. The institution has developed along lines very similar to those used by Western welfare states in taking care of their poor. In Yemen, as in other Arabic countries, a special Ministry of Waqfs and Religious Guidance controls the distribution of religious charitable endowments.

Fasting The ninth month of the lunar year, Ramadan, is the month of fasting. During Ramadan, Muslims abstain from eating, drinking, smoking and sexual intercourse between sunrise and sunset. Extra prayers and recitations of the Koran are encouraged, since the purpose of fasting is to bring people closer to God.

The considerable effort needed to fulfil this religious requirement greatly contributes to each individual's sense of belonging to the Muslim community – everybody shares this experience at the same time. Fasting also has a great influence on the daily routines of any predominantly Muslim country because all daily activities are, of necessity, kept to the lowest possible level. Ramadan is not a detested month, though. In fact, Muslims love it; fasting during the daylight hours gives them a reason to feast in the dark. Nights are lively, joyous occasions and many people stay awake all night, leaving sleep for the afternoons.

Pilgrimage Every Muslim who can afford to do so should make the pilgrimage to the holiest of cities, Mecca, at least once in their lifetime. The reward is considerable: the forgiving of all past sins. The *hajj* pilgrimage takes place every year during Dhul-Hijja, the last month of the Muslim calendar. Pilgrimages can also be made at other times of the year.

Since Yemen shares a border with Saudi Arabia, a very high percentage of Yemenis perform this ceremonial journey. Of the 1.6 million hajj pilgrims who enter Saudi Arabia each year, between 7% and 8% are Yemenis. This figure does not include the many Yemenis who work in Saudi Arabia and perform the pilgrimage while there.

LANGUAGE
Arabic is the language spoken in Yemen. Radio broadcasts and daily newspapers are in Arabic, which is the official language. The exception is the evening TV news, which is in English. Having some Arabic at your command makes all the difference.

Coping Without Arabic
Many Yemenis speak a non-Arabic language. We encountered a few old men who spoke excellent Italian; in the 1930s, Mussolini made Abyssinia (today's Ethiopia) a colony of Italy, and these Italian speakers came to Yemen from Eritrea. Migration still occurs from various African countries, spreading African languages which will probably not be familiar to you.

Some Yemenis speak Russian because the Soviet Union has played a major role in developing the basic infrastructure (and the military) in both parts of the country since the revolutions. In the southern governorates, Russian was the most important non-Arabic language during the 23 years of communist rule and, in the Tihama region, you can still see road signs written in the Cyrillic alphabet. The People's Republic of China also gave generous aid in the form of work brigades, but we haven't observed the Yemenis' ability to speak Chinese.

Today, English is the most important non-Arabic language. It is widely understood by older Yemenis in the southern governorates because of the region's colonial past. After the revolution and the civil war, the new government of the YAR recognised the need for education in general, and knowledge of English in particular. So, even in the most remote mountain villages, you'll quickly be surrounded by children eager to brush up on their English. The schooling programme is still young, however, and many English greetings are used synonymously, such as 'Hello', 'how are you', 'I love you', 'no friend', 'thank you' and 'I'm sorry'.

However, it is getting easier for English-speaking travellers in Yemen. You can already get along fairly comfortably in San'a and Aden using just English. Compare this to the mid-1980s, when all San'a's street signs were in Arabic and you couldn't get a taxi from the centre of San'a to the airport if you didn't know that airport should be pronounced 'mata:r', with very dark a's (pronounced at the back of the mouth).

If you get really stuck, the staff of a government office in a town of reasonable size will usually manage to fetch a fairly able interpreter within 30 minutes or so. Don't expect this to happen in remote mountain villages, though.

Exactly why the younger generation does not speak English better is hard to tell. Certainly, it is not for want of trying. We have been shown exercise books from advanced classes: the students solve impressive grammatical drills with little difficulty. However, only a small fraction of what is learnt is actually applied to the spoken language. This is due partly to the scant opportunities for practice and partly to the weak links between the written and spoken language of their mother tongue. To appreciate this, we must look briefly at the history of the Arabic language.

Classical Arabic

The holy book of Islam, the Koran, was dictated to Muhammad by Allah (God) in the early 7th century AD – the literal meaning of 'Koran' is 'recitation'. The Koran was dictated in the language of Muhammad which, at that time, was used only in parts of the Arabian Peninsula. It was then mainly a spoken language; the earliest known written examples date from the previous century. The Koran was written down around the time of the Prophet's death and, by the end of the Umayyad Caliphate in 750 AD, differing versions had disappeared and the text had found its final form.

The Koran is the word of Allah and is thus final; not a dot can be changed. During the first centuries of its existence, Islam spread rapidly throughout the Middle East and North Africa and, with it, the language of the Koran, previously unknown to the new converts. To protect Allah's word from foreign influences (which were threatening to force the language into a process of evolution), the Islamic scholars codified Arabic by introducing precise grammatical and lexical rules consistent with the usage in the Koran. The result of this work is known as 'classical Arabic', the language used by early Islamic poets and writers. It is still in active ceremonial use and is taught in the Koran schools.

Colloquial Arabic

With the written form of the language frozen, only spoken Arabic could evolve. Across a vast geographical area and over more than a thousand years, the evolution led to a wide collection of colloquial dialects. The decline of Arab civilisation in the colonial era (from the 15th to the 19th centuries AD) led to the unforeseen isolation of Arab people from one another, speeding up the differentiation of various dialects. In the 20th century, pan-Arab ideals and modern communications have had the opposite effect.

While French and Italian developed from Latin over a similar period of time into two distinct languages, the dialects of Arabic cannot be classified as separate languages, a fact largely attributable to the influence of the Koran. Yet, this does not mean that the dialects are always mutually intelligible. While a Saudi sheikh may readily understand the appeals of an Egyptian beggar, a Yemeni farmer might have serious difficulties bargaining in a Moroccan marketplace.

There are dozens of Arabic phrasebooks on the market, most of which are of questionable value in Yemen, since they describe a different dialect. With a phrasebook of Maghrebi, Egyptian, Levantine or Iraqi Arabic, you can probably get your questions understood. However, they will not help you much in understanding the answers. Worse still, the books may teach you Modern Standard Arabic.

To my knowledge, there is no Yemeni Arabic phrasebook, but any book that concentrates on Peninsular Arabic should do the job. If you are serious about the language, there is a 10,000-word Yemeni Arabic-German-English dictionary: *Jemenitische*

Wörterbuch by Jeffrey Deboo (Verlag Otto Harassowitz, 1989).

There is considerable variation between dialects in different parts of the Arabian Peninsula. Nevertheless, the inhabitants of this area usually understand each other and this situation improves all the time because of better communication and increased economic activity. There are even different dialects within Yemen; the Sumarra Pass is a linguistic watershed often mentioned in treatises on this subject. In practical terms, this means that even if you are able to get your message across, you may have difficulties understanding what you are told or asked.

Modern Standard Arabic
The spoken forms of Arabic never found their way onto paper. The language of the Koran was so highly appreciated that colloquial dialects were considered a sign of linguistic degeneration and not worthy of being written down. This attitude still prevails.

On the other hand, the vocabulary and idioms of classical Arabic reflect the traditional tribal Bedouin society, therefore a more suitable means was needed to convey information and ideas in the modern world of mass media, international communications, politics and advertising. Over the past 100 years, a new form of Arabic has emerged – Modern Standard Arabic. This 'streamlined' version of classical Arabic is capable of expressing modern concepts in new words and idioms.

Modern Standard Arabic is taught alongside classical Arabic in all Arabic countries and is understood by every educated Arab. It is the language children learn to read and write. It is used in all 'serious' communication, from formal speeches to novels, and films to legal documents. It is also a useful means by which two Arabs from different countries can speak with each other. Moreover, it is the language Westerners are generally taught in Arabic courses all over the world – for most students, it is quite a shock to realise how far it really is from the spoken forms of the Arabic language.

Modern Standard Arabic was created when Arab people started to free themselves of colonial rule and needed not just a tool to communicate with each other but also a symbol of Arab unity. Thus, the language contains very few words borrowed from Western languages; new words are derived from old Arabic roots. This is probably one of the reasons that so few Westerners actually learn Arabic – there are no familiar words with which to start.

Alphabet & Transliteration
The Arabic script is cursive, and is written from right to left. The shape of a letter depends on its position in the word and most letters assume four different shapes. There are no capital letters and only one set of type is used; instead, there is a rich variety of calligraphic styles ranging from the simple (for taking quick notes) to the very decorative (for ornamental use).

The alphabet has 28 consonant characters, 18 of which represent sounds also used in English, while the rest will sound unfamiliar to native English speakers. Three of the consonants are semivowels and these can represent consonants, long vowels or diphthongs. Short vowels are never written. There is considerable variation in the pronunciation of vowels in different areas and pronunciation variants also occur with some consonants.

Transliterating Arabic into Latin script is an inherently difficult problem to which a final solution has not yet been found. There are a couple of 'scientific' systems as well as a plethora of nonscientific systems in use today. I own half a dozen books about the language and each uses a different method of transliteration. One consequence of all this is that you will see Arabic names written in various ways in Western newspapers and on maps.

Although your ear will not distinguish the emphatic consonants from their ordinary counterparts, they audibly affect the nearby vowels, making them darker (ie they are pronounced at the back of the mouth). Thus, *ay* is pronounced as in 'why' if there is an emphatic present in the word but is otherwise pronounced more as in 'way' (though not quite). With the exceptions of 'ayn and ghayn, other sounds should be utterable for a native speaker of the English language.

The following table shows Arabic letters and their corresponding translitera-

tions. You will notice that there is an exact and an informal system of transliteration. In the phraselist I have used the exact transliteration. Throughout the rest of this book, I have used the informal transliteration for place names because it's easier to read but I have also presented an exact pronunciation

Transliteration Table & Pronunciation Guide

Arabic	Name of Letter	Transliteration Exact	Informal	Pronunciation
ا	'alif	a:	aa	as in *father*
ب	ba:'	b	b	as in *big*
ت	ta:'	t	t	as in *tongue*
ث	tha:'	th	th	as in *thin*
ج	ji:m	j	j	as in *jam*; or in some countries like *g* in *go*
ح	Ha:'	H	h	strong *h* from back of throat, like blowing on spectacles to clean them
خ	kha:'	kh	kh	like *ch* in Scottish *loch*
د	da:l	d	d	as in *dim*
ذ	dha:l	dh	dh	like *th* in *this*
ر	ra:	r	r	pronounced with a quick tap of the tongue against upper gum; as in Spanish *caro*
ز	za:	z	z	as in *zip*
س	si:n	s	s	as in *sock*
ش	shi:n	sh	sh	as in *shoe*
ص	**sa:d**	**s**	s	emphatic *s*, as in *sum*
ض	**da:d**	**d**	d	emphatic *d*; as in *dumb*
ط	**ta:'**	**t**	t	emphatic *t*; as in *tar*
ظ	**za:'**	**z**	dh	emphatic *dh*; a bit like *z* in *czar*
ع	'ayn	'	'	a glottal stop; a bit like the missing 't' when a Cockney says 'bottle'
غ	ghayn	gh	gh	a gutteral sound like Parisian *r*
ف	fa:'	f	f	as in *fat*
ق	qa:f	q	q	like *k* made further back in throat; or *g* as in *go* (common in Yemen)
ك	ka:f	k	k	as in *king*
ل	la:m	l	l	as in *lamb*
م	mi:m	m	m	as in *man*
ن	nu:n	n	n	as in *name*
ه	ha:'	h	h	as in *ham*
و	wa:w	w	w	as in *wet*; or
		u:	u	long *u* as in *mood;* or
		aw	aw	diphthong as in *how*
ى	ya:'	y	y	as in *yes*; or
		i:	i	long *i* as in *meet;* or
		ay	ay	diphthong as in *why* or in *way*

and transliteration for geographical names. For many names, more than one transliteration is in common use; I will list some of them. For example, for Yemen's capital you will see San'a (**s**an'a; Sana, Sanaa). Within the brackets, the exact pronunciation is given first, followed by one or more alternative spellings.

The Arabic alphabet consists of 28 consonants. There are four vowel sounds in Arabic that are not represented in the alphabet:

'   glottal stop, like the non-voice before *Oh Lord!*
a   as in *hat*, or *hut* (with emphatics)
i   as in *hit*
u   as in *put*

Phrases

Familiarity with some local phrases is particularly useful when travelling in Arabic countries. The behaviour of the Arabs is highly ritualised and everyday conversation consists of some 50 to 100 very common phrases. If you know them well, you should get by quite smoothly. It's also a good idea to learn the numerals – besides the obvious practicalities, you'll get much better prices if you can bargain in Arabic. Unfortunately, the numerals are among the most difficult words for a Westerner to pronounce.

The following phrase list has common phrases in colloquial Yemeni Arabic. (You can find very different phrase lists in other books.)

Greetings & Civilities
Hello.

(greeting)	*is-sala:mu 'alaykum*
(response)	*wa 'alaykum is-sala:m*
Goodbye.	*ma'a s-sala:ma*

Good morning.

(greeting)	***s**aba:H il-khayr*
(response)	***s**aba:H in-nu:r*

Good evening.

(greeting)	*masa:' il-khayr*
(response)	*masa:' in-nur*

How are you?

(to a man)	*kayf Ha:lak*
(to a woman)	*kayf Ha:lik*
(to a group)	*kayf Ha:lkum*
Fine, thanks.	*il-Hamdu li-lla:h/ bi-khayr il-Hamdu li-lla:h/ il-Hamdu li-lla:h bi-khayr*

And you?

(to a man)	*wa inta?*
(to a woman)	*wa inti?*
(to a group)	*wa intkum?*

Please.

(to a man)	*min fadl-ak*
(to a woman)	*fadl-ik*
Thank you.	*shukran*
You're welcome.	*'afwan*
Yes.	*aywa/na'am*
No.	*la:*
Excuse me.	*'afwan*
What? (pardon)	*aysh?*
I'm sorry. (forgive me)	*ana muta'assif*

Language Problems

Do you speak Arabic?	*titkallam 'arabi?*
Do you speak English?	*titkallam ingli:zi?*
A little.	*shwayya*
I don't understand.	*mush fahim*
I don't speak Arabic.	*mush atkallam 'arabi*
Please write it down.	*mumkin titkub*
I don't have a pen.	*ma: fi: qalam*

Small Talk
What's your name?

(to a man)	*aysh ismak?*
(to a woman)	*aysh ismik?*
My name is ...	*ismi ...*

Where are you from?

(to a man)	*min wayn inta?*
(to a woman)	*min wayn inti?*
(to a group)	*min wayn intkum?*

I am/We are from ... *ana/iHna min ...*
   Australia *ustura:liya*
   Finland *finlanda:*
   France *faransa*
   Germany *alma:niya*
   UK *brita:niya*
   USA *amri:ka*

How do you like *kayf al-yaman?*
Yemen?
Yemen is a beauti- *al-yamanbilad*
ful country. *jami:l*
May I take a photo? *mumkin su:ra*

He's my ... *huwa ...*
   son *waladi*
   brother *akhi*
   father *abi*
   husband *zawgi*

She's my ... *hiya ...*
   daughter *binti*
   sister *ukhti*
   mother *ummi*
   wife *zawgati*

OK. (acceptable) *tammam/kwayyis/*
  tayyib
OK. (understood) *khala:s*
Never mind. *ma'laysh*

Accommodation

Is there a hotel *fi funduq hina:?*
here?
Is this house a *ha:dha l-bayt*
hotel? *funduq?*
Do you have a free *fi: takht/kursi?*
bed in the dorm?
Do you have a free *fi: ghurfa?*
room?
(No, we are) full. *malya:n*
I want to see the *mumkin ashu:f al-*
room first. *ghurfa*
Is there a bathroom? *fi: Hamma:m?*
Is there hot water? *fi: ma:i Ha:rr?*
How much is it per *ka:m riyal bi-l-*
night? *laylat al-wa: Hida?*
It's not good, the *mush tammam, ma:i*
water is cold. *ba:rid*

This is dirty, I'd *ha:dha: wasikh,*
like a clean one. *mumkin na**dhi**:f*
I want to speak to *mumkin atkallam*
the manager, please. *ma'al-mudi:r*

key *mifta:H*
towel *munsafa*
toilet paper *warakat hamma:m*

Getting Around

I want to go to ... *ashti aru:H ...*
Where is the bus *wayn al-maktab al-*
office? *ba:sa:t?*
Does this bus go to *ha:dha: l-ba:s ila:*
Ta'izz? *ta'izz?*
Does this taxi go to *ha:dha: t-taksi ila:*
Ibb? *'ibb?*
How much is it *ka:m riyal ila: ...?*
to ...?
One ticket/two *tadhkira/tadhkirayn*
tickets to ..., please. *ila: ..., min fa**d**lak?*
How far to the *ka:m ki:lu ila: l-*
airport? *ma**t**ar?*
Let's go! *yalla!*

Around Town

Where is the ...? *wayn ...?*
   bank *maktab al-bank*
   hospital *mustashfa*
   market *su:q*
   pharmacy ***s**aydali:ya*
   police station *maktab ash-*
      shurta
   post office *maktab al-bari:d*
   tourist office *maktab as-*
      siya:Ha

Is it far from/near *ba'i:d/qari:b min*
here? *hina?*

At the Checkpoint

papers *waraka*
passport *jawa:z/ba:sbu:r*
tour permit *ta**s**ri:H*

Food

Two glasses of tea, *mumkin ithnayn*
please. *sha'i*

I'd like to see (what's) in the kitchen, please.	*mumkin ashu:f fi: l-matbakh*
I would like some ...	*mumkin ...*
I'd like a fork and knife, please.	*mumkin shawka wa sikki:n*

beef	*laHam baqari*
brains	*mukh*
bread	*khubz*
chicken	*dija:j/tiqayq*
coffee	*qahwa*
drink (cold)	*ba:rid*
fish	*samak*
liver	*kibda*
mutton	*ghanami*
pepper	*filfil*
potatoes	*bata:ta*
restaurant	*mat'am*
rice	*ru:z*
salt	*milH*
sugar	*sukkar*
traditional tea	*sha'i talqi:m*
teabag	*sha'i libtun*
tea with milk	*sha'i ma' Hali:b*
tea without milk	*sha'i aHmar*
water	*ma:'i/muya*

Shopping

Do you have ...?	*fi: 'ind-kum ...?*
bananas	*mawz*
grapes	*'anab*
oranges	*burtuqa:li*
cigarettes	*saja:yir*
matches	*kabri:t*
a loaf of bread	*Habbat khubz*
two loaves of bread	*Habbatayn khubz*
a bottle of water	*shi:shat ma:'i*
two bottles of water	*shi:shatayn ma:'i*

How much is this?	*bi-ka:m ha:dha?*

bigger	*akbar*
smaller	*asghar*
cheap	*rakhi:s*
expensive	*gha:li*
money	*flu:s*

Time & Dates

What time is it?	*as-sa'a kam?*

When?	*mata?*
now	*ha:lHi:n/da:lHi:n*
today	*il-yawn*
tonight	*il-yawn **saba:H***
tomorrow	*bukra*
yesterday	*ams*
In half an hour.	*ba'd nuss sa:'a*
In an hour.	*ba'd sa:'a*
In a couple of hours.	*ba'd sa:'atayn*

Numbers

The clock dial is a good way to become familiar with Arabic numbers. The term 'Arabic numbers' generally refers to the positional number system, *not* to the symbols used in Western countries. Don't let the visual similarity of some Western and Arabic number symbols confuse you. Pay attention to the order of the words in numbers from 21 to 99.

The numerals read as follows:

0	***s**ifr*
1	*wa:Hid*
2	*ithnayn*
3	*thala:tha*
4	*arba'a*
5	*khamsa*
6	*sitta*
7	*saba'a*
8	*thama:niya*
9	*tisa'a*
10	*'ashra*
11	*Hida'sh*
12	*ithna'sh*
13	*thala:ta'sh*
14	*arba'ta'sh*
15	*khamsta'sh*
16	*sitta'sh*
17	*saba'ta'sh*
18	*thamanta'sh*
19	*tisa'ta'sh*
20	*'ashri:n*
21	*wa:Hid wa 'ashri:n*
22	*ithnayn wa 'ashri:n*
30	*thala:thi:n*
40	*arba'i:n*
50	*khamsi:n*
60	*sitti:n*
70	*sab'i:n*

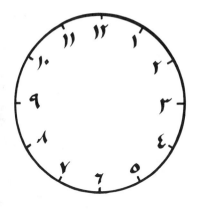

Arabic clock face

80	*thama:ni:n*
90	*tis'i:n*
100	*miya*
200	*miyatayn*
300	*thala:thmiya*
400	*arba'miya*
1000	*alf*
2000	*alfayn*
3000	*thala:that a:la:f*
6666	*sittat a:la:f wa sittmiya wa sitta wa sitti:n*

Body Language

The Arabs are famous for being able to communicate the most complex ideas through gestures, both standard and improvised. The Yemenis are no exception. Body language tends to be universal and you should have no problems understanding or speaking it yourself, although there are some important differences.

The Western 'OK' sign of thumb touching forefinger in a circle, for example, is obscene, referring to a woman's vagina. Familiar gestures include the biker's 'thumb's up' signal – a universal expression of agreement or support – and the Western 'up yours' gesture, a severe insult in Yemen, as elsewhere.

To beckon someone, put the fingers of your right hand together, hold the hand downwards and motion towards yourself.

'No' can be expressed by raising both eyebrows. Blinking with both eyes simultaneously means 'yes'.

If you hold the thumb and forefinger of the right hand stretched out at right angles to each other with the other fingers curled into the palm, facing the speaker, then wave the whole hand back and forth a couple of times, it conveys a general interrogative sense which applies to a wealth of situations.

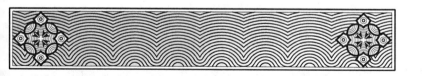

Facts for the Visitor

VISAS & EMBASSIES

Everybody needs a visa to enter Yemen and it is easy to get one. Any Yemeni consulate will issue you an entry visa as long as there is enough room in your passport (one blank page will be needed).

At the time of writing it was also required that you are not an enemy of Yemen – a citizen of Israel. If Israel has even granted you a visa, you can forget about your trip to Arabia Felix – at least until you acquire a new passport. Yemen was very slow to recognise the 1993 breakthrough in the peace process between the PLO and Israel, not sending their first government-level observer to the negotiations until late 1994. However, if the peace process progresses smoothly, this restriction may well be abolished by the time this book is printed.

The entry fees vary from embassy to embassy but are generally about US$30 for citizens of the country where the embassy is located, and twice or thrice that for other applicants. The period covered by an entry visa also varies. They may be valid from one to three months, with visas issued by far-off embassies tending to be valid for longer periods.

The maximum duration of stay is written in the entry visa and is often two months. This is not definitive, however. The actual date by which you have to either exit the country or apply for an extension will be specified in the stamp which you get upon entry into Yemen, so don't let the markings in your entry visa affect your plans in any way.

Entry Visa

The visa application forms must be completed in duplicate (triplicate or quadruplicate at some embassies), so you will need two (to four) photographs.

The form asks you the customary questions about your person and passport. For your religion, it is perfectly safe to write

'Christian' – Arabs think that Christians believe in the same God they do but are incompletely informed because they haven't received the message of Muhammad.

Traditionally, the same applies for Jews but, given the continually troublesome relationship between the Arabs and Israel, I would think twice before proclaiming myself a Jew. Yemen traditionally saw the Palestinian question as the pivot of its Arab policy and an active PLO faction has been based in the country since Israel ousted the organisation from Lebanon in 1983. Furthermore, Yemen was one of the last Arab countries to recognise the 1993 peace accord between the PLO and Israel. At the grass-roots level, a movement 'to Resist the Normalisation Process with the Zionist Entity' was organised in late 1994. Other religions are probably safe but stating 'none' might create a stir among the highly religious Yemenis.

If you apply for a tourist visa, the purpose of the visit will obviously be 'sightseeing' or simply 'tourism'. In this case, a return air ticket is needed to prove that you will only be in the country temporarily. Since prospective travellers may be unwilling to buy a ticket before getting the visa, this is not a hard and fast rule in practice, at least when you are dealing with an embassy in the Western world. They are probably stricter on this point in places such as eastern Africa, where flocks of people are trying to emigrate to countries with more promising economic futures.

In giving details of your profession, I don't recommend that journalists admit theirs unless invited for an official visit; otherwise, the trip might turn official anyway! If you're travelling on business, you will need a reference in Yemen – a letter from the Yemeni company or organisation with which you are dealing. The letter must state, in detail, the reasons for your trip and the name and address of the Yemeni referee.

Residence Visa

Residence visas are issued at the border provided you already have the entry visa. At the San'a International Airport this happens automatically. If you arrive in Yemen by land or by sea, you'd better check the stamps in your passport. The residence visa is a rectangular stamp reading 'Leave to enter for one month' (or whatever period is valid in your case) in Arabic and English. It is usually placed on the same page in your passport as the entry visa.

If you haven't got this stamp and you plan to stay in the country for more than seven days, you will have to register at the Immigration Office in San'a, Ta'izz, Aden or al-Hudayda within seven days of arrival.

The length of time you are entitled to stay in Yemen is usually one month, regardless of what your entry visa says. In San'a the stamp is bilingual, but if the dates are written in Arabic numerals only, ask any English-speaking Yemeni to read them to you – they will be only too eager to help and will probably use the opportunity to study the details of your strange passport thoroughly!

Visa Extensions

If you need to stay more than a month in Yemen, you can get two-week extensions of your residence visa from the Immigration Office of the Ministry of Interior at no cost. There are immigration offices in San'a, Ta'izz, al-Hudayda and Aden (see the maps of those cities).

Re-Entry Visa

If you are working in Yemen, re-entry visas are granted for short-term leaves. You can get your re-entry visa from the immigration office.

For tourists, there are no such arrangements so, if you decide to visit Djibouti, Eritrea or some other nearby destination (relatively cheap from San'a or Aden), you will need a new entry visa from that place. It might be best to plan your trip so that you arrive in Yemen once only.

Yemeni Embassies

Yemen has embassies in most of the Arab countries, as well as in many European, African and Asian countries and the USA. If it is difficult for you to get to a Yemeni embassy, you can apply for your visa by post; just order the application forms and you'll receive further instructions in a week or two. Embassies in Western capitals have application forms in Arabic as well as in relevant Western languages. We have used London and Bonn several times and found the method reliable and reasonably fast, although the obligatory use of registered mail when sending passports and cheques adds somewhat to the cost.

If your country's postal service is unreliable or you are not on a tight budget, you could plan your route to Yemen to include a stop of a few days in a nearby capital. Better still, if you include the visit to Yemen in your grand tour of north-east Africa or the Middle East, you can obtain your Yemeni visa in almost any capital city en route. The visas usually take 48 hours to issue. The Yemenis are sometimes flexible – once we got visas from Djibouti the next day – but sometimes definitely inflexible, so don't count heavily on this. Most Yemeni embassies are only open in the mornings and close at noon.

In non-Arab countries, the addresses of embassies of Yemen are:

Canada
    Suite 500, 56 Sparks St, Ottawa, Ontario, K1P 5A9 (☎ 2306136)
China
    4 Dong Chi Men Wai St, Beijing (☎523346, 523991, 523748)
Czech Republic
    Washingtonova 17, 12522 Prague 1 (☎ 222411)
Djibouti
    Plateau du Marabout, 127/4 Ahmad Ibrahim Building, PO Box 1913, Djibouti (☎ 352975/6)
Eritrea
    Tesfalidet St, PO Box 11040, Asmara (☎ 209422)
Ethiopia
    Role International Rd, PO Box 664, Addis Ababa (☎ 181260/5)
France
    21 Ave Charles Floquet, 75007 Paris (☎ 43066622)

Germany
Adenauerallee 77, 5300 Bonn (☎ 220273, 220451, 261490/9)
Waldstrasse 15, 1110 Berlin (☎ 4800391)
India
B55, Pashami Marg, Vasant Vihar, New Delhi 110057 (☎ 674064, 674743, 674472, 674124, 674391)
Italy
Via Verona 3, Int 4-00161, Rome (☎ 4271018, 4270811, 4270281)
Japan
4-chome, Nishi-Azabu, Minato-ku (106), Tokyo (☎ 34997151/2)
Netherlands
Surinamestraat 9, 2585 GC The Hague (☎ 653936/7, telex 33290)
Pakistan
H No 46, St 12, F, 6/3, PO Box 1523, Islamabad (☎ 821146/7, 828441)
Russia
2 Neopalimovskij Per 6, Moscow (☎ 2461814, 2464427, 2461554)
Switzerland
Kistlerweg 2, 3006 Bern (☎ 444885)
UK
41 South St, London W1 (☎ 4914003, 6299905/6/7/8)
USA
Suite 860, Watergate Six Hundred, 600 New Hampshire Ave NW, Washington, DC 20037 (☎ 9654760/1, 8654781)
United Nations, 8th floor, 747 3rd Ave, New York, NY 10017 (☎ 3551730/1)

Embassies of Yemen are in the capital cities of all Arab countries except Bahrain. Apply for your visa in person.

Foreign Embassies in Yemen

Addresses of some non-Arab diplomatic representations in San'a are:

China
Az-Zubayri St (☎ 275337)
Czech Republic
As-Safiya al-Gharbia al-Junubiya (☎ 247946)
Djibouti
Southern Ring Rd (☎ 245792)
Eritrea
Baghdad St (☎ 209422)
Ethiopia
Hadda Rd (☎ 208833)
France
Al-Bawniya Area (☎ 268832)
Germany
Rd No 22, Hs No 9-49 (☎ 216756/7)

Hungary
As-Safiya, St 5, Hs 9 (☎ 216250)
India
Az-Zubayri, St 8, Bldg 6 (☎ 241980)
Italy
St 29, Bldg 5 (near Muhammad 'Ali ash-Shawkani St) (☎ 265616)
Japan
Ring Rd as-Safiya al-Gharbiya (☎ 207536)
Netherlands
Hadda St (after Ring Rd) (☎ 215626/7/8)
Pakistan
Ring Rd (near Hadda St) (☎ 248813/4)
Russia
26th September St (☎ 78272, 203142)
UK
al-Hamadani St (☎ 215630/1/2/3)
USA
Sa'wan St (☎ 238842/52)

DOCUMENTS

All visitors to Yemen require a valid passport and visa. Those travelling from places where cholera and yellow fever are prevalent require international vaccination certificates. Visitors flying in directly from Western Europe no longer need any vaccination certificates.

At the Checkpoint

There are road blocks and checkpoints all around the country, and passengers are frequently asked to produce their passports or ID cards. Foreign travellers were formerly required to have tour permits in order to visit any regions or towns outside San'a. This system was abolished by the unification of the country in 1990, but sometimes soldiers at the checkpoints are still asking for *tasri:h*. There are rumours that Yemen's system of tour permits will be re-established, but so far visitors are free to come and go. Showing your passport is enough.

Some people living in Yemen advise against showing your actual passport at checkpoints, but instead to show copies of your passport – the pages with your photo and visa. You can always tell them your passport is in San'a.

There are photocopiers in almost every photo studio in San'a as well as other cities. One convenient studio is by the narrow shopping alley that leads from the park in front of the General Tourist Corporation to Gamal Abdul Nasser St. A copy should not cost you more than YR 15 or so.

The Arabic word for 'copy' is *sura* (or **s**u:ra); the same word is used for a photo or picture.

CUSTOMS

Most tourists arrive in Yemen through the San'a International Airport. Aden's facilities are more modern and the capacity of its airport is greater, but the airport fell into disuse during the siege of Aden in May-July 1994 and has yet to recover.

You must first fill in the blue arrival card. This will have been handed to you on the plane if you flew Yemen Airways; otherwise, you can pick one up in the arrival hall. You will find most of the answers in your passport.

You must supply an address in Yemen, even if you simply supply the address of a hotel in San'a. This is just a formality and nobody will be interested in it afterwards – the form just has to be completed.

The card is then handed, with your passport, to the immigration officer, who will stamp it with the entry date.

The customs procedures tend to be time-consuming because every bag and pack must be opened, be it closed by locks, ropes or seals. Strangely, however, their contents are usually inspected in a most casual way. If possible, choose a queue containing only foreigners – the one Yemeni standing ahead of you with only a small attaché case is probably holding the place for his two wives and four brothers, who'll carry the 20 or 30 pieces of their luggage!

Also, don't try to get your handbag past the examination – at the exit, there will be an armed guard who's not going to let you pass with an unmarked bag. By the way, this 'guards watching guards' method is a typical Yemeni phenomenon and you will encounter it many times during your stay. Just ask the inspector to mark every piece of your luggage even if they don't look into all of them.

Imports

You are allowed to bring 200 cigarettes, 50 cigars or 250 grams of pipe tobacco into Yemen. Alcoholic beverages are prohibited within the country but non-Muslims can bring in one litre. Women are allowed to have 'reasonable' quantities of cosmetics and jewels with them. If you come by land, you are permitted to have 50 litres of gasoline for your car.

Pornographic material is prohibited, of course, in this Islamic country. Your magazines may be examined and video cassettes seized for closer inspection (you can reclaim them a few days later at the Ministry of Information or the immigration office).

Computers (even electronic typewriters) have caused some travellers trouble in the past, however we had no problems travelling with our computer on our last visit. Regulations change, so to be safe, enquire about the current regulations at the embassy while applying for your visa.

Other regulations are not likely to affect the average tourist. You are allowed to bring in gifts not exceeding US$25 in value, domestic animals holding international health certificates, and so on. If you are a business person, you are allowed to bring samples of your products as well as brochures and other promotions aids, provided you take them with you when you leave the country.

Exports

You are permitted to export anything you purchase in Yemen. This doesn't include, of course, items of historical value – you can't take with you the nice marble capital you found lying in the sands near the Ma'rib Dam. Officially, all articles more than 40 years old belong to the national heritage and cannot be exported without permission from the General Tourism Corporation. Don't be alarmed, though, because the silverware you bought in the suqs is probably not as old as you imagine.

MONEY
Currency
Before unification in 1990, both Yemens had currencies of their own: the riyal in the YAR and the dinar in the PDRY. Both currencies continued to be used throughout Yemen from unification until the civil war of 1994, though it was much more common to see riyals used in the southern part of the country than dinars in the north. After the civil war ended in the victory of the northerners, the dinar also fell rapidly into disuse in the south. Still, no monetary union was ever officially declared, and the dinar is still legal tender.

The riyal is denoted in this book by the abbreviation YR. There is both a coin and a banknote worth 1, 5 and 10 riyals and banknotes of 10, 20, 50, 100 and 200 riyals. The notes are easily distinguished since they are bilingual; values are printed in Arabic on one side and in English on the other. You soon learn to recognise them by their colours. The coin values are shown only in Arabic.

Of more numismatic than practical interest today, the dinar (YD) was divided into 20 shillings or 1000 fils, so that a shilling was worth 50 fils. Occasionally, you may still receive 50, 100 or 250 fils coins as change in the southern governorates. The shilling was a unit used in speech for convenience; the coins and banknotes always show their value in fils and dinars. The aforementioned coins are referred to as 1, 2 and 5 shillings respectively. You are rather unlikely to encounter dinar bills, but there were 250 and 500 fils banknotes as well as banknotes worth 1 and 5 dinars, the latter often referred to as 20 and 100 shilling notes.

Exchange Rates
The official exchange rate at the time of writing is:

US$1 = YR 50

However, the Yemeni government has actually defined four different official exchange

rates for the US$ and confirms the 'officially approved parallel market rate' also! So, at the time of research Yemen had the following exchange rates for the dollar:

Foreign Ministry Rate	US$1 = YR 5
Subsidised Import Rate	US$1 = YR 40
Customs Import Rate	US$1 = YR 18
Diplomatic Community Rate	US$1 = YR 25
Parallel Market Rate	US$1 = YR 165

The official bank rate for bank notes is the same as the subsidised import rate. It remained fixed at YR 12 from 1990, when the parallel market rate was less than 10% higher, to April 1995, when the official bank rate was less than 10% of the parallel market rate. The government then drastically raised the official bank rate overnight to YR 50.

Inflation has been rampant in unified Yemen. The government has been unable (some say unwilling) to balance the budget, and the ever-growing deficits have been covered simply by printing new money without any controls. In early 1995 the government's debt to the Central Bank of Yemen was approaching YR 200,000 million.

In January 1994 the parallel market dollar rate was about YR 60, while in July 1994, immediately after the war, the dollar jumped up to YR 130, only to fall back to YR 80 when confidence again built up. In mid-1995 a tourist was able to change dollars for close to YR 165, however Yemeni business people were getting up to 30% more for their greenbacks.

The net effect of the instability of the riyal has been a serious 'dollarisation' of the economy: businesses have started to cite their prices in US dollars only, because riyal-based budget planning has turned impossible. In regard to the effect on travellers, this applies specifically to airlines, tour operators and many hotels frequented by Western tourists. You'd better think twice before complying to demands to pay in dollars; whenever you shell out dollars for any service you are probably paying three to eight times the riyal price a Yemeni would

Price Increases
In April 1995 the Yemeni government finally decided to bite the bullet and introduced stiff economic measures: the subsidised import rate was raised to YR 40; private moneychangers were once more arrested; the price of gas was doubled to YR 12 per litre; and shop prices were fixed by law. Predictably, demonstrations broke out all around the country, resulting in three deaths and several injuries in Aden.

Consequently, the riyal prices for transport listed in this book are likely to date quickly. It remains to be seen how other prices and the parallel market rate will develop, but it is a safe bet that your dollar prices will go up too – at the time of research Yemen was exceptionally favourable for the dollar tourist. ■

pay. With airlines you have no choice as only Yemeni nationals can buy tickets with riyals, but you can always say no to dollar hotels – there are plenty of alternatives.

Changing Money

You can't buy Yemeni riyals abroad, but all major Western currencies are accepted in Yemen. The problem is where to change them on arrival. There is an exchange counter in the arrival hall of the San'a International Airport, before passport control, but it seems to be irregularly staffed. You will find a couple of other bank offices at the San'a airport. These are open only from 8 am to noon and, in practice, perhaps from 9 to 11 am. Quite possibly, they never open at all. In Aden, there is a branch office of the state bank after you pass the passport control. In any case you will only get the official bank rate here.

You will need local money to leave the airport. If you arrive during business hours (that is, 8 am to 1 pm), you could get a taxi and ask the driver to take you to a moneychanger first. Another alternative is to change money with an airport worker, local passenger, anybody. If you offer a profitable enough bargain, any Yemeni will be eager to do some banking with you – if they don't happen to have the money, they'll borrow it – so it might be a good idea to carry about US$20 worth of small notes when entering Yemen. However, don't change more than necessary here, as the rates are better elsewhere.

All major world currencies are recognised in Yemen. As only Yemeni currency can be used in daily transactions, you have to exchange your money for local currency. You will also have no problems changing US dollars, British pounds, French francs or German marks. On the other hand, it is difficult to change minor currencies; even the francs of nearby Djibouti are exchanged at lousy rates, if at all.

The US dollar is recommended – despite growing distrust in the US dollar elsewhere, the exchange rate in Yemen seems to be steadily improving. US$100 bills will get you somewhat better rates than smaller denominations. Bring only notes dated 1990 or later – in that year the US Treasury introduced microprinting to fight counterfeits, and Yemeni moneychangers automatically deem all older dollar bills forged. Further changes are planned for the fine details of the paper and printing in years to come, so always ask for the latest models and check with your bank before accepting your sheaf of greenbacks.

Moneychangers You can change your money either in commercial banks at official rates or with moneychangers in the suqs of larger cities. The moneychangers offer market rates – at the time of writing some were 700% better than the banks – but using them is not exactly legal.

In fact, moneychangers get forcibly outlawed by the government every now and then. Until the mid-1980s, authorised moneychangers operated from small offices in the city centres in the YAR, but in early 1988 the government jailed these entrepreneurs and their offices vanished. They returned with flashy signs in the early 1990s, but in December 1994 a campaign against them was again launched by the Central Bank of Yemen. Some 40 of them were imprisoned in San'a only on the pretext of offering better rates than the officially approved parallel market rate. Others continued in the streets instead.

Your best bet for changing money is in the suqs, an area where traditional values of the Yemeni society are the strongest and the government's influence is at its weakest.

Banks Should a correction of the official exchange rate occur, or if you have to use a bank for any other reason, choose an international one such as Bank Indo-Suez; they are usually the most flexible, and English is more likely to be spoken. Some banks may not offer exchange services at all. Banks are open from 8 or 9 am until noon, every day except Friday and other holidays. On Thursdays they are open for shorter hours, in the morning only.

Hotels The biggest hotels also change money at official rates, while some smaller hotels charge rates only slightly less than the street rates.

In smaller towns, you will probably not be able to change any money at all. In fact, you should not count on being able to change money anywhere outside of the bigger towns. At the time of writing moneychangers were abundant in San'a, Ta'izz and Aden, easily found in al-Mukalla and Ibb, but nonexistent in Hajja or Zabid. Surprisingly, even al-Hudayda is not a good bet for changing money.

Travellers' Cheques
You can change travellers' cheques in most banks at bank rates. Some moneychangers also accept them. However, if you decide to use travellers' cheques stick to major worldwide companies, and be sure not to rely on them exclusively.

Credit Cards
For a budget traveller, credit cards are simply useless in Yemen, and for everybody else they are of limited use. They are only accepted in a few five-star hotels, airline offices, tour operators and big-town jewellery shops specialising in selling to tourists. American Express is about the only recognised card.

Carrying Cash
I recommend that you use cash instead of travellers' cheques and credit cards as it is easier to handle and relatively safe to carry around – if there is a country left in the world where crime is rare, it must be Yemen. Despite alarming reports of car hijackings, kidnappings and robberies after the unification, the victims have almost exclusively been working for oil companies or the government, and the motivation has been as much political as economical. Ordinary tourists are usually safe, and attempts on their belongings are extremely rare – visitors have reported only one incident or so per year to us here at Lonely Planet.

Theft is restrained here by a set of values that have remained beyond question for 1400 years. It is not because Shari'a, the Islamic law, orders the right hand of a thief to be cut off – it is because theft is virtually nonexistent in this culture. If you drop your wallet in the suqs it will probably be handed back to you. You will see locals walking in the streets counting thick bundles of banknotes in their hands; similar behaviour in a Western capital would probably provoke an act of street violence. Foreigners may have no such qualms, however, so keep an eye on your fellow travellers.

Of course, reasonable precautions are advisable. Carrying most of your cash in a money belt under your clothing should be enough. Many Yemenis have travelled abroad a lot since the revolution and some might have begun to think that stealing from a non-Muslim is not so bad after all, since non-Muslims steal from one another routinely. Certainly, overcharging for services is not seen as robbery, so don't boast of your wealth. On the other hand, we have never heard about anybody being cheated while changing money in the suqs.

Costs

Is Yemen cheap or expensive? Things have changed considerably since the first edition of this book, and are likely to continue to do so, not necessarily in the same direction as in the past. From 1984 (when we visited Yemen for the first time) up to the research of this edition, the US dollar value of the riyal had dropped by eleven-twelfths. Correspondingly the value of domestic products and services had dropped by three-quarters if measured in US dollars, while simultaneously rising three or four or six-fold, sometimes twelve-fold, in riyals.

Costs naturally depend on what you are after. If you conform to the traditional Yemeni lifestyle, you can travel very cheaply here, but if you demand steak grilled medium, beer and private guided tours, you will find that it was only the flight ticket that was cheap. If you try something in-between, you will probably find Yemen is still reasonably cheap.

Yemen ranks among the poorest 40 countries in the world if measured by the per capita Gross Domestic Product (GDP). People have to be able to meet their daily needs using little money. Basic food is cheap, for example. A glass of tea or a loaf of bread costs YR 10 to YR 15 and you can have a simple but nourishing dinner in a street-level San'a restaurant for about YR 400. A live chicken sells for YR 150 in the market while the bill for a grilled one in a restaurant is YR 400 to YR 600.

As for hotels, you'll find everything from absolutely basic inns at YR 300 per bed to Western-style five-star deluxe hotels charging US$210 a night. Transport, your third main expense, is not overwhelmingly expensive as long as you don't hire a car for your personal use. The longest bus hauls take four hours and cost YR 200 in the former YAR, 12 hours and YR 400 in the southern governorates. A service taxi may charge 30% to 50% more for the same distance.

On the other hand, imported items are expensive because the riyal has been devaluating against Western currencies in recent years. Luxury goods are readily available, however, since about every fifth Yemeni was working abroad in the 1980s, effectively spreading the word about the fruits of modern technology.

Tipping

This questionable practice simply doesn't exist in Yemen and you would be wise not to introduce or encourage it. Service is included in restaurant and hotel prices. Fares for taxis and other such financial arrangements are best negotiated in advance.

Bargaining

Contrary to what you might expect, Yemen is not a place where time-consuming bargaining is the rule. Grocery prices are always fixed and, even in the suqs, bargaining is rare, often impossible. This doesn't mean you should pay whatever you are asked. Use your judgement and compare the prices offered by different traders; if you have the time and opportunity, check prices in different suqs. You will also find a few things that are unique to each suq.

When a trader quotes a price, it is often final (or close to it). It may not be the same price that would be asked of a fellow Yemeni and it probably includes a 'foreigner's tax'. However, it is final in the sense that it is your price and, because you seem able to afford it, you won't be offered a lower one.

Exceptions to this rule are hotel prices and private taxis, which are often negotiable if suspiciously high. Western tourists have also introduced the art of bargaining to the silver suqs of San'a and other bigger cities, where you should find out the right prices by comparing the offerings of different traders.

PLANNING YOUR TRIP

It pays to plan your visit to Yemen beforehand. Take at least a cursory look through this book and decide which places you want to see and in what order. However, leave room for change. One of the most fascinating aspects of Yemen is that you may run across curious things that are not documented anywhere. You might walk to a small village not drawn on any map and local residents will take your hand and lead you to some astonishingly well-preserved pre-Islamic structures or strange geological formations.

Itineraries

The number of asphalted roads in Yemen is increasing rapidly but the lack of road connections will still have a big effect on your touring plan. For example, the only useful route from Ibb to Zabid is via Ta'izz – there are alternatives but they are either impractical or off limits.

Most visitors short on time restrict themselves to the northern provinces only, traversing the big triangle between San'a, Ta'izz and al-Hudayda. This takes at least a week but, depending on your means of transport, how many towns you visit en route and what kind of accommodation you find acceptable, may take much longer. Sa'da and Shihara can be visited on one trip from

San'a. Even if you hire a private taxi for the trip, you'd better allocate at least four days to visit these two towns.

Visiting the eastern governorates introduces much longer distances. A visit to Hadhramawt from San'a will easily take two weeks if you are using ground transport. There are plenty of alternatives and choosing between them depends on how you want to balance your time and money. You may choose to go to Aden first, from there to al-Mukalla and, finally, to Say'un in Hadhramawt, spending three full days in buses or taxis between these towns, plus the days spent exploring the towns. On return you may skip Aden and take a shortcut via al-Baydha from al-Mukalla to San'a. The shortest and most expensive route between San'a and Say'un goes straight over the desert via Ma'rib – two days in taxis. In any case, the complete trip will be as long as one from Amsterdam to Istanbul, or Stockholm to Rome. Flying in one or the other direction is worth considering if it fits into your budget.

Due to the range of accommodation in San'a, visitors like to use the city as a base for excursions. Ma'rib is one of the places visited by most tourists (too) hurriedly; they leave San'a early in the morning, sit in the car most of the day and return late in the

---

Yemen's Weekly Markets

When planning your trip, take into consideration the system of weekly markets. While large cities like San'a, Ta'izz and al-Hudayda have suqs that are open every day, the smaller villages conduct business one day a week only. Farmers and craftspeople from the neighbourhood gather at these weekly markets to sell their products, making the suqs colourful social events. The system serves not only commerce but also helps to pass information (and time).

Market day differs from village to village and it pays to visit at least some of them. If you visit the Tihama, you should try to see Bayt al-Faqih's Friday market, which has been deservedly famous for hundreds of years. Some villages have few permanent inhabitants and, consequently, are almost dead except on market day; examples are Suq at-Talh near Sa'da and Suq al-Khamis in the northern Tihama. In other villages, the market may be quite small but still creates a clearly different atmosphere to other days of the week.

Weekly markets are very common in the northern part of Yemen and in the Lahej and Abyan governorates in the south. The system is known in most Arab countries but nowhere else has it gained such widespread acceptance. This ancient practice was documented by the Danish explorer Carsten Niebuhr in the 18th century, who commented on the extraordinarily large number of markets. And they show no signs of dying out – recent counts show that the introduction of permanent roadside markets by the main asphalted highways and of Western-style supermarkets in the cities has had no impact on the number of weekly market sites. ■

Top: House in Rayda
Bottom: Highland village in al-Mahwit Province

Top: Village in Hajja Province
Bottom: Mud houses in Old Mar'ib

evening. There are excellent roads from San'a to Hajja, Shibam, Thilla, at-Tawila, al-Mahwit and Manakha, and any of these towns can be comfortably visited in one or two days. On the other hand, these towns lie in the mountain area which is best suited to trekking; you could spend weeks walking and hitchhiking along the dirt roads from town to town.

Off-Limit Areas

Just half a decade ago, most of Yemen was off limits to travellers. The PDRY was one of the most reclusive countries in the world, and could only be visited on invitation or in a tour group paying US$3000 to US$4000 for a 16-day tour, not including flights to and from the country. The YAR maintained an elaborate system of tour permits which demanded travellers plan their trip beforehand and list the places they would like to visit; from the list a government official selected those ones suitable for a visit. On unification all limitations were officially abolished and basically you are free to travel wherever you wish in the country.

However, many former limitations still apply, enforced by the local tribes. Some villages are time and again not recommended for tourists, which means you can't arrange transport: there is no shared taxi and no tour operator that will take you to certain places. If you try to hitchhike or manage to hire a private taxi, you may be shown away at the checkpoint.

Most of the border areas are off limits for reasons that can be easily understood: the desert borders are not clearly defined and border disputes have been all too common in this part of the world throughout the 20th century. Recent oil discoveries in the central deserts and the deterioration of the Saudi-Yemeni relationship have certainly exacerbated this problem. Oil-production areas are also off limits. At many towns and villages a mountaintop may be in military use, and you are not allowed to approach the place too closely.

Another reason is that certain areas, especially in the northernmost part of the country, are not under complete government control. Moreover, the influx of tourists in the late 1980s and early 1990s has caused the inhabitants of some much-visited mountain villages to grow surly towards Western visitors. Of course, the Yemeni government is also not willing to let tourists wander in areas where they are not absolutely safe. You might feel that this is overly protective but there have been some nasty incidents.

As matters stood at the time of research, tour operators in San'a were not taking travellers to places like the Shihara mountain and Baraqish. Some places, such as Sirwah and Suq al-'Inan, have been completely off limits for many years. Since the situations change from season to season, it pays to go and ask some tour operators even if you are not planning to use their services. If they don't want to take you to a certain village it might be a good idea to drop the place from your agenda.

The tour operators get instructions from the General Tourist Corporation, a state-run company for tourist services in al-Hasaba, northern San'a. If you have a pressing need or desire to visit some place you suspect problematic, you can contact them to get the official view. They also have branch offices in a number of towns, giving information on local conditions, but these offices are of limited usability.

In some cases, you need local guidance in order to visit a place restricted to visitors. If the restrictions are due to tribal tensions, it is only the local folks who know the current situation and trouble spots. Sometimes visiting an archaeological site or remote village may involve driving through the areas of several tribes, so guides from each tribe are needed, and your journey may prove costly.

What happens if you travel in off-limits areas on your own? This depends on where you try to go. In some remote nonmilitary areas, you might get through because of loose controls. Take care, though. In 1993 and 1994, before the civil war, hijacking foreigners as tools to blackmail government was trendy in certain regions. As far as we know, similar incidents have not occurred after the war, but listen for the latest developments.

The Time Factor

If you make firm day-by-day plans, they have no chance of being realised completely. There are 1001 details that can go wrong; Murphy's Law says that they will go wrong and you'd better believe it.

The most obvious thing that can go wrong is your schedule. Everything takes more time in southern Arabia than it would in your home country. The bus that leaves at 7 am will actually leave an hour later (or half an hour earlier, causing you to miss it!), 200 km in a taxi will take five hours (because of lunch, prayers and checkpoints on the road) and buying a bottle of Coke takes half an hour (you only have 100 riyal notes and the shopkeeper has no change).

This is all the more frustrating when there are things you have to do at certain times. Banks and government offices are open only in the morning; everything is closed in the afternoon. You will also want to visit certain places on certain days because of the system of weekly markets. The best advice is to allow plenty of time and make your schedule flexible enough to accommodate the inevitable delays.

Length of Stay By now, you should have some idea of how long to stay in Yemen. Staying one week will probably turn out to be very expensive because you will want to come back and see what you missed. If you maintain a frenzied pace and use expensive private taxis every now and then, two weeks will give you enough time to see most (but definitely not all) of the historical towns in the northern part of the country, though you'd need another couple of weeks for the southern governorates. The most extensive organised tours in Yemen take two weeks and cost more than US$1000 per person (not including flights to and from Yemen). A three or four-week visit is good for an independent traveller; you'll have ample time to visit all the famous sites, you can wander around in the mountains (a must in Yemen, even if

hiking is not your cup of tea) and you have a chance to change your plans if you find something you didn't expect.

The Weather Factor

There is no ideal season during which to visit Yemen because climatic conditions vary so greatly between regions. The Yemenis themselves, in their inimitably optimistic way, recommend that you visit the country 'any time'. This is sound advice because, at all times, some region is sure to be at its best.

If you have more than a passing interest in the Tihama region or are planning to visit Aden and Hadhramawt, summer is certainly the season to avoid. The Arabian Peninsula is said to be one of the most hostile places on earth to human habitation and you'll really believe this if you visit the coastal areas of Yemen in summer. The air is extremely humid and hot, there is no rain and the wind carries sand everywhere, particularly under your clothes.

If you visit the Tihama in December, you may still think the air extremely humid and hot, and the windblown sand just as much of a problem. However, rest assured that it's worse in July. The coastal areas are always hot and, even during the rainy seasons, the sands are seldom wet enough to resist the wind. This makes things very dusty. The Hadhramawt valley has more pleasant temperatures and dry air in the winter.

By contrast, the highlands can get quite cold in winter. From late November to early January, San'a has nightly frosts and, in the mountains, it is chilly indeed. Even in October and February, you will need some warm clothes in the early morning and after sunset.

May to early August is dry and hot everywhere and you probably won't need heavy clothing, even if you plan to do extensive trekking in the highest mountain areas at this time. (As a rough guide, the temperature goes down by more than 0.5°C but less than 1°C for every 100 metres you climb.) There are no clouds, the sun shines from 5 am to 6.30 pm and the weather may turn out to be unbearably hot. You soon learn why the

Trekking & the Weather Factor

Trekking can be anything but enjoyable when you encounter a torrent delivering 10 cm of water in just a couple of hours. It is easy to get caught by a rainstorm because the mornings are often deceptively bright and warm, and the clouds don't gather until the afternoon. Heavy mountain rains can be extremely dangerous to trekkers because the cascading water carries rocks the size of small cars down the slopes. And, of course, you won't be able to see the mountains because of the clouds!

The temperatures are highly dependent on the continuity of sunshine, too; a cloud obscuring the sun may drop the temperature by a dozen degrees in a few minutes. So, if you plan to do extensive trekking in the rainy season, you will need light, warm, wind-proof and water-resistant clothes and boots. The worst rainfalls occur in the Ibb province and in the western mountains – some of the best areas for trekking.

The periods just after the rainy seasons – April/May and September/October – are ideal for trekking. The roads are drying fast, there is plenty of water flowing in bigger wadis and even un-irrigated fields and groves are green, yielding their harvest. Nevertheless, the rains are a sight in themselves so, if you want to see as many faces of Yemen as possible in a few weeks, it is worth visiting Yemen in March/April or September. This is usually the best time to visit, although if it's a particularly wet year, the mountains will be permanently obscured by clouds. ∎

Yemenis offer no services in the afternoons; your own level of activity will also peak in the mornings and evenings.

In addition to temperature, there is another factor to consider: water. The dry seasons are really dry; from late October to early February and from May to June, there are perhaps three rainfalls in San'a and, though it may rain throughout the summer in the Ibb region, most of the country is parched for at least eight months of the year.

If architecture is higher on your list of priorities than nature, this may sound all right. However, as most of the roads and streets in Yemen are not asphalted, heavy traffic and turbulent winds continually raise huge clouds of dust. Another drawback is that during the dry winter months (almost half of the year), most of the fields lie barren. Half the trees have dropped their leaves and those trees that do have foliage left are so brown with dust that you might not even notice. You simply won't understand how Yemen earned the epithet 'the Green Land of Arabia'.

The rainy seasons – the lighter one in March/April and the heavier one in August/September – offer pleasant temperatures of 20°C to 30°C in the high plateau areas and, even in the mountains, you won't need heavy clothing. However, what is dust during the dry season becomes mud when it rains. You may find that small dirt roads along the wadis – plenty of them around here! – are untraversable, even with a 4WD vehicle, so you'd best stick to the main roads.

WHAT TO BRING

When packing for your trip to Yemen, be selective. The less weight you take with you, the happier you will be. Yemen today is quite a modern country and, with a few exceptions, you will be able to buy any commodities you might need.

In the supermarkets of Yemen's bigger cities, you can buy all the little things you need for personal hygiene, from tissues to toothpaste and toilet paper (and, nowadays, sanitary napkins and tampons). Don't expect to find these items in smaller villages, though.

Bring supplies of medicine for minor ailments: Band-aids and iodine for small wounds, charcoal and salt tablets, painkillers and so on. If you travel in winter, it is advisable to bring some eardrops and medicine for colds. Vitamin tablets are also worth considering if your stay is not a very short one; given the hygiene conditions, you can't get vitamins in the normal way from fresh vegetables (these should be avoided – see

Diarrhoea under Health). If you have a chronic ailment requiring special treatment, bring whatever is needed with you.

Yemeni towns are loaded with pharmacies that stock all the wonders of modern medicine, even those banned in the Western world because of harmful (even lethal) side effects. No prescriptions are asked for; in fact, the pharmacy staff often have to do the doctor's job when customers drop in to discuss their problems and ask for solutions. Often, the customer is offered half a dozen alternatives. If you are a doctor and know your medicines, you can probably find one for any curable disease. However, if you are looking for a particular medicine, don't count on finding it. The pharmacy you happen to choose might not have that particular preparation in stock or you might not Arabicise your pronunciation sufficiently to be understood.

It's also a good idea to bring a torch (flashlight) with you; when night falls, Yemeni towns and villages are lit dimly, if at all. Even the biggest cities suffer from frequent power outages.

TOURIST OFFICES
There is no tourist office representation of Yemen abroad. The General Tourist Corporation, the official tourist information bureau of the former YAR, still has offices in San'a, Ta'izz and al-Hudayda, but virtually all you can get from them is some tea and a nice chat with a friendly official, who will answer your queries but is unlikely to volunteer any information. In San'a they run a relatively well-stocked souvenir shop also. In the southern part of the country no similar organisation is presently functioning.

BUSINESS HOURS & HOLIDAYS
Government offices and banks are open weekdays (Saturday to Wednesday) from 8 or 9 am to about noon or 1 pm and are closed in the afternoon. Post offices in the northern provinces are an exception; they are also open from 4 to 8 pm. On Fridays and other holidays the offices stay closed,

and on Thursday they tend to be open shorter hours in the morning only.

The private sector has more flexible hours of business and most shops and restaurants are open mornings and evenings, closing for a few hours in the early afternoon for qat time. The exact schedule varies according to the day of the week, the district and the individual entrepreneur.

The Calendar
An essential consideration when timing your trip to Yemen is the Muslim calendar, which is used alongside the Gregorian calendar familiar to Westerners. All religious feasts are celebrated within the framework of the Muslim calendar, while secular authorities arrange their activities according to the Christian system.

The Muslim year is based on the lunar cycle and is divided into 12 lunar months, each with 29 or 30 days. Accordingly, the Muslim year is 10 or 11 days shorter than the Christian (solar) year. The Muslim festivals thus gradually move through the Christian year, completing a full cycle every 33 years or so.

When planning your trip to Yemen, take note of what month Ramadan occurs in that year. Visiting a strongly Muslim country like Yemen during Ramadan can be a trying experience unless you are a frequent traveller in the Arab countries and know what you're doing.

The Muslims' rules of abstinence may be quite hard to observe, especially the one forbidding drinking during daylight hours (even if Ramadan falls during a hot summer month). As a non-Muslim, you may drink and eat whenever you wish, provided you don't do it under the eyes of the believers – do it only in your hotel room.

Given the afternoon temperatures (even in winter), people's activity level is extremely low during Ramadan. Many shops are closed, banks and government offices have even shorter opening hours than usual, bus timetables have fewer entries and it is difficult to get a taxi during the day. Every kind of business is at a standstill.

The first four days of the Shawwal month immediately following Ramadan mark the 'Id al-Fitr festival of breaking the fast. Another major holiday is the 'Id al-Adha, or 'Feast of Sacrifice'. It begins on the 10th of the Hajj, the month of pilgrimage, and celebrations continue for up to six days. Do not count on getting any weekday business done on these days.

Muslim Holidays

The dates of Muslim holidays up to the year 2000 are listed in the following table. If you compare these dates with those given by other sources, you may find that these are consistently one day later. The explanation is that, according to the Muslim calendar, a day begins at sunset, while in the Christian calendar a day begins at midnight. The Muslim dates given here correspond to the morning according to the Gregorian calendar, as most of your daily activities are likely to happen within that part of the 24-hour cycle. It should be noted that Muslim holidays offer very little for a Western traveller to see or take part in, as they are family occasions.

Secular Holidays

The dates of these holidays are set according to the Christian calendar:

May
    Labor Day (1st)
    Day of National Unity (22nd)

September
    Revolution Day (26th)
October
    National Day (14th)
November
    Independence Day (30th)

The two Yemens observed each others' national days before unification and now both days are national holidays in the unified country. The intensity of celebrations of either one depends on which part of the country you are in.

You should also take into account that if a holiday falls on a Wednesday or a Sunday, the Yemenis eagerly take the opportunity to enjoy a 'long weekend' (from Wednesday to Friday or from Friday to Sunday). This means that most shops will be closed for these three days.

USEFUL ORGANISATIONS

The Yemen Language Center (☎ 205125), in San'a, offers courses in Arabic language, useful for those working or residing in the country for a lengthy time. Their address is PO Box 16961, San'a.

POST & TELECOMMUNICATIONS

Postal services are relatively developed in Yemen, and you can send your postcards and mail in fair confidence that your friends will receive them. Sometimes mail gets from San'a to Europe in only four days, sometimes it takes two weeks. However, sending mail from small villages is usually not possible, and mail sent from towns around the country first goes

Table of Muslim Holidays

Hijra Year	New Year	Prophet's Birthday	Ramadan Begins	'Id al-Fitr	'Id al-Adha
1416	31.05.95	09.08.95	22.01.96	22.02.96	29.04.96
1417	19.05.96	28.07.96	10.01.97	10.02.97	18.04.97
1418	09.05.97	18.07.97	31.12.98	31.01.98	08.04.98
1419	28.04.98	07.07.98	20.12.99	20.01.99	28.03.99
1420	17.04.99	26.06.99	09.12.99		

to the hub in San'a or Aden, which slows the transport and introduces chances for mishandling. Rates are reasonable; for example, a postcard to Europe costs YR 20.

Mail can be received from San'a poste restante, although don't count on the service. Big hotels belonging to international chains also serve their customers.

Telephone services have advanced rapidly since unification country, and there are phones in most hotels. Public payphones were traditionally rare, but TeleYemen has recently opened International Telecommunications Centres in several towns, much needed since many Yemenis live abroad. These offices have phone booths with dial-direct service to any country in the world. They can also be used for domestic calls. The centres use one of two methods for payment: you either buy a plastic phone card loaded with several minutes' worth of connection units, or pay a deposit and collect the unused amount after your call. Overseas rates are comparable to those in Western countries. The introduction of cellular phones has made it possible for private entrepreneurs to offer phone services at varying rates in more and more remote towns around the country. However, it's still not possible to call home from small villages.

All major hotels in Yemen used to have telex, but today the better ones have telefax; rates vary depending on the hotel, the number of pages, the destination, and the time and day of transmission.

The country code for Yemen is 967. The phone services are automatic in the towns of the western part of the country but to the eastern part and many rural areas you still have to place your calls through an operator. Area codes for some of the most important towns and districts are:

1	San'a
2	Aden
3	Al-Hudayda
4	Ta'izz, Ibb, Jibla
51	Sa'da
6	Dhamar, Ma'rib
61	Al-Bayda
7	Hajja, 'Amran

TIME

Yemeni time is three hours ahead of GMT/ UTC. No daylight savings system is applied in summer.

When it's noon in San'a or Aden, the time elsewhere is:

Los Angeles	1 am
New York	4 am
London	9 am
Paris, Rome	10 am
Perth, Hong Kong	6 pm
Sydney	8 pm
Auckland	10 pm

ELECTRICITY

The electricity voltage is around 220 volts, 50 cycles. To use electricity in hotels, bring a universal plug for your appliances. Wall outlets are of various makes; I have counted no less than four different systems in use. The round-pin two-pronged variety are most common, but carry an adaptor if you want to be sure.

Along with the general deterioration of Yemen's economy, power failures have become more and more common in recent years. While in 1990 only the remote Province of Sa'da suffered from daily blackouts, in 1994 scheduled power outages were applied even in San'a, probably due to the fact that some power plants got destroyed during the civil war.

LAUNDRY

While some of the biggest and most expensive hotels provide a laundry service in San'a, you'll most often find yourself at the washbasin of your hotel bathroom. The dry-cleaning outlets all around San'a and other cities are mainly geared to handle the jackets of Yemeni men – your shirts and underwear are not accepted here.

WEIGHTS & MEASURES

Yemen uses the metric system; traditional weights and measures have long since fallen into disuse.

BOOKS

A surprising number of books about Yemen have been written by Westerners in the last 25 years or so. There are also quite a few volumes from earlier times. Many of those books were printed once only, are difficult to find and are limited in coverage. The many academic studies and project reports may be rich in information but are often poor in readability. Most of the published books are about the YAR. They may not be among those you find on the shelves of your local bookshop, though. If you plan to buy books about Yemen, your best option is to buy them either before or after your trip. Don't count on finding any in Yemen itself. However, the Taj Sheba and Sheraton hotels in San'a have souvenir shops worth checking for books about Yemen in English, French and German, although these selections are not extensive.

In fact, in Yemen you can hardly find anything printed in Western countries except *Time* and *Newsweek* magazines. Although there are plenty of bookshops in San'a and quite a few in Ta'izz, al-Hudayda, Aden and al-Mukalla, their selections are almost exclusively in Arabic. In San'a, a couple of bookshops by Qasr al-Jumhuri occasionally have some English titles available. In Aden, street vendors at Main Bazaar St sell second-hand books. But if you need some reading to help you fall asleep at night, pack your favourite paperbacks just to be sure.

General Reading

The ultimate work on any aspect of Yemen is the fabulous *San'a – an Arabic Islamic City* by Serjeant & Lewcock (1983). This tome, published by Scorpion Press and the World of Islam Festival Trust, is a limited-edition (2000 copies) luxury volume and contains everything you might ever want to know about Yemen in general and old San'a in particular. I have seen it a few times in London bookshops but have never had the $300 with me!

Pinguin Verlag has published *Yemen – 3000 Years of Art and Culture of Arabia Felix* (1987), another collection of thorough articles on specific topics in Yemeni history and culture. This 500-page tome has been published in English and German.

A more modest volume is Michael Jenner's *Yemen Rediscovered* (Yemen Tourism Company, 1983), a general description of Yemen. Another book in a similar vein is Jacques Hébert's *Yemen – Invitation to a Voyage in Arabia Felix* (Azal Publishing, 1989), which covers the northern part of the country only. This book has awakened in many people the desire to see Yemen's wonders for themselves. These texts are not particularly informative, but both books have many good photographs. Both of these books are widely available and have also been published in German and French.

Concept Media have a coffee-table book containing perhaps the most wonderful photographs of Yemen: *Arabian Moons – Passages in Time Through Yemen* by Pascal & Maria Marchaux (1987).

People & Society

A brilliant study of a single but all-embracing aspect of life in Yemen deserves special attention: Shelagh Weir's *Qat in Yemen – Consumption & Social Change*. This lively little book tells you far more about the daily life of today's Yemeni than its title would suggest. A not so brilliant but emotionally loaded and popular book is Zana Muhsin's *Sold*, memoirs of the daughters of a Yemeni-British couple who were brought up in the UK but forced to marry into a most backward village in the Yemeni mountains. This Gothic horror story about culture shock gives you an emphatically unbalanced view of the country.

Eric Hansen's *Motoring with Mohammed* (Vintage Books, 1991) is a hilarious account of a Westerner trying to retrieve his travel diaries lost in a shipwreck in the Red Sea.

History

The first written information about Yemen dates back to the era of Herodotus. However, a general reader will probably want to start with something less ancient. The absolute classic is Carsten Niebuhr's *Travels Through Arabia & Other Countries in the East* from 1792, a scientific but lively description of a famous Danish expedition to Arabia Felix. A great part of this book describes Yemen, where the expedition spent a lengthy period from December 1762 to August 1763 – mostly in the Tihama but with visits to Ta'izz and San'a. Unfortunately, it is hard to get your hands on even though it was reprinted in Beirut in 1965 – try academic libraries.

Interesting insights into Yemen of the early 1900s are found in Freya Stark's travel books from Southern Arabia. While Ms Stark's books are definitely habit-forming, I will here only recommend *The Southern Gates of Arabia* (1936), in which she describes her journey to the Hadhramawt. The book was reprinted several times in the 1980s and is easy to find.

For those interested in Yemen's more recent history, especially developments immediately before, during and after the revolutions, I highly recommend Fred Halliday's *Arabia without Sultans*, published by Penguin Books in 1974 and reprinted many times. If you are able to see through the Marxist parlance adopted by the author, this book gives a detailed and quite accurate account of the recent development of the peninsular countries, with some 180 pages devoted to the Yemenis. Other books on Yemenis and Yemen by the same author include *Arabs in Exile – Yemeni Migrants in Urban Britain*, and *Revolution and Foreign Policy: the Case of South Yemen 1967-87*, published by IB Tauris in London (1992).

Architecture

If architecture is what you're after, Fernando Varanda's *Art of Building in Yemen* (MIT Press, 1982) is outstanding. This hefty volume contains all the photos you are likely to snap in the northern provinces. The readable text is full of facts, and almost every page is illustrated.

The southern governorates are best covered in Salma Samar Damluji's *A Yemen Reality – Architecture Sculptured in Mud and Stone* and *The Valley of Mud Brick Architecture*, published by Garnet Publishing in 1991 and 1992 respectively. The books include hundreds of photographs plus thorough explanations of the construction methods in the southern part of Yemen.

Travel Guides

The tradition of guidebooks on Yemen spans only a few years, from the early 1980s. Available in Yemen only is Fritz Piepenburg's 1988 *New Traveller's Guide to Yemen*, a reworking of the same author's 1983 pioneering edition. Published by Yemen Tourism Company, it contains a general overview of the region and its history as well as lengthy descriptions of 'major sightseeing tours' in Yemen.

However, as the book is something of a semiofficial guide to the country, the author is extraordinarily shy in presenting any detailed information on present-day reality in Yemen. Because the sightseeing tours described are those offered by Yemen Tourism Company, a lone traveller relying on this book may face some surprises on the road, since the conditions out there are not necessarily the same for loners as for groups. The practical information is in condensed form and is considerably out of date.

In some bookshops you may still find copies of the fully official guidebooks of the former Yemens: *Tourist Guide of Yemen Arab Republic* and *Tourism in Democratic Yemen*. These books mainly offer gorgeous colour plates and are of historical interest only.

A recent work is APA Publications' 1990 *Yemen*, part of their Insight Guides series, edited by Joachim Chwaszcza. This work of more than 300 pages by a dozen authors has plenty of excellent photographs of both the old and new Yemen. Written just before unification, the book only grants five text pages to the southern governorates.

MAPS

For the trekker planning to spend a couple of weeks in the Yemeni mountains, no information about the roads and paths exists on paper – the only source of information is locals speaking wildly differing dialects of Arabic in each village.

The Michelin road atlases that cover a third of a continent are probably the best maps generally available in the West.

Another option is the *Touristic Map of the Republic of Yemen*, published by Deutsch-Jemenitische Gesellschaft eV (Kronenstr. 11, D-79100 Freiburg, Germany). It is a road map in a 1:1,000,000 scale with contours and 'hints for tourists' such as 'picturesque town', 'hotel, European standard' and so on.

The best available map of the country is the *Tourist Map of Republic of Yemen*, prepared by the Survey Authority in San'a for the General Tourism Authority in 1993. It shows roads and contours in a 1:1,500,000 scale, and spells placenames in both English and Arabic. It is available in Yemen from the General Tourist Corporation and from several bookshops and stationers in the cities.

Some town maps are also available in Yemen. The General Tourist Corporation used to have rather useful street maps of San'a, Ta'izz and al-Hudayda. These show the location of government institutions, hotels and mosques in the early '80s – the only problem is that often only the mosques remain in the same places. Unfortunately, these maps seem to be out of print now and only very poor-quality imitations are available.

In fact, the Yemeni governments have traditionally seemed to think that selling maps is like putting weapons into enemy hands. Although extensive cartography is being done and plenty of high-quality maps have already been printed by the Survey Authority, these are not available to the general public. You can see fairly detailed maps of the country and of smaller towns in the offices of some tour operators or at the Salah Museum in Ta'izz, but these maps are not sold anywhere. I hope that the civil war of 1994 has reduced the number of enemies to the point that maps can finally be declassified.

MEDIA
Newspapers & Magazines
Yemeni newspapers were government controlled prior to unification: *al-Jumhuriya* (The Republic) and *ath-Thawra* (The Revolution) were run by the former YAR while *14. Uktubir* (14 October) stems from the PDRY. After unification, more than 100 independent newspapers were quickly founded, many with political motivation. Though hampered by economical problems, scarce paper supplies and harassment by high officials from the ruling parties, these papers have played an important role in the development of the political culture in the country.

Perhaps most interesting is Yemen's only English-language newspaper, the *Yemen Times*. It defines itself as 'an Independent Economic & Political weekly', and the ruthlessness of its attacks against the government and the president measure the current level of freedom of the Yemeni press. It was started in 1990 by Dr Abdulaziz al-Saqqaf, a professor in the San'a University, who has been arrested once and harassed many times by officials because of his paper. In 1995 the US National Press Club awarded him the International Prize for Freedom of the Press – the first Arab journalist to receive this honour. You can buy the paper at the newsstands and stationers in the bigger cities.

The freedom of the Yemeni press was compromised, however, in accordance with the Memorandum of Understanding signed with Saudi Arabia. For the Saudis, who strictly control their domestic press, a free Yemeni press was a problem, and they managed to persuade the Yemeni government to ensure that no offending material be published about Saudi Arabia in the Yemeni press. This allowed the Ministry of Information to reintroduce a level of censorship in Yemen.

The availability in the past of a couple of Saudi Arabian English-language dailies – *Arab News* and *Saudi Gazette* – once measured the warmth of relations between Saudi and Yemeni governments. During our latest trip these newspapers were nowhere to be found, indicating an icy phase between the two neighbours. Should the relations improve, *Arab News* is recommended for those interested in religious questions because of its twice-weekly page 'Islam in Perspective'. This features scholarly advice on applying the principles of faith to daily questions such as divorce, breast-feeding, heritage and so on.

Also available in Yemen are *Time* and *Newsweek* magazines. You'll find them at some centrally located newsstands in the bigger cities (San'a, Ta'izz, al-Hudayda and Aden) and at a couple of luxury hotels in San'a.

Radio & TV

Radio broadcasts in Yemen are mainly in Arabic, but there are some news reports in English also; for example, on Radio San'a at 10 am.

There are two TV channels for the entire country (one broadcasting from San'a, the other from Aden) and all programmes are in Arabic, except for the 7.30 and 10.00 pm news which are broadcast in English. Satellite antennas were legalised in 1991. Despite the fact that a permit from the Ministry of Information is still needed to purchase one, they are spreading fast. In 1994 there were already some 5000 satellite dishes installed around the country, and in many top-class hotels you can tune into familiar channels.

FILM & PHOTOGRAPHY

Film is readily available in bigger cities, though not in remote villages.

Taking photos of people in Yemen is tricky because Islamic tradition explicitly prohibits the making of portraits of people. Never photograph anybody without first asking permission. It is not customary to photograph women, even veiled women. If you do, you must always ask permission from a woman's male companion, not from the woman herself. Generally, photography is more acceptable in the Tihama than in the mountains. People are most reserved about it in the northern mountains.

In the past, tourists taking photos of Yemenis without prior negotiations have lost their equipment – the subject has simply snatched the camera from the foreigner's hands and thrown it violently against rocks. Show your camera and utter the phrase *mumkin sura*. Many will not grant your

request and, if they refuse, you should point your camera in some other direction.

On the other hand, many Yemenis, especially those of the TV generation, not only tolerate posing for pictures but insist on being photographed. The problem with these people is that their idea of a good photo is very different from yours – they will grin in horrible poses, pretending to kill each other with their daggers or playing tricks, to the accompaniment of uncontrolled laughter. It seems that only a true professional or a devout amateur can take good pictures of merry Yemenis.

If someone poses quietly for you and, after the click of your camera, stretches out a hand, they are *not* asking for money. The custom of posing for money is nonexistent in Yemen and you should not establish it – Yemenis are quick to learn new habits, so be careful not to encourage any decadent behaviour. The subject is asking for the picture, which they probably want to keep. Yes, instant photography has arrived in Yemen and that kind of equipment may have been their only exposure to cameras. Be careful not to offend.

It is also easy to run into difficulties when you aim your camera at an inanimate object. Military installations and buildings are strictly prohibited subjects and, in a country ruled by the military, there are plenty of them around. You are bound to come across this situation if you do some photographing outside tourist groups, so you'd better know the Arabic word for 'forbidden': *mamnu'*.

It is easy to understand why airports, checkpoints and communications stations are all mamnu' – they are sensitive subjects in most countries. The old fort on top of the hill, half of it in ruins, is probably still in use, so it is also mamnu'. A soldier passing by may forbid you to take a picture of a mosque not because of the mosque itself but because of the neighbouring police station, which is (of course) mamnu'.

HEALTH

Travel health depends on your predeparture preparations, your day-to-day health care while travelling and how you handle any medical problem or emergency that does develop. While the list of potential dangers can seem quite frightening, with a little luck, some basic precautions and adequate information few travellers experience more than upset stomachs.

Travel Health Guides

There are a number of books on travel health:

Staying Healthy in Asia, Africa & Latin America, Dirk Schroeder, Moon Publications, 1994. Probably the best all-round guide to carry, as it's compact but very detailed and well organised.

Travellers' Health, Dr Richard Dawood, Oxford University Press, 1992. Comprehensive, easy to read, authoritative and also highly recommended, although it's rather large to lug around.

Where There is No Doctor, David Werner, Macmillan, 1994. A very detailed guide intended for someone, like a Peace Corps worker, going to work in an underdeveloped country, rather than for the average traveller.

Travel with Children, Maureen Wheeler, Lonely Planet Publications, 1995. Includes basic advice on travel health for younger children.

Predeparture Planning

Health Insurance A travel insurance policy to cover theft, loss and medical problems is a wise idea. There are a wide variety of policies and your travel agent will have recommendations. The international student travel policies handled by STA Travel or other student travel organisations are usually good value. Some policies offer lower and higher medical expense options but the higher one is chiefly for countries like the USA which have extremely high medical costs. Check the small print:

* Some policies specifically exclude 'dangerous activities', which can include motorcycling or even trekking. If such activities are on your agenda you don't want that sort of policy.
* Policies which pay doctors or hospitals direct are probably useless in Yemen, as are policies which ask you to call a centre in your home country for an assessment of your problem. Instead, you should be prepared to pay on the spot; keep all relevant documentation and claim when you return home.

* Check if the policy covers ambulances or an emergency flight home. If you have to stretch out you will need two seats and somebody has to pay for them!

Medical Kit It's wise to carry a small, straightforward medical kit. A possible kit list includes:

* Aspirin or Panadol – for pain or fever.
* Antihistamine (such as Benadryl) – useful as a decongestant for colds, allergies, to ease the itch from insect bites or stings or to help prevent motion sickness.
* Antibiotics – useful if you're travelling well off the beaten track, but they must be prescribed. Bring the drug with you: the prescription would probably be useless in Yemen due to differences in brand names.
* Kaolin preparation (Pepto-Bismol), Imodium or Lomotil – for stomach upsets.
* Rehydration mixture – for treatment of severe diarrhoea. This is particularly important if travelling with children.
* Antiseptic, mercurochrome and antibiotic powder or similar 'dry' spray – for cuts and grazes.
* Calamine lotion – to ease irritation from bites or stings.
* Bandages and Band-aids – for minor injuries.
* Scissors, tweezers and a thermometer (note that mercury thermometers are prohibited by airlines).
* Insect repellent, sunscreen, suntan lotion, chap stick and water purification tablets.

Ideally, antibiotics should be administered only under medical supervision and should never be taken indiscriminately. Overuse of antibiotics can weaken your body's ability to deal with infections naturally and can reduce the drug's efficacy on a future occasion. Take only the recommended dose at the prescribed intervals and continue using the antibiotic for the prescribed period, even if the illness seems to be cured earlier. Antibiotics are quite specific to the infections they can treat; stop immediately if there are any serious reactions and don't use it at all if you are unsure if you have the correct one.

Health Preparations Make sure you're healthy before you start travelling. If you are embarking on a long trip make sure your teeth are OK; in Yemen, a visit to the dentist would be the last thing you'd want to do.

If you wear glasses take a spare pair and your prescription with you. Losing your glasses can be a real problem, since getting new ones in Yemen could turn out to be next to impossible.

If you require a particular medication take an adequate supply, as it may not be available locally. Take the prescription, with the generic rather than the brand name (which may not be locally available), as it will make getting replacements easier.

Immunisations Vaccinations provide protection against diseases you might meet along the way.

No vaccinations are required to get an entry visa into Yemen, as long as you don't come from or through a country infected with yellow fever or cholera. Even though proof of vaccination is not required, as the Yemeni officials advised us, 'for your own sake, do some vaccinations'. Tropical diseases can be hard to eradicate, especially in the heat of Tihama or the southern coast, and a tourist passing through is just as likely to develop them as the Yemenis.

All vaccinations should be recorded on an International Health Certificate, which is available from your physician or government health department.

Plan ahead for getting your vaccinations: some of them require an initial shot followed by a booster, while some vaccinations should not be given together. Most travellers from Western countries will have been immunised against various diseases during childhood but your doctor may still recommend booster shots against measles or polio, diseases still prevalent in Yemen. The period of protection offered by vaccinations differs widely and some are contraindicated if you are pregnant.

The possible list of vaccinations includes:

Cholera Some countries may require cholera vaccination if you are coming from an infected area, but protection is not very effective, only lasts six months and is contraindicated for pregnancy.

Tetanus & Diphtheria Boosters are necessary every 10 years and protection is highly recommended.

Hepatitis A The most common travel-acquired illness which can be prevented by vaccination. Protection can be provided in two ways–either with the antibody gamma globulin or with a new vaccine called Havrix. Havrix provides long term immunity (possibly more than 10 years) after an initial course of two injections and a booster at one year. It may be more expensive than gamma globulin but certainly has many advantages, including length of protection and ease of administration. It is important to know that being a vaccine it will take about three weeks to provide satisfactory protection–hence the need for careful planning prior to travel.

Gamma globulin is not a vaccination but a ready-made antibody which has proven very successful in reducing the chances of hepatitis infection. Because it may interfere with the development of immunity, it should not be given until at least 10 days after administration of the last vaccine needed; it should also be given as close as possible to departure because it is at its most effective in the first few weeks after administration and the effectiveness tapers off gradually between three and six months.

Yellow Fever Protection lasts 10 years and is recommended. You usually have to go to a special yellow fever vaccination centre. Vaccination is contraindicated during pregnancy but if you must travel to a high-risk area it is probably advisable.

Communal Hygiene

To understand the Yemeni concept of public hygiene, we must remember that, as recently as the early 1960s, the Yemeni economy was completely based on recyclable materials. No 'waste' existed; everything was useable and anything that was thrown away was immediately absorbed in a process of natural circulation. This applied not only to rural agricultural communities but also to cities where cattle have always been raised. So, for example, in San'a, even the human excrement was dried, carefully collected and used as fuel in public bathhouses. The ashes were, in turn, sold to gardeners to be used as fertiliser.

The revolution brought the 20th century to this medieval society but has so far been unable to change the habits of 4000 years. Waste is still treated as though it were organic but nowadays gets thrown around in all neutral, loosely defined areas such as streets and roadsides; it's a pity that tin cans, plastic bags and used cars are of no use to the ecosystem! Water pipes have been introduced to the towns and villages before sewage systems; the result is that what was previously dried up into neat cakes now flows along the streets. The problem is considerably worse in the northern part of the country than in the once centrally planned PDRY.

All this tends to shock some Westerners, who interpret the ubiquitous 'wrecking yards in the streets' as a sign of an uncivilised society. It is not. Rather, it is the outcome of a violent collision between two cultures. The West has taken several hundred years to solve this problem; eventually, the Yemenis will also come to terms with it. In fact, they have already started. The old part of San'a today is a much cleaner place than it was in the mid-1980s.

Personal Hygiene

The most important thing to realise is that what you see on the roadsides is not a threat to your health. The Yemenis do wash themselves and epidemics no longer scourge the country. This is certainly an aspect of life that has radically changed for the better since the revolution. Tap water is now available throughout the country and the thumping of water pumps in the modern Yemeni countryside is as characteristic a sound as the chirping of crickets.

In the restaurants, soap and tap water are available for customers to wash their hands before the meal. Since Yemenis eat with their fingers instead of with knives and forks, they tend to use the tap for washing after the meal, too. But don't jump to the conclusion that they are overly hygienic in their everyday routines; it is still best to exercise some caution when choosing your food.

Basic Rules

Care in what you eat and drink is the most important health rule; stomach upsets are the most likely travel health problem but the majority of these upsets will be relatively minor. Don't become paranoid; trying the local food is part of the experience of travel, after all.

Water The number one rule is *don't drink anything but bottled water and soft drinks.* Street-side vendors offering tempting cold fruit juices make their ice from tap water, and their products should be avoided – the same applies to any ice-cooled drinks, even if served in the better hotels.

Mineral water, including Shamlan, Hadda and Azal, and soft drinks, including Canada Dry and Coca-Cola, are available all over the country, even in the smallest villages. At many rural road intersections there are tiny shacks selling biscuits, water and soft drinks. You don't need to bring any means of water purification to Yemen unless you intend to do extensive trekking in very sparsely populated areas.

Mineral water comes in handy plastic bottles of 0.75 or 1.5 litres. You should always carry a couple of them with you. Beware of bottles refilled with tap water, occasionally sold in more remote places; always check that the cap of the bottle has the plastic seal intact.

Tea or coffee should always be OK, since the water should have been boiled, but watch out for tea served from thermos bottles – if it is not hot any more it may not be safe, since the thermoses are washed seldom. Only boiled milk should be drunk; yoghurt is safe. If you like your tea with milk, you still may have no problem since they most often serve canned milk, safe especially if opened in your presence.

Food There is an old colonial adage which says: 'If you can cook it, boil it or peel it you can eat it...otherwise forget it'. Salads and fruit should be washed with purified water or peeled where possible. Prepackaged ice cream is OK but rare in Yemen. Thoroughly cooked or grilled food is safest but not if it has been left to cool or if it has been reheated. Take great care with shellfish or fish and avoid undercooked meat. In general, places that are packed with travellers or locals will be fine, while empty restaurants are questionable. Bread is best bought from bakeries or streetside vendors when it's newly baked and hot.

Nutrition If food is poor or limited in availability, if you're travelling hard and fast and therefore missing meals, or if you simply lose your appetite, you can soon start to lose weight and place your health at risk.

Make sure your diet is well balanced. Eggs, beans and lentils are all safe ways to get protein. Fruit you can peel (bananas, oranges or mandarins for example) is always safe and a good source of vitamins. Try to eat plenty of grains (rice) and bread. Remember that although food is generally safer if it is cooked well, overcooked food loses much of its nutritional value. If your diet isn't well balanced or if your food intake is insufficient, it's a good idea to take vitamin and iron pills.

In the hot climate of Yemen, make sure you drink enough – don't rely on feeling thirsty to indicate when you should drink. Not needing to urinate or very dark yellow urine is a danger sign. Always carry a water bottle with you, and several on long trips. Excessive sweating can lead to loss of salt and therefore muscle cramping. Salt tablets are not a good idea as a preventative, due to the danger of overdosing; it is better to carry table salt with you and add it to your food. If you suddenly feel tired after sweating a lot, try putting some salt on your palm and licking it.

Everyday Health Normal body temperature is 98.6°F or 37°C; more than 2°C higher is a 'high' fever. A normal adult pulse rate is 60 to 80 per minute (children 80 to 100, babies 100 to 140). You should know how to take a temperature and a pulse rate. As a general rule the pulse increases about 20 beats per minute for each °C rise in fever.

Respiration (breathing) rate is also an indicator of illness. Count the number of breaths per minute: between 12 and 20 is normal for adults and older children (up to 30 for younger children, 40 for babies). People with a high fever or serious respiratory illness (like pneumonia) breathe more quickly than normal. More than 40 shallow breaths a minute usually means pneumonia.

Many health problems can be avoided by taking care of yourself. Wash your hands frequently – it's quite easy to contaminate your own food. Clean your teeth with purified water rather than straight from the tap. Avoid climatic extremes: keep out of the sun when it's hot, dress warmly when it's cold. Avoid potential diseases by dressing sensibly. You can get worm infections through walking barefoot. You can avoid insect bites by covering bare skin when insects are around, by screening windows or beds or by using insect repellents. Seek local advice: if you're told the water is unsafe due to sharks, don't go in. In situations where there is no information, discretion is the better part of valour.

Medical Problems & Treatment

Potential medical problems can be broken down into several areas. Firstly there are the problems caused by extremes of temperature, altitude or motion. Then there are diseases and illnesses caused through poor environmental sanitation, insect bites or stings, and animal or human contact. Simple cuts, bites and scratches can also cause problems.

Self-diagnosis and treatment can be risky, so wherever possible seek qualified help. Although we do give treatment dosages in this section, they are for emergency use only. Medical advice should be sought before administering any drugs.

An embassy or consulate can usually recommend a good place to go for such advice. So can five-star hotels, although they often recommend doctors with five-star prices. (This is when that medical insurance really comes in useful!) In most parts of Yemen standards of medical attention are so low that for some ailments the best advice is to return to San'a (or even to get on a plane and leave the country).

Climatic & Geographical Considerations

Sunburn In Yemen you can get sunburnt surprisingly quickly, even through cloud.

Use a sunscreen and take extra care to cover areas which don't normally see sun – for example, your feet. A hat provides added protection, and you should also use zinc cream or some other barrier cream for your nose and lips. Calamine lotion is good for mild sunburn.

Prickly Heat Prickly heat is an itchy rash caused by excessive perspiration trapped under the skin. It usually strikes people who have just arrived in a hot climate and whose pores have not yet opened sufficiently to cope with greater sweating. Keeping cool but bathing often, using a mild talcum powder or even resorting to air-conditioning may help until you acclimatise.

Heat Exhaustion Dehydration or salt deficiency can cause heat exhaustion. Take time to acclimatise to high temperatures and make sure you get sufficient liquids. Salt deficiency is characterised by fatigue, lethargy, headaches, giddiness and muscle cramps and in this case salt tablets may help (see the Nutrition section as well). Vomiting or diarrhoea can deplete your liquid and salt levels. Anhydrotic heat exhaustion, caused by an inability to sweat, is quite rare. Unlike the other forms of heat exhaustion it is likely to strike people who have been in a hot climate for some time, rather than newcomers.

Heat Stroke This serious, sometimes fatal condition can occur if the body's heat-regulating mechanism breaks down and the body temperature rises to dangerous levels. Long, continuous periods of exposure to high temperatures can leave you vulnerable to heat stroke. You should avoid excessive alcohol or strenuous activity when you first arrive in Yemen's hot climate.

The symptoms are feeling unwell, not sweating very much or at all and a high body temperature (39°C to 41°C). Where sweating has ceased the skin becomes flushed and red. Severe, throbbing headaches and lack of coordination will also occur, and the sufferer may be confused or aggressive. Eventually the victim will become delirious or convulse.

Hospitalisation is essential, but meanwhile get patients out of the sun, remove their clothing, cover them with a wet sheet or towel and then fan continually.

Fungal Infections Hot weather fungal infections are most likely to occur on the scalp, between the toes or fingers (athlete's foot), in the groin (jock itch or crotch rot) and on the body (ringworm). You get ringworm (which is a fungal infection, not a worm) from infected animals or by walking on damp areas, like shower floors.

To prevent fungal infections wear loose, comfortable clothes, avoid artificial fibres, wash frequently and dry carefully. If you do get an infection, wash the infected area daily with a disinfectant or medicated soap and water, and rinse and dry well. Apply an anti-fungal powder like the widely available Tinaderm. Try to expose the infected area to air or sunlight as much as possible and wash all towels and underwear in hot water as well as changing them often.

Infectious Diseases
Diarrhoea The disease you are most likely to catch in Yemen is some form of diarrhoea. A change of water, food or climate can all cause the runs, but diarrhoea caused by contaminated food or water is more serious, and the most usual cause of the condition in Yemen. The best precaution is to avoid everything that is not hot when brought to your table. Fresh vegetables and unpeeled fruits are the most common source of problems, as they are often washed in contaminated water – don't eat them. Nor should you drink anything but bottled water or soft drinks. Bread is usually safe – either dry bread from stores or the greasy bread that is baked in the outdoor restaurants just before you eat it.

Despite all your precautions you may still have a mild bout of travellers' diarrhoea but a few rushed toilet trips with no other symptoms is not indicative of a serious problem. Moderate diarrhoea, involving half-a-dozen loose movements in a day, is more of a nuisance. Dehydration is the main danger with any diarrhoea, particularly for children where dehydration can occur quite quickly. Fluid replacement remains the mainstay of management. Weak black tea with a little sugar, soda water, or soft drinks allowed to go flat and diluted 50% with water are all good. With severe diarrhoea a rehydrating solution is necessary to replace minerals and salts. Commercially available ORS (oral rehydration salts) are very useful; add the contents of one sachet to a litre of boiled or bottled water. In an emergency you can make up a solution of eight teaspoons of sugar to a litre of boiled water and provide salted cracker biscuits at the same time. You should stick to a bland diet as you recover.

Lomotil or Imodium can be used to bring relief from the symptoms, although they do not actually cure the problem. Only use these drugs if absolutely necessary – eg if you *must* travel. For children Imodium is preferable, but under all circumstances fluid replacement is the most important thing to remember. Do not use these drugs if the person has a high fever or is severely dehydrated.

In certain situations antibiotics may be indicated:

- Watery diarrhoea with blood and mucous. (Gut-paralysing drugs like Imodium or Lomotil should be avoided in this situation.)
- Watery diarrhoea with fever and lethargy.
- Persistent diarrhoea for more than five days.
- Severe diarrhoea, if it is logistically difficult to stay in one place.

The recommended drugs (adults only) would be either norfloxacin 400 mg twice daily for three days or ciprofloxacin 500 mg twice daily for three days.

The drug bismuth subsalicylate has also been used successfully. The dosage for adults is two tablets or 30ml and for children it is one tablet or 10ml. This dose can be repeated every 30 minutes to one hour, with no more than eight doses in a 24-hour period.

The drug of choice in children would be co-trimoxazole (Bactrim, Septrin, Resprim) with dosage dependent on weight. A three-day course is also given.

Ampicillin has been recommended in the past and may still be an alternative.

Three days of treatment should be sufficient and an improvement should occur within 24 hours. However, if your condition lasts longer than a week, it is probably serious. There are plenty of possible causes but you should see a doctor. It is recommended that you fly directly to your home country but, for severe cases, an immediate cure may be needed; try the al-Kuwayt Hospital (Mustashfa al-Kuwayt) in San'a.

There are anecdotal reports that *Lactobacillus acidophilus*, available as the French preparate Biophilus, is helpful in the prevention of diarrhoea. However, there is currently no medical evidence which confirms this, and you'd be wise to contact you doctor before leaving your home country.

Giardiasis The parasite causing this intestinal disorder is present in contaminated water. The symptoms are stomach cramps, nausea, a bloated stomach, watery, foul-smelling diarrhoea and frequent gas. Giardiasis can appear several weeks after you have been exposed to the parasite. The symptoms may disappear for a few days and then return; this can go on for several weeks. Tinidazole, known as Fasigyn, or metronidazole (Flagyl) are the recommended drugs for treatment. Either can be used in a single treatment dose. Antibiotics are of no use.

Dysentery This serious illness, which some foreigners have caught in Yemen, is caused by contaminated food or water and is characterised by severe diarrhoea, often with blood or mucous in the stool.

There are two kinds of dysentery. Bacillary dysentery is characterised by a high fever and rapid development; headache, vomiting and stomach pains are also symptoms. It generally does not last longer than a week, but it is highly contagious.

Amoebic dysentery is often more gradual in the onset of symptoms, with cramping abdominal pain and vomiting less likely; fever may not be present. It is not a self-limiting disease: it will persist until treated and can recur and cause long-term health problems.

A stool test is necessary to diagnose which kind of dysentery you have, so you should seek medical help urgently. In case of an emergency the drugs norfloxacin or ciprofloxacin can be used as presumptive treatment for bacillary dysentery, and metronidazole (Flagyl) for amoebic dysentery.

For bacillary dysentery, norfloxacin 400 mg twice daily for seven days or ciprofloxacin 500 mg twice daily for seven days are the recommended dosages. If you're unable to find either of these drugs then a useful alternative is co-trimoxazole 160/800 mg (Bactrim, Septrin, Resprim) twice daily for seven days. This is a sulpha drug and must not be used by people with a known sulpha allergy.

In the case of children the drug co-trimoxazole is a reasonable first-line treatment. For amoebic dysentery, the recommended adult dosage of metronidazole (Flagyl) is one 750-mg to 800-mg capsule three times daily for five days. Children aged between eight and 12 years should have half the adult dose; the dosage for younger children is one-third the adult dose.

An alternative to Flagyl is Fasigyn, taken as a two-gram daily dose for three days. Alcohol must be avoided during treatment and for 48 hours afterwards.

Cholera Cholera vaccination is not very effective. The bacteria responsible for this disease are waterborne, so attention to the rules of eating and drinking should protect the traveller.

Although the disease is not very common in Yemen any more, precautions are still recommended. The disease is characterised by a sudden onset of acute diarrhoea with 'rice water' stools, vomiting, muscular cramps and extreme weakness. You need medical help – but treat for dehydration, which can be extreme, and if there is an appreciable delay in getting to hospital then begin taking tetracycline. The adult dose is 250 mg four times daily. It is not recommended for children aged eight years or under nor for pregnant women. An alternative drug

is Ampicillin. Remember that while antibiotics might kill the bacteria, it is a toxin produced by the bacteria which causes the massive fluid loss. Fluid replacement is by far the most important aspect of treatment.

Viral Gastroenteritis This is caused not by bacteria but, as the name suggests, by a virus. It is characterised by stomach cramps, diarrhoea, and sometimes by vomiting and/or a slight fever. All you can do is rest and drink lots of fluids.

Hepatitis Hepatitis is a general term for inflammation of the liver. There are many causes of this condition: drugs, alcohol and infections are but a few.

The discovery of new strains has led to a virtual alphabet soup, with hepatitis A, B, C, D, E and a rumoured G. These letters identify specific agents that cause viral hepatitis. Viral hepatitis is an infection of the liver, which can lead to jaundice (yellow skin), fever, lethargy and digestive problems. It can have no symptoms at all, with the infected person not knowing that they have the disease. Travellers shouldn't be too paranoid about this apparent proliferation of hepatitis strains; hepatitis C, D, E and G are fairly rare (so far) and following the same precautions as for A and B should be all that's necessary to avoid them.

Viral hepatitis can be divided into two groups on the basis of how it is spread. The first route of transmission is via contaminated food and water, and the second route is via blood and bodily fluids. Hepatitis A and E are spread by contaminated food and water, while hepatitis B, C and D are spread by contact with blood and bodily fluids.

Hepatitis A This is a very common disease in most countries, especially those with poor standards of sanitation. Most people in developing countries are infected as children; they often don't develop symptoms, but do develop life-long immunity. The disease poses a real threat to the traveller, as people are unlikely to have been exposed to hepatitis A in developed countries.

The symptoms are fever, chills, headache, fatigue, feelings of weakness and aches and pains, followed by loss of appetite, nausea, vomiting, abdominal pain, dark urine, light coloured faeces, jaundiced skin and the whites of the eyes may turn yellow. In some cases you may feel unwell, tired, have no appetite, experience aches and pains and be jaundiced. You should seek medical advice, but in general there is not much you can do apart from resting, drinking lots of fluids, eating lightly and avoiding fatty foods. People who have had hepatitis must forego alcohol for six months after the illness, as hepatitis attacks the liver and it needs that amount of time to recover.

The routes of transmission are via contaminated water, shellfish contaminated by sewerage, or foodstuffs sold by food handlers with poor standards of hygiene.

Taking care with what you eat and drink can go a long way towards preventing this disease. But this is a very infectious virus, so if there is any risk of exposure, additional cover is highly recommended. This cover comes in two forms: gamma globulin and Havrix. Gamma globulin is an injection where you are given the antibodies for hepatitis A, which provide immunity for a limited time. Havrix is a vaccine where you develop your own antibodies, which gives lasting immunity.

Hepatitis B This is also a very common disease, with almost 300 million chronic carriers in the world. Hepatitis B, which used to be called serum hepatitis, is spread through contact with infected blood, blood products or bodily fluids, for example through sexual contact, unsterilised needles and blood transfusions. Other risk situations include having a shave or tattoo in a local shop, or having your ears pierced. The symptoms of type B are much the same as type A except that they are more severe and may lead to irreparable liver damage or even liver cancer. Although there is no treatment for hepatitis B, a cheap and effective vaccine is available; the only problem is that for long-lasting cover you need a six-month course. The immunisation schedule requires two injections at least a month apart followed by a third dose five months after the second. Persons who should receive a hepatitis B vaccination include anyone who anticipates contact with blood or other bodily secretions, either as a health-care worker or through sexual contact with the local population, particularly those who intend to stay in the country for a long period of time.

Hepatitis C This is a recently defined virus. It is a concern because it seems to lead to liver disease more rapidly than hepatitis B.

The virus is spread by contact with blood – usually via contaminated transfusions or shared needles. Avoiding these is the only means of prevention, as there is no available vaccine.

Hepatitis D Often referred to as the 'Delta' virus, this infection only occurs in chronic carriers of hepatitis B. It is transmitted by blood and bodily fluids. Again there is no vaccine for this virus, so avoidance is the best prevention. The risk to travellers is certainly limited.

Hepatitis E This is a very recently discovered virus, of which little is yet known. It appears to be rather common in developing countries, generally causing mild hepatitis, although it can be very serious in pregnant women.

Care with water supplies is the only current prevention, as there are no specific vaccines for this type of hepatitis. At present it doesn't appear to be too great a risk for travellers.

Salmonellosis This is a large family of bacteria usually causing stomach upset and fever, common in Yemen. It is spread by poor hygiene and most typically contracted through eating contaminated food. Chicken not properly cooked, vegetables washed with impure water and cold sauces a few days old are typical sources. There are a thousand or so variants of this germ. Typhoid fever and paratyphoid fever are the most extreme diseases caused by bugs in this family, but there are about 2000 or more species with effects varying from mild stomach unease to violent diarrhoea and high fever, requiring hospital care. Treatment with antibiotics is needed in severe cases. The only precaution is to avoid unsafe food and drink. No vaccination is available because of the numerous variations of the disease. However, for the one or two per cent of people who carry the so-called HLA-B27 factor in their blood, any variant of salmonellosis may cause potentially crippling joint damage. Should you test positive for this factor, you'd better be extremely careful in choosing your food in Yemen.

Typhoid Typhoid fever is another gut infection that travels the faecal-oral route – ie contaminated water and food are responsible. Vaccination against typhoid is not totally effective and it is one of the most dangerous infections, so medical help must be sought.

In its early stages typhoid resembles many other illnesses: sufferers may feel like they have a bad cold or flu on the way, as early symptoms are a headache, a sore throat, and a fever which rises a little each day until it is around 40°C or more. The victim's pulse is often slow relative to the degree of fever present and gets slower as the fever rises – unlike a normal fever where the pulse increases. There may also be vomiting, diarrhoea or constipation.

In the second week the high fever and slow pulse continue and a few pink spots may appear on the body; trembling, delirium, weakness, weight loss and dehydration are other symptoms. If there are no further complications, the fever and other symptoms will slowly go during the third week. However you must get medical help before this because pneumonia (acute infection of the lungs) or peritonitis (perforated bowel) are common complications, and because typhoid is very infectious.

The fever should be treated by keeping the victim cool and dehydration should also be watched for. The drug of choice is ciprofloxacin at a dose of one gram daily for 14 days. It is quite expensive and may not be available. The alternative, chloramphenicol, has been the mainstay of treatment for many years. In many countries it is still the recommended antibiotic but there are fewer side affects with Ampicillin. The adult dosage is two 250-mg capsules, four times a day. Children aged between eight and 12 years should have half the adult dose; younger children should have one-third the adult dose.

People who are allergic to penicillin should not be given Ampicillin.

Tetanus This potentially fatal disease is found in undeveloped tropical areas. It is difficult to treat but is preventable with immunisation. Tetanus occurs when a wound becomes infected by a germ which lives in the faeces of animals or people, so clean all cuts, punctures or animal bites. Tetanus is also known as lockjaw, and the first symptom may be discomfort in swallowing, or stiffening of the jaw and neck; this is followed by painful convulsions of the jaw and whole body.

Rabies Rabies is found in Yemen as in many countries and is caused by a bite or scratch by an infected animal. Dogs are a noted carrier. Any bite, scratch or even lick from a mammal should be cleaned immediately and thoroughly. Scrub with soap and running water, and then clean with an alcohol solution. If there is any possibility that the animal is infected medical help should be sought immediately. Even if the animal is not rabid, all bites should be treated seriously as they can become infected or can result in tetanus. A rabies vaccination is now available and should be considered if you are in a high-risk category – eg if you intend to work with animals or investigate the rare Yemeni wildlife closely.

Tuberculosis Tuberculosis is a lung disease commonly spread by coughing or by unpasteurised dairy products from infected cows, and is widespread in developing countries. Milk that has been boiled is safe to drink; the souring of milk to make yoghurt or cheese also kills the bacilli. It is also passed by sharing unclean eating and drinking utensils and the like, so if you enjoyed chewing qat with Yemenis in a dormitory of a cheap hotel and smoking that huge *mada'a* (water pipe), I'd advise that you check your lungs when you get home. The disease is curable.

Young children are more susceptible than adults and vaccination is a sensible precaution for children under 12 travelling in endemic areas.

Bilharzia Bilharzia is carried in water by minute worms. The larvae infect certain varieties of freshwater snails found in rivers, streams, lakes and particularly behind dams. The worms multiply and are eventually discharged into the water surrounding the snails.

They attach themselves to your intestines or bladder, where they produce large numbers of eggs. The worm enters through the skin, and the first symptom may be a tingling and sometimes a light rash around the area where it entered. Weeks later, when the worm is busy producing eggs, a high fever may develop. A general feeling of being unwell may be the first symptom; once the disease is established abdominal pain and blood in the urine are other signs.

Curing the disease may take quite some time and liver damage may be permanent. As the disease is common in Yemen, you should resist the temptation to join Yemenis having a great time swimming in a wadi. Avoiding swimming or bathing in fresh water where bilharzia is present is the main method of preventing the disease. Even deep water can be infected. If you do get wet, dry off quickly and dry your clothes as well. Seek medical attention if you have been exposed to the disease and tell the doctor your suspicions, as bilharzia in the early stages can be confused with malaria or typhoid. If you cannot get medical help immediately, praziquantel (Biltricide) is the recommended treatment. The recommended dosage is 40 mg/kg in divided doses over one day. Niridazole is an alternative drug.

Diptheria Diphtheria can be a skin infection or a more dangerous throat infection. It is spread by contaminated dust contacting the skin or by the inhalation of infected cough or sneeze droplets. Frequent washing and keeping the skin dry will help prevent skin infection. A vaccination is available to prevent the throat infection.

Sexually Transmitted Diseases Sexual contact with an infected sexual partner spreads these diseases. While abstinence is the only 100% preventative, using condoms is also effective.

Gonorrhoea and syphilis are the most common of these diseases; sores, blisters or rashes around the genitals, discharges or pain when urinating are common symptoms. Symptoms may be less marked or not observed at all in women. Syphilis symptoms eventually disappear completely but the disease continues and can cause severe problems in later years. The treatment of gonorrhoea and syphilis is by antibiotics.

There are numerous other sexually transmitted diseases, for most of which effective treatment is available. However, there is no cure for herpes and there is also currently no cure for AIDS. Even though the latter is common in nearby parts of Africa, there are so far no reported cases from Yemen. Using condoms is the most effective preventative.

HIV/AIDS HIV, the Human Immunodeficiency Virus, may develop into AIDS, Acquired Immune Deficiency Syndrome. While HIV is common in nearby parts of Africa, there are few reported cases from Yemen so far. In many developing countries transmission is predominantly through heterosexual sexual activity. This is quite different from industrialised countries where transmission is mostly through contact between homosexual or bisexual males, or via contaminated needles shared by IV drug users. Apart from abstinence, the most effective preventative is always to practise safe sex using condoms. It is impossible to detect the HIV-positive status of an otherwise healthy-looking person without a blood test.

Any exposure to blood, blood products or bodily fluids may put the individual at risk. HIV/AIDS can also be spread through infected blood transfusions; most developing countries cannot afford to screen blood for transfusions. It can also be spread by dirty needles – vaccinations, acupuncture, tattooing and ear or nose piercing can potentially be as dangerous as intravenous drug use if the equipment is not clean. If you do need an injection, it may be a good idea to buy a new syringe from a pharmacy and ask the doctor to use it. Fear of HIV infection should never preclude treatment for serious medical conditions. Although there may be a risk of infection, it is very small indeed.

Insect-Borne Diseases

Malaria Malaria occurs mainly in the Tihama and in the southern coast, where it is spread by mosquito bites. If you are travelling in endemic areas it is extremely important to take malarial prophylactics. Symptoms include headaches, fever, chills and sweating which may subside and recur. Without treatment, malaria can develop more serious, potentially fatal effects.

Antimalarial drugs do not prevent you from being infected but kill the parasites during a stage in their development.

There are a number of different types of malaria. The one of most concern is falciparum malaria. This is responsible for the very serious cerebral malaria. Falciparum is the predominant form in many malaria-prone areas of the world, including Africa, South-East Asia and Papua New Guinea. Contrary to popular belief cerebral malaria is not a new strain.

The problem in recent years has been the emergence of increasing resistance to commonly used antimalarials like chloroquine, maloprim and proguanil. Newer drugs such as mefloquine (Lariam) and doxycycline (Vibramycin, Doryx) are often recommended for chloroquine and multidrug-resistant areas. Expert advice should be sought, as there are many factors to consider when deciding on the type of antimalarial medication, including the area to be visited, the risk of exposure to malaria-carrying mosquitoes, your current medical condition, and your age and pregnancy status. It is also important to discuss the side-effect profile of the medication, so you can work out some level of risk versus benefit ratio. It is also very important to be sure of the correct dosage of the medication prescribed to you. Some people have inadvertently taken weekly medication (chloroquine) on a daily basis, with disastrous effects. While discussing dosages for prevention of malaria, it is often advisable to include the dosages required for treatment, especially if your trip is through a high-risk area that would isolate you from medical care.

Primary prevention must always be in the form of mosquito-avoidance measures. The mosquitoes that transmit malaria bite from dusk to dawn and during this period travellers are advised to:

- wear light-coloured clothing
- wear long pants and long-sleeved shirts
- use mosquito repellents containing the compound DEET on exposed areas (overuse of DEET may be harmful, especially to children, but its use is considered preferable to being bitten by disease-transmitting mosquitoes)
- avoid highly scented perfumes or aftershave
- use a mosquito net – it may be worth taking your own

While no antimalarial is 100% effective, taking the most appropriate drug significantly reduces the risk of contracting the disease.

No one should ever die from malaria. It can be diagnosed by a simple blood test. Symptoms range from fever, chills and sweating, headache and abdominal pains to a vague feeling of ill-health, so seek examination immediately if there is any suggestion of malaria.

Contrary to popular belief, once a traveller contracts malaria he/she does not have it for life. One of the parasites may lie dormant in the liver but this can also be eradicated using a specific medication.

Malaria is curable, as long as the traveller seeks medical help when symptoms occur.

Cuts, Bites & Stings

Cuts & Scratches Skin punctures can easily become infected in hot climates and may be difficult to heal. Treat any cut with an antiseptic solution and mercurochrome. Where possible avoid bandages and Band-aids, which can keep wounds wet.

Bites & Stings Bee and wasp stings are usually painful rather than dangerous. Calamine lotion will give relief and ice packs will reduce the pain and swelling. There are some spiders with dangerous bites but antivenenes are usually available. Scorpion stings are notoriously painful and can be fatal to children and elderly people. Scorpions often shelter in shoes or clothing.

Snakes There are several poisonous species of snakes in Yemen. To minimise your chances of being bitten always wear boots, socks and long trousers when walking through undergrowth where snakes may be present. Don't put your hands into holes and crevices, and be careful when collecting firewood.

Snake bites do not cause instantaneous death and antivenenes are usually available. Keep the victim calm and still, wrap the bitten limb tightly, as you would for a sprained ankle, and then attach a splint to immobilise it. Then seek medical help, if possible with the dead snake for identification. Don't attempt to catch the snake if there is even a remote possibility of being bitten again. Tourniquets and sucking out the poison are now comprehensively discredited.

Bedbugs & Lice Bedbugs live in various places, but particularly in dirty mattresses and bedding. Spots of blood on bedclothes or on the wall around the bed can be read as a suggestion to find another hotel. Bedbugs leave itchy bites in neat rows. Calamine lotion may help.

All lice cause itching and discomfort. They make themselves at home in your hair (head lice), your clothing (body lice) or in your pubic hair (crabs). You catch lice through direct contact with infected people or by sharing combs, clothing and the like. Powder or shampoo treatment will kill the lice and infected clothing should then be washed in very hot water.

Women's Health

Gynaecological Problems Poor diet, lowered resistance due to the use of antibiotics for stomach upsets and even contraceptive pills can lead to vaginal infections when travelling in hot climates. Keeping the genital area clean, and wearing skirts or loose-fitting trousers and cotton underwear will help to prevent infections.

Yeast infections, characterised by a rash, itch and discharge, can be treated with a vinegar or even lemon juice douche or with yoghurt. Nystatin suppositories are the usual medical prescription.

Trichomonas is a more serious infection; symptoms are a discharge and a burning sensation when urinating. Male sexual partners must also be treated, and if a vinegar-water douche is not effective medical attention should be sought. Flagyl is the prescribed drug.

Pregnancy Most miscarriages occur during the first three months of pregnancy, so this is the most risky time to travel as far as your own health is concerned. Miscarriage is not uncommon, and can occasionally lead to severe bleeding. The last three months should also be spent within reasonable distance of good medical care. A baby born as early as 24 weeks stands a chance of survival, but only in a good modern hospital. Pregnant women should avoid all unnecessary medication, but vaccinations and malarial prophylactics should still be taken where possible. Additional care should be taken to prevent illness and particular attention should be paid to diet and nutrition. Alcohol and nicotine, for example, should be avoided.

Women travellers often find that their periods become irregular or even cease while they're on the road. Remember that a missed period in these circumstances doesn't necessarily indicate pregnancy. There are health posts or Family Planning clinics in many urban centres in developing countries, where you can seek advice and have a urine test to determine whether or not you are pregnant.

WOMEN TRAVELLERS

Women can visit Yemen without a male companion. However, Western feminist attitudes are simply irrelevant here. Respect the values of your host country. A woman's place in Yemeni society is, by and large, at home with the family and there is nothing you can do about this.

Dress appropriately and behave modestly. Naive Western women have attracted sexual harassment by smiling at men or looking them in the eyes in public. For young teenage boys in the streets of the cities, a lone Western woman is an interesting challenge. Avoid physical contact with them and don't hesitate to show your anger if one actually touches you. Not showing your anger is seen as encouragement.

In the area of transport, buses are preferable to long-haul service taxis. If the bus is full, you will be seated next to another woman. If you have to use a taxi alone, you might want to buy both of the front seats so you can sit alone with the driver. Be prepared to be asked some extra questions at the checkpoints, though.

Some hotels and restaurants do not serve lone women at all. Choose the more expensive hotels of the two-sheet category at least and restaurants frequented by tourists. In shops, you may be served only after the men, including those who enter after you.

DANGERS & ANNOYANCES

Although Yemen is a most enjoyable and safe country to travel in, there are certain details you should be aware of.

Security

In the northern provinces (Ma'rib and al-Jawf, parts of Sa'da and Hajja, northern Shabwa), the general security seems to become time and again a genuine problem. Yemen is a heavily armed society: the number of firearms in the country is estimated at 60 million, or four times the population. All kinds of armament from hand grenades to anti-aircraft Stingers can be freely purchased at special arms suqs around the country, so it is no wonder that whenever tribal disputes develop into full-blown conflicts the casualties are high. If you are warned about some regions the tour operators are not including in their itineraries and taxi drivers are reluctant to take you to, don't play Lawrence of Arabia and go by yourself – the area may be suffering from open warfare!

The period between the unification and the 1994 civil war showed a marked unpopularity of the government among the Bedouins and mountain-dwellers of these areas, leading to cars stolen at gunpoint and hijackings of diplomats or oil workers. In a few cases tourists got inadvertently involved. Despite the high publicity these incidents inevitably draw, the danger should not be exaggerated. No Westerners ever got killed or even injured – the target has been the government, and foreigners have only been accidentally affected or served as instruments in the negotiations. After the war almost no such incidents have been reported, but then foreigners had not yet returned en masse at the time of this writing.

Attitudes Towards Westerners

As in any recently opened country, tourism has had its effects on Yemen, and attitudes towards Western travellers seem to fluctuate along with the numbers.

The late 1980s saw an unprecedented tourist boom in the YAR, only accelerating in the couple of years after unification. In 1992, 83,100 travellers visited Yemen on tourist visas, and while many of them came from Arabic countries, still 47,800 were from Europe, three times the number of the mid-1980s. Some Western travellers may not have shown appropriate respect to the Yemeni way of life or, perhaps, the sheer weight of numbers has been too much for the villagers.

In fact, it seems that while cases of unfriendliness towards travellers were slowly but steadily becoming more frequent in recent years, the decline in tourist flow after the 1994 civil war has returned the Yemeni hospitality to its former level. Our last visit was as enjoyable as our first in the mid-1980s.

In the early 1990s, children in some regions had taken to throwing rocks at tourists. Whether they were just playing (*intifada*), with tourists in the role of Israeli soldiers, or whether they were being encouraged by their parents is unclear. Some much-visited highland towns and villages – Manakha, Hajja and Shihara, for example, or Sa'da in the north – were no longer as enjoyable. While the rocks hardly ever hurt you physically, they could certainly spoil your humour. Should you encounter this kind of behaviour, the best but not perfect precaution is not to hurry and talk patiently with the flocks of children around you while proceeding steadily.

Beggars

The Muslim religious requirement to give alms means that beggars appear here and there in Yemen. However, they seem to have been told that non-Muslims do not know about the obligations written in the Koran, so they are not likely to bother you. If someone tries to get some baksheesh from you, they will usually be steered away by an embarrassed Yemeni.

You will definitely come across more beggars in the Tihama than in the highlands. Probably due to African influences, the coastal beggars are more pushy than those in the highlands. In Aden and a few other towns there are hordes of Somali refugees that have managed to escape from the refugee camps, with no hope of jobs or regular income. But, even here, you should have no difficulties with beggars.

WORK

Yemen has a most serious unemployment problem, so job opportunities for foreigners are limited to the extreme: all vacancies are advertised with the requirement or preference of Yemeni nationality. Western oil companies operating in Yemen employ high-skilled professionals fluent in Arabic, but otherwise your chances of finding well-paid work in Yemen are slim. You will need a letter of introduction from your Yemeni contact in order to obtain a work visa.

The Netherlands, Germany, France and Italy have the most extensive development aid programmes in Yemen, so your chances of participating in one such programme on a paid or voluntary basis are the highest if you are a citizen of one of these countries.

Useful mainly to US citizens, enquiries about academic scholarships for field work in Yemen can be sent to the American Institute for Yemeni Studies, 155 E 58th St, Chicago, IL 60637, USA. This organisation also has an office, library and hospice in San'a. Send enquiries to PO Box 2658, San'a.

ACTIVITIES
Trekking

Trekking is an excellent way to get to know the Yemeni mountains, and the country offers many fine regions suitable for exploring on foot. However, trekking in Yemen is nothing like trekking in the Swiss Alps or in the Yellowstone National Park, in that in Yemen it is absolutely unorganised. There are no marked trails, no maps, no guidance. Yemenis won't understand why you want to walk: if you ask for directions you're likely to be shown to the nearest dirt road used by shared taxis or Toyota pick-ups. Basically you are on your own.

Equip yourself with a compass, containers for drinking water, a tent and warm clothes. Water purifiers and some condensed food might be useful – you will be able to buy foodstuffs and bottled drinks in most of the villages you'll come across but sometimes you might not reach one before dark. Yemen is a most unevenly populated country. Choose a densely inhabited region with a friendly and hospitable population such as the Haraz mountains near Manakha or the al-Mahwit Governorate.

Don't go during Ramadan or religious festivals, since you'd be the only one moving around and needing to buy things. Eating and drinking might pose a big problem for you during Ramadan.

Erecting your tent near a village is sure to attract a lot of children. It is very unlikely you would be able to camp unnoticed anywhere. It is courteous to ask permission to camp from the sheikh of the village. In some regions camping is not welcomed at all – as a rule of thumb trekking is not recommended anywhere east of San'a. Sometimes you will be invited to sleep on the rooftop of a house.

Diving & Snorkelling
The Yemeni seas are rich in fish, and snorkelling is popular among Western expatriates working in projects near the coastal areas, either for the sheer joy of watching the underwater life or catching the fish. The al-Khawkha beaches are most frequented by water-sports enthusiasts, but there are good beaches north of al-Hudayda and near Bir 'Ali also.

However, water sports are not popular among Yemenis, and there is no equipment rental anywhere in the country. You have to bring everything from your home country, which obviously limits all kinds of water sports for a short-term visitor.

You are also on your own when it comes to security: there are no warning systems against sharks, strong currents or sharp rocks. Unless you have a guide or a friend who has visited the place before, you'd be unwise to embark on this alone.

HIGHLIGHTS
Yemen is a country of 3000 years of recorded history, and the Yemenis are proud of their historical sites, eager to show them to foreigners. Few visitors can resist visiting **Ma'rib**, and the nearby **Baraqish** is, by appearance, even more spectacular.

However, Yemen is not another Italy or Egypt: time has not handled Southern Arabia gently, and most of the ancient cities today consist of rubble and very modest ruins. It is not the impressive ruins but the sense of history which makes Yemen such a fascinating destination. Sites like **Qana**, **Shabwa** or **Timna'** have little to see but plenty to experience.

The more recent history of Yemen is best reflected in the many fine mosques, most of which are, unfortunately, inaccessible to infidels. Still, there are many mosques revealing their beauty to the outside, too: the old centres of **San'a**, **Zabid** and **Ta'izz**, or the towns in **Wadi Hadhramawt** abound with breathtaking works of art. The mosques of **Yifrus**, **al-Janad**, **Jibla** and the **al-Amiriya** mosque in Rada' also make a visit to these small towns worthwhile.

The variety of architectural styles unique to Yemen is incredible, and should any mountain village of Yemen be cut from its roots and moved to Europe, America or Australia, it would create a permanent attraction and sure-fire fee collector. Take your camera to old San'a, Sa'da, Ma'rib, Manakha, Zabid, Habban, Shibam and Tarim, and you will leave Yemen with an amazing collection of photographs.

Yemen is an extremely mountainous country, and the geological attractions are numerous. While it is no match for the Himalayas, the interest value of Yemen is enhanced by the Yemeni tradition of building houses and villages on the most inaccessible mountaintops, making the Yemeni mountains a truly special place to visit. **Kawkaban** and **Shihara** are prime examples included in every ready-made tour, but **at-Turba** is definitely worth a visit also. Furthermore, you can enjoy less celebrated locations anywhere in the mountain governorates; the **Haraz** mountains near **Manakha** and the whole of the **al-Mahwit** Governorate are good for trekking on your own. The unique socio-geological feature of **Wadi Hadhramawt** is definitely not to be missed.

However, it is the unique culture and

way of life of the Yemeni people that will probably leave you with the most lasting memories. Visit their suqs, use their shared taxis, overnight in hotels in traditional tower houses. You may disagree with their habits of chewing qat every afternoon or carrying heavy armament they so often have not hesitated to use. Yet, it is difficult to find a people so friendly and hospitable towards strangers, and so eager to please and make friends with you.

ACCOMMODATION

In Arabic, there are two words for hotel: *funduq* and *u:ti:l (util)*. These words have equivalent meanings and can be used interchangeably; the latter is a borrowed word while the former is original. The international word is most often seen (also in the Latin alphabet) above the entrances of newer hotels on the assumption that foreign visitors will represent significant market potential in the near future.

Some Westerners believe that funduqs constitute a special family of traditional Arabic inns, while utils are more modern, Western-style hotels. This misconception is actively supported by Arab tour organisers, who recognise here a chance to charge more for something seen as traditional, exotic accommodation. Funduq can only be translated as 'hotel' and is the word you should use when trying to find one.

The traditional form of accommodation is the so-called one-riyal funduq, well known to the few travellers who visited the YAR in the 1970s. You may have heard or read stories about these or about the legendary hospitality of Peninsular Arabs in general. According to these stories, cheap hotels abound even in the remotest and tiniest tent villages and, should there not be one, villagers will compete for the honour of being accepted as host for a traveller, the sheikh (the elected elder in the village) usually winning the contest. The overall atmosphere is warm and kind, the visitor will be served free tea or coffee and there is always excellent food ready.

Despite this image, Yemen has never been a predominantly Bedouin society and the inhabitants of stable agricultural settlements are traditionally more reserved towards strangers. Moreover, motorised vehicles, especially 4WDs, have virtually eliminated the need for an extensive network of cheap hotels. It is sad but true that, nowadays, on the outskirts of Yemeni villages, you will hardly ever find those small groups of beds under big trees that once offered the cheapest possible accommodation. Still, there is a good choice of reasonably priced hotels in the northern provinces.

In classifying Yemeni hotels, we must replace the conventional no-star to five-star system with the Yemeni no-sheet to two-sheet system (based on what you will find on the beds).

No-Sheet

The lowest level of accommodation is still cheap by Western standards. In any town or bigger village in the northern provinces, you should be able to find a place to stay for YR 300 to YR 350 a night. For this price, you will get a bed with no sheets but plenty of blankets and pillows. The bed may have legs or it may be just a mattress on the floor. It is always absolutely filthy; the bedding is never washed during its lifetime – Yemen is an arid land and precious water is not wasted on this kind of thing. You will not know the true meaning of the word 'filthy' until you have stayed in no-sheet accommodation.

Despite the general filth, these inns can be used if you bring your own sheets (or just don't mind the dirt!). For many people, a sleeping bag does the job of sheets quite comfortably but, as you don't need it for warmth, it may be needlessly heavy to carry around. Even though the nights can be rather chilly in the mountains, there are always more blankets available than you will need and, in the coastal areas, you'll prefer some form of cooling. All that is required is something to separate you from the hotel bedclothes.

As for your own hygiene, *hammam* in these places usually means a toilet, not a bathroom. In bigger towns, running cold water is usually available. Sometimes, there's even a cold shower but, more often, you'll only get a tap and bucket. In smaller towns, running water is seldom available and the innkeepers provide full buckets of water in the hammam. In the one-storey houses of the Tihama, there is seldom any sewerage system and the toilet consists of a small hole dug in the ground.

The beds – 10, 20, 30 or even more – are usually in one large hall. This means no women. In some places, there are also smaller rooms with only four or six beds and, if the inn is not full, you may have such a room all to yourself (and your companion). You often have to pay for every bed, however, though that may not be too bad if the cost is YR 300 a bed and you have no choice.

Getting a private room is a good idea even for males; the big dormitory is going to be noisy late at night and early in the morning. You can be sure that a TV set will be watched keenly until midnight and will be played at full volume to keep it audible over the general conversation. The air is not only polluted by noise; the smoke from water pipes is heavy. After a few weeks in Yemen, you will appreciate some privacy anyway.

There are inns of this category in all the bigger northern towns, usually concentrated near the bus and taxi stations and the central markets. Though they seldom have signs, even in Arabic, the inns are easy to find – when you arrive in a town, just ask the driver for a *funduq rakhi:s* (cheap hotel). If you don't look too rich, you will be shown a nearby house.

In many of these inns, the main dormitory is on the ground floor and is wide open to the street. Wherever you see a large hall with Yemeni men lying on beds, watching the street life and smoking those ubiquitous water pipes, you know you have found a chance for a cheap overnight stay.

One-Sheet

The next step upwards is a one-sheet hotel, with beds at about YR 300 to YR 500.

The single sheet is placed on the mattress and is often no wider than the mattress itself – it does not necessarily resemble what you know as a sheet. Sometimes, there are even two sheets. The essential thing about hotels in this category is that the sheets are changed not when the customers change but according to a set schedule – once a week in busy seasons and about once a month when the occupancy level in the hotel is low.

The hammams in this kind of hotel usually offer facilities undreamed of a mere 20 years ago. Tap water is always available, cakes of soap may appear by the sink and, increasingly often, small boilers offer you the luxury of a warm shower. The bathrooms are not clean and you won't want to enter one barefoot. However, with suitable equipment, you can get yourself very clean quite comfortably here. The bathrooms also have doors and locks so that females can use them. After a few days excursion in the countryside, it will look like paradise.

Otherwise, hotels in the no-sheet and one-sheet categories are pretty similar. Both may have large dormitories, though the one-sheet variety is more likely to have rooms as well and may even have just smaller rooms. Neither category offers single rooms and even doubles are rare; rooms with three or four beds are usually the smallest available. The pricing is always per bed; if you want the whole room, you pay for every bed in it.

There are no hotels of this standard in villages or smaller towns. On the other hand, where there is demand for this type of accommodation, there is usually also some competition, so you will have a choice.

Two-Sheet

This kind of hotel is usually found only in cities and big towns. The prices range from YR 400 to YR 1000 per person per night.

In a two-sheet hotel, the two sheets look like Western-style sheets and are changed at least with changes of guests, perhaps even every other day. There are no big dormitories– only rooms. Double rooms are usually the smallest, though singles are sometimes available. Prices are set by the room.

What you should look for, of course, is hygiene. If you choose a clean hotel in the lower price range intending to pay YR 800 to YR 1000 for a double, *don't* choose one with private bathrooms. A common bathroom in the corridor is usually much better because it gets cleaned every day and, if you are not satisfied with it, you can try another bathroom further down the corridor.

A private bathroom will cost you at least YR 200 and delivers its distinctive stench (and, possibly, its cockroaches) directly to your room. If you invest in one, what do you do when the toilet refuses to flush? The staff suddenly won't speak English and, even if you can get somebody to have a look at it, there will be nothing they can do to fix it – why don't you take the bucket and flush it yourself? Moreover, the sewerage system is slow to suck away any water so, when you take a shower, the excess water streams under the door and comes to rest in a pool next to your bed. No, private bathrooms belong to the luxury category in Yemen.

In the Tihama and on the southern coast, you will probably be willing to pay for air-conditioning. In no-sheet and one-sheet categories, air-conditioning is generally unknown but even the most basic two-sheet hotels offer you some kind of fan, with or without cooler (the price is different, of course). In some cheaper hotels, you will find rooms with or without a fan; you will probably automatically be offered one with a fan but, if you don't feel like paying the extra YR 200 to YR 300, you could ask if they have rooms without air-conditioning. You won't find air-conditioning in two-sheet hotels in the highlands – during winter, you'll hope for heaters instead but they, too, are nonexistent.

There are restaurants in some two-sheet hotels but meals are not included in the room prices. The general rule seems to be that, if the restaurant is at the top of the hotel building, it has few customers and the food will

be tasteless and pricey. However, if the restaurant is on the ground floor and opens onto the street, it may be rather good. If plenty of locals eat there, you can bet that the food is cheap and tasty; if there are also plenty of foreign diners, it may even be safe to eat.

Deluxe

Although many Yemeni hotels bear the name *diluks*, there are not too many luxury hotels here. If you're willing to pay YR 2000 to YR 5000 and up per night for fabulous Western-style service, you can do that in San'a and, in a less opulent style, in Aden, Ta'izz and al-Hudayda.

General Thoughts
Room Inspection When choosing a hotel in Yemen, it is quite acceptable to take a look at the rooms offered before making a decision. In the bigger towns, there are plenty of alternatives and it might be worth wandering around and making some price and quality comparisons. When you have asked about the availability and prices of rooms, simply say *mumkin ashuf* to the person at the desk; they will be all too glad to show you the room. Saying *mumkin ashuf al-hammam* will get you a look at the bathroom if it is in the corridor.

Bathrooms In the more basic hotels, the bathrooms are exclusively Yemeni style, with squat-type toilets. In some two-sheet hotels, there may be a choice between this 'Arabic' variation and the 'French-style' bathroom, with sit-down toilet and, perhaps, a bathtub. There may even be a bidet. The Arabic-style bathroom is recommended; French toilets require you to show quite a bit of flexibility and balance to maintain a standard of hygiene.

When you are offered facilities, *don't* accept anything without trying it. Check that turning the taps does produce a flow of water and that the drain actually takes it away. It is quite common to see a water heater hanging on the wall but, to get warm water, it must be connected. The thermometer needle on the side of the boiler may point to 60°C but the water may actually be icy. *Don't* believe them if they say it can be fixed; if it is not fixed then and there, it will not be fixed at all. A boiler with no red light on is a dead boiler.

Prices At the time of research, the Yemeni economy was suffering from the worst turbulence since the revolutions. With inflation running absolutely out of control, over 100% per year, hotel owners face tough choices in setting their prices. The riyal price level an average Yemeni can afford is ridiculously low for a foreigner changing his or her greenbacks in the parallel market, the equivalent of a few dollars only.

Consequently, some hotel owners have set a double standard, charging foreigners variably from 50% to 700% more than Yemeni nationals. You may disagree with this strategy; if so, choose another hotel. Unfortunately, the situation is changing so fast that the pricing information given in this guide simply cannot be accurate. Rules of thumb to ensure paying Yemeni prices are as follows:

- Paying in US dollars instead of riyals guarantees a price hike of at least 200%.
- In hotels publishing room prices on the wall of the reception, be sure to compare the equality of prices given in Latin and Arabic alphabet.
- If in doubt, compare the prices with those of nearby hotels and with your earlier experiences.

In the older one or two-sheet hotels, the price level for a two-sheet double at the time of research was from YR 600 to YR 1000, well on par with the general inflation for food and transport prices during the past ten years. In contrast, the lowest and highest price categories seem to have seen spectacular price hikes in recent years. Finding a bottom-end no-sheet or one-sheet hotel charging less than YR 300 for a bed was surprisingly hard, making the whole category absolutely not cost-effective. New hotels, on the other hand, were seldom doing business below YR 1000 per room or person per night, and the upper limit of US$210 for a double was set by the luxury hotels in San'a and Aden.

A sad but inevitable consequence of increased tourism is that hotels in some remote but much-visited villages are charging absolutely ridiculous sums for basic accommodation. In fact, the price level in San'a was among the lowest in the country during our visit. The other hotel in Kawkaban, for example, falls into the no-sheet category but its prices belong to the upper two-sheet category. The house is a nice, traditional stone tower with plenty of rooms from which to choose, the atmosphere is friendly and you will be served tea and genuine Yemeni food. Nevertheless, it is not clean and charging YR 400 per person is simply ridiculous; a Yemeni would never accept it. This is not the worst example; sometimes, the price is not twice or thrice but 20 times too high.

Some innkeepers seem to think that foreigners come to Yemen because they have run out of ways to spend their money. With this in mind, they try to help by charging the highest possible price when they would give similar services to a Yemeni for free. The illusion that all travellers are wealthy is maintained by the drivers who bring tour groups from San'a to distant destinations and boast to locals about the high fees.

This is not something to get angry about. However, it is important that you refuse to pay unreasonable prices for anything; otherwise, you just make it difficult for the travellers who arrive there next week. If you have any choice, it is better not to even try bargaining; simply make it clear that the price is insane and leave.

Sleeping Outdoors

Some people have slept out in a sleeping bag under the big Yemeni sky. While their letters describe overwhelmingly positive experiences, these individuals have taken quite a risk. Scorpions and snakes are common in Yemen and your warm body certainly attracts them in the cold of a mountain night.

It is advisable to bring a tent, however small, if you plan to rely on your own lodging. Erecting a tent near a village is, however, likely to attract considerable attention among the local children. In a few places, such as al-Khawkha or Bir 'Ali, tents have been used by tour operators for years and are no longer objects of curiosity.

FOOD

The Yemeni diet is simple. Sorghum and other cereals constitute the bulk of the daily diet, while fenugreek (the celebrated *hilba* soup), vegetables, rice and beans are also common. Meat, milk, eggs and fruit are traditionally the food of the upper social classes but labour emigration and the resulting influx of money to village families have brought these items to the tables of most Yemenis. Fish is a natural part of the diet in the Tihama and along the southern coast.

The most important food in Yemen is bread. The Yemenis prefer warm bread and, where wood for the ovens can be afforded, baking is done once or twice daily. There are several varieties of bread: *khubz tawwa* (ordinary bread fried at home), *ruti* (bought from stores) and *lahuh* (a festive pancake-type bread made of sorghum).

As in all Middle Eastern countries, *kebabs* are cheap and readily available but Yemen also has its own culinary treats. The national dish is a thick, fiery stew called *salta*. It contains lamb or chicken with lentils, beans, chickpeas, coriander, spices and any other kitchen leftovers and is served on a bed of rice. Yemenis also like their *shurba* – a cross between a soup and a stew. Varieties include *shurba bilsan* (a lentil soup) and *shurba wasabi* (lamb soup). They are served with a thin Arabic bread brushed with clarified butter and a paste made from fenugreek and coriander. In the heat of the afternoon, *shafu:t* (a green yoghurt soup) is refreshing.

A typical Yemeni dessert is *bint al sahn*, an egg-rich, sweet bread which you dip into a mixture of clarified butter and honey. Yemeni suqs, particularly in the Tihama, have many delicious fruits on offer. Peaches and figs have been cultivated here for thousands of years; bananas, papayas, melons and mangoes are more recent introductions.

The main meal in the day of a Yemeni is lunch. You can verify this if you're in a bus or shared taxi at noon; the bus will stop in village and discharge all the locals into the snack bars, leaving disoriented tourists to wait in their seats, wondering whether to join the Yemenis or play it safe and stay by the bus. Dinner, served after the sunset prayer, is more modest.

Restaurants

In Yemen, restaurants are places to eat; they are not places of social interaction, as you might expect if you have visited some other Arab countries. Most socialising in Yemen happens at qat parties (see Qat in Facts about the Country).

Bad news for the homesick: there are almost no Western-style restaurants in Yemen. There are no McDonald's, no bratwurst and no continental breakfasts, though there is a Pizza Hut in Aden. Only the restaurants in the most expensive hotels (and most hotels in the south) serve Western-style food and their idea of Western-style is simple: no spices.

Good news, though, for the connoisseur: there are plenty of restaurants everywhere serving tasty Yemeni food. Yemeni men never seem to eat lunch at home and restaurants are also crowded at dinnertime. Restaurants abound in big cities as well as in the smaller towns. In the biggest cities you will even find a few foreign restaurants that serve Lebanese or Ethiopian food.

Tourists may find that eating in restaurants is a somewhat risky business. Restaurants are no exception to the general standards of hygiene in Yemen. Choosing the most crowded places at least ensures that the food is not tainted but, even then, you should be careful when choosing your meal. Not only are you forced to refrain from eating fresh vegetables; you should also avoid eating anything that isn't hot when brought to your table, though bread is usually safe. *Never* drink water from the standard plastic jars on the table – always order Shamlan or Hadda or whatever brand of bottled water may be available. Canada Dry is safe, too.

This shouldn't stop you from eating out – just don't take unnecessary risks. Yemeni restaurants have many pleasant surprises but even experienced travellers can easily develop diarrhoeal diseases if they are careless with their diet.

Many restaurants hang the menu on the wall; only a few bring a conventional written menu to your table. Generally, the menu is in Arabic only, often hastily written with a ball-point pen. Sometimes, though, you may encounter minor calligraphic wonders. The selections are usually huge; even tiny restaurants often sport menus of 30 dishes. This doesn't mean they are all available – some may be reserved for holidays only. If you ask the waiter to recommend something, dishes such as liver or meat will probably be suggested.

Table manners are Arabic, that is locals do not use a knife or fork. Sometimes, they eat with a spoon. More often, however, they bring food to the mouth with the right hand and bread. In some big-city restaurants, there may be more Western-style equipment available. The left hand is considered impure and it is customary to refrain from putting it to your mouth.

DRINKS

Nonalcoholic Drinks

Tea & Coffee The everyday drink in Yemen is tea, drunk from small glasses; it's sometimes flavoured with cardamon or a leaf of mint. *Sha'i talqi:m*, or traditional tea, is delicious and warmly recommended, although *sha'i libtun*, or teabags, are rapidly gaining acceptance. Tea can be enjoyed either with milk *(sha'i ma' Hali:b)*, or without *(sha'i Hmar)*. It is always sweet to the extreme; sugar is the first thing Yemenis put in the kettle when boiling water for tea.

Qahwa, or coffee, is not as common as tea, although you can get it too from most restaurants. Coffee is made from either coffee beans themselves *(bunn)*, very strong, or from coffee-bean shells *(qirsh)*, not strong at all. Coffee, too, is always very sweet, and is often flavoured with ginger and other spices.

Water Safe drinking water is no longer a problem in Yemen. Bottled mineral water and soft drinks are now readily available even in the tiniest villages; even mere cross-roads have tin shacks selling water to passers-by.

Alcohol

The Koran explicitly rules alcohol out of the lives of Muslims and this rule is easy to follow in Yemen – you simply cannot find alcohol in supermarkets or restaurants. The sweet grapes of Rawdha are grown not for wine but for raisins. Non-alcoholic beer is available in some supermarkets but even this is rare. Liquor is totally forbidden in the northern provinces, as it has been for centuries.

The British, however, depended on beer and built a brewery in Aden during their colonial rule. Strangely, the brewery survived not only the revolution of 1967 but the entire period of Communist rule on the pretext that some inhabitants of Aden follow other religions and, of course, foreign project workers and sailors have to be served, too. It was only in the civil war of 1994 that the Seera brewery was finally bombed to pieces and the beer-serving restaurants of South Yemeni hotels were torn down.

The ban on alcohol does not mean that you can't find liquor, even in the northern part of Yemen, if you are sufficiently determined. Muslims know that alcohol is not a sin for non-Muslims and Yemenis feel they must provide full service to tourists. Some top-end tourist hotels in San'a, Aden, Ta'izz and al-Hudayda still sell alcohol in some secrecy. You don't have to be a hotel resident to buy a bottle; you can simply walk up to the restaurant and place your order. However, most often you can't enjoy it in the restaurant but have to take the bottle away. Whisky is almost always available and beer is also common but wines are rare.

The catch is that alcoholic drinks are intolerably expensive; a can of beer may cost more than YR 10,000 in San'a, for example. As it has travelled a long way through innumerable checkpoints, this is understandable. The main smuggling port before unification was al-Makha and, if you drive the Tihama road from Ta'izz to al-Hudayda, many a passer-by will try to attract your attention around Mafraq al-Makha. They are trying to sell you alcohol; presumably, in this region, you should get the best prices in Yemen.

Some Yemenis working overseas have come to know alcohol as a poor substitute for qat. They know that God is forgiving, so they maintain the habit after they return. Some have driven themselves into a situation where they eat qat in the afternoon like any good Yemeni but drink whisky later in the evening so they can sleep well. It is a sad story; often, these people have returned home to unemployment and the years abroad have alienated them from farmer's work. Instead of returning to their home villages, they settle in the big cities, live in cheap hotels and use up their savings on qat and alcohol.

THINGS TO BUY

Yemen is not exactly a popular shopping stop and some visitors find it difficult to find any typical Yemeni products that could serve as nice souvenirs. Yemen lacks many of the traditional 'Arab' items that are popular tourist buys.

Even the most 'Yemeni' objects are often not of Yemeni origin; it is quite possible that your souvenir is made in India or Lebanon. Those huge, richly ornamented water pipes, so requisite in every Yemeni funduq, usually come from India.

Jewellery

Among the places most frequented by tourists in Yemen are the silver markets in the suqs of San'a and Ta'izz, where old and old-looking silverware is sold. Often, some corals, pearls and pieces of amber, glass and ceramic are combined with the silver. You can find necklaces, earrings, noserings, bangles, chains, amulets and small containers on chains used to carry verses of Koran.

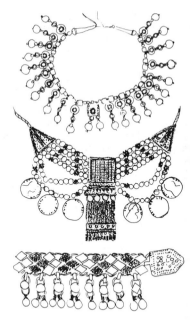

Traditional silver jewellery

To fully appreciate what you can buy, we must take a look at the interesting history of the Yemeni silverware. The Yemeni class structure has always differentiated people on the basis of occupation. For example, the *jazzars* (butchers) formed one – not particularly highly valued – social group; the *shaqi* (day labourers) made up another low-prestige social group. Although the occupations are not hereditary by definition, it is often impossible for the son of a butcher to get another job, and marriages generally are arranged exclusively within the group.

From *himyar* times, or from time immemorial, the Jews of Yemen have served as the country's silversmiths. They were always an extraordinarily important branch of craftspeople in Yemen because silver jewellery has traditionally been a convenient and popular means of paying the bride wealth without which no Yemeni marriage

The Marie Theresa Thaler
A special form of silverware in Yemen is the Maria Theresa thaler, a coin originally brought to the Middle East from Austria by Napoleon, who conquered Egypt in 1798. The Ottoman Turks brought the coin to Yemen, where it served as the currency until the end of the imamate; it has remained in limited use even since the revolution. This imported coinage was far from ideal as a form of currency; its supply depended on the condition of trade routes from Austria and its value fluctuated with the international value of silver. You can buy this genuine Yemeni item for a few tens of riyals. Don't be fooled by the date on the coin, though; all Maria Theresa thalers bear the date 1780 even though they were minted in later centuries – actually, they only went out of production in 1960. ∎

could be arranged. However, the silversmiths were never of high social status, since the Jews were despised and oppressed.

When the Jews emigrated from Yemen in 1949 and 1950 to the newly founded state of Israel, the Yemeni imams realised that their country was going to lose an important pool of skilled workers. They therefore declared that no Jewish silversmith could leave the country before teaching their skills to a Yemeni. However, due to the short time available, the Yemeni silversmiths were mere apprentices when the masters left to fulfil Isaiah's prediction: 'They shall mount up with wings, as eagles.' The Yemeni Jews were carried to Israel from Aden in a major airlift operation code-named 'Magic Carpet'.

The quality of the workmanship was never quite regained, as anyone who visits the suqs of Yemen's larger cities can verify. The silversmiths' shops abound in old and old-looking silverware but, if you take a closer look at the objects for sale, you may find defects: a missing piece here and a broken joint there, often some missing chains replaced by threads of cloth or other substitutes. The shopkeeper may volunteer to fix these if you point them out, immediately finding spare parts below the counter. The result is a 'perfect' piece that will not fall apart when you wear it but you are left wondering how original it is.

Indeed, it is a fact that most Yemeni silverware isn't very old. When a Bedouin woman dies, all her silverware is melted down to make new jewellery. On the other hand, the townspeople and farmer families keep their precious things for several gener-

ations; the women own their jewellery and it functions as their insurance in case of divorce or similar catastrophe. It is passed along in the family in the form of gifts, bride wealth and inheritance, always at the woman's discretion.

The third main group of jewellery consumers is the religious elite. They demonstrate their status with fashionable clothing, elaborately embroidered belts for their silver *dhumas* (daggers), and other ceremonial weapons.

Much of the silverware is offered only to tourists and is made to look old by treating it with chemicals. The 'silver' is never very pure and many pieces have hardly any silver content at all. Many wares made of tin plate are not intended to be sold as silver but, since they are sold in silversmiths' shops, tourists often wish to believe more than they are told. But why worry? If you like it, buy it. Do some bargaining – the Yemenis won't lower the price much, if at all, but there are plenty of shops to choose from.

Nowadays, gold jewellery is very popular among the Yemenis and goldsmiths abound. However, the objects do not look very 'Yemeni'. Some people say that gold can be bought at rather low prices in Yemen when compared to Western countries, so there is a chance for profit. This is because gold is sold by the gram, with no value added for the workmanship, and no import taxes are imposed. If you want to explore this, you should know your prices and be able to judge the purity of the product. Gold is probably cheaper in al-Hudayda or Ta'izz than in San'a.

Jambiyas

An object that is indisputably typical of countries in Southern Arabia is the curved dagger worn by men on a special belt at their waist. The make and look of the dagger differs greatly according to the region and the tribe, as well as the social status of the owner. The tradition was banned in the south during the period of Communist rule but has been continued in the northern provinces without a break.

In Yemen, the sharply curved tribesman's dagger – called a *jambiya* – is kept at the front of the body with the tip of the sheath pointing to the right. The elite, such as a *qadhi* or a *sayyid*, wear their daggers on the right side of the body. These daggers are called dhumas and their design is more slenderly curved. Dhumas and their belts are usually richly ornamented with silver and gold, while jambiyas often expose the base materials, cloth and leather, beneath sparse cloth ornaments.

Dhumas and jambiyas serve mainly ceremonial purposes and are not meant for actual use (although Yemeni men are all too eager to demonstrate their ability to fight). The design of the blades ensures that you can't do anything with them. They are objects of pride and are often inherited. The prices of these pieces are absolutely insane; while you may obtain a simple jambiya for a couple of hundred riyals, more ornate dhumas with silver and gold decorations can cost thousands of riyals. An old one once owned by a much-respected qadhi may cost hundreds of thousands of riyals.

The most highly valued daggers have handles made from African rhinoceros horn. In fact, Yemen is the chief consumer of this rare material, jeopardising the survival of the entire species.

Guns

The second Ottoman occupation of the northern part of Yemen relied heavily on the use of modern firearms imported from Western Europe. Germany, Italy and France supported Turkey's colonisation of the Arabian Peninsula in order to weaken the British influence in the Middle East. Accordingly, plenty of firearms flowed into Yemen from these countries and many ended up in the hands of the rebelling Yemenis.

Due to this history, there are lots of old guns in Yemen, sold today in the silver suq of San'a. You can find French-made Gras Cavalry carbines, Italian Vetterli-Vitali rifles and German Mauser rifles, all from the 1870s or later decades. Prices are reasonable compared to those current in middle Europe. A 100-year-old rifle in working condition may be sold for a couple of hundred riyals. Old pistols and swords may also be offered for sale.

Buying these weapons is not recommended, and doing so may create difficulties with the customs office in your home country, or Yemen, or other countries you may pass through with this equipment. Also remember that, although the shopkeepers will happily sell you objects they claim to be antique, it is against Yemeni law to export objects over 40 years old without specific permission.

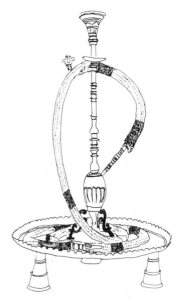

Mada'a – water pipe made in India

Water Pipes

Other impractical souvenirs include the huge water pipes (called *mada'a*) you see men smoking in every funduq of the country. The equipment includes a brass tripod stand onto which the water bowl is placed and which also serves as a support for the hose (up to two metres long) when it is not being used. On top of the vertical tube is the funnel-shaped tobacco and coal-holder, which is made of pottery.

A typical mada'a is about one metre high with a tripod stand some three-quarters of a metre in diameter. Prices vary according to the materials and workmanship.

Music Cassettes

Local music is one of the best souvenirs you can find. In Yemen, the locals listen to Arabic and Yemeni styles rather than to Western-style disco or rock music. Musical traditions differ greatly in various parts of the country, with Tihami, San'ani and Hadhrami styles clearly distinguishable from each other.

As in most Arabic countries, records do not exist in Yemen and most music is sold in cassette form. This is because electronic sound reproduction arrived late in these countries, cassettes are less prone to damage caused by dust and sand, and because the vast majority of all recordings sold in the Arab world are bootleg copies. If you listen to a recording in a suq cassette stand and decide to buy it, the owner of the shop will probably record a new copy for you then and there (so don't think you can purchase your audio souvenir on your last hurried morning before leaving the country).

One benefit of this is that recordings are fairly inexpensive in Yemen; the price of a cassette should not exceed YR 70. However, the quality of sound ranges from barely satisfying to incredibly bad. My advice is to purchase more cassettes than you actually want, and from several vendors. The cost will be negligible when compared to the expense of getting to the country.

Everyday Items

Commonplace consumer goods produced locally, though not exactly spectacular, often make nice, useful souvenirs. In many suqs, you can find beautiful and very colourful fabrics, baskets and clay pots. A variety of spices is readily available, as is bunn and qirsh. Vacuum-packed Mocha coffee is sold in supermarkets under the brand name of 'Yemen Cafe'.

Another sensory indulgence, frankincense, is still available in the Yemen. In San'a, you can see Black African ladies selling *luba:n*, or several varieties of incense for a few tens of riyals per small lump. Smell it or chew it; when burned, it releases its fragrance very efficiently – a cool alternative to the Indian 'dhoops' so loved by the hippies of the 1960s.

Things You Won't Buy

Many things that you would expect to be sold in an Arab country are not to be found in the Yemen. For example, there are no Oriental-looking Yemeni carpets. Almost all rugs with some colour are imported and many can only be described as tasteless. A carpet featuring puppies dressed as humans in a London-style pub looks very strange as a piece of interior decoration in a Yemeni house!

You probably won't buy Yemeni clothes, either – at least if you are male. Typical male attire is a *futa*, or skirt, ending a little below the knees and worn with a shirt and jacket that look as though they were imported from the Western world (but really aren't). This is a nice combination but not one that is likely to become fashionable elsewhere.

For women, a much better variety is available, from the urban black veils and dresses in the suqs of San'a and Ta'izz to the very colourful garments in local markets. Expect to draw loud and excited attention if you try those pieces on and, once you do so, don't expect to be able to bargain much – by your actions, you have already accepted the price.

Getting There & Away

AIR
To/From Europe
Direct flights from Europe to San'a are offered by Yemenia from Amsterdam, Frankfurt, Larnaca, London, Moscow, Paris and Rome; there are one to three flights a week. ALYEMEN flies directly from London to Aden. Air France flies weekly

---

Air Travel Glossary
Apex Apex, or 'advance purchase excursion' is a discounted ticket which must be paid for in advance. There are penalties if you wish to change it.

Baggage Allowance This will be written on your ticket: usually one 20 kg item to go in the hold, plus one item of hand luggage.
Bucket Shop An unbonded travel agency specialising in discounted airline tickets.
Bumped Just because you have a confirmed seat doesn't mean you're going to get on the plane – see Overbooking.

Cancellation Penalties If you have to cancel or change an Apex ticket there are often heavy penalties involved, insurance can sometimes be taken out against these penalties. Some airlines impose penalties on regular tickets as well, particularly against 'no show' passengers (see No-Shows).
Check In Airlines ask you to check-in a certain time ahead of the flight departure (usually 1½ hours on international flights). If you fail to check in on time and the flight is overbooked the airline can cancel your booking and give your seat to somebody else.
Confirmation Having a ticket written out with the flight and date you want doesn't mean you have a seat until the agent has checked with the airline that your status is 'OK' or confirmed. Meanwhile you could just be 'on request'.

Discounted Tickets There are two types of discounted fares – officially discounted (see Promotional Fares) and unofficially discounted. The lowest prices often impose drawbacks like flying with unpopular airlines, inconvenient schedules, or unpleasant routes and connections. A discounted ticket can save you other things than money – you may be able to pay Apex prices without the associated Apex advance booking and other requirements. Discounted tickets only exist where there is fierce competition.

Full Fares Airlines traditionally offer first class (coded F), business class (coded J) and economy class (coded Y) tickets. These days there are so many promotional and discounted fares available from the regular economy class that few passengers pay full economy fare.

Lost Tickets If you lose your airline ticket an airline will usually treat it like a travellers' cheque and, after inquiries, issue you with another one. Legally, however, an airline is entitled to treat it like cash and if you lose it then it's gone forever. Take good care of your tickets.

No Shows No shows are passengers who fail to show up for their flight, sometimes due to unexpected delays or disasters, sometimes due to simply forgetting, sometimes because they made more than one booking and didn't bother to cancel the one they didn't want. Full fare passengers who fail to turn up are sometimes entitled to travel on a later flight. The rest of us are penalised (see Cancellation Penalties).

On Request An unconfirmed booking for a flight, see Confirmation.

---

from Paris, KLM has twice-weekly flights from Amsterdam, and Lufthansa has twice-weekly flights from Frankfurt. Alitalia, Austrian Airlines, British Airways, Sabena and Swiss Air also serve Yemen. Economy-class return fares to San'a start from US$1250.

Many of the Arab countries' national carriers also offer flights from Europe to San'a via their respective capitals. Saudia used to be the most convenient but has currently suspended flights to Yemen. The fares of EgyptAir are among the most economical.

Surprisingly, one of the cheapest ways to fly to Yemen from most Western European

Open Jaws A return ticket where you fly out to one place but return from another. If available this can save you backtracking to your arrival point.

Overbooking Airlines hate to fly with empty seats and since every flight has some passengers who fail to show up (see No Shows) airlines often book more passengers than they have seats. Usually the excess passengers balance those who fail to show up but occasionally somebody gets bumped. If this happens guess who it is most likely to be? The passengers who check-in late.

Promotional Fares Officially discounted fares like Apex fares which are available from travel agents or direct from the airline.

Reconfirmation At least 72 hours prior to departure time of an onward or return flight you must contact the airline and 'reconfirm' that you intend to be on the flight. If you don't do this the airline can delete your name from the passenger list and you could lose your seat. You don't have to reconfirm the first flight on your itinerary or if your stopover is less than 72 hours. It doesn't hurt to reconfirm more than once.

Restrictions Discounted tickets often have various restrictions on them – advance purchase is the most usual one (see Apex). Others are restrictions on the minimum and maximum period you must be away, such as a minimum of 14 days or a maximum of one year. See Cancellation Penalties.

Standby A discounted ticket where you only fly if there is a seat free at the last moment. Standby fares are usually only available on domestic routes.

Tickets Out An entry requirement for many countries is that you have an onward or return ticket, in other words, a ticket out of the country. If you're not sure what you intend to do next, the easiest solution is to buy the cheapest onward ticket to a neighbouring country or a ticket from a reliable airline which can later be refunded if you do not use it.

Transferred Tickets Airline tickets cannot be transferred from one person to another. Travellers sometimes try to sell the return half of their ticket, but officials can ask you to prove that you are the person named on the ticket. This is unlikely to happen on domestic flights, on an international flight tickets may be compared with passports.

Travel Agencies Travel agencies vary widely and you should ensure you use one that suits your needs. Some simply handle tours while full-service agencies handle everything from tours and tickets to car rental and hotel bookings. A good one will do all these things and can save you a lot of money but if all you want is a ticket at the lowest possible price, then you really need an agency specialising in discounted tickets. A discounted ticket agency, however, may not be useful for other things, like hotel bookings.

Travel Periods Some officially discounted fares, Apex fares in particular, vary with the time of year. There is often a low (off-peak) season and a high (peak) season. Sometimes there's an intermediate or shoulder season as well. At peak times, when everyone wants to fly, not only will the officially discounted fares be higher but so will unofficially discounted fares or there may simply be no discounted tickets available. Usually the fare depends on your outward flight – if you depart in the high season and return in the low season, you pay the high-season fare. ■

countries has been with Russian Airlines. After the demise of the USSR, the Soviet company Aeroflot was divided and there now exists several national airlines in various Commonwealth of Independent States (CIS) countries. The international flights to and from Moscow are handled by Russian Airlines, which is still using the Aeroflot name. Aeroflot has one weekly flight to San'a. The fare from Moscow to San'a is only US$750 for a 10 to 35-day excursion ticket. Connecting flights to/from European centres are free, so the trip is cheap even from Paris.

Don't go to the Aeroflot office yourself; you will be charged a fare that is the same as your own national carrier would charge in business class (should it fly the route). Instead, find a travel agency specialising in cheap flights to Asia and/or Africa; they will probably offer Aeroflot flights. Be prepared to reserve your ticket several months before your trip because the flights are usually fully booked well in advance.

If you use this service, you will have to stop in Moscow and, since the timetables are not necessarily synchronised with connecting flights between your country and Yemen, you may have to stay overnight (or even two or three nights) in Moscow. If you have plenty of time in Moscow, you might also want to visit the city. I heartily recommend this but, as you'll need to reserve one or two hours for customs and another two hours for the bus/metro ride to the centre of Moscow, the excursion will take at least one whole day. You have to apply for a transit visa before you start off. This usually takes at least a week to be issued; you need a photo and US$10 to US$20. The dates and hours of your visit will be written onto the visa, so you have to decide your date of return beforehand.

To/From Africa

From East Africa, it is easy and relatively cheap to reach Yemen by air. Yemen's national carrier, Yemen Airways, flies directly to Khartoum, Addis Ababa, Asmara

and Djibouti from San'a and Aden. Air Tanzania now flies weekly from Dar es Salaam via Zanzibar to Aden. Prices do vary: at the time of research a one-way economy-class flight from San'a to Djibouti was US$110; to Asmara the cost was US$150.

Ethiopian and Sudanese airlines also serve the country.

To/From the Middle East

You should have no difficulties reaching Yemen from Middle Eastern countries. Egypt Air, Gulf Air, Iraqi Airlines, Kuwait Airlines, Royal Jordanian and Syrian Airways all serve the country, and Yemen Airways offers direct flights to many Arab capitals. The most notable omission in the list is Saudia.

To/From Asia

Yemen Airways flies directly to Karachi and Bombay. You can look for cheaper fares from various other airlines flying either directly from India or Pakistan or via more circuitous routes. Aeroflot, for example, flies from Singapore or India to Moscow and then connects to San'a. A flight to Amman in Jordan and a connection from there to Yemen is another possibility.

Pakistan International Airlines has a weekly flight from Karachi to San'a, continuing to Nairobi, and back. Air India and Cathay Pakistan also serve Yemen.

To/From Australia

There are no direct connections between Australia and Yemen and, although many flights between Australia and Europe operate via the Gulf States in the Middle East, that route is likely to be expensive. Royal Jordanian has flights between Amman and Singapore and has plans to extend the service to Sydney.

Several carriers now have fares from Australia to the Middle East – Gulf Air offers services to Abu Dhabi, Al-Ain, Dubai, Fujairah, Ras al-Khaimah and Sharjah from A$1775, and to Jeddah, Muscat, Bahrain, Dhahran, Doha, Kuwait and Riyadh from

A$1829. Vietnam Airlines fly weekly from Melbourne and Sydney to Saigon (stopover allowed), then to Dubai; fares start at A$850 one-way and A$1500 return.

Plenty of other carriers fly to the region from Australia, including Malaysian, Cathay Pacific, South African, Singapore and Thai. However, often the cheapest way is to fly with Qantas or British Airways to Asia, then with Pakistan International (via Karachi); fares start from about A$1000 one-way and A$1500 return.

To/From the USA

There are no direct flights from the USA to Yemen; it is probably best to fly to your destination via Europe. Combination flights are offered by major airlines.

LAND
To/From Europe

There are no bus lines crossing Yemeni borders, so the next alternative to flying is to drive your own car. This is interesting but impractical, and could be very costly.

Occasionally, Yemen's relationship with its neighbours makes the option impossible. The border between Oman and Yemen was not opened until late 1992. The only route – the coastal road through Salalah – is very long and tiring, and very few travellers have taken this option so far. From Saudi Arabia, only the Tihama road from Jizan to Bajil is open, but the real problem is getting to Saudi Arabia in the first place.

You will need a transit visa to Saudi Arabia (no tourist visas are available), which you can obtain only if you have an entry visa to Yemen.

The transit visa is valid for three days only, so you *must* get through this vast country within that time. This shouldn't be a problem – Saudi Arabian highways are asphalted and in good condition and your car is obviously in excellent shape or you wouldn't even think about driving in Yemen! In practice, you can only get Toyotas repaired in Yemen, since other makes of car are rare here. Diesel engines are not recommended because it is difficult to find fuel for them in either Saudi Arabia or Yemen – they were even forbidden a few years ago, as were Fords. Note also that unleaded gas is not available in Yemen. For the trip to and from Yemen, an ordinary car will do but if you plan to visit smaller villages in Yemen, you will definitely need a 4WD vehicle.

No matter what your vehicle, you must get a *carnet de passage en douane*. You'll also need hefty insurance: should you be involved in an accident in which a Saudi or Yemeni citizen dies, you will be held liable for considerable compensation and may end up having to pay millions of riyals to the victim's family. As you might have major problems trying to get your insurance work done in Yemen, check the procedures with your insurance company beforehand in case you have to leave your vehicle in Yemen.

The Tihama road is asphalted and presents no problems. Yemeni customs and immigration formalities are handled in Haradh. The paperwork is extremely time-consuming – expect to spend anything from a few hours to a full day at the border. In San'a, you'll have to obtain a separate permit to return to Haradh.

SEA

There are ship connections between Africa and Yemen. However, while Aden is the most widely served port in the country, passenger services are currently next to non-existent, and your options are limited to cargo ships. There are regular cargo ships to al-Hudayda from Port Sudan in the Sudan and from Massawa in Eritrea. From Assab in southern Eritrea there are occasional connections on freighters, too, to al-Makha and al-Hudayda.

From Djibouti to al-Makha a most erratic smuggling trade flourishes. Schedules, prices and ticket conditions are available locally.

TOURS

Several tour agents in Central Europe, especially in Germany, organise tours to Yemen.

A typical package tour takes two weeks, hurries through half or two-thirds of the towns and villages described in this book and costs anything from US$2000 upwards. Some examples are:

New Adventure in Steinbackweg 13, D-69118 Heidelberg, Germany (fax 49 6221 80931), offers 15-day tours in all parts of Yemen for DM 3000 to DM 3500. They also offer trekking and camel-riding trips.

Karawane Tours in Weisshausstr. 25, D-50939 Köln, Germany (fax 49 221 4200364) have a similar selection of tours for small groups. They offer to send you their catalogue in return mail.

SSR-Reisen from Zürich, Switzerland (☎ (1) 2423000), offers 16 days in the northern part of the country for SwF 3990 and 14 days in the south for SwF 4300. A combination four-week tour is available for SwF 5950.

LEAVING YEMEN

The departure procedure is straightforward: customs, ticket check and passport control. You are required to arrive at the airport two hours before the scheduled flight time.

The airport tax is US$10 for foreign destinations and is payable in Yemeni currency at the check-in counter.

Getting Around

AIR

For the average independent traveller, flight services inside Yemen are only to be considered if you are in a hurry and plan to combine Hadhramawt with a visit to the highlands. Otherwise, ground transport is cheap, frequent, reasonably fast and offers a chance to see the unforgettably varied Yemeni landscapes.

The two independent Yemens each had a national carrier – Yemenia in the YAR and al-Yemda in the PDRY. Both companies operated domestically as well as abroad. After unification, these companies announced that they would unite to form a company called Yemen Airways. However, as the country headed towards the civil war of 1994, this did not happen, and today Yemen has two airlines hovering on the brink of bankruptcy. To add to the confusion, each one is using two names: Yemenia called itself Yemen Airways for a while but seems now to be sticking to the old name Yemenia, while al-Yemda is burying the past and uses the name ALYEMEN Airlines instead.

The airlines are making losses because they charge Yemenis in YR while their costs are in US$. (Airlines use the official exchange rate of YR 50 for US$1). Foreigners must pay in US dollars but Yemenis get their tickets currently at about one-third of the real price.

Domestic economy-class tickets used to cost about three times as much as ground transport fares but the latter have come down in price, not keeping up with the exchange rates. First-class flights are available only from San'a to Ta'izz and Aden, obviously for connecting international flights. Add to this the exorbitant taxi fares to and from the airports and you will easily end up spending another 50%.

There are good links between large cities, with several flights a day (usually morning and afternoon, plus occasional midday departures) between San'a, Aden, Ta'izz and al-Hudayda, as well as daily return flights to Say'un and al-Mukalla. Airlines also serve many smaller towns.

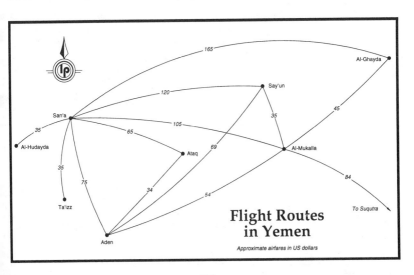

Flight Routes in Yemen

Approximate airfares in US dollars

The San'a International Airport was built by West Germany in 1973 and supplied with planes from Saudi Arabia. In 1977, Saudi Arabia helped to found Yemenia and owns 49% of the company – an uneasy arrangement given the recent lows of Saudi-Yemeni relations. The Aden International Airport was expanded in the late 1980s with Soviet aid, and sports a huge, modern terminal building. However, in 1990, the company still operated a fleet of ancient de Havilland DHC-7 propeller-powered aircraft, alongside some more up-to-date Boeing 707s and 737s.

You should have no difficulty getting tickets. There are plenty of travel agencies and airline offices in San'a, Ta'izz and al-Hudayda (fewer in Aden) and most of them sell Yemenia and/or ALYEMEN tickets. English is widely spoken at these places.

At most travel agencies, you will probably be given a schedule. Don't be astonished to see some strange destinations: Sa'da, Ma'rib, al-Buq, al-Jawf. It doesn't necessarily mean that you can fly to these places. The Ma'rib airport is, for the time being, used for military and industrial purposes and no passenger flights were in operation when we asked ('There is a problem with the airport in Ma'rib – why don't you use a taxi?'). Al-Buq (near al-Baydha) and al-Jawf (north of Ma'rib) are also not for civilian use – at least, not for the use of foreign civilians.

BUS

There are two main forms of land transport in Yemen: bus and service taxi. Of these, taxis are the more original and you should at least try them – they have a real Arabic feel. Buses work the same as buses do everywhere in the world, and there are no cultural barriers to cross in using them.

Buses were introduced to Yemen in the mid-1980s. The bus companies – the General Transport Corporation of the North and Yemen Land Transport Company of the South – enjoyed a period of rapid expansion, but recently the trend has reversed. The bus services seemed to be deteriorating when we last visited, with fewer connections and more worn-out equipment. Still, buses are the cheapest way to get around in Yemen, and the service is punctual and reliable.

Unfortunately the bus windows are made of grey or brown glass to reduce the heat of the sun, and often they cannot be opened. This means that you can't take photos en route. Furthermore, the buses are filled with unbearably heavy tobacco smoke.

The buses go wherever there are asphalted roads. New bus routes were opened yearly during the 1980s keeping pace with road construction, and the 1990 unification opened four new connections across the former border. However, the civil war of 1994 heavily affected the latter connections and brought the bus services in the southern part of the country to a virtual standstill. The routes below should be used only as a guide. Buses are best suited to long-haul travel – from San'a to Ta'izz or from Aden to al-Mukalla for instance. You can easily use them to get from a terminal city to a smaller town en route (from Ta'izz to Ibb, for example) but you may find that a trip from, say, Yarim to Dhamar is best done by taxi.

Buying a Ticket

Usually, you cannot buy tickets on the buses – you have to buy them from ticket offices beforehand. There are ticket offices at every bus terminal and, occasionally, at stops along the way. Timetables exist only for departures from terminals, not for those from intermediate stops. Ticket offices are usually open about 30 minutes to an hour before buses depart and close immediately after the bus leaves. At an intermediate stop, the ticket office may only be open for the time the bus stops there. If there is room in the bus, you may succeed in halting it almost anywhere by the roadside, though you can't count on this.

You will find it hard to locate a ticket office much in advance of your planned departure. You are not expected to do such advance planning in Yemen; you should act in a more Yemeni, spontaneous manner. We had the following conversation with a local and it illustrates a profound difference

Bus Timetable

From	To	Departures am	pm	Duration (hours)	Price (YR)	Stops
Aden	Al-Mukalla	6.00		12	800	Lawdar, Habban, 'Azan, Bir'Ali
Aden	Ataq	6.30		6	600	Lawdar
Aden	'Azan	6.30		6	600	Lawdar, Habban
Aden	Ta'izz	7.00		3	400	Lahej, Ar-Rahida
Al-Hudayda	Harad	6.00		3	240	Al-Qanawis, Suq al-Khamis, Suq 'Abs
Al-Hudayda	Ta'izz	7.00 8.00	2.00	4	360	Bayt al-Faqih, Zabid, Hays, Al-Juma'a, Mafraq al-Makha
Al-Mukalla	Say'un	6.00		5	600	Shibam, Al-Qatn
San'a	Al-Hudayda	5.30 6.30 7.30 10.00	1.30 2.00	4½-5	400	*either* Mafha, Manakha, Al-Qadm, Bajil *or* Ma'bar, Madinat ash-Sharq, Bajil
San'a	Al-Mahwit	10.00	2.00	3	260	Shibam, At-Tawila
San'a	Ma'rib	*7.00	2.00	3	300	none
San'a	Rada	10.00	1.30	3	240	Ma'bar, Dhamar
San'a	Sa'da	7.00	2.00	5	360	Amran, Khamir, Al-Harf
San'a	Ta'izz	5.30 6.30 7.30 10.00	1.30 2.00	4½-5	360	Ma'bar, Dhamar, Kitab, Ad-Dalil, Ibb

The buses mostly follow the same timetable for travel in the opposite direction (* indicates a different departure time).

between Yemeni and European ways of thinking:

Where can we find the bus ticket office here?
  There is none here.
But can we get a bus here?
  No, the bus has gone already.
But can we get a bus tomorrow morning?
  Yes, of course.
So can we buy the ticket in the bus?
  No, you must buy them in the ticket office.
You said there is no ticket office here?
  Tomorrow there will be.
Where, then?
  Just here.

You need to arrive well before the bus is due to leave. On crowded lines like those in San'a, Aden, al-Hudayda and Ta'izz, this may mean getting there a full hour before the scheduled departure time, especially on weekends. There may be one or more buses going to your destination but all tickets may already be sold 30 minutes before the bus leaves.

The main San'a bus station, Bab al-Yaman, may be confusing and you might have some problems finding the right bus. The destinations are marked on most buses but, if your knowledge of Arabic is limited to what you've read in this book, you probably won't be able to recognise the one you want. Moreover, there may be more than one bus going to a particular city and, if you take the wrong one, you will be politely asked to move over just before the bus leaves and you could end up sitting in a much worse seat than you had intended. Although the seats are not reserved, the tickets are sold for specific buses anyway. The bus number is marked on the front bumper, again in Arabic only. You should be able to compare this with the number on your ticket.

City Bus

In cities and major towns, you can find minibuses (called *dhabar)* and larger buses to serve very local transport needs. The fares are a few riyals per person. The cheapest buses link San'a's major gates and squares; these city buses wait until they are full, with the driver shouting the name of the destination to everyone who passes by. Once full, they drive fast and charge everybody YR 10.

The cities of the north also have plenty of black-striped minibuses that drive along pre-defined routes and pick up passengers from the streets. The drivers are very alert; if you simply stand by the roadside waiting for the chance to cross the street, they will swarm around you offering their services. Prices are generally YR 10 to YR 20 per person. This is an ideal form of public city transport – cheap, reliable and fast. You'll find that the only problem is not knowing the routes, which makes it difficult to find the right bus. Generally, any minibus will become a private taxi if you mention a destination that is not on the route, so remember to check the price before getting in.

TAXI

There are two types of taxi in Yemen: *sarwis*, or service (shared) taxis, and *inqiz,* or private taxis.

Service Taxi

Service taxis are well known in many Arabic countries. In Yemen, they run on predetermined routes, say, from San'a to Shibam or from Shibam to at-Tawila. All bus routes are also served by service taxis and the taxis travel on nonasphalted roads as well. Service taxis have no timetables – they wait until they are full and then leave. This may take anything from a few minutes to a few hours. Usually, service taxis have seats for four or

six people but they are not considered full until they have six or 10 passengers, respectively. More people are sometimes crammed in if the passengers know each other. Once, I saw a man, his two wives and three children in the front seat in addition to the driver – nobody complained.

Taxis are invariably so old that you can't help wondering what keeps them going. Although their maintenance may seem to have been totally neglected, the driver makes the interior of the taxi very cosy: dashboards are decorated with fancy Arabic-style textiles and the mascots that hang from the rear-view mirror include classic calligraphy, such as 'Allah' or 'Muhammad', etched in brass.

The atmosphere in a service taxi is very warm and positive. Passengers often form a spontaneous community, enjoying lunch and prayers together during stops (which are inevitable if the trip takes more than a couple of hours). It pays to make an effort to communicate with the other passengers. If you do, you will be more easily accepted and will be granted privileges otherwise not available, such as views of remarkable mosques and villages by the road or extra photo stops. Yemenis like talkative people, especially in the afternoon.

Service taxis use different stations to the buses. Often, a service-taxi station is a little way from the centre of town along the road the taxis take so, depending on traffic routes, there are usually a few stations in each town.

Taxis are easy to recognise in Yemen: they are painted white with broad horizontal stripes and a big circle on the driver's door. Often the taxi's route is painted in Arabic inside the circle. Ordinary city taxis and short-haul service taxis have black stripes, while the stripes on long-haul service taxis are coloured according to the route served.

route	stripe colour
San'a to Al-Hudayda	blue
San'a to Sa'da	brown
San'a to Ma'rib	yellow
San'a to Ta'izz and Aden	green
Ta'izz to Al-Hudayda	red
Al-Hudayda to Al-Harad	red

Fares There are a couple of important things to remember about taxi fares. First, you always pay for a seat in the taxi – that is, the fares are per person. Second, the price must always be negotiated before you sit down. If you are part of a couple or group and you ask for the fare to a particular destination, the driver will tell you one price; multiply it by the number of persons in your group to get the total fare.

Generally, service taxi fares are fixed and non-negotiable. Nevertheless, a Westerner is likely to be charged something extra by way of a 'foreigners' tax', so be wary. If there are local passengers around, you will almost certainly get the right price the first time. If you are alone, you will probably be quoted a price that's too high. It might be a good idea to loiter around for a while, ask the fare from different individuals (such as drivers to other destinations) and listen keenly when locals ask the same question.

If you agree on an amount and get into the car, no more bargaining can be done; you have to pay the agreed fare. An agreement must always be honoured in Yemen. If you accept a price and sit in the car alone, and the taxi then starts off immediately without waiting for other passengers, you are paying for all the empty seats as well (about five to 10 times the cost of a single seat). The driver is not cheating you; rather, you are being given especially good service because you seem able to afford it.

If you want to complain, you should have some idea about the prices beforehand. Distances don't tell the whole truth because road conditions vary widely in Yemen. To estimate the cost yourself, ask the driver how long it will take to reach your destination. They will probably not want to give you an overestimate, since you might then abandon the trip altogether, but too short a time would show that the price is too high. You are therefore likely to get a reasonable answer.

A rule of thumb is that a car should cost something in excess of YR 1200 to YR 1400 per hour. A journey from San'a to al-Hudayda (240 km on a winding but good asphalted road) takes about five hours, so a fare of YR 800 per person is typical for an eight to 10 passenger taxi. Here, the price is somewhat high because it is a bus route; Yemenis consider a service taxi more comfortable than a bus, so you can expect the taxi fare to be 15% to 50% higher than the corresponding bus fare. On some less-traversed routes, a regular taxi service may not exist but locals may offer a 4WD Toyota and a driver at a price that works out at around YR 2000 to YR 3000 per hour.

Sometimes, after waiting at the station for a couple of hours, it is agreed that there just won't be enough passengers for the taxi to be considered full. In such cases, an extra charge is calculated and added to each passenger's fare.

Even when you are not going to ride the whole distance, you will often be asked to pay the full fare; this depends on how confident the driver is of picking up new passengers at the place where you'll be getting out.

Use your judgement in deciding whether to accept these kinds of conditions; often, you'll be able to find alternatives. If you get into a taxi at a halfway point, you should always be entitled to a rebate.

Private Taxi

The distinction between public buses and private taxis is very vague in Yemen. Some small taxis drive (mostly along certain cheap routes) seeking extra passengers on every street corner ('public'), while others will drive you anywhere, treating you as the owner of the car ('private'). Each charges appropriately. Even a huge bus will sometimes turn into a private taxi when a tourist is obviously at a loss and keeps asking how to get to a certain place. You should be able to get almost anywhere within the city boundaries for well below YR 300 in San'a and less than YR 200 in Ta'izz or al-Hudayda, though some patience may be required to find the right taxi.

Sometimes, private taxis can be a nuisance because drivers love to offer you better service than you actually need. Suppose you want to get to a service-taxi station to leave a city for some distant destination but you don't know where the station is. From any point in any city, the appropriate fare should be no more than YR 200. However, the driver may insist on driving you right to your final destination for around YR 10,000. Don't try to argue; just take another taxi – there are always plenty of them around.

CAR RENTAL
Car With Driver

Car rental in the Western sense of is new and rare in Yemen. Cars are usually hired complete with driver and are available either on the streets or from local travel agencies. A 4WD vehicle with a driver will cost you at least YR 10,000 a day and, if you travel long distances (for example, to Ma'rib and back within a single day), expect the cost to be well over YR 18,000.

If you are alone or with a small group, these prices are vastly above those you would be charged for using service taxis or buses. However, if you are with five or more people, it might be a good idea to check some of the travel agencies. An additional benefit is that the driver will act as a guide; some travel agencies have English, German or French-speaking drivers. This can also be a nuisance, though, since the driver may insist on taking an active part in your decision-making on where to go next, how long to

stay in each place, where and what to eat, where to stay overnight and so on. You will probably pay the driver's expenses, too, since it is courteous to express your gratitude for good service, so include that in your estimate of the costs.

The many travel and tour agencies in San'a include:

ABM Tours
    PO Box 10420, San'a (☎ 270856)
Bazara Travel & Tourism
    Zubayri St (near Hadda St), San'a (☎ 285925)
Universal Travel Company
    Bawniya St, PO Box 10473 San'a (☎ 272861)
Yemen Arab Tourism Agency
    PO Box 1153, San'a (☎ 224236)

There are plenty of other tour agencies around Ali Abdul Mogni St and az-Zubayri St. Phone them first to confirm current street addresses.

Car Without Driver

Renting cars without drivers is a concept that didn't reach Yemen until the mid-1980s but there are already some offices on az-Zubayri St and Hadda St in San'a. This is a cheaper way to rent; YR 6000 to YR 8000 a day. The smallest 4WD vehicles cost about YR 7000. To this, you must add the cost of fuel (YR 12 per litre).

Gasoline is *bitru:l* in Arabic. The petrol gauges come from Saudi Arabia, so don't be

---

The Hazards of Driving in Yemen

Don't think about renting a 4WD vehicle unless you know what you're doing. You need to be very experienced in handling such a vehicle because the mountain tracks are difficult to traverse. A Yemeni driver seems to be able to get a car across anything a goat can climb but they have been doing so for years. Driving for hours and hours along such routes is exhausting. There are no reliable maps because tracks in the lowlands often change seasonally. Never rely on meeting friendly souls at every crossroad to show you the right track – Yemen is a most unevenly populated country and, in some areas, you can drive for hours without seeing another human being.

When driving along Yemeni roads, you are subject to Islamic and tribal law. This means, among other things, heavy financial penalties if you happen to harm somebody through careless driving. In the case of a fatal accident, the foreigner is always assumed to be guilty of carelessness. You may have to pay millions of riyals if you cause the death of a man, half the amount if you kill a woman and less again for children. During Ramadan and the pilgrimage season, the penalties are doubled.

Remember – you can't expect local shepherds to fix the car if something goes wrong with it. ■

surprised to see riyals and halalas on the display. These are Saudi riyals; one Saudi riyal is 1000 halalas. In any case, the gauges are calibrated to show the cost in Yemeni riyals.

WALKING & HITCHING

Many people come to Yemen with the principal aim of wandering through the mountains from village to village. The country offers some of the best opportunities in the world for this, especially in the mountains north-west of San'a, or around Ibb and Ta'izz. There, the distances between villages are short, a few hours on foot at most, and there are plenty of open-minded and helpful people to assist you with any problems you might encounter on your trek.

For longer hauls, it is easy to get a ride in Yemen, except on the asphalted roads served by buses and taxis. Many poorer Yemenis rely entirely on cheap (occasionally free) rides from passing vehicles. Although many tourists join the crowd in hitch-hiking, it is not an entirely safe way of getting around, and just because we explain how it works doesn't mean we recommend it.

You'll see plenty of open-platform trucks travelling along the highways, roads and tracks of Yemen carrying anything from one to 20 people in addition to their cargoes. Often, you will find it easy to join these passengers – just wave the vehicle down and greet the driver and passengers cordially before asking where they are going and whether it is OK to climb onto the platform. Usually, it will be. Sometimes, you will even be invited to have a seat, and somebody will move over to the platform to make room for you.

It is perfectly possible to get a ride in any vehicle. Soldiers and police often pick up tourist hitchhikers, while well-educated Yemenis may want to practise their English. You are less likely to get a ride on a busy route frequented by buses and service taxis than on quieter roads or tracks. On the other hand, in remote areas where tourists are rare, people may worry about their own safety and avoid contacting strangers, which may make it difficult to get a ride.

Don't behave as though you are taking the driver's hospitality for granted. They expect you to talk with them and to answer their questions. If they don't ask any, volunteer information about yourself. If they speak only Arabic and you don't, talk with them in your own language; at least you have body language in common. If, for some reason, they don't want to talk with you, they will let you know but it is better if they decide this, not you.

After the ride, always offer some money; not too much, definitely less than you would pay for a seat in a service taxi, but not too little either – be careful not to make your offer offensive. They may not take it or they may take it without a word of thanks – either way it's all right.

Some Yemenis have heard wild rumours about foreigners paying astronomical amounts for rides of a few km; they may ask crazy prices when you ask for a ride, such as thousands of riyals for a 30-minute drive. Fortunately, these people are still rare, at least for the time being, and you should not add to their number. Turn them down – this kind of situation is not good for you, it is not good for Yemen and it is not good for those who will come after you.

San'a

Yemen's capital, San'a (**s**an'a; Sana, Sanaa), is in the northern provinces. As the bustling capital of a not-so-small country, it has the usual traffic jams and environmental problems, but it boasts one of the biggest open-air museums in the world. Rather than displaying lifeless relics, San'a preserves the age-old way of living. For 1500 years it was a legendary town; few Europeans had ever visited San'a and it earned fame as a city never exposed to foreign influence. Then, quite suddenly, in the latter half of the 20th century, it became an integral part of the modern world. However, the Pearl of Arabia Felix still exists, perhaps in more fascinating form than ever, in the midst of modern suburbs and beneath the dust clouds raised by motor vehicles.

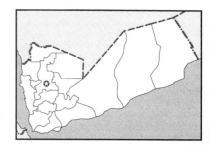

History

According to Yemeni folklore, San'a was founded by Noah's son Shem and is one of the first sites of human settlement. Legend says that Shem came to Yemen from the north seeking somewhere to settle and chose the place shown to him by a bird. The legend still flourishes in San'a and the town bears the nickname 'Sam City'.

After Shem, other religious notables (Jewish, Christian and Muslim) lived here. At one point the city was called Azal, after the sixth son of Biblical Joktan (Qahtan in Arabic) to whom all South Arabian tribes trace their origins. Today, Azal is the brand name of a bottled mineral water.

Spoken tradition also tells us that, at some point during the Sabaean and Himyarite times, around the beginning of Christian times, there was a huge palace somewhere in or near present-day San'a. The palace, Ghumdan, was said to be 20 storeys high. Bronze lions guarded each corner and the alabaster roof was apparently so thin and translucent that the

Street scene in San'a

unnamed king could see the birds flying above the palace.

In the 10th century AD the famous Yemeni historian al-Hamdani reported on developments some 800 years before his time. According to his account, it was the Sabaean king Sha'r Awtar who, in the late 2nd century AD, built a wall around the palace of Ghumdan, thus starting the tradition of making the city a walled one. The name San'a literally means a fortified city.

The oldest reliable records of San'a date from the 1st century AD; however, these give us little information about the city's changes in status. A few centuries later, San'a suddenly appeared as the capital of the Himyarite kingdom. Exactly when Dhafar lost its place as the capital to San'a is not known, but in 525 AD, when the Aksumites from Ethiopia conquered the Himyarites, San'a had served as the capital during the reigns of more than one king.

Scriptures from that period describe the Qalis in San'a as a splendid cathedral built of teak with gold and silver nails, housing an ebony pulpit with gold and silver plating. (The word 'Qalis' is derived from the Greek word 'ecclesia', which means church.) It was a place of pilgrimage for the Christians of Arabia; even today, some inhabitants of old San'a may stop a tourist and point out the place where the Qalis is supposed to have stood.

Nothing is left of these monuments. The Persians came some 50 years after the Ethiopians, and again only scriptures testify to their presence in San'a. In the course of only a few years following the arrival of Islam in Yemen in 628 AD, the palaces of non-Muslims were destroyed, as were many of the city's other buildings. The Great Mosque of San'a was built using the stones.

During subsequent centuries San'a often served as a capital, either of the whole of Yemen or of a small region in the midst of the highland plains. The city prospered greatly at these times. Often, however, it was humiliated and destroyed by new sultans seizing power from old rulers and moving the throne elsewhere.

The first troubles occurred soon after the Islamic expansion. Early in the 9th century, Yemenis fought to free themselves from the rule of the Abbasid caliphs of Baghdad; San'a was destroyed by the troops of the legendary Caliph Harun ar-Rashid in 803 AD. About 100 years later, destruction came at the hands of a closer rival: in 901 AD the emerging Zaydi state conquered San'a for

the first time. The year 1187 AD was another black year for San'a – a series of dynastic battles for power severely damaged the city.

At the beginning of the 16th century, Mamelukes from Egypt briefly occupied Yemen and succeeded in taking San'a. In 1548 came the Turks. They held the city for some decades and left in 1636, only to return to Yemen over 200 years later, in 1849, conquering San'a in 1872. Again, their power was highly disputed and they had to give up San'a several times while fighting against the troops of the Zaydi imams. San'a again suffered greatly from recurring battles.

It was only after the 1912 Treaty of Da''an (in which the Turks agreed to retreat from the Yemeni highlands, leaving the region under the rule of Imam Yahya) that San'a started to enjoy the benefits of peaceful development. In 1918 the city became the capital of the independent Kingdom of Yemen.

San'a's next crisis came in February 1948, when the so-called 'Free Yemenis', a group of Shafa'i merchants and other opponents of the imamic rule, killed Imam Yahya outside San'a. They proclaimed Abdullah al-Wazzir the new imam. However, with support from the Saudis, Yahya's son Ahmad recaptured power, killed al-Wazzir and let Zaydi tribespeople loot the city. Al-Wazzir's head was staked on top of a flat rock near the Bab al-Yaman gate, where it stayed for weeks as a warning to others. A main street in San'a was later named after Muhammad Mahmud az-Zubayri, a leader of the revolutionary group.

After the coup attempt, Ahmad moved the capital to Ta'izz. However, San'a remained an important highland centre and, shortly after the 1962 revolution, it again became the capital of Yemen. In fact, the 1962 revolution began in San'a when Imam Ahmad's son Muhammad al-Badr was proclaimed the new imam following his father's death. On 26 September, a week after the transfer of power, the newly appointed head of the imam's bodyguard, Abdullah as-Sallal, ordered army tanks to

Enchanting San'a

Despite the furious pace of recent urban development, the old San'a, especially the eastern part, has remained relatively intact. The city wall has been broken in several places to let cars and motorcycles enter the narrow streets, and steel water pipes crisscross both the lanes and the outer walls of the houses. Even with these modern additions, San'a is a remarkable town; many houses are more than 400 years old and all are built in the same 1000-year-old style.

In fact, old San'a is internationally regarded as such a unique part of the human cultural heritage that, in December 1984, UNESCO launched an international campaign to safeguard the city. (At the same time, a campaign was launched to protect the city of Shibam in Wadi Hadhramawt, PDRY.) The San'a operation was expected to cost US$223.5 million (YAR contribution US$500,000) and take five years, but the deadline has been extended a few times, the latest occurring in 1994.

What makes San'a so special? Two things immediately stand out. First, the *medina*, or old walled centre of the city, is one of the largest completely preserved medinas in the Arab world. From Suq al-Baqr in the centre of the old city, you can walk more than half a km in any direction, barely encountering 'Western' or 'modern' architecture – only a couple of schools built in the early 1990s spoil the whole image. Second, the architecture of San'a is distinctly different from that found anywhere else in the world; there are comparable gems elsewhere in Yemen but they are smaller and more difficult to reach.

San'a houses represent a fascinating mix of Yemeni styles and materials. The first few floors are built of dark basalt stone and the next storeys of brick. Brown, sun-dried bricks constructed from local mud were exclusively used up to as late as 1990, but in recent years red bricks have come into use with this age-old material. Occasionally the top floor has a mud coating. Outer walls are typically ornamented with elaborate friezes, and plastering with white gypsum is used imaginatively.

The *takhrim* windows, with their complex fretwork of superimposed round and angular shapes, are traditionally made of alabaster panes, though coloured glass has become a substitute in the 1990s. The small panes of different colours make a night walk in the streets of San'a an unforgettable experience.

Takhrim windows

The houses of the eastern part of the medina, especially those to the east of the *sa'ila* (the seasonal river, or wadi, that crosses the city in a north-south direction), are more prestigious than those in the western part. These tower houses have five or six floors, each floor serving a different function. The ground floor is typically used to house animals and for bulk storage. There is often also an excrement room – a small chamber that collects waste from the toilets of the upper floors, to be used as fuel. The rooms on the 1st floor often serve as storage spaces for agricultural products and household items. The 2nd floor may include the *diwan*, or reception room, for guests.

Yemeni tower houses belong to extended families, so the next two or three floors are generally used as bedrooms for the several generations of families occupying the house. Use of the rooms may vary by the season: colder rooms are used during summer while warmer ones are favoured in winter. The kitchen is somewhere on one of these storeys, usually equipped with a well going straight through the lower storeys.

On the top floor is the most privileged room of the house: the large *mafraj*, or the 'room with a good view', where the owner's guests gather to chew qat in the afternoons. The *manzar*, a separate attic on the roof, serves the same purpose as the mafraj. ■

San'a houses

shell al-Badr in his palace in San'a. The next day, Yemen was proclaimed the Yemen Arab Republic.

Al-Badr survived, fled to the mountains and, from there, organised armed resistance against the new leaders. The resulting civil war lasted through the rest of the 1960s, success fluctuating between the Royalists and the Republicans. On 1 December 1967 the Royalists laid siege to San'a. The siege lasted for 70 days but ultimately failed and the civil war was finally brought to an end in 1970.

Since the civil war San'a has experienced unprecedented growth, doubling in size every four years. In 1962 the city wall was completely intact, embracing the whole city and separating it from the green fields immediately outside. A 1964 map shows that large sections of the city wall had been destroyed and new suburbs built; by the mid-1980s the city had spread in all directions, swallowing the nearby villages and covering hundreds of hectares of fertile fields. During the same period the population of the city grew from 55,000 to almost 500,000.

In 1990, when the two Yemens united, San'a became the capital of the new Republic of Yemen, which further accelerated the growth of the city. In the 1994 census its population was 972,000. Clearly, the growth is out of control; it has been estimated that the ground water reservoir beneath the San'a basin will be depleted before the year 2010.

Orientation

San'a is best defined in terms of its main squares. Maydan at-Tahrir (the Square of Liberation, or Tahrir Square) is at the point joining the separate parts of the old city. This square is the postrevolutionary centre of the city; it is the terminal point of intercity bus lines and there are several important government offices nearby. Bab al-Yaman, the Gate of Yemen, south of the old city's eastern part, was the most important part of the city in the Turkish era and it continues to gather great crowds. The largest city market in Yemen, Suq al-Milh, borders the gate.

Less important squares include Bab ash-Sha'ub, to the north of the old town, and Maydan al-Qa', in the western part of the old city. These, too, are connected to Maydan at-Tahrir by bus.

Information

Tourist Office The office of the General Tourist Corporation (spelt Cooperation on some local maps) is at the western end of Maydan at-Tahrir.

The Handicraft Exhibition (souvenir shop) of the office is worth checking; even if you don't purchase their silvery jambiyas or colourful Tihami clothes, you can check the top price levels for bargaining in the suqs, and get all the maps the Yemeni officials have decided are suitable for general sale. There is also a good selection of postcards, posters and other works of art. The shop is open from 9 am to 1 pm.

The headquarters of the General Tourist Corporation are in Hasaba, in the northern part of San'a. If you are serious about visiting more obscure places and would like to enquire about the security situation, this is the office to visit. A taxi takes you there for YR 100.

Money There are plenty of banks in the vicinity of Maydan at-Tahrir which exchange both cash and travellers' cheques. In Suq al-Milh you can find private enterprisers exchanging cash only. US$100 banknotes tend to get you better rates than smaller notes, even though the moneychanger probably has only thick piles of 20 riyal notes to offer in return.

Post The main post office is at the southeastern corner of Maydan at-Tahrir. Postcards can be purchased at the main entrance (cheaper from the General Tourist Corporation or bookshops).

Telephone For calls inside Yemen, use the coin-operated phones in the main post office. No phone directories are available but the staff at the counter will gladly assist you with numbers.

For overseas calls, there are several International Telecommunication Centres in

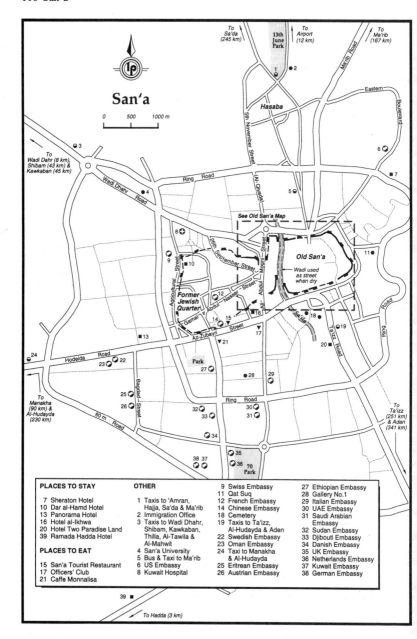

San'a

0   500   1000 m

PLACES TO STAY

7 Sheraton Hotel
10 Dar al-Hamd Hotel
13 Panorama Hotel
16 Hotel al-Ikhwa
20 Hotel Two Paradise Land
39 Ramada Hadda Hotel

PLACES TO EAT

15 San'a Tourist Restaurant
17 Officers' Club
21 Caffe Monnalisa

OTHER

1 Taxis to 'Amran,
   Hajja, Sa'da & Ma'rib
2 Immigration Office
3 Taxis to Wadi Dhahr,
   Shibam, Kawkaban,
   Thilla, Al-Tawila &
   Al-Mahwit
4 San'a University
5 Bus & Taxi to Ma'rib
6 US Embassy
8 Kuwait Hospital

9 Swiss Embassy
11 Qat Suq
12 French Embassy
14 Chinese Embassy
18 Cemetery
19 Taxis to Ta'izz,
   Al-Hudayda & Aden
22 Swedish Embassy
23 Oman Embassy
24 Taxi to Manakha
   & Al-Hudayda
25 Eritrean Embassy
26 Austrian Embassy

27 Ethiopian Embassy
28 Gallery No.1
29 Italian Embassy
30 UAE Embassy
31 Saudi Arabian
   Embassy
32 Sudan Embassy
33 Djibouti Embassy
34 Danish Embassy
35 UK Embassy
36 Netherlands Embassy
37 Kuwait Embassy
38 German Embassy

San'a. A central one is at Qasr al-Jumhuri St, three blocks from Ali Abdul Mogni St. You pay a deposit for the minimum three-minute's call (YR 360 to Europe at the time of writing).

A handy phonecard service is some 10 minutes walk from the junction of Ali Abdul Mogni St and az-Zubeiry St, operated by TeleYemen. Walk west on az-Zubeiry St, then turn right along the small street with the sign 'St No 36'. TeleYemen is on a corner a couple of blocks from the junction, near the Chinese Embassy. It is open from 8 am to 10 pm. Cards are available in denominations of YR 200, YR 400 and YR 600.

Visa Extensions Visa extensions can be obtained at the Immigration Office in Hasaba, in the northern part of town. It is halfway between Maydan at-Tahrir and the San'a International Airport, near the station for taxis to Sa'da and other northern destinations. A service taxi takes you there from Maydan at-Tahrir for YR 20 per person – ask for *Hasaba, maktab al-jawa:za:t* (passport office). This is simple to pronounce and the drivers will probably understand you.

Travel Agencies Flight bookings can be made at any travel agency on Ali Abdul Mogni St between Maydan at-Tahrir and az-Zubeyri Sts, or along az-Zubeyri St between Sa'ila and Hadda Sts.

Bookshops Finding English books in Yemen is no easy task (see Books in the Facts for the Visitor chapter). The souvenir shops in the Taj Sheba and Sheraton hotels are worth checking, although their selections are limited. Otherwise, try the bookshops on Qasr al-Jumhuri St.

Maps The Survey Authority map of San'a (1:10,000 and 1:2500, 1982) is good but difficult to find. Poor-quality hand-drawn imitations are available at newsstands, bookshops and souvenir shops in old San'a, and on Ali Abdul Mogni St and Qasr al-Jumhuri St.

Medical Services The Yemeni hospitals are seriously understaffed and medical standards are dismally low. If possible, don't undergo major treatments or operations in Yemen; arrange for first aid only and fly back to your home country or one which is better equipped. The hospital of choice among the expatriates in San'a is the Kuwait Hospital (☎ 203282) on Kuwait St, near the junction of the Wadi Dhahr Rd.

Emergency With a myriad of helping hands all around it is unlikely you will need to handle any emergency in San'a yourself. Emergency phone numbers include:

Police (*shurta* in Arabic)	☎ 199
Traffic Accidents	☎ 194
Fire Brigade	☎ 191

The Old City

The most imposing sight in San'a is the city itself. You can walk around it for days, finding more and more fascinating houses, mosques and suqs. Many places in the city have distinctly different characters at different times of the day and on different days of the week – it is the people who bring San'a alive.

The eastern part of the old city is a great place to explore. Make sure you carry twice as much film as you think you will need. Plenty of mosques raise their minarets high above the roofs of the beautiful tower houses; unfortunately, though, entering a mosque is practically impossible for a Westerner. Hammams, or bathhouses, abound in the city, many dating from the Turkish era. There are separate hammams for men and women, and it is possible for a visitor to have an inexpensive bath in one. A local guide may help you feel more comfortable in these places.

Don't ignore the gardens of San'a – there are hectares of them within the walls of the old city, although they might easily escape your eyes because they are private and mostly walled, visible only from the backyards of the houses or mosques. They are improbable oases in this vast urban environment. In previous times the city was self-sufficient in vegetables and fruit; the gardens are actively cultivated to this day.

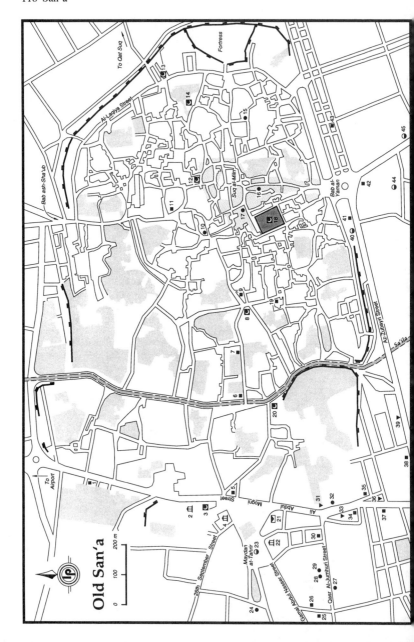

Old San'a

PLACES TO STAY

1	Sam City Hotel
5	Funduq an-Nazir
6	Sultan Palace Tourist Hotel
7	Dar Saad Tourist Hotel
9	Taj Talha Hotel
11	Sendbad Hotel
19	Old San'a Palace Hotel
25	Hotel Arwa
26	Hotel al-Khayam
30	Hotel Alexander
34	Gulf of Oman Tourist Hotel
35	Plaza Hotel
37	Taj Sheba Hotel
38	Middle East Tourist Hotel
41	Hotel as-Salam
42	Himyar Land Hotel
43	Reidan Palace Hotel

PLACES TO EAT

31	Palestine Restaurant
33	Shazarwan Restaurant
36	Teahouse of 26th September
39	Al-Afrah Restaurant

OTHER

2	National Museum
3	Al-Mutwakil Mosque
4	Musem for Arts & Crafts
8	Qubbat Talha Mosque
10	Handcraft Centre ('Women Branch')
12	Al-'Aqil Mosque
13	Qubbat al-Bakiriya Mosque
14	Salah ad-Din Mosque
15	Site of Qalis
16	Samsarat an-Nahas (Handcraft Centre)
17	Samsarat al-Mansura (National Art Centre)
18	Great Mosque
20	Qubbat al-Mahdi Mosque
21	Post Office
22	Military Museum
23	Buses to Bab al-Yaman, Bab ash Sha'ub & Qa'al-Yahud
24	General Tourist Corporation
27	Bookshop
28	International Telephone Centre
29	Bookshop
32	Cinema
40	Bus Office, Buses to Al-Hudayda, Ta'izz, Ibb & Al Mahwit
44	City Bus & Taxi Station
45	Taxis to Ta'izz, Al-Hudayda & Aden

that point though, some friendly souls may approach to ask where you want to go; boundaries between public streets and private courts are vague here and you are being gently reminded that the privacy of homes is inviolable in an Arabic city.

The paving of the main streets of old San'a is of recent origin, having started in the late 1980s with Italian aid. Before the introduction of motorised vehicles, paving was unnecessary; people, goats, camels and donkeys trampled the soil down, so dust was no problem. With only 30 or so rainy days per year, mud was no problem either; the torrential rains were hardly enough to wash away loose debris from alleys.

Unfortunately, after the revolution, modern technology began to pulverise the streets of San'a. An encounter with a Toyota jeep on an unpaved street leaves you spitting dust and the traffic raises giant dust clouds that constantly blanket the city. This phenomenon is greatly amplified by the cement factories just outside the city.

The other part of the old city, to the west of Ali Abdul Mogni St, has newer buildings and is less likely to elicit gasps of admiration. Its many grocery stores, supermarkets and electronic shops abound in imported goods – Japanese Nikon cameras, Dutch Philips vacuum cleaners, Finnish Kantolan biscuits, Australian nonalcoholic Swan beer – demonstrating a prosperity that makes it hard to believe that Yemen still ranks among the least developed countries in the world.

Nevertheless, a walk in this part of the city is rewarding; most of the old embassies have their offices in Bir al-'Azab (at the westernmost end) and many beautiful old houses remain. The former Jewish quarters, Qa' al-Yahud (also called Solbi), can be found south-west of Maydan al-Qa'. Many houses have been destroyed, but with luck, you can still find an original one, identifiable by the Star of David above the door or windows. Otherwise, these clay houses are modest in the extreme. Under imamic rule, Jews were not allowed to build houses higher than nine metres, so their houses often had basements, a rarity in Yemen.

Although the old city covers a large area, you hardly need a map. The overall structure of the city steers you along the main routes. If you enter the smaller alleys, you may soon find they are dead ends. Before you reach

The City Wall

The best remaining examples of San'a's city wall are by the western side of the Sa'ila and by az-Zubeiry St, between Sa'ila and Bab al-Yaman. The wall was originally built of mud only; the stony part was built in 1990 as an act of restoration, preserving the structure but destroying its spirit.

Parts of the wall also exist on the northern side of the medina, near Bab ash-Sha'ub. On the south-eastern tip of the walled city, the old citadel is elevated, surrounded by massive walls. It is used by the military forces and cannot be visited.

Suq al-Milh

The central market area begins at Bab al-Yaman and extends all the way past the Great Mosque, half a km to the north from the Bab. Bab al-Yaman itself was built in the 1870s by the Turkish occupiers and looks almost as alien as the fountain in front of it, built by South Koreans in 1986.

The suq is open daily but is best visited in the morning, when activity peaks, or between 6 and 7 pm. After entering Bab al-Yaman, you encounter an ever-expanding variety of commodities for sale. Although the area is called Suq al-Milh, or the Salt Market, salt is a minor sales item in this market. The market zone actually consists of some 40 smaller suqs, each specialising in a clearly defined sector of business.

Traditionally, each suq was under the control of the *shaykh as-suq*. Within each suq there was (and still is) a *samsara* (plural *sama:sir)*, a building that served as both a storehouse for the wares and an inn for those bringing the wares for sale. Today these buildings have largely fallen into disuse, and there are restoration projects for the most important sama:sir. Fifteen important sama:sir can still be found next to the corresponding suqs, recognisable by their decoratively tiled brick facades and their location within the suq area.

Many of the goods are left out in the open overnight; men called *shaykh al-layla* guard them from small watchtowers. There used to be a central samsara (Samsara Muhammad Ibn al-Hassan) for storing money and other precious items but this tradition ended in 1948: after a murder attempt, Imam Ahmad ordered his tribespeople to loot San'a, including the samsara.

Along the central alley of the suq, Samsarat an-Nahas has been renovated into a handcraft centre, housing several small shops that mainly target tourists. On the roof of the house you can enjoy magnificent views over old San'a. Another handcraft centre (signposted 'Women Branch') can be found to the west of Suq al-Milh. It specialises in modern carpetry with motifs copied from photos of Yemeni national symbols, crafted by local women.

Near Bab al-Yaman, jambiyas, music cassettes and other items from the past and present are sold. Deeper in the suq better defined sub-suqs emerge, many of them selling mainly traditional products, although imported wares are not uncommon. In the actual Jambiya Suq you have a good opportunity to watch the complicated crafting of the ceremonial weapons. The silver market largely bases its prosperity on tourists paying high prices but many of the silver goods on sale have been made in the suq or imported from India. You may be lucky enough to see a genuinely old piece brought from the Yemeni countryside, distinguished by its astronomical price.

The spice market is by far the most pleasantly scented place in Yemen. Vegetables, qat, corn, raisins, pottery, clothes, carpentry and copper, to mention just a few, has a suq of its own.

Qat Suq

To the east of the old city is a more modern market, the walled Qat Suq. This vast wholesale market primarily sells qat but has a range of other products, including chickens, cows, grain and firewood.

Open every day, the Qat Suq is recommended if you enjoy crowds and a busy atmosphere.

The Great Mosque

For Muslim visitors, the place to visit in

Bathing in the Hammams of San'a

In old San'a you will see several modest single-storey buildings with many cupolas on the roof, apparently for public use. Few travellers realise that they are actually *hammams*, or bathhouses, and sometime mistake them for mosques without minarets. Public baths abound everywhere in Yemen, and in the old city of San'a there are more than fifteen of them. Foreign visitors seldom dare to visit of the bathhouses, which is a pity since the experience is pleasant and memorable.

Yemenis love hot baths, and the bathhouses offer several pools of different temperatures. The bathhouses have wells of their own. The cold water pool is most often nearest to the entrance, while the warm and hot pools are in separate rooms further inside the building. Many Yemeni bathhouses are built according to a traditional plan, which places three warm and three hot pool rooms in adjacent rows, each having a domed ceiling with small windows which allow sunlight in.

As you travel from room to room you will notice an inclination, as the hotter parts of the buildings are dug below the surface of the earth. This helps to preserve energy: the climate of San'a is chilly for a large part of the year, and minimising the surface area of outer walls keeps the warmth inside the building. The baths are open eighteen hours a day, from very early in the morning until very late in the evening, so the afternoon heat only helps for a short while.

The water is heated in a separate boiler at the rear of the building. Hypocausts and vents direct heat to the hot and warm rooms. In addition, hot water flows to the pools from the well and boiler via a system of pipes. In the past, human excrement gathered from the city was burned in the ovens; today oil has replaced this traditional fuel. In many parts of this volcanic country hot springs provide the heat, but this is not the case in San'a.

The baths are strictly, but not permanently, segregated: a particular bathhouse may be visited by males on one day and by females on another. On your first visit, you may feel more comfortable with a local guide – entering the bathhouse alone will inevitably attract attention from the locals.

Leave your shoes and valuables with the keeper of the place and enter the changing room to undress. Never undress completely – use a *futa*, or loincloth, to cover your private parts. There are shelves for your clothes in the changing rooms. Before entering the innards of the bathhouse it is considerate to wash your feet.

You next proceed directly to the hot rooms, where the bath attendants will pour hot water all over you. You may sit down and enjoy the heat and steam for a while. Most people come with their friends; bathing is a social event, and hushed chattering fills the air. Once you have had enough of the heat you move to one of the more temperate rooms, where you finally wash yourself. You may apply soap yourself or let a friend or a bath attendant – but never a stranger – do it for you. Once you have rinsed off the soap, you move to one of the small, dark side rooms to wash under the loincloth.

After one last douse in the coolest room, wrap yourself in a towel, remove your loincloth and return to the changing room to dry yourself. You may sit here for some time to cool off. Tea or coffee is available. For those wishing to pray, there is a *mihrab* on the wall towards Mecca.

There is no fixed price for the bath – guests pay the keeper according to their wealth. For family occasions, or gatherings of friends before festivities, the entire bathhouse can be rented by the hour. ∎

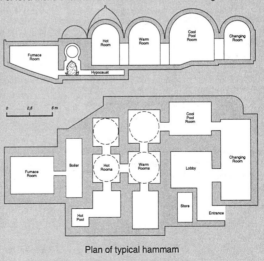

Plan of typical hammam

San'a is, of course, al-Jami' al-Kabir, or the Great Mosque, on the westernmost side of Suq al-Milh.

The mosque was built around 630 AD, in the very first years of Islam's presence in Yemen, when the Prophet Muhammad was still alive. Since then it has been severely damaged and restored many times; by 705 the original building was greatly enlarged, in 875 it suffered severe flood damage, and in 911 it was badly damaged during wars against the Qarmatians. In the 12th century the mosque and both its minarets were restored. It is from this period that most of the present structures date, although even the Turkish occupiers later contributed to the mosque's inner decorations.

The Great Mosque is built in strictly Islamic style. Within the great square of walls are all the requisites of a Muslim place of worship: it has a fountain and an ablution pool for the ritual washing before prayer; the most richly decorated *mihrab* wall indicates the direction of Mecca; the imam conducts the Friday worship from the *minbar*, or pulpit, by the mihrab wall; and the muwadhdhin responds to the imam during the sermon from the *dikka*, or platform, in the centre.

Entrance is usually not granted to non-Muslims. The straight walls effectively hide the mosque's beauty from outsiders and even the minarets are difficult to see because the densely built city makes it impossible for you to observe them from a distance. If you take a hasty peek through the main door into the solid hall of columns, believers are likely to inform you that you'd do better somewhere else.

Other Mosques

Of greater interest to non-Muslims are those mosques that reveal their beauty from the outside. You can choose from quite a variety in this 'city of 64 minarets'.

Salah ad-Din Mosque, in the eastern part of the city, is built in pure Yemeni style, while the Qubbat Talha, in the western part of the medina, shows Turkish influence in its cupolas.

The small al-'Aqil Mosque raises its beautiful minaret, brightly lit at night, over Suq al-Milh. The relatively recent al-Mutwakil Mosque on 5th November St, near the northernmost corner of Maydan at-Tahrir next to the National Museum, was built in Turkish style by Imam Yahya in the early 20th century.

The Qubbat al-Bakiliya, in the easternmost part of the old city, is perhaps the most imposing of all, partly because of its location by broad al-Laqiya St, where the mosque is easy to inspect from a distance. The building work was started in 1585 AD and completed in the early 1600s, during the first Turkish occupation. The mosque was restored in 1878 AD, again by the Turks who had returned to Yemen in the latter part of the 19th century. Its 11 cupolas are built in Turkish style, while the brick minaret is Yemeni.

In the late 1980s several new mosques were built in the modern parts of San'a. The sheer size of these massive concrete constructions makes them striking but not exactly pleasing to the eye. A very good example is the ash-Shuhada Mosque, next to the taxi stations south of Bab al-Yaman.

National Museum

The National Museum is on Ali Abdul Mogni St, some 100 metres north of Maydan at-Tahrir, next to al-Mutwakil Mosque. It is housed in Dar as-Sa'd (House of Good Luck), a former royal palace built in the 1930s. The museum moved there in 1987 from Dar ash-Shukr (House of Thanks), an older and smaller imamic palace in the Mutwakil estate, when its collection grew too big.

The National Museum is open daily from 9 am to noon and from 3 to 5 pm, except on Friday when it's open in the morning only. The entrance fee is YR 30 per person. The museum occupies five floors, each with several rooms and a different theme. The small ground floor is for foreign exhibitions; when we visited, we saw ancient European items, including old Roman statues lent by Germans, with labels in German and Arabic.

The 1st floor houses a permanent exhibition of the pre-Islamic history of Yemen, with rooms dedicated to ancient kingdoms such as Saba, Ma'rib, Ma'in and Himyar. Plenty of finds from archaeological excavations are on show here, along with interesting maps.

The 2nd floor presents Yemen's Islamic past. Rooms feature Koranic calligraphy, copperware and coins, as well as information on towns of significant Islamic achievement, such as Dhafar, Dhi Bin and Zabid. A slide show runs hourly.

The 3rd floor showcases 20th-century Yemeni folk culture. In this ethnographical section there are plenty of traditional scenes that can still be seen in the Yemeni countryside (though they are vanishing fast). Agriculture, fishing, jambiya-making, carpentry, pottery, carpet-weaving, costumes, jewellery, even San'a weddings each have a small room here.

While the 1st, 2nd and 3rd-floor exhibits are labelled in English and Arabic, the 4th floor is obviously meant exclusively for Arabs, since all labels are in Arabic only. Among other things, there is a collection of photographs of Yemen and of (currently) friendly Arab countries; Egypt and Iraq used to have permanent rooms, but at our last visit, this part of the exhibition was closed.

Museum for Arts & Crafts

A new collection called the Museum for Arts & Crafts opened in April 1995. It is by Maydan at-Tahrir in Dar ash-Shukr. It consists of the spill-over from the National Museum and specialises in traditional Yemeni household items and everyday customs.

Both museums have benefited from expert assistance and financial support from the Netherlands.

Military Museum

The Military Museum, on the south-western corner of Maydan at-Tahrir, is easy to spot: the building is exuberantly decorated with military hardware. The museum tells the story of Yemen from a military point of view, as seen by the government. The civil war of 1994 has yet to make its mark in the exhibitions.

Plenty of equipment is on show in the two storeys and in the small courtyard of the building, and major historical events are depicted in text and photographs. Look out for small items such as a stamp which reads 'The Free Mutawakkelite Kingdom Fights Egyptian Imperialistic Aggression'.

The museum is open daily from 9 am to noon and from 4 to 8 pm; it is closed on Fridays and on the last Thursday of each month. The entrance fee is YR 10, plus YR 10 if you want to take photos.

Arts

Traditionally, Yemeni visual arts – calligraphy, jewellery and architecture – were Islamic only. The depiction of living things, especially human beings, was prohibited by the Islamic faith for centuries and this ban has only recently been selectively lifted. TV and the ubiquitous portraits of political leaders have made it possible for art in the Western sense to enter Yemen.

The pioneer of San'a's art scene, German-educated artist Fuad al-Futaih, owns Yemen's first art gallery, which opened in 1986. Gallery Number One displays the work of both Yemeni and visiting artists. YIt is a 15-minute walk from the junction of az-Zubeiry St and Ali Abdul Mogni St: walk south on Ali Abdul Mogni St until you reach St No 15 (Khartum St, formerly al-Mujahid St), turn right and, after a couple of blocks, you will come across the tiny gallery.

Fuad al-Futaih is also the director of the National Art Centre in old San'a, which has exhibitions of Yemeni and foreign artists. It is in the Samsarat al-Mansura house on the north-western side of Suq al-Milh, near the Great Mosque. The exhibitions are open from 9 am to 12:30 pm and 4 to 7 pm.

Organised Tours

In addition to the tours listed in the Getting Around chapter, organised tours are also arranged by some hotels in old San'a such as the Dar Saad and the Sultan Palace Tourist Hotel.

Places to Stay

San'a offers the widest variety of hotels in Yemen. Prices range from YR 200 to US$210 per night, though it is probably not a good idea to choose the cheapest alternatives here since elsewhere in the country you may not have a choice.

There are many reasonably priced hotels in the environs of Maydan at-Tahrir and Bab al-Yaman.

Places to Stay – bottom end

If you want to spend the night in a dormitory, don't need to wash anything but your hands and face and don't mind cold water, there are several bargains to be found. For rock-bottom prices try the no-sheet *Funduq Wadi Bana*, opposite Bab al-Yaman, in the corner where the city buses arrive from Maydan at-Tahrir.

A little better is the one-sheet *As-Salam Hotel*, on the other side of az-Zubeiry St. Triples are YR 550 and hot water is available 'tomorrow'.

Slightly better again is the *Funduq an-Nazir*, in a side street off Ali Abdul Mogni St, opposite the post office on Maydan at-Tahrir. In this one-sheet hotel, four of you can share one room for around YR 200 each. Amazingly, the shower in the public bathroom has hot water.

Places to Stay – middle

Most hotels in central San'a are in the YR 300 to YR 600 per person range. At this price you get one or two-sheet beds in double or triple rooms; singles are occasionally available. Check the hot water availability before you check in.

Reidan Palace Hotel (☎ 245686) is a little way off Bab al-Yaman; walk east on either of the streets extending from az-Zubeiry St. Triples (YR 750) are the minimum room size in this hotel. Its public bathrooms feature warm showers and a cleanliness that is exceptional in the one-sheet category.

The *Himyar Land Hotel*, opposite Bab al-Yaman, is in a central but exceptionally noisy place. In this one-sheet hotel, you get doubles for YR 600 and a level of hygiene that is very Yemeni.

The *Middle East Tourist Hotel* (or Funduq ash-Sharq al-Awsat as-Siyahi), is on az-Zubeiry St, between the Sa'ila and Ali Abdul Mogni St. Doubles with private bathroom cost YR 1200. This is quite a clean two-sheet hotel.

Ali Abdul Mogni St has several two-sheet hotels with fully equipped shared bathrooms. These places are in varying condition and offer doubles from YR 600 to YR 1200. They were built in the early 1970s in contemporary Egyptian style. The newly renovated *Gulf of Oman Tourist Hotel* has strikingly tidy doubles for YR 1000. The neighbouring *Shabwa Hotel Tourism* and *Hotel al-Mohra* are not too bad either. *Funduq al-Iskandariya* (Alexander Hotel) is a couple of blocks off the main street, on Qasr al-Jumhuri St, and offers singles and triples.

If you continue along Qasr al-Jumhuri St for a few blocks and turn right, you'll come to the *Arwa* and *al-Khayam* hotels. Both are two-sheet hotels with doubles for YR 600 and both are relatively clean. The Arwa has shared bathrooms while the al-Khayam has reasonably clean private bathrooms.

A little more expensive is the *al-Ikhwa Hotel*, a couple of blocks behind Taj Sheba. At YR 1100 for a very clean double with private bath and TV, this hotel is certainly worth the expense. However, their prices seem to fluctuate, so take care.

There is a selection of less central but newer and cleaner hotels along Ta'izz Rd, to the south of Bab al-Yaman. The big two-sheet *Two Paradise Land Hotel* offers triples with private bathroom for YR 1200 and has doubles with shared bathroom for YR 600.

Palace Hotels San'a has a special class of hotel not found in other towns of the country. Many old tower houses in the old town were converted into hotels in the early 1990s. Although these houses were never actually palaces, their prices guarantee that Yemenis never use them. For a Western traveller they can still be relatively cheap, offering a convenient chance to see the interior of a traditional house.

Instead of beds they invariably have Yemeni-style mattresses on the floor. Shared toilets and bathrooms are new additions. Most of them also have a restaurant in the *manzar* (attic) of the house.

Sendbad Hotel to the north of Suq al-Milh has very clean doubles for YR 1400. A couple of blocks to the west is *Taj Talha Hotel*, near the Qubbat at-Talha Mosque. Doubles cost YR 1200, but the price is negotiable.

Old San'a Palace Hotel in the south-west part of the old city has singles/doubles for YR 800/1200. *Sultan Palace Tourist Hotel* (☎ 331842), next to the bridge that crosses the Sa'ila, charges YR 1200 for a double, including breakfast. The owner runs a tour service, but it's a good idea to compare his prices with those offered elsewhere.

The central *Dar Saad Tourist Hotel* has given up trying to adjust their riyal prices to keep up with inflation and charges US$15 for doubles which are not that much better than those of the previous hotels. They also run a tour service.

The traditional *Dar al-Hamd* has been in business since the late 1970s. It is in the western centre of San'a, only a km from Maydan at-Tahrir and charges US$20 for a double.

Places to Stay – top end

If money is not a concern and your travel agent has made advance reservations, you'll stay at *Taj Sheba* (☎ 272372), on Ali Abdul Mogni St. This gorgeous hotel belongs to an Indian hotel chain and has everything you'll ever need in a hotel (doubles US$210).

If you don't want to stay in the city centre, you could choose the modern *San'a Sheraton* (☎ 237500, telex 2222 SHSAN YE) in the same price range. It's on the Ring Rd in the eastern suburbs. *Ramada Hadda Hotel* (☎ 215214, telex 2227 RAMADA YE) is on Hadda St. This international hotel could do with a renovation.

Also close to the centre is the *Sam City Hotel* (☎ 270752) at 5th November (al-

Qiyada) St (US$25 for a double). This was one of the luxury hotels in San'a but was closed in the late 1980s after it was officially found out to sell alcohol. It stayed closed for a few years and opened after a renovation a couple of years ago. They have a roof-top restaurant with fine views but serve tasteless food at inflated prices. A similar high-rise hotel in the centre of the city is the brand new *Plaza Hotel* (☎ 274346) at Ali Abdul Mogni St, next to the Teahouse of 26th of September. They have singles/doubles at YR 1750/2360.

By the end of 1996 a new five star hotel complex is expected to open in Bir al-'Azab, converted from five traditional Sana'ani houses situated in beautiful park surrounds, having formerly served as the premises of the US embassy.

Places to Eat

Yemeni men like to eat out so San'a is full of restaurants. There are not too many of them in the old city but, immediately outside it along the main streets, you will find innumerable small eateries that would be called snack bars in the Western world. Further off in the suburbs, restaurants also prosper. All have basic Yemeni menus and are not exactly exotic.

Middle Eastern The best selection of restaurants can be found near Bab al-Yaman and Maydan at-Tahrir.

The *Shazarwan Restaurant* is near the Gulf of Oman Tourist Hotel, opposite the cinema on Ali Abdul Mogni St and very near the Teahouse of 26th September. It is clean and busy; anything you can buy here is probably safe and the cooks certainly know their job. The grilled chicken is some of the best you will find in Yemen at only YR 350.

Opposite the Shazarwan, next to the cinema, you can find the *Palestine Restaurant*, which is a bit more expensive. They have a vast chicken-grill by the door and their shawarma (the huge vertical spit of lamb meat) is tasty and so popular that portions seem to be carved out often enough to ensure the freshness of the meat. However, several travellers have become ill after eating here.

On az-Zubeiry St between Ali Abdul Mogni St and the Sa'ila, the excellent and cheap *al-Afrah Restaurant* has menus which are brought to the tables. This is a very rare occurrence in Yemen; usually there is just one menu (in Arabic) hanging on the wall. The 'Dry Cleaning' sign in the rear of the place shows you where to wash your hands. Another good but much more expensive restaurant with English menus is the tiny *Ash-Sham Restaurant* in az-Zubeiry St on the other side of Ali Abdul Mogni St, just past the Sayf Ben Thi Yazin St junction.

In the small street parallel to Ali Abdul Mogni St, between the post office and Qasr al-Jumhuri St, there are a couple of inexpensive fish restaurants.

San'a Tourist Restaurant near the TeleYemen office on St No 35, north of az-Zubeiry St, is an Ethiopian restaurant, with a huge Italian-style espresso machine in the front and *injera* tables in the back rooms.

Western You won't find hamburgers, pizzas, bacon or fried eggs in Yemen. The only Western-style fast-food chain was *Kentucky Fried Chicken* but they've pulled out of the country, leaving only their signs behind.

All over the streets of the newer parts of San'a, you can find small stalls serving takeaway french fries.

First-class hotels have restaurants serving Western-style food with prices to match. *Taj Sheba* hotel, for example, has a Western (as well as Yemeni) buffet every night which costs YR 1500.

For a genuine Italian cappuccino, *Caffe Monnalisa* in Hadda St, 100 metres from the junction of al-Zubeiry St, is unbeatable. The owner returned to Yemen from Italy during the tourist boom of the early 1990s. He used to offer fantastic Italian food. Maybe he'll resume if enough of you keep asking.

Sweets Near the junction of Hadda St and az-Zubeiry St are several shops selling

Arabic sweets. The *Lebanese Pastry Shop* has a variety of Middle Eastern desserts as well as ice cream.

Tea If all you want is a glass of tea, you might enjoy the balcony on the 1st floor of the hotel on Bab al-Yaman, which has excellent views of the bustling square below. Other recommended places abound in the city, most of them on ground level extending into the street. Many serve excellent greasy loaves of bread *(khubz)* for YR 10 in the evenings; we became fond of the place behind the main post office.

The real place to be is the *Teahouse of 26th September*, where the local low-income intelligentsia gather with their newspapers and course books to see and be seen. It's on Ali Abdul Mogni St, opposite the Taj Sheba Hotel, halfway between Bab al-Yaman and Maydan at-Tahrir. The place is a park restaurant (relatively rare in Yemen); it's enjoyable to sit in the shade of the trees, sipping *libtun* and watching the crazy traffic of San'a's main street.

On the opposite corner of the junction of Ali Abdul Mogni and az-Zubeiry Sts, there is the *Officers' Club*, which can be visited by nonmilitary personnel.

Entertainment

Nightlife in Yemen is not exactly 'fast'. With no bars or nightclubs, you might like to watch a football match at the stadium on the Qasr al-Jumhuri St. The stadium is also used for the TV filming of folk-dance performances on major national holidays.

The cinemas in San'a mostly show Egyptian and Indian titles, with an occasional 1970s Spaghetti Western from Italy bringing. However, to follow the plot you need to be fluent in Arabic, as foreign movies are usually dubbed in Egypt for the local market. Still, the atmosphere makes the experience worthwhile, even if you can't follow the plot. A central cinema is on Ali Abdul Mogni St, next to the Palestinian Restaurant.

The Taj Sheba, Sheraton, Dar-al-Hamd and Ramada Hadda hotels have occasional evening banquets and folk-dance perfornances, usually coinciding with Western holiday seasons and at considerable cost. Take a look at the *Yemen Times* for their advertisements.

Getting There & Away

There are a few bus and taxi stations in San'a, each serving a different direction.

South & West Buses to Ta'izz, al-Hudayda and al-Mahwit leave from Bab al-Yaman (actually, from a couple of hundred metres west of the Bab, on az-Zubeiry St). You can't miss the station as there are plenty of buses there. Taxis to Ta'izz and al-Hudayda leave from the huge taxi station on Ta'izz Rd, just south of az-Zubeiry St behind the houseblocks. If you want to use the old and picturesque San'a to al-Hudayda road you have to go to the taxi station at the western end of az-Zubeyri St; a minibus takes you there for YR 20.

North-West If you are going in the direction of Wadi Dhahr, Thilla, Shibam, at-Tawila, Kawkaban and al-Mahwit, you'll find the taxi station inconveniently in Matbah, some five km to the north-west of Maydan at-Tahrir. Take a taxi for YR 200. Minibuses going round Ring Rd take you close enough for YR 20, but you have to ask for directions and walk a few blocks from the stop. The taxis bear black stripes, just like city taxis.

North Brown-striped taxis going to 'Amran, Hajja and Sa'da leave from Hasaba, at the junction of the Sa'da and airport roads. Black-striped minibuses will take you there from Maydan at-Tahrir for YR 20 per person.) Buses in the same direction leave from the station in al-Jomhuriyya St, half a km north of Bab ash-Sha'ub, where the city bus leaves you.

East You can find buses to Ma'rib leaving from the same station as the northbound buses. Yellow-striped taxis operate from the square next to the bus station.

Getting Around

To/From the Airport The official fare between the airport and the city centre is displayed on a sign on the taxi station at the airport, but few taxis are willing to take you for that price. The official fare is YR 600, but YR 800 is commonly demanded. If you walk a hundred metres from the door of the airport towards the city, you can find shared taxis for YR 40 per seat.

If you can't find a shared taxi from the city to the airport, you can always take a black-striped minibus from the Maydan at-Tahrir to Hasaba for YR 10 per person, walk across the Sa'da Rd junction and catch another minibus to the airport for the same price. Obviously you aren't in a hurry if you choose this option and it's certainly not practical if you have plenty of luggage or your plane leaves at an odd hour.

Bus San'a is an easy place to move around because the public transport system is extremely comprehensive. The most important subcentres, around Bab al-Yaman, Bab ash-Sha'ub and Maydan al-Qa', are linked with Maydan at-Tahrir by city buses. These buses wait at the stations for passengers and the drivers stand beside their buses, yelling their destinations. Buses leave when all seats are full, and cost YR 10 per person. The route between Maydan at-Tahrir and Bab al-Yaman is served most frequently.

Black-striped minibuses shuttle along main streets such as az-Zubeiry St, Ali Abdul Mogni St (the airport road), Hadda St and parts of Ring Rd. The usual fare is YR 10 per person, YR 20 for longer hauls. Beware of empty minibuses whose drivers agree to take you wherever you want to go; they quickly turn into private taxis charging YR 400 or more. Check the price before entering the vehicle.

Taxi Black-striped shared taxis often operate on the same principle as minibuses, driving back and forth along a certain street. The cost may vary from YR 20 to YR 30 per person, according to the length of the ride. Again, bargain before entering the vehicle but don't argue if the price is not right, just choose another shared taxi – at least five others will be there waiting for you.

Almost any black-striped car may choose to operate as a private taxi, charging you a few tens of riyals for the ride. Within the urban area there is no reason to use private taxis, unless you are uncertain about how to get to your destination. Even then, be prepared to encounter a driver no wiser than yourself.

Around San'a

There are several places of interest on the outskirts of San'a, near the borders of the San'a basin. They are suitable for half or full-day excursions from the capital.

AR-RAWDHA

(ar-rawza; ar-Rawdah, Raudah)

This village is eight km north of San'a's centre, just to the east of the airport road. It is surrounded by large vineyards and, in earlier times, served as a summer resort for the imam. Today it is a suburb of San'a and highly recommended by Yemeni tourist officials.

Things to See

Apart from the lively **market** on Sunday mornings, there are a couple of architectural sights in ar-Rawdha.

The **Rawdha Palace Hotel**, in the middle of the village, was originally built to serve as a residence of the imam. It is a perfect example of San'a's architecture and offers the visitor a chance to see the interior of a multistoreyed house built of stone and clay bricks. You can also admire the beautiful landscapes from its roof. For a room you usually need to have a reservation in advance, best arranged by a travel agency.

The **Mosque of Ahmad ibn al-Qasim** stands very near the palace and is noteworthy for its outer walls and for the minaret, decorated with Koranic verses. Imam Ahmad, a grandson of Qasim al-Kabir, ruled between 1676 and 1681. (The mosque in Dhawran, in

the 'Anis Mountains, was built at the same time – for details, see Dhawran in the Dhamar chapter.)

Further into the village is an underground building with only cupolas standing. This is the **Hammam of ar-Rawdha**, a bathhouse built by the Turks in typical Turkish style.

Getting There & Away

The best way to get to ar-Rawdha is to take one of the minibuses that abound in Al Abdul Mogni St by Maydan at-Tahrir, to Hasaba (YR 10 per person). From there take a black-striped taxi to ar-Rawdha. A seat in a shared taxi costs only YR 20 but you will gladly be offered a whole taxi for YR 400 so be careful.

The best day to visit ar-Rawdha is Sunday, the village market day, when buses shuttle from Bab al-Yaman to ar-Rawdha and back between early morning and noon. A ticket costs a mere YR 20.

BAYT AL-HUQQA

(bayt al-Huqqa)

Some 23 km north of San'a, in the direction of 'Amran, lies a small village named Bayt al-Huqqa. The site of an ancient settlement, it is rich in Himyarite relics. In the 1920s German archaeologists carried out a research project here; the most precious finds are now in San'a's National Museum. However, many stones from ancient temples have been reused in present buildings, and ornaments as well as animal figures can be observed on the walls of the houses in Bayt al-Huqqa.

According to researchers, the temple of al-Huqqa and the water cistern belonging to it were built in the 3rd century BC. The temple was destroyed in an eruption of the nearby volcano in the 3rd century AD.

Getting There & Away

Bayt al-Huqqa is not served by regular taxis. You can reach it by private taxi or you can take a service taxi to 'Amran. Get out where a dirt road starts to the right just before the village of al-Ma'mar, some 20 km from San'a, and walk the last five km. The road

PERTTI HÄMÄLÄINEN

PERTTI HÄMÄLÄINEN

Top: Ramlat as-Sab'atayn desert
Bottom: Village in the Habban region

PERTTI HÄMÄLÄINEN

BETHUNE CARMICHAEL

Top: Modern mural in Aden
Bottom: Cafe in Aden

leads you past the village of Bayt al-Hawiri and continues to al-Jahiliya – turn left before reaching that village.

WADI DHAHR

(wa:di: **z**ahr)

Only 15 km or so north-west of San'a lies Wadi Dhahr, a fertile and very pleasant valley of small villages and clay-walled orchards, green all year round and growing all kinds of fruits of the Mediterranean variety. Dar al-Hajar, a building that has developed into some kind of symbol of Yemen, serves as a landmark in the valley.

You'll find it rewarding to spend a few hours walking in the valley and surrounding mountains, where the green gardens are a striking contrast to the reddish and brownish sandstone of the wadi's rocky edges. Walking upstream (to the west, out of the area covered by the Wadi Dhahr map), you come to the village of Bayt Na'am. Continuing from there, you can reach the very beginning of the wadi.

Thursday is the day when weddings are celebrated in the area, and on Friday mornings you have a chance to watch locals dancing the weddings away in the open. Come after 9 am but before noon and drop away from the taxi just before the road starts to descend in the wadi.

Qaryat al-Qabil

To the north of Dar al-Hajar, Qaryat al-Qabil is a beautiful little village with a small Friday market. It is shadowed by an impressive stone wall formed over millions of years by fast-flowing waters. (You may find it difficult to imagine the fast-flowing waters if you visit during the dry season, but in 1975, the villages in the wadi were severely damaged by floodwaters eight metres high.) Here you can enjoy the Yemeni sense of harmony by observing the way a constructed environment is incorporated into the giant frame of nature; the houses seem to have grown out of the bedrock.

The region was already inhabited in Himyarite times; if you look carefully towards the precipice, you should spot

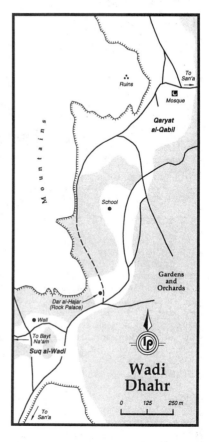

several caves. The ruins of fortifications on nearby hilltops probably date from the days of Turkish occupation but some may have even more remote origins. Continuing north along a path past the village cemetery and through the fields in the bottom of the wadi, you will find some ancient rock paintings of animals and hunters by the wadi bank near a small house. Ask the children for directions.

Heading east from the village, you come to an asphalted road that leads to the San'a to Sa'da highway, offering you an alternative route back to the capital.

Dar al-Hajar – the Rock House

Dar al-Hajar, the Rock House (or Rock Palace), is a remarkable building atop a protruding rock formation in Wadi Dhahr. Pictured in every other book about Yemen, it has become a symbol of the country itself. If you have defined your destination only vaguely as Wadi Dhahr, the driver will probably drop you here.

The five-storey palace was built in the 1930s by Imam Yahya as a summer residence. Building a palace in such an extraordinary place was not his idea; there were already ruins of a prehistoric building on top of the hill. The well penetrating the rocks by the house is said to be original.

The palace is government property and stayed empty from the revolution to 1990, when a 'renovation and furnishing project' was started. It was still going on in 1994. Rumour has it that the palace will be developed into a 1st-class hotel with a casino (!) on the top floor. Another rumour is that the remarkable structure will serve as the official residence of the president. Visit it as long you can, it is worthwhile for the chance to inspect the elaborate takhrim windows and enjoy the scenery from the roof. The entrance fee is YR 50. ■

Dar al Hajar

Getting There & Away

It is easy to reach Wadi Dhahr from San'a: black-striped taxis leave from the car park a couple of blocks north of Maydan at-Tahrir and will take you to Wadi Dhahr for YR 50 per person. The road down to the wadi branches from the asphalted San'a-Shibam road about nine km from San'a, then descends into the valley at a place called Suq al-Wadi.

THILLA

(thilla:; Thulla, Thula)

About 54 km north-west of San'a is a remarkable ancient town, Thilla. It is built at the eastern foot of a mountain, near a large gently sloping basin of terraced fields, with a fortress on the mountaintop to shelter the inhabitants during crises. It is an excellent example of the system of defence that has so efficiently protected Yemenis against foreign invaders.

Thilla is a rare example of an almost perfectly preserved highland town of stone tower houses. The walled town with its paved streets is entirely built with stones from the mountain, so that from a distance you would hardly suspect the presence of a town here. Walking in its alleys, lanes and the old suq is a pleasing experience; friezes and wall textures give the houses variation despite the fact that all are built from the same material.

Thilla has always been a free town. During the Turkish occupation in the 16th century, it remained unconquered, with Imam Muttahir Sharaf ad-Din leading the successful battle against aggressors equipped with firearms.

Near the northern and southern gates you'll find well-preserved aqueducts and beautifully carved water cisterns. More cisterns can be found by the fortress on top of the mountain, which provided the population with drinking water in times of crises. Old domes mark the graves of imams.

Unfortunately the fortification on top of the hill is not easily visited. A walk along the steep path would take only 20 minutes but the guards by the locked gate at the beginning of the path usually won't let you through. If you want to try, walk straight through the town from the eastern gate (where taxis leave you) to find the beginning of the path. We were once permitted to enter for a small fee.

A visit to Thilla can be combined with a visit to Shibam and Kawkaban (see the al-Mahwit chapter) since the towns are so close to each other, but visiting both may turn out to be too much for a single day. There are modest hotels in each of these three towns, so a couple of days for a leisurely trip makes good sense, with a possible extension to at-Tawila and al-Mahwit.

Places to Stay

Thilla has a no-sheet hotel in an old-style tower house. You can find it behind the post office *(maktab al-bari:d,* sign in Arabic only), which is by the central square, where Thilla's small Tuesday market takes place. The Thilla hotel charges YR 275 for a bed in rooms of various sizes.

Getting There & Away

You can reach Thilla from San'a by taking a taxi from Harat al-Musbana, a couple of blocks north of Maydan at-Tahrir. There are few direct connections to Thilla but the black-striped taxis and minibuses leave frequently for nearby Shibam; a seat costs only YR 100. You have to exit at *mafraq* Thilla, a crossroads a couple of km before Shibam; from there it is nine km to Thilla but you are likely to get a ride to your destination from any car passing by. The road is asphalted all the way to Thilla.

HADDA

(hadda; Haddah)

The village of Hadda, in the foothills of Jabal Hadda, is just 10 km south-west of San'a along a good asphalted road. It is recommended for those on a tight schedule who wish to visit a typical mountainside village by the San'a basin.

Hadda has beautiful terraced almond and walnut orchards as well as peach, apricot and other fruit trees. The orchards are watered by a controlled stream that flows through the village. The path through the orchards to the upper part of the village has several pleasantly shaded resting places suitable for picnicking and it is amusing to witness a Yemeni family with a portable TV set enjoying a holiday in the open .

From the slopes of the mountain, above the village, a grand view towards San'a opens between two mountains. From here you can continue to other mountain villages and even to Bayt Baws (see later in this chapter), less than 10 km to the east.

Getting There & Away

The cheapest way to travel to Hadda from San'a is to take a YR 10 minibus along az-Zubeiry St to its junction with Hadda St, then a black-striped taxi to Hadda (YR 40 at most). The road goes past the Hadda hotel, the oldest of the 1st-class hotels in the northern part of Yemen. On the mountainside east of Hadda you'll see several tiny villages which depend on the small streams that flow down the mountain for their livelihood.

BAYT BAWS

(bayt baws; Beit Baws)

The easternmost of the villages, Bayt Baws, is seven km from Hadda and is the mountaintop village closest to San'a. On top of a small (by Yemeni standards) rocky outcrop, the village is of ancient origin, as the Sabaean inscriptions on a stone near the village gate testify. A small cistern beneath the far side of the village once served as the sole water reservoir, but today, water is carried up by the motorised pumps that are now so common in Yemeni villages.

On the San'a side of the village, near the fields in which the villagers work, there is a newer subvillage with a new school building. Schools and water pumps are ubiquitous in the Yemeni countryside, demonstrating the government's firm intention to preserve the vitality of rural regions and to prevent the movement of the rural population from villages to towns and cities.

However, the people of Bayt Baws did not appreciate the government-donated water pipes and have all but deserted their mountaintop settlement and moved down to the new village.

San'a Province

The Province of San'a is the largest in the northern part of Yemen, stretching from as far south as Kusma, between Dhamar and Bayt al-Faqih, to as far north as Suq al-'Inan, east of Sa'da. A highland province, it has large cultivated plateaus at an altitude of more than 2000 metres and desolate mountains of more than 3000 metres. By the main roads to the west and north, there are a few towns and villages of interest; visits to these can be easily combined with tours to more distant destinations.

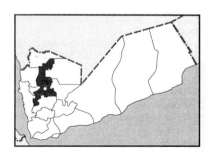

JABAL AN-NABI SHU'AYB
(jabal an-nabi: shu'ayb; Dzebel Nabi Shoeib)
The highest mountain in Yemen (actually, in the entire Arabian Peninsula), is the 3660-metre Jabal an-Nabi Shu'ayb, which stands a mere 30 km from San'a as the crow flies. To visit the mountain, take a bus or a taxi heading west from San'a along the old al-Hudayda Rd to the small village of Matna, 25 km away. From there a dirt road leads up to the mountain, branching several times to reach the small villages scattered around the south-eastern slopes.

Further along the al-Hudayda road, before the small Thursday market of Suq Baw'an, 34 km from San'a, another scenic road branches off to the right. The road winds 18 km along the western slopes of Jabal an-Nabi Shu'ayb to reach al-'Urr, a village with a Tuesday market.

MANAKHA
(mana:kha; Manakhah)
In the Haraz Mountains 90 km to the west of San'a stands the proud mountain village of Manakha, at an altitude of 2200 metres. The centre of the intensely cultivated terraced countryside and benefiting from ample monsoon rains gathered by the western mountains, Manakha is an important market town for villages on the surrounding mountain slopes.

The village had a strategic location during the Ottoman occupation of Yemen; from here it was possible to protect the supply lines between San'a and al-Hudayda, in the Tihama. The Turks installed their cannons in the mountains and effectively blocked the lower roads.

For today's occupiers, Western backpackers, Manakha is an excellent base for trekking. Small villages and hamlets lie scattered everywhere between the terraces that extend across the steepest slopes. Many visitors have suggested that the majestic spirit of the mountains can be felt more intensely in Manakha than anywhere else in Yemen.

Places to Stay
There is an old-style no-sheet hotel in a traditional Manakhan house. This place is frequented by Western tour groups and its prices may be high, varying according to the season (and the customer?) from YR 350 to YR 750 per person (check the price beforehand). You might want to try bargaining if it is a quiet day.

Just by the entrance of the village, on the right-hand side, next to the gas station, is another hotel. It is owned by the same family and the prices are similar.

The *Manakha Tourist Hotel* is a newish establishment with beautiful stained-glass windows and plastered walls, built by Jewish

Trekking in the Province of San'a

Short Treks The Ismaili villages with their decorated houses provide a wonderful area for trekking; al-Khutayb, the most important place of pilgrimage for members of the small sect, lies only about five km downhill, south-southeast from Manakha. To reach it, walk through Manakha and follow the southbound road on the eastern side of the town; keep asking the locals for the right route. The roads, tracks and footpaths uphill to the west lead to other picturesque villages which overlook al-Khutayb and Manakha itself. From al-Kahil a steep footpath leads back to Manakha. Jabal Shibam, the highest peak of the Haraz region at almost 3000 metres, stands to the south of Manakha, a couple of km south-west from al-Khutayb.

The Haraz region is full of old fortified villages built on hilltops. One of the finest examples, the tightly built al-Hajjara, is five km south-west of Manakha. Take the road that branches from the western side of town, in front of the Manakha Hotel. The four and five-storey stone houses of al-Hajjara can already be spotted in the distance. The village, dating to the 12th century AD, served as an important fortification during the Turkish occupations of Yemen. Continuing another five km to the west brings you to Jabal Masar (jabal masa:r) and exposes you to several more fine villages in the area.

Long Treks If you came to the Yemen with trekking in mind and with plenty of time and appropriate survival facilities (such as tent, compass, water purifier, suitable shoes and clothes), you might consider leaving Manakha on foot for a trek of several days. This is a challenge: no maps exist, paths are not marked and the locals can't understand why you are walking, showing you the way to the nearest taxi route instead of the village you are seeking. Be prepared to get lost, and make sure you carry enough food and water (you will drink at least seven litres a day, depending on the time of year).

One possibility is to go south from Jabal Shibam or from al-Hajjara, reaching the village of al-'Urr in a few hours, then turning westwards and following the road by a small wadi. Walking for a couple of days through the green landscape, with its many small villages, will eventually bring you to a suq village called 'Ubal ('uba:l), by Wadi Siham and the Ma'bar to Bajil highway. Here you have a choice of directions: either back to the highlands or onward to the Tihama. By now you have descended almost 2000 metres from Manakha.

On the other hand, you might want to leave Manakha for the north, with al-Mahwit as your destination. This can best be done from Khamis bani Sa'd, 45 km west from al-Maghraba (see al-Mahwit). A much less frequented and much harder route directly north from al-Maghraba to ar-Rujum by the at-Tawila to al-Mahwit road will take several days (or more) and will give you plenty of chances to get lost in this fascinating land. Recommended for only the most experienced trekkers, the route takes you along Wadi Day'an down to Wadi Surdud (wa:di: surdu:d), a descent of 1000 metres from al-Maghraba. Continuing south-west along the wadi takes you to Khamis bani Sa'd; to the north-east, along Wadi Ahjar, is Shibam. Heading in a northerly direction along one of the wadi's side valleys, you will eventually end up somewhere by the at-Tawila to al-Mahwit road, exhausted. Sorry, no reliable maps are available.

Warning The Ismaili sect keeps many holy shrines and tombs in the villages of the Haraz Mountains and the nearby al-Haima region. In early 1995 religious Zaydi zealots attacked many of these sites, bombing and destroying the shrines. In one particularly ghastly incident the bones of Idris Bin Hassan Imadul Din al-Qurashi, a holy man buried some six hundred years ago in the village of Shibam in Haraz, were dug out and the adjoining shrine was destroyed. The tensions that built up in the region will no doubt be over once you arrive, but it might still be a good idea to enquire about the present security situation before setting afoot. ■

craftsmen from Sa'da. Prices are YR 350 per bed.

For rock-bottom prices it's better to stay in the small no-sign funduq in al-Maghraba, on the San'a to al-Hudayda road. A night in one of their dormitories costs just YR 300.

A very pleasant alternative is to spend one night in *al-Hajjara Hotel* in al-Hajjara. This village receives less tourists than Manakha and at YR 350 for a bed in a beautiful dormitory, the place is a steal; good, cheap meals are also available.

Getting There & Away

Manakha is only a few km from the old San'a to al-Hudayda road, so it is well served by the buses and taxis operating on that route. An excursion from San'a to Manakha takes at least two days, so you might want to make a detour to the town when travelling from one end of the highway to the other.

Buses and taxis to al-Hudayda leave from Bab al-Yaman in San'a; buy a ticket to the village of al-Maghraba (82 km from San'a), a small roadside market where buses and taxis usually stop for lunch. The fare to al-Maghraba is YR 180 by bus; a taxi may want to charge you all the way to al-Hudayda, expecting to get no new customers from al-Maghraba.

From al-Maghraba, a six-km road takes you up to Manakha. Local taxis charge YR 60 for the ride, but if you don't plan to do extensive trekking in the region, walking the distance will provide you with some of the finest photo opportunities of your visit. The not-too-distant village to the west, al-Hajra, is a former market site on the old San'a to al-Hudayda road.

Getting away may involve a long wait for a taxi in al-Maghraba. A better alternative is to take the San'a or al-Hudayda bus. For schedules, remember that al-Maghraba is about halfway between these two cities.

'AMRAN

('amra:n; Amran)

'Amran is a walled town in the middle of fields, 50 km north-west of San'a. It is on the San'a to Sa'da highway, where the modern Hajja road heads west. The fields by the junction were completely built over in recent times, so you only see the modern suburbs of 'Amran unless you get out of the car.

A visit to the old part of the town is well worth it, especially on Friday, 'Amran's market day. The town has mixed stone and clay architecture; ground floors are often built only of stone, higher floors are made of clay bricks and mud, and roof parapets have raised corners. The appearance of the houses is similar to the San'a tower houses, although they are more modest and have features bor-rowed from the eastern Bani Husaysh style. Some houses have stones with pre-Islamic inscriptions.

'Amran's town wall is made of stone, exceptional in this area of mud architecture. The old suq of 'Amran is also noteworthy because of its round stone columns support-ing a roof above the shops. The construction is similar to that found in the market of Kuhlan. The original market is today dwarfed by the roadside market on the Hajja road.

Places to Stay

You are unlikely to stay overnight in 'Amran, however, there is some very modest accommodation on the highway.

Getting There & Away

'Amran is best visited while travelling to see Hajja to the west or Sa'da to the north. Buses to 'Amran leave San'a from Bab ash-Sha'ub. Brown-striped taxis have their base in Hasaba, by the airport road, and charge YR 100 per seat.

RAYDA

(rayda; Raidah)

The old Tuesday market of Rayda is 22 km north of 'Amran. Buses and taxis to Sa'da may stop here for cigarettes, qat or water. Rayda is interesting mainly because it is an excellent example of how traditional tribal rule is alive and well in Yemeni society. In 1979 Bayt Harash, a new market village with modern facilities, was built just two km off the road to the east. Bayt Harash also func-tions as a Tuesday market, and contrary to expectation, both markets continue to prosper. The explanation is that the market in Rayda is controlled by the Bakils, while Bayt Harash was founded by Hashid tribes. Despite the apparently bold leap the Yemenis have taken into the 20th century, the old set of values continues to govern their thinking.

DHI BIN

(dhi: bi:n)

Thirty km along the dirt road to the north-east from Rayda, you will arrive in the

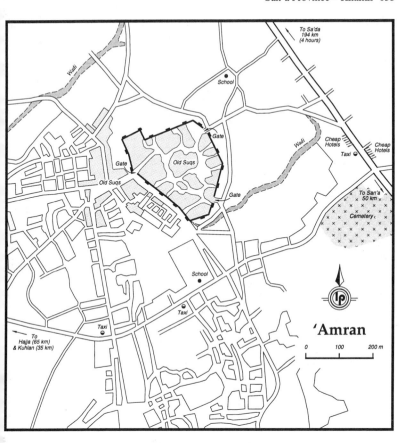

village of Dhi Bin, famed for its 13th-century mosque. A few hundred metres before the village, a steep path ascends to the beautiful mountain village of Dhafar and to the ruins of an ancient fortification. The extent of the ruins is huge, second only to that of Baraqish in al-Jawf, but very little is known about the history of Dhafar. Excavations started in the late 1980s and should shed some light on the site's past.

Although the mosque has been depicted on a postcard published by the General Tourism Corporation of San'a and the Dhafar fort ruins are among the most impressive to see, the place is not officially recommended to visitors due to security problems. At the time of research it was possible to visit the place by hiring a car (with driver) from a tour company, for YR 8000 or so per day.

KHAMIR
(khami:r)

Khamir is another small market town in the heartlands of the tribal region. It's on the San'a to Sa'da highway, 22 km north of Rayda. Market day is Sunday.

HUTH

(Hu:th)

Huth, the biggest town between 'Amran and Sa'da, has a Friday market and some very modest hotels waiting for misscheduled travellers arriving from Shihara (see the Hajja section in the Hajja chapter) in the dead of night. Huth is 118 km from San'a and 120 km from Sa'da.

SUQ AL-'INAN

(su:q al-'ina:n)

Suq al-'Inan is a village in the Barat Mountains, remarkable for its distinctive architectural style. Houses are built of mud, using the zabur technique common in Sa'da, even though stone is plentiful in the region. The main ornamental effect comes from the striking use of colour, with broad stripes of red and yellow ochre alternating in the facades and round the windows, where white plastering is also used. (You may have already glimpsed a few such houses north of Huth from the main road to Sa'da.) Suq al-'Inan has a Monday market.

Getting There & Away

The bad news about Suq al-'Inan is that you won't see it: visiting it on your own would be very difficult. No shared taxis are available in this most sparsely populated region and the local inhabitants tend to be surly towards strangers. Not even tour operators are willing to risk driving you there.

Should things change, getting to Suq al-'Inan would involve a 36-km drive from Huth in the direction of Sa'da, arriving in the village of al-Harf. From there, a very stony path leads north-east to Suq al-'Inan (65 km).

Al-Mahwit

Although the Province of al-Mahwit, north-west of San'a and south of Hajja, has the smallest area of all the North Yemeni provinces, it has several places that are worth visiting. The age-old twin towns of Shibam and Kawkaban are on the agenda of any ready-made tour of Yemen. So are the towns of at-Tawila and al-Mahwit, important marketplaces of the highlands, although they can't boast a glorious history.

The stone architecture of the province is related to that of Thilla, east of Shibam. Stone decorations include friezes, inlays and carefully worked-out openings; large, beautiful windows are set very low, almost at floor level. The windows are often surrounded by two narrow takhrims, very typical of this area.

Al-Mahwit is also one of Yemen's most beautiful mountain provinces and its many villages and paths make the area excellent for trekking. The inhabitants of the region are among the most friendly in Yemen and are used to backpackers. The many paths and small roads link the towns to each other and to the neighbouring provinces; an intrepid traveller could walk from at-Tawila to Hajja, for example, in a few days.

This is a fast-developing area and the newly asphalted road that leads from Shibam to al-Mahwit provides good connections from San'a. A legacy from the centuries gone is thriving in al-Mahwit: this is one of the most famous coffee growing regions in the country.

SHIBAM
(shiba:m)
Yes, there is another Shibam in Yemen: the Shibam in the Hadhramawt valley, a town famous for its extraordinary skyscraper architecture. The Shibam of al-Mahwit in the north is a smaller town with a less arresting appearance but with quite a past. It stands on the edge of the San'a basin, and Jabal Kawkaban, a mountain with a large flat

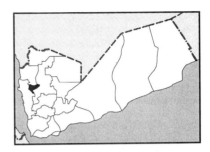

summit, starts its steep ascent just behind the town, rising from 2500 metres to 2850 metres.

The town is worth a visit mainly because of its dramatic location and its lively Friday market.

History
Shibam was an inhabited area well before Islam came to Yemen. During the 1st century AD it served as a capital, not of Yemen but of a small and short-lived independent

---

The Historic Fart
Shibam has the honour of being the only place in Yemen to host a tale from the *Thousand and One Nights*.

In the tale, a man fouls up his wedding ceremony by letting out a tumultuous fart at the peak of the festivity. In utmost shame, the man flees the scene, riding his horse all the way to India and finally settling there. Years later he decides to put an end to his exile and returns home to Yemen. On the outskirts of his adored village, he dismounts by a house and happens to overhear a conversation through a window. A young girl asks her mother about her age and is told that she was born 'on the day of Husayn's historic fart'. Facing the horror of the fact that his fart will never be forgotten or forgiven, the man mounts his horse and rides away, this time for ever. ■

'state'; these states were common in the highlands when the Kingdom of Saba was weakening and the Himyarite state, with its capital, Dhafar, was rising. Both Sabaean and Himyarite inscriptions can be found on stones reused in the city gate of Shibam, in the mosque and in other older constructions; you may be able to spot a few. Some stone pillars in the old market area are of Sabaean origin.

From 845 AD to 1004 AD Shibam was again the capital, this time of much of the highlands, when the Bani Ya'fur dynasty ruled here. They built the Shibam mosque on the site of a Himyarite temple.

Places to Stay

Many travellers have enjoyed the basic no-sheet *Funduq Hanida*, where you can overnight in traditional Yemeni style at varying prices (YR 200 to YR 600 or more) To find the funduq, walk down the at-Tawila road from the central market square until you see a small arch, some 30 metres on your right. Go through the arch and you will find the modern-looking house directly in front of you.

Getting There & Away

Black-striped taxis shuttle to Shibam from San'a. The taxi station is in Matbah, northwest of San'a, by the start of the Wadi Dhahr and al-Mahwit roads. The fare is YR 100 per person, and the 45-km drive takes about one hour.

KAWKABAN

(kawkaba:n; Koukaban)

If you don't feel like trekking and climbing mountains, preferring cosy hotel rooms and guided half-day tours instead, Kawkaban is *the* place in Yemen to visit for a taste of the Yemeni passion for building villages on the most inaccessible mountainsides. Here you can enjoy the country from an eagle's point of view.

Kawkaban, on top of Jabal Kawkaban, which shadows Shibam, was built to serve as Shibam's fortification. During crises, the inhabitants were evacuated to the fortress.

Several water cisterns carved out of the rock collected water during the rainy seasons and grain silos were filled during the years of peace, so the population was able to survive a crisis of almost any length. The door of the town's only gate is still closed and locked each night.

The only way up – the steep path winding its way from Shibam – was easily defended; many an attacker found their sophisticated guns useless against Yemenis throwing rocks down from the cliffs. It was only during the civil war of the 1960s that Kawkaban was defeated, like many of Yemen's other famous mountain fortresses. Most of its buildings were then bombed from aeroplanes, so today the town is partly in ruins.

From the edge of the cliff there is, besides the sheer 350-metre drop, a very good view over the vast fields below. Far to the left (north), a mountain is visible; the low-lying town of Thilla and its mountain fortress are nine km from Shibam and are heartily recommended for a visit (see Thilla in the San'a chapter). On the southern horizon, you may be able to see the peak of Jabal an-Nabi Shu'ayb, the highest mountain in Yemen at 3660 metres.

Places to Stay & Eat

The *Hotel Jabal Kawkaban* and *Kawkaban Hotel* stand side by side in the north-east part of the village. Entering the main gate, head straight through the village, past the market area along the alley of shop huts of stone, then across the even top of the mountain.

These old-style Yemeni tower houses offer charming no-sheet accommodation for tourists. The former is a very basic and rather filthy, and charges an outrageous YR 1200 for a double with a cold common shower. The latter is used by many tour organisers and apparently adjusts their prices according to demand. We were quoted YR 750 for a cleaner room, and hot water was available in the common shower. In any case, the prices include an outrageous scenery tax.

The Kawkaban Hotel has a reasonably good restaurant where you can get tasty Yemeni food at reasonable prices.

Trekking in the Province of Al-Mahwit

The province of al-Mahwit is arguably the best place to trek in Yemen. The distances are not overwhelming, the mountain scenes are breathtaking and the people are among the friendliest in the country. Many trekking routes will take you to or from a neighbouring province in just a few days. Plan your trek carefully; don't rush in unprepared, seduced by the beautiful scenery. Stock up on food and water and bring along a tent. Lastly, don't underestimate the difficulty of some routes.

From al-Mahwit or at-Tawila, it is possible to head north towards Hajja and Kuhlan (see Hajja), crossing the westwards-flowing Wadi La'a on the way. The adventurous will find countless unmapped footpaths and dirt roads here. A good halfway destination is the 3240-metre Jabal Maswar, some 35 km south-east of al-Mahwit. Extraordinarily beautiful terraces abound on the slopes of the mountain. To the east of the mountain, almost directly north of at-Tawila (some 20 km), is a village called Bayt 'Adhaqa.

From here you can continue north-west to Hajja or north to Kuhlan, still using small footpaths. Or, if you prefer the luxury of a Toyota, you may opt for the eastbound dirt road to 'Amran, joining with the 'Amran to Kuhlan asphalt road after 17 km, halfway between the towns.

Still another possibility is the very scenic southern road east from Bayt 'Adhaqa, leading all the way to Thilla, 31 km away (see the San'a Province chapter).

Alternative routes to al-Mahwit from the San'a to al-Hudayda road have already been mentioned (see also Manakha). Twenty-six km from al-Mahwit, on the road to Khamis bani Sa'd, the road forks; the right-hand branch winds its way along the northern slopes of Jabal Hufash and the Jabal Milhan mountains, eventually connecting with the at-Tur to Dayr Dukhna road in the at-Tur basin. This is a very long alternative route to the northern Tihama (130 km from al-Mahwit to Dayr Dukhna). ∎

Getting There & Away

The walk from Shibam to Kawkaban takes at least one hour – probably longer because you'll stop every now and then to admire the majestic scenery. Take a good stock of film. The footpath is paved and easy to walk, though somewhat steep; it starts from behind the big mosque.

There is hardly a village in Yemen that is not served by 4WD Toyotas, and Kawkaban is no exception. There is now an asphalted road which starts from Shibam and goes round the mountain but it's not a very scenic route. However, the road has saved the village from desertion – like many other mountain-top villages, Kawkaban was gradually being deserted as its inhabitants moved down to more conveniently accessible quarters. (There is a second footpath up, leaving this road halfway to Kawkaban and offering an alternative walking route.)

AT-TAWILA

(at-tawi:la; at-Taweelah)
At-Tawila is a smallish town built beside a short ridge of mountains facing south, the houses framed by majestic boulders. Stretched along the slope, the old town is squeezed between the road and the mountain wall, having perhaps earned its name from this feature (tawila means long). Newer suburbs have also spread down to the other side of the road.

A walk on the steep mountain paths above the town offers a good view over at-Tawila and a glimpse of the other valley behind those huge rocks. The four peaks from west to east are al-Mahdhur, al-Munqur, ash-Shamsan and al-Husn; al-Qarani is further to the north-east. There are old fortifications on most of these peaks but they are inaccessible because of military restrictions.

Places to Stay

There are a couple of modest hotels near the at-Tawila taxi station. The one-sheet as-Sala:m Hotel (spelt Alsslam on the sign) has doubles for YR 500; a no-name no-sheet place across the square charges YR 300.

Getting There & Away

At-Tawila is easily reached from Shibam in

a shared taxi (YR 100, 1¼ hours) or from San'a (YR 160, 2¼ hours). Walking the 29 km from Shibam to at-Tawila is highly recommended; between the towns, the road rises to mountains well over 3000 metres high. Around at-Tawila there are plenty of small villages and cultivated terraces with shade trees, rare elsewhere in Yemen.

AL-MAHWIT
(al-maHwi:t; al-Mahweet)

Al-Mahwit is the larger of the province's two towns. It is a beautiful mountain town, with the oldest houses atop the central hills and the new settlement spilling down the slopes. Splendid views over the valleys are often obscured by clouds in the rainy season. The mountains around al-Mahwit are just as beautiful as those of the Haraz region around Manakha.

Places to Stay

Al-Mahwit has a few old-style no-sheet hotels with no signs outside. Ask the locals, they will be all too eager to find you a place to stay. Prices are around YR 350 a bed per night in double rooms. *Funduq an-Nil* at the western end of the market area offers beds in a dormitory for about YR 350 – watch out for fleas. There's a new hotel by the main road passing by al-Mahwit, close to the market area, just one block downhill from Funduq an-Nil; rooms cost from YR 1500 to YR 2000.

Getting There & Away

The road from Shibam to at-Tawila continues along an agricultural valley, passes by the small Monday market of ar-Rujum and climbs the slopes of the al-Mahwit mountain, eventually reaching al-Mahwit. The taxi fare for the 26-km ride from Shibam is YR 160 per person, and from San'a, YR 240.

The province also has a narrow projection to the south of al-Mahwit, extending all the way to the San'a to al-Hudayda road, where a small Thursday market village, Khamis bani Sa'd, marks the beginning of the dirt road to al-Mahwit. No taxis serve this route but it is possible to get a ride on the platform of a Toyota. Allocate at least five or six hours (two days if you are on foot) for the 60-km ride; vehicles use the Wadi Sari' as the road, then pass by the Friday market of Juma'a Sari' and start the long ascent to al-Mahwit. The slopes are a perfect example of rural Yemeni landscape – all are terraced and under intense cultivation, with small hamlets scattered everywhere.

Hajja

The Province of Hajja, north-west of San'a and al-Mahwit, is an oddity on the Yemeni map. It is quite a large province, stretching from Yemen's highest mountains to the northern Tihama. The country's road network traverses Hajja in several directions; however, the different parts of the province have little in common, and to get from one town to another, you often have to leave the province and re-enter it by another road.

For a traveller, the most interesting places to visit are Hajja, the provincial capital and Shihara, an extraordinary mountain village in the northern part of the province. The northern Tihama rarely sees tourists other than the few who enter the country by land from Saudi Arabia.

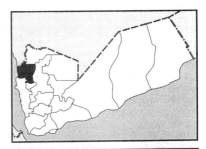

HAJJA
(hajja; Hajjah, Haddzhah, Haggah)
Hajja is a modern town of 50,000 inhabitants, boasting one of the very first traffic lights in Yemen. The town is on top of a mountain; indeed, several peaks are completely built over. It has relatively few attractions; a small market area and some mosques are not enough to draw masses of tourists to the town. Instead, people come to see the environs of the town – countless villages on the tops and slopes of the terraced mountains in the heart of the Yemeni highlands. The Hajja road alone makes a trip to Hajja worthwhile, even if you just take the next taxi back.

Despite its modern outlook, Hajja is an old settlement, first mentioned in historical documents from the 14th and 15th centuries AD. Once the town briefly served as the capital of the Zaydi state. Hajja owes its importance to its strategic location, from which it has been possible to control vast areas of the heavily cultivated and populous mountainous Tihama area in the at-Tur basin by Wadi Mawr.

The inhabitants of Hajja have paid dearly

The bridge of Shihara

for this privilege in the course of history; during the Turkish occupation of Yemen, this Zaydi stronghold was often defeated, although the Turks also put a great deal of effort into developing the town. During the late years of the imamate, Hajja was both a stronghold of the dynasty as well as an activity centre for dissenters, so it is no wonder that the town was heavily bombarded during the civil war of the 1960s. Most of the city has been built since the revolution of 1962.

The Turks started building the al-Kwal'a citadel on top of Hajja's highest peak, and it later served the Zaydi imams while the country was not occupied. The imamic rule depended heavily on the custom of taking hostages from rebelling tribes, so the citadel has large underground prisons. Some older houses feature decorations in the Turkish style, while new houses sport some very bold colour combinations on their facades, unique in Yemen.

The al-Hawra Mosque was built in the final phases of the Turkish occupation, completed in 1907 AD. With no domes and a minaret only nine metres high, it is uncharacteristic of an Ottoman mosque. The mosque has both a male and female section.

Hajja offers a reasonable variety of accommodation, so it is a feasible base for trekking in the vicinity.

Places to Stay – bottom end

There are a couple of very modest hotels near the central taxi station, with no signs. Coming from the direction of San'a, from the central junction take the next street on your right and ask anybody for *mumkin funduq rakhi:s*. The hotels offer doubles to quadruples for YR 270 per bed, with no sheets or one very dirty sheet. There are shared bathrooms in the corridor but no shower or hot water.

Places to Stay – middle

Hajja Tourist Hotel (or Funduq Hajja Siyaha) (☎ 220196) is a satisfactory two-sheet hotel built in modern Yemeni style to European standards. It belongs in the upper-middle class (or, in Yemen, the lower-deluxe class), offering very clean doubles in the YR 600 to YR 900 price range. The private bathrooms have hot water and showers that work, and there is a restaurant in the hotel.

The hotel is out from the centre of the town, 20 minutes' walk from the central taxi station. From the central crossroads, take the road uphill (coming from San'a, to the left). The winding road climbs and then drops, going round the mosque, an old cistern and a school. There are a few crossroads; ask the locals for directions. The hotel has been closed a couple of times in the past few years, apparently due to low season, so ask somebody before starting out.

Places to Stay – top end

Funduq Ghamdan Hajja (or Ghamdan Hotel Hajah) (☎ 220420) stands on top of the hill to the west of central Hajja; you can walk there in 10 minutes from the central crossroads (coming from San'a, to the right). The Ghamdan offers doubles for YR 1400 or so.

Getting There & Away

Hajja is easily reached from San'a on the asphalt road. Buses don't currently serve the town, but taxis leave from Hasaba, at the junction of the airport and Sa'da roads, and cost YR 340. The 115-km ride takes from 2½ to three hours.

This road offers spectacular views, especially the 65-km stretch between 'Amran and Hajja. The road first climbs to an altitude of 2800 metres, slowly ascending through terraced slopes. By the time you reach the outskirts of the 'Amran basin, some of the worst effects of the oil boom in the Middle East are evident – the labour force was drained from the Yemeni countryside, to work on construction projects in Saudi Arabia and the Gulf States, which left terraces untended. After just a couple of years of neglect, heavy rains had washed the fertile soil from the terraces, exposing the stones and leaving the form of the terraces visible.

After crossing the highest pass, the road descends in steep serpentines all the way down to Wadi Sharas, a mere 1000 metres above sea level. This descent of almost two km provides quite a variety of climates, scenery, vegetation and plantations. The Chinese-built road itself warrants a second look; this remarkable feat of engineering is marked by a small observation platform near the village of Kuhlan. Here you can stop to admire the harmonious alignment and construction of the road.

In Suq Sharas, there is a small Sunday market built where the road crosses the river at the bottom of the valley where you can enjoy the striking contrast between Yemeni and Chinese aesthetics – a Chinese pavilion stands in the midst of the shopkeepers' modern tin shacks.

After crossing the wadi, the road again ascends to Hajja, 1700 metres above sea level.

Until the 'Amran-Hajja road was built, the only route traversable by car was the dirt road from Dayr Dukhna on the Tihama highway, and this road still offers an interesting alternative (see Around al-Hudayda in the al-Hudayda chapter). The road is still bad, but will probably be tarred in the next couple of years. The taxi fare between al-Hudayda and Dayr Dukhna is YR 200, plus another YR 200 to al-Hudayda.

KUHLAN
(kuHla:n; Kohlan)

Halfway between 'Amran and Hajja, just after the observation platform, there are a couple of crossings to the right (northern) side of the road. The signs read 'Hesn Kohlan'. This small mountain-top village is well worth visiting and is highly recommended for those on a tight schedule as it is easily accessible – the roads are good and the village is just behind the mountain.

Kuhlan is a very good example of a Yemeni mountain village. It is built on a slope so steep that the ground floor of one house is above the roof of the next. Monday, market day, is the best day to visit; the road nearer Hajja leads directly to the suq. The shops are framed by porticoes with stone columns, similar in style to those you can find in the suq of 'Amran.

A climb to the top of the mountain involves following serpentine paths through or around the village. The citadel on top of the mountain is for government use and cannot be entered. The path to the left of it leads over the mountain and back to the Hajja road.

SHIHARA
(shiha:ra; Shaharah)

Shihara is one of the most famous mountain fortress villages in Yemen. Situated on top of the 2600-metre Shihara mountain in an area otherwise averaging an altitude of 1500 metres, the almost inaccessible village of Shihara has long been a base for armed conflict. During bygone centuries it served more than once as an asylum for the Zaydi imams when foreign occupiers threatened their power. The inhabitants of the village have always been suspicious of strangers and eager to defend themselves to the very end if needed. Even today visitors find the Shiharans among the most reserved of Yemenis.

During the 16th and 17th centuries Shihara played an important role as a base for resistance to the Ottoman Turks, who occupied most of the Yemeni highlands at various times. The defence, led by Imam Qasim al-Mansur Bi-llah and completed by his son Imam Mu'ayyid in 1635, was largely conducted from Shihara. The fierce battles of this conflict caused so many casualties among the occupying forces that Yemen came to be known as 'the grave of the Turks'. During the second Turkish occupation in the 1800s and early 1900s, Shihara remained the western landmark of the area of 'independent tribes' on Turkish maps of Yemen.

During the civil war of the 1960s, Shihara again served as a headquarters, this time for the Royalists in their struggle against the Republicans. This time, however, new technologies of warfare brought defeat to Shihara for the first time – the Republicans used their air strength to heavily bombard the village, inflicting severe damage. Houses that collapsed in the air raids can still be seen today, although many have been rebuilt in traditional style.

The architecture of Shihara does not favour abundant decoration. The stone houses have up to five storeys but feature little more than dented friezes and a few small round or cruciform openings above the upper facade windows. White plastering is often used around the windows, splashed from inside with little care. Here you can find perfect examples of original, almost archaic, Yemeni mountain architecture.

Shihara has plenty of water cisterns, dug in amphitheatre form deep into the rock. By one count, there are 23 water cisterns; one of the biggest is in the centre of the village, near the mosque. These cisterns were built during the first Ottoman occupation so that the inhabitants would be able to survive the dry season while besieged by the enemy.

The village actually consists of two parts, located on neighbouring mountain peaks. They are connected over a 300-metre deep gorge by a stone bridge, a remarkable feat of early 17th-century engineering. The bridge construction plans, prepared by famous architect Salah al-Yamani, called for three separate arches, one on top of another, but only the topmost arch remains today.

Places to Stay

The price of an overnight stay in one of the no-sheet dormitories at *Funduq Shihara* varies greatly. Some people tell stories about staying there for YR 300, while others have been charged YR 900 per person. This old-style Shiharan stone house is principally used by tour groups yearning for the 'exotic', so the prices have been inflated. With no tap water in the bathroom, YR 300 would seem about right but foreigners tend to get over-charged for any service around Shihara. Why complain? Tea and simple food are available.

The only other accommodation around Shihara is that offered by people who serve tourists privately. Take care – you could be badly overcharged. Although some travellers tell of the hospitality they received from Shiharan families, this is not the general rule. In al-Qabai, for example, there is a house claiming (rather fancifully) to be a funduq. It charges around YR 600 per person for a roof, four walls and earthen floor – nothing else. The nearest modest hotels are in Huth.

Getting There & Away

Shihara is one of the few places in Yemen to have been spoiled by excessive tourism. As recently as the mid-1980s, Shihara was something of a challenge for independent travellers, being one of the hardest places to reach on your own. Today the thrill is all but gone, replaced by compulsory spending. During the tourist 'boom' of the late 1980s the Shiharans converted their hostility and suspicion towards strangers into greed for the travellers' seemingly plentiful money. A few years ago official regulations required all tourists visiting Shihara to use a tour operator. Although such regulations no more apply, most visitors still choose this option. San'a tour operators will provide you with a car and driver for US$80 to US$100 a day. Local transport is in short supply and not much cheaper.

Although Shihara is only 163 km from San'a, you still need a full day to reach it and another day to get back, plus the time you spend there. After 118 km you reach Huth, a smallish town by the San'a to Sa'da highway and 120 km from Sa'da. It is only 45 km from Huth to Shihara but, as road conditions are rather bad here, the journey to the foothills of the Shihara mountain may easily take a few hours.

Eighteen km west of Huth along a stony, bumpy mountain road is al-Ashsha, a small village with a few grocery shops. Continuing along the fertile, subtropical Wadi al-Wa'ar, past the date, banana and papaya plantations, you come to the tin shacks of Suq al-Ahad, 12 km south-west of al-Ashsha. This Sunday market serves the surrounding rural area.

The village of al-Qabai, at the foot of Jabal Shihara, is 15 km west of Suq al-Ahad. From al-Qabai the 1400-metre ascent to Jabal Shihara (2600 metres) begins: it's a very steep road and a very unpleasant drive.

The locals will force a car change at al-Qabai. The San'a tour operators are not allowed to drive you to the top of the mountain, so you have to hire a local car for the staggering sum of about YR 7000. This fee is charged for every car load arriving from San'a – if you have hired a car for a small group and happen to meet up with another group here, you can't team up to fill one Shiharan 4WD. Two cars arriving from

San'a means two Shiharan Toyotas climbing the mountain, even if each vehicle is carrying just one tourist!

The better option is to walk up, enjoying the extraordinary views from the terraced and qat-growing slopes of the mountain. However, you need to be in excellent physical shape to do this because the trip will take at least five to seven hours. Walking all the way to the top will vividly demonstrate to you why the Turks were not able to conquer the village on top of the mountain!

There are four small villages by the road. Immediately after the third of them, Hababa, the road branches. The road to the right is a very steep path and leads straight to the smaller part of Shihara. The famous bridge that joins this part of Shihara to the main village can already be sighted from near the junction. The left-hand fork is easier but longer; it winds around the mountain and passes the Thursday market of Suq al-Khamis, yet another village of tin shacks. Here the road branches, with the right-hand path starting the final ascent to Shihara through the Bab an-Nakhla gate.

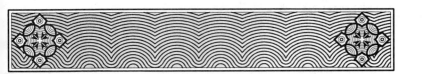

Sa'da

Sa'da, Yemen's northernmost province, deserves respect. Its capital, the town of Sa'da, is the birthplace of Zaydism, the most powerful spiritual school of Islamic thought in Yemen. The province provides a home for numerous mountain tribes still clinging to their independent status – in the 1960s, during the civil war in the YAR, the proud tribes of Sa'da were the last to drop their weapons and accept Republican rule in the new state. It was also here that the 1990 unification of the Yemens faced its most stubborn resistance.

The province's northern border with Saudi Arabia is largely undemarcated, while to the east, the province merges into the sands of ar-Ruba' al-Khali, the vast Arabian desert. Saudi influence, both good and bad, has been visible here throughout the history of independent Yemen. In quiet times, the Saudis have actively smuggled consumer goods across the border; in restless times they have provided weapons and ideological support to Yemeni internal resistance.

Most visitors to Yemen come to Sa'da, though some, after visiting other parts of Yemen, are not particularly impressed with Sa'da. For them, it is just another old town with Toyotas and Peugeots cramming its streets. The province is relatively sparsely populated and most of its villages are in the mountains west of Sa'da, where tourists don't go; the highway steers you through the desolate plateaus of Yemen to the town of Sa'da and back again.

Nevertheless, Sa'da is a place worth visiting. Here you can appreciate the solemn traditions of an ancient town that has been abruptly thrown into the late 20th century. Sa'da also has a distinctively original architectural style, which is striving to survive the introduction of concrete and tin.

Small things mean a lot: the lone young soldier walking towards us on top of the city wall, stopping and gesturing for a photo with his kalashnikov, didn't utter a word – he just nodded his thanks and hurried past after the click of the shutter. He left us more than a

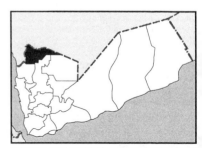

Village on the outskirts of Sa'da

memory on film; his actions carried a culture spanning 1000 years.

SA'DA
(sa'da; Sadah, Saadah)
The city of Sa'da was originally walled and stood in the midst of fields. Sa'da is still a walled city, but is now surrounded by

146

suburbs as well as fields. Although it was badly damaged during the civil war of the 1960s and the city wall was broken in the 1970s to make way for motor vehicles, much of the original town is still intact. The few startlingly modern government houses built next to the city wall seem quite out of place.

History

In Sa'da, as elsewhere in the country, Yemenis are eager to point out that their town was inhabited before the arrival of Islam. Located halfway between the cities of Ma'in (to the south-east) and Najran (to the north), near the beginning of Wadi Najran and in the midst of a basin 35 km long, Sa'da must have been an excellent stopping place for camel caravans on the incense road. But those days have left little behind.

The first written account of Sa'da town dates back to the 10th century AD, when the famous Yemeni historian and geographer al-Hamdani included it in his description of South Arabia. By that time, Sa'da was already important because of the introduction of Zaydism at the end of the previous century.

In 901 AD, Yahya bin Husayn bin Qasim ar-Rassi (an outsider from Basra, Iraq) proclaimed himself the imam and made Sa'da his capital. He was a highly religious man, representing the Shi'a sect of Islam, and had spent years in Madina learning the teachings of Zayd ibn 'Ali (697 to 740 AD) – hence the name Zaydism. Yahya had been called to Sa'da from Madina in 892 to mediate between warring Hashid and Bakil tribes; at first he refused but, in 897, he returned and settled the quarrel most successfully, eventually founding a unified state and becoming its head. He was to be known as 'al-Hadi ila-l-Haqq' (the leader to the truth).

Zaydism is a Shi'a subsect and is found only in northern Yemen (see Population & People in the Facts about the Country chapter). Zaydi teachings are considered excellent support for the idea of a state, as they emphasise the difference between a person's private and public duties and rights.

The Zaydi state is led by the imam.

According to Zaydi principles, anyone who meets certain conditions can be elected to the post of imam. There are 14 conditions on the list, such as being male, being born free and healthy, paying one's taxes and knowing the Koran. The 11th and 12th conditions are the most restrictive of all. They state, in essence, that the imam must be chosen from those descended directly from 'Ali and Fatima, the son-in-law and daughter of the Prophet.

This system effectively created a religious nobility, the sada (see Social Classes in the Facts about the Country chapter), a collection of families who had all the power. During the 1000 years of Zaydi rule, the number of members of the sada class rose to 50,000. These people held most of the government positions, while the land remained mostly in the possession of ordinary tribespeople. Tribal justice and imamic rule were often on a collision course through the centuries, but generally the sada have been highly respected.

Imam Yahya ruled until the year 911. The three imams following him continued to rule from Sa'da but, from then on, the capital was moved to other towns, such as Hajja or San'a. It was not until 1597, when Imam al-Mansur al-Qasim ibn Muhammad made Sa'da his base for the war against the Ottoman Turk occupiers, that the town again became the capital of the Zaydi state. In 1636, when the Turks were finally thrown out of the country, the capital was again moved to San'a. Sa'da, however, remained the spiritual capital of the country, the holy city of the Imamate.

In 1962 the last imam, al-Badr al-Mansur, was dethroned by the revolution that laid the foundation of the YAR. Imam al-Badr fled to the mountain area north-west of Sa'da to lead a fruitless campaign against the new leaders. The civil war lasted for seven years; even today it is in the northernmost part of the country that the power of the Republican government is at its weakest.

At the beginning of the 1990s the Sa'da region was the centre of opposition to the unification of the two Yemens. Indeed, the town and its religious aristocracy stood to

A City of Elegance
Sa'da is a perfect example of the *zabur* architecture that is common on the plateaus of the eastern and northern highlands, where stone is scarce but clay is abundant. Zabur means laying clay courses on top of each other, letting one layer dry as the next one is built. Walls of the houses are typically at least half a metre thick, thinning towards the higher floors.

In Sa'da, the technique has yielded a town unique in style and appearance. The corners of the houses are raised from the base, continuing the difference in the levelling of the clay to the roof and in contrast with the horizontal lines of the clay courses. The walls are carefully finished with a mud coating, leaving the courses clearly visible, even emphasised. Small horns mark the roof corners. On the edge of the roof are parapets decorated with a number of small arches, plastered white with lime, like the horns in the corners. Alabaster-paned windows feature elaborate carvings and lime plastering. The effect is one of distinctive elegance and grace. ∎

Sa'da house

lose the most in the process. The loosening of Yemeni economic ties with Saudi Arabia left Sa'da out in the cold, with the commercial centre of the country moving to the distant port of Aden. Moreover, the unification left the 'liberal' laws of the south intact for the moment, to the dismay of the *ulama* (religious scholars and leaders) of Sa'da, who were horrified by such ideas as educated and unveiled women working for a salary. They finally got their vengeance in the 1994 civil war.

Orientation & Information

The carriers leave you in front of Bab al-Yaman, Sa'da's southern gate. The hotels, restaurants, bus office, taxi station, police and hospital are on San'a St, within a few km of the city wall.

There used to be an office of the General Tourist Corporation here, but it has gone with the closure of the mountain road from Saudi Arabia.

Things to See

The holiest place of the Zaydis is the **Great Mosque of Sa'da**, built in the 12th century. Imam Yahya, the founder of Zaydism, is buried here with 11 later imams, under 12 cupolas. You'll have to be satisfied with looking from the outside; don't even think about entering the mosque. The same applies

to another remarkable mosque, the **an-Nisari Mosque**, further into town. The fortification on the central hill today serves as a government office (read: military base), so it can't be entered either.

Don't be discouraged – the town itself deserves your attention. Despite some modern buildings just outside the old town, Sa'da is excellently preserved in zabur style and the **town wall** remains largely intact. Built of clay during the days of Imam Yahya, the wall was originally wide enough for a donkey to draw a cart along. Although parts of the wall have collapsed into rubble, it is still possible to walk around the town on top of it, and a restoration project is proceeding. You may have to step down here and there, but this is the best way to appreciate the beauty of Sa'da. The place to start is by the Bab al-Yaman gate; immediately on entering the old town, take the narrow alley to your right, next to a silver vendor's shack.

Of special interest is **Bab Najran**, the northern gate, surrounded by imaginatively twisted walls. Enemies fighting their way through the winding alleys by this gate certainly had a problem. Remember to exercise some discretion when aiming your camera at the private clay-walled gardens which are exposed to people walking on the town wall.

The next best way to see Sa'da is to walk

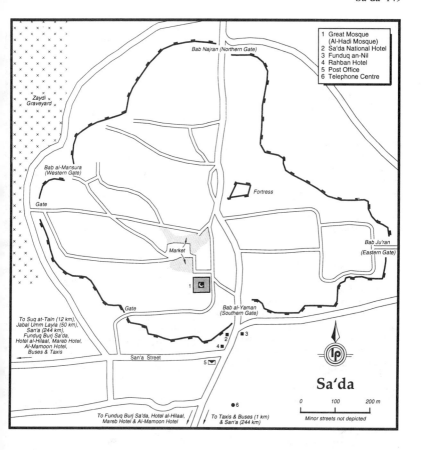

Sa'da

1 Great Mosque
  (Al-Hadi Mosque)
2 Sa'da National Hotel
3 Funduq an-Nil
4 Rahban Hotel
5 Post Office
6 Telephone Centre

Bab Najran (Northern Gate)

Zaydi Graveyard

Bab al-Mansura (Western Gate)

Gate

Fortress

Market

Bab Ju'ran (Eastern Gate)

Gate

Bab al-Yaman (Southern Gate)

To Suq at-Tain (12 km), Jabal Umm Layla (50 km), San'a (244 km), Funduq Burj Sa'da, Hotel al-Hilaal, Mareb Hotel, Al-Mamoon Hotel, Buses & Taxis

San'a Street

To Funduq Burj Sa'da, Hotel al-Hilaal, Mareb Hotel & Al-Mamoon Hotel

To Taxis & Buses (1 km) & San'a (244 km)

0   100   200 m

Minor streets not depicted

the streets of the town, though you see less. In the town, the **market** is worth seeing. Though permanent, it also functions as a Sunday market, when it is greatly enlarged. From the moneychangers, who lay their wares on cloths spread on bare earth, you can buy a Maria Theresa thaler, the silver coin used as the sole monetary object before the revolution and still in limited use.

Just outside the town, to the west of the town wall, is a huge 'empty' field surrounded by a modest wall. This is the **Zaydi graveyard**, by far the biggest and oldest in Yemen. You are allowed to enter, and can observe innumerable elaborately carved stone plates and tombstones. A few small domes here and there mark the graves of the imam's distinguished relatives and other learned Zaydis.

Places to Stay – bottom end

The one-sheet *Funduq an-Nil* (Nile Hotel) offers singles, doubles and dormitories but is not among Yemen's cleanest places to stay. Shared bathrooms feature showers, even warm ones if you switch on the boilers and wait a couple of hours. A bed in a double room costs YR 300 to YR 400.

If you are on a really tight budget, you can get a bed in a double room for YR 200 by forgoing the luxury of warm water and choosing the *Sa'da National Hotel*, opposite.

Funduq Burj Sa'da has a sign in Arabic only. This no-sheet hotel is on San'a St, 1½ km towards San'a. Triples cost YR 700.

Places to Stay – middle
Sa'da has plenty of hotels along San'a St, within one or two km from the old town. *Hotel al-Hilaal*, a traditional one-sheet inn, is remarkably clean for its class. Quadruples are the smallest available rooms; a bed costs YR 250. The *Mareb Hotel* is a bit classier. It offers two-sheet doubles with shared bathrooms for YR 700.

Furthest from town, the two-sheet *al-Mamoon Hotel* (☎ 2203) is the newest and cleanest of those built at the end of the 1980s. It has very friendly staff, singles for YR 800, doubles for YR 1200 and one bathroom to every three rooms. Similar is the close-by *Queen Bilqis Throne Hotel*

The *Rahban Hotel* is a two-sheet hotel in a modern house, curved like a dhuma and most conveniently positioned just outside the old town – taxis bring you right to the front door. Singles/doubles with private bathrooms go for YR 800/1200.

Places to Eat
Several eateries along San'a St offer modest but tasty food. The *Yemen Unity Restaurant* has received favourable mentions from travellers. Inside the city walls, there are also a few places around the market area where you can find something good to eat. Try the *United Arab Coffee Shop*.

Getting There & Away
From San'a, Sa'da is best reached by bus or taxi. Buses leave from Bab ash-Sha'ub at 7 am and 2 pm; the fare is YR 360. Brown-striped taxis will take you to Sa'da any time for YR 400 a seat; the taxi station is at Hasaba. The 244-km trip takes about four hours.

AROUND SA'DA
You can conveniently visit a number of places around Sa'da. In the immediate environs of the town, there are plenty of very beautiful small villages built in zabur style. It's worth taking a walk along the Wadi Sa'da for a few hours.

Walking a few km south-southeast from Bab al-Yaman along the wadi, you will reach the beautiful village of Raqban (raqba:n). A km or two further on is the mouth of the very narrow Wadi 'Abdin (wa:di: 'abdi:n). On the left bank of the wadi you will see an old fort, as-Sinnara. It is well worth a visit and travellers are occasionally granted entry.

Immediately to the east of Sa'da, a 15-minute walk from Bab al-Yaman, near some old water cisterns, you can find huge pre-Islamic rock engravings with an ibis motif. Six km south-southwest of Bab al-Yaman is the village of Ghuraz. There are rumoured to be pre-Islamic cave drawings seven km north of town; you'll need a local guide.

Suq at-Talh
(suq at-talH)
Suq at-Talh, a Friday/Saturday/Sunday market, is some 12 km from Sa'da, in the direction of Najran. This is the biggest market in the province. Here you can buy anything you would expect to find in a Yemeni market, including cattle, qat, fruit and pottery.

Suq at-Talh used to be one of the most extraordinary places in Yemen. It was the largest market for commodities imported from Saudi Arabia. Hundreds of trucks and jeeps brought wares across the border and the goods were sold directly from the vehicles. You could buy anything: building materials, automatic rifles, consumer electronics, hand grenades – you name it.

Legal? Well, is smuggling legal in a place where sheikhs of the Bakil tribes have more power than the government? In the late 1980s the governments of the YAR and Saudi Arabia reached an agreement to stop smuggling. The deterioration of Saudi-Yemeni relations during the Gulf crisis of 1990 and the Yemeni civil war of 1994 were further blows for Suq at-Talh, and today, it is a mere shadow of its former self.

Still, the border region is difficult to control, and a significant proportion of the cars in use in Yemen are driven around unregistered, with no taxes paid on them. In early 1995 the Yemeni government again launched an attack against smuggling with new legislation, but it remains to be seen if it will be enforced.

Umm Layla

The Umm Layla (Mother Night) mountain, some 50 km north-west of Sa'da along the asphalt road that leads to the Saudi Arabian border, is as far north as you can go in Yemen. The sandstone mountain is bizarrely eroded and the drawings sculpted into its rocks date back to the days of the incense trade. It takes 1½ hours to climb the mountain and the scenery makes it worthwhile.

Al-Hudayda

The Province of al-Hudayda stretches across the Tihama coastal plains from al-Khawkha in the south to al-Luhayya in the north. The width of the province averages 50 km, from the coast to the foothills of Yemen's western mountains. It is widest where major wadis (Wadi Mawr in the north, Wadi Siham just south of al-Hudayda, and Wadi Zabid in the south) have eaten their way deep into the mountains, extending the coastal plain.

The heat and humidity of al-Hudayda is extreme, and sandy winds blow daily, yet the province has played a major role in the country's agricultural output. While al-Hudayda lacks the spectacular architecture and ancient sites that abound in other parts of the country, with its radically diverse population it is a striking contrast to the mild climate and more homogeneous people of the highlands.

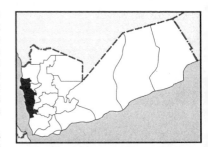

AL-HUDAYDA

(al-Hudayda; Hudaydah, Hodeida)
Al-Hudayda is the capital city of the Province of al-Hudayda and is Tihama's Rome: all roads lead to the city. Since every bus and long-haul taxi line starts or terminates here, it is impossible to pass the city by when visiting the Tihama. You will probably arrive in al-Hudayda by bus or taxi from the direction of San'a or Ta'izz. The third (less probable) alternative is to approach from the north, from either Hajja or Saudi Arabia.

On the trip from Ta'izz the scenery is quite monotonous; the Soviet-built Tihama highway offers few surprises.

There are two asphalted roads between San'a and al-Hudayda. The northern road, which passes near Manakha, was built in the late 1950s and early 1960s. It is a spectacular feat of Chinese engineering and serves as a model of how to build a mountain road whilst preserving the beauty of the landscape. This is the route taxis usually take; buses use both roads.

Tihama reed huts

The less scenic southern road branches off the San'a to Ta'izz road at Ma'bar, penetrates the mountains abruptly and descends to Madinat ash-Sharq, then follows the vast Wadi Siham to join the northern road before Bajil. The path of this road, built in the early 1980s, treats the landscape much more ruthlessly. Rocks have been blasted away wherever necessary, with little attention to aesthetic considerations. Moreover, the agricultural valley of Wadi Siham seems to be a developing area whose small settlements are rarely as eye-catching as those on the northern route.

Wherever you decide to stop en route, don't get your first impressions of the Tihama from Bajil. This industrial city demonstrates the worst aspects of poor planning: the neighbouring cement factory has been positioned so that the prevailing winds carry cement dust (plenty of it!) all over the town. Instead, if you arrive on a Monday morning, you might want to stop in al-Marawi'a (al-mara:wi'a), just 20 km from al-Hudayda. This lively little village has a Monday market. It's a substitute for Bayt al-Faqih if visiting that village on a Friday doesn't fit into your schedule.

History

Al-Hudayda is a young city. Although it was a verifiable port in the early 1500s, Carsten Niebuhr, the chronicler of the famous Danish expedition in the 1760s, makes almost no mention of the town, describing al-Luhayya and al-Makha as the ports of Yemen. Al-Hudayda, along with most of the northern Tihama, was destroyed in 1809 when the Wahhabi forces marched south from the Jizan area. It was not until 1830, after the British had started developing Aden, that the Ottoman Turks began to make al-Hudayda an efficient port and thus diminished the importance of al-Makha.

But the Turks were not strong enough to keep enemies from destroying their efforts. Recurrent wars devastated the Tihama for 100 years, peaking around WW I, when the al-Hudayda population dropped from 40,000 in 1911 to a mere 2000 in 1918, after Italians and Britons in turn had bombarded the city from the sea. Peace came to the Tihama only after the Saudi-Yemeni war, and since 1934 al-Hudayda has been allowed to develop without disturbance.

The start was slow, however. Imam Yahya ibn Muhammad's isolationist foreign policy was of little use to a port. After his death in 1948 the pace quickened as Imam Ahmad

cautiously tried to open some doors to the outside world. Ahmad's achievements include cooperation projects with China (the San'a to al-Hudayda road) and the Soviet Union (the al-Hudayda port).

The real boom for the city began after the revolution and especially after the civil war, in the explosive years of the foreign (import) trade. Since 1970 the port has been among the most congested in the world, with waiting times for unloading of up to six months. The city itself has been evolving rapidly, pushing the reed huts of local fishers out of the path of modern concrete buildings and asphalted streets.

The unification of the two Yemens left al-Hudayda as the second most important port in the new country. Its growth rate is expected to slow down remarkably now that Aden has stolen its place as the trade capital of the country. On the other hand, the expulsion of Yemenis from Saudi Arabia in late 1990 doubled the population of al-Hudayda almost overnight, since most of the Yemeni workers returned along the coastal route, and many chose to settle in al-Hudayda.

Today al-Hudayda is Yemen's fourth largest city, with a population of more than 300,000. Most of the province is rural; the rest of the population of almost 1.8 million lives in towns and villages of less than 30,000 inhabitants.

For travellers al-Hudayda is the dullest city in the entire country. It has almost no visible history, most of the city's buildings were built during the last few decades, it is on the coastal plain, with no topographical attractions, and it has no 'sights'. You won't miss much if you avoid visiting al-Hudayda altogether.

Orientation

It is fairly easy to find your way around al-Hudayda. Since you'll probably arrive from the east or south, or from the direction of San'a or Ta'izz, you will be left at the main street, San'a St, which enters the city from the east. The most interesting area is between San'a St and the coastline.

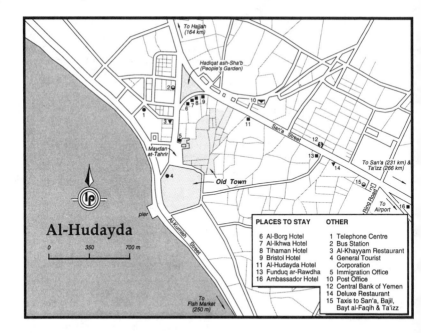

Al-Hudayda

0   350   700 m

PLACES TO STAY

6 Al-Borg Hotel
7 Al-Ikhwa Hotel
8 Tihaman Hotel
9 Bristol Hotel
11 Al-Hudayda Hotel
13 Funduq ar-Rawdha
16 Ambassador Hotel

OTHER

1 Telephone Centre
2 Bus Station
3 Al-Khayyam Restaurant
4 General Tourist
   Corporation
5 Immigration Office
10 Post Office
12 Central Bank of Yemen
14 Deluxe Restaurant
15 Taxis to San'a, Bajil,
   Bayt al-Faqih & Ta'izz

Continuing along San'a St to the very end, you will come across what must be the most modern and best-kept park in all of Yemen: Hadiqat ash-Sha'b (the People's Garden). Here you can watch people spending their time around the huge fountains, which are gorgeously illuminated at night. Southwards, in the direction of the seashore, there are a couple of similar open spaces, leading eventually to Maydan at-Tahrir (Tahrir Square), just one block from the sea and next to the old suq area.

Everything you need in al-Hudayda lies within one or two km of the People's Garden – bus stations, taxis, accommodation, the 'old' city, shops, markets, pharmacies, banks and the fishing port. Al-Hudayda is a fairly large city and you might easily exhaust yourself walking around the modern suburbs to the north of San'a St.

Information
Tourist Office There is a branch office of the General Tourist Corporation in the old city. Those entering Yemen by sea may be particularly interested in visiting the office. The 1983 map of al-Hudayda is available here, or at any other branch. Of the three city maps available in Yemen, this one contains the least information. Most travellers spend only a day or so in al-Hudayda, so a detailed map is not required.

Money There are banks around the People's Garden but many of these seem to concentrate on activities other than exchange. Private moneychangers are best found in the suq area but are not plentiful. Should you have trouble finding a moneychanging service, go to the Bank of International Credit & Commerce, to the west of the People's Garden. Another choice is the Central Bank of Yemen office on San'a St, near the Yemen Airways office – this bank also changes travellers' cheques.

Post The GPO is one block off the main street, north of the bus station on San'a St. Any postcards you send out of Yemen go through San'a, so sending them from here won't speed up the delivery time.

Telephone For phone and telex services there is an office of Cable & Wireless a few hundred metres west of the hotel cluster by the People's Garden. It operates like the office in San'a. You can also make overseas calls from the GPO.

Things to See & Do

Al-Hudayda does not offer the traveller an overwhelming array of attractions. The architecture consists mainly of concrete and cement blocks dating no further back than the 1960s.

In the morning you'll probably enjoy walking southwards by the shore, along al-Kurnish St. The **fishing port** further to the south abounds with fishers returning with a good catch to sell at the adjoining fish market. Many fishers still use wooden vessels built in the traditional way. These boats are worth taking a few photos of but be careful not to aim your camera at objects that might be regarded as military – and there is plenty of military interest in a port.

Some visitors have gone swimming a few km further south and also to the north of the city, for a change from the highlands. Females, however, may have some trouble with inquisitive locals.

The oldest part of al-Hudayda is formed by the **Turkish quarters** near the old market area and features some beautiful but rotting buildings. The typical old Red Sea house is three or four storeys high with wooden balconies and window covers (signs of Turkish influence) and beautifully plaster-decorated walls. One of the best examples faces the Red Sea by al-Kurnish St. This fine building with a rare dome on its roof has not been in use for years and was badly damaged by moist onshore winds. Restoration began on the house in 1990.

Indian influence is also evident in the doorway decorations of some of the older houses. This is hardly surprising, since craftspeople used to follow sailors and traders to the port cities of the Red Coast; the 20th century has put an end to this kind of cultural exchange.

The **market** itself is as lively as any Yemeni market, beggars (there are more of them here than anywhere else in Yemen) and sailors from diverse countries contribute to the atmosphere. The **old market quarters** are behind the eye-catching Turkish gate. Some people say that gold jewellery is cheaper here than in San'a or Ta'izz – perhaps a chance for a bargain. But remember – if there is a place in Yemen where you may be cheated or robbed, it is al-Hudayda.

Places to Stay

There is quite a variety of hotels in al-Hudayda – you can spend anything from a few tens of riyals to a few hundred riyals for an overnight stay. While there are probably plenty of alternatives elsewhere in the city, there is little reason to look outside the two-km stretch of San'a St from the taxi station to the People's Garden, which has a variety of Yemeni hotels.

Places to Stay – bottom end

If you arrive by taxi from San'a or Ta'izz and walk a couple of blocks along San'a St, you will find a couple of hotels on the left-hand side of the street. A no-sheet, no-sign *dormitory*, wide open to the street and with doors the size of the wall, offers modest lodging for males who arrive late in the evening, start again early in the morning and have no need for luxury.

Another choice is the legendary one-riyal *hotel* by the market area, a noticeable white building, now charging YR 300. The huge dormitory on the 1st floor has no walls, so the warm Red Sea winds caress you to sleep.

Places to Stay – middle

Funduq ar-Rawdha is a two-sheet hotel where an air-conditioned double with private bathroom costs YR 850. While definitely not very clean by Western standards, this one is acceptable if the price suits you and if you don't feel like carrying your baggage any further. There is another place of this type half a km further along, on the same side of the street – the *al-Hudayda Hotel* (☎ 226100). It has similar prices and friendly service but is often full.

The biggest cluster of hotels is on the southern side of the People's Garden, where you'll find four hotels. You might consider investing a few riyals in a local taxi ride instead of walking from the taxi station – the buses take you much closer.

The *Tihama* (☎ 239558) and *al-Ikhwa* hotels, are popular with backpackers and sailors, and they offer reasonable accommodation in the lower two-sheet category. Prices for a double start at around YR 850 (private bathroom and air-conditioning cost an extra YR 150 to 250 each). Ask to see the rooms before making a decision, though. In general, you should not pay for a private bathroom here – bathrooms in the corridors are no less filthy but at least you have a choice. If you do want one, make sure there's running water. The cockroaches are not dangerous.

The *al-Borg* is surprisingly cheap; rooms with one double bed and a clean private bathroom cost YR 950 (other hotels topped YR 1250 for similar but less clean rooms). The hotel also has a nice but overpriced rooftop restaurant.

It's a wise idea to get a room with air-conditioning because the temperature doesn't drop when night falls. Also, insisting on hot water doesn't necessarily make sense in the Tihama, since cold tap water is seldom particularly cold. The water has probably been stored in a tank on the roof of the house, with the sun heating it all day, so a shower is warm in the evening and cold in the morning – as it should be.

Places to Stay – top end
If money is of no concern, you'll probably choose the *Bristol* (☎ 239197, telex 5617) and stay in a room with a view of the People's Garden. The hotel is in the Yemeni deluxe category and you'll get the best al-Hudayda has to offer. Prices are in dollars – a double room costs US$65.

The most Western-style hotel in al-Hudayda is undoubtedly the *Ambassador* (☎ 231247), on San'a St, a few hundred metres from the taxi station in the direction of San'a. This hotel, frequented by businesspeople and government officials, has singles/doubles with bath, air-conditioning and TV at prices slightly higher than those at the Bristol.

Places to Eat
There are restaurants along San'a St and more in the market area between the Red Sea and the People's Garden.

Al-Andlus at 26 San'a St is a reasonably priced place and popular with backpackers. *Al-Khayyam Restaurant*, on the street running from the People's Garden to Tahrir Square, is popular among the expatriate community of al-Hudayda, though it is not cheap. Tahrir Square has a good no-name fish restaurant; you can buy your fish from the market and bring it here to be cooked in their ovens. On San'a St you may try the *Royal Golden* or the *Deluxe*.

Fish is great for lunch. Fishers bring their catch ashore in the mornings and it's fresh at noon. I would think twice, however, before eating fish for dinner – the cold storage facility in the fishing port may be the only one in the entire city, and a day in the open in al-Hudayda makes anything stink, especially a dead fish! Lunch is the main meal of the day for the Tihamis. For religious reasons, shellfish is rarely eaten in the restaurants, though you will see plenty of it in the fishing port if you visit early in the morning.

At the market you can buy any fruit, from banana to papaya or watermelon, at prices somewhat lower than in the mountains. The fruit is sometimes fresher, too.

Getting There & Away
There are two practical ways of getting to and from al-Hudayda – bus and taxi. There are also two impractical ways – plane and

boat. As few international flights land at the al-Hudayda airport, flying to this city is a bit complicated. As for boats, every other visitor to Yemen seems to have contemplated entering or leaving the country by sea. However, there are no passenger routes to al-Hudayda, so the only way to do it would be to board a cargo ship from Port Sudan or some other improbable place. The precious few I know who have actually had the chance to do this decided against it, considering it too dangerous! Only consider it if you're desperate.

Bus The bus station is on the north-south street just to the west of the People's Garden. For schedules, see the Getting Around chapter. The timetable (in Arabic only) is inside the ticket office. The office is open one hour before the buses leave.

The fares to San'a and Ta'izz are YR 360 to YR 400 depending on the type of connection. You can also buy a ticket to an intermediate stop (see the table of bus routes in the Getting Around chapter).

Taxi The station for taxis to the east and south is further along San'a St. There are always plenty of taxis waiting for passengers heading in the direction of San'a or Ta'izz. While taxi fares are YR 40 to YR 100 higher than the bus fares, taxis are a viable alternative to buses on these busy routes. You should not have to wait more than 30 minutes for a taxi to fill up, unless you arrive in the quiet hours of the afternoon or at midnight.

North of Al-Hudayda

You must have more than a passing interest in the Tihama if you want to visit the coastal areas north of al-Hudayda. These are certainly not tourist areas: the few funduqs in the region are definitely of the lowest class, the weather is unbearably hot and humid, and most of the roads (other than the al-Hudayda to Jizan highway) are miserable dirt roads. A trip to al-Luhayya, for example, makes a very long day even if you hire a private car, and you have to find a driver willing to drive from 6 am until late evening. Otherwise you would also have to stay overnight somewhere – and the locals are not used to seeing tourists camping nearby!

Indeed, the General Tourist Corporation discourages individual visits to places of the northern Tihami such as al-Luhayya. While Harad certainly belongs to the border area, it should still be possible to visit areas along the main road as far north as Suq al-Khamis, even Suq 'Abs.

AS-SALIF
(as-sali:f)
This old port town, by the strait that separates the Kamaran island from the mainland, is the site of age-old salt quarries, still in operation. Today it stands out as the end point of oil pipes from the Ma'rib/al-Jawf area and is off limits to tourists (as is the Kamaran island). There are no buses and very few shared taxis, but if you have a car, you can approach the town by taking the coastal road north of al-Hudayda. Turn left some 14 km after al-Hudayda and drive for another 50 km to reach as-Salif. There are several fine beaches along the road, and even some relatively desolate ones, which are convenient if inquisitive Yemenis make you feel a little self-conscious.

The Kamaran island has not been developed and is off limits to tourists.

AZ-ZAYDIYA
(az-zaydiya; al-Zaydiyah)
Back on the Jizan Rd, 50 km north of al-Hudayda, the road passes az-Zaydiya, northern Tihama's largest town. This is also the largest brick settlement in the northern Tihama (brick architecture is common in the southern Tihama; Zabid and Hays are brilliant examples. Az-Zaydiya is said to be a major producer of dhumas.

AL-QANAWIS
(al-qana:wis)
Al-Qanawis, 20 km further on, is another brick village. From this point on, the typical reed

architecture of the Wadi Mawr area becomes dominant, giving the landscape an eerie 'African' feel. Halfway between al-Qanawis and Wadi Mawr is the Dayr Dukhna crossroads; the road to the right leads to Hajja.

AZ-ZUHRA
(az-zuhra; al-Zuhrah)
Twenty-five km from al-Qanawis, a few km after you cross Wadi Mawr, you will see a gravel road on your left. The road leads first to az-Zuhra and then on to al-Luhayya, 60 km off the main road.

There is nothing special to see in az-Zuhra, but the region's hundreds of round huts are the finest examples you will find of Tihami reed architecture of African origin. The huts may look primitive from a distance, but if you walk inside the village among the houses you'll suddenly feel very small. The biggest huts may be up to six metres in diameter and six metres high – hardly primitive!

If you are lucky enough to be invited inside a house, you will see that the floors and walls are completely surfaced with mud all the way up to the domed ceiling, leaving no visible sign of the reed structure. The walls are often painted with bright colours and lively motifs, and household utensils hang conveniently from the walls.

A few km south of az-Zuhra is the village of ar-Rafi'i (ar-ra:fi'i:). It has a Sunday suq and an old Turkish fort that was later used by the imams as a winter resort.

AL-LUHAYYA
(al-luHayya; Loheyah)
The old port of northern Tihama, al-Luhayya, had its heyday from the 15th to the early 19th centuries. Today it is a small fishing village. Its small rectangular reed houses are built in a completely different style from those in az-Zuhra. The few remaining (and rapidly decaying) Red Sea houses stand alongside the ruins of many others, reminding the visitor of the city's past importance. A major attraction is the central mosque, built by Ottoman Turks in the 19th

century, with its three big domes and 14 smaller ones in two neat rows.

SUQ AL-KHAMIS
(su:q al-khami:s)
About 40 km to the north of al-Qanawis and a couple of km off the main road is a small village that seems completely desolate for most of the week. The name of the village, Suq al-Khamis, literally means 'Thursday Market', and that's what it is – a marketplace with very few permanent dwellers. On Thursday mornings the village abounds with hundreds of traders and their customers from nearby villages. There are several hundred similar suqs in northern Yemen but this one is the most important in the northern Tihama.

GETTING THERE & AWAY
There is a bus service from al-Hudayda to the northern Tihama up to Harad near the Saudi border. It runs along the asphalted Jizan road to Saudi Arabia. You can abandon the bus in az-Zaydiya, al-Qanawis, al-Ma'ras and Suq al-Khamis, or Suq 'Abs in Hajja.

If none of these places is your destination, you could try to get a taxi or hitch a ride from a crossing. However, you would still be better off hiring your own car from al-Hudayda. The bus continues to Harad, though this is unlikely to be your destination, since it is a border station and individual travellers are not permitted into Saudi Arabia (unless they drive their own vehicle, in which case they require a transit visa; Saudi Arabia is still not granting tourist visas).

An interesting alternative exists for those who want no more than a glimpse of the northern Tihama and who are equipped with an adventurous mind and plenty of time – the Hajja taxi.

The Hajja taxi station is located inconveniently far from the city centre, by the Jizan road. You need a taxi for a disproportionate YR 200 to get there. The route from al-Hudayda to Hajja goes 100 km north along the asphalted road past az-Zaydiya and al-Qanawis to Dayr Dukhna (where you may have to change cars and wait for a couple of hours for the next one to fill with passengers). It then turns east onto a dirt road that leads to Hajja, some 70 km away via at-Tur. Expect this latter part of the trip to take at least twice as long as the first. The so-called road is very bumpy requiring a 4WD vehicle. As matters stand now, the overall cost of the trip is YR 300 to YR 400 per person. The experience is worth it as long as you don't suffer from car sickness.

South of Al-Hudayda

The Tihami towns and villages of greatest historical and modern-day interest lie to the south of al-Hudayda.

AS-SUKHNA
(as-sukhna)
This small, modest bath resort in the foothills of Jabal Bura' has a few hot springs and used to be one of the imams' winter palaces. There are persistent rumours that the present government has plans to develop this place into a tourist attraction.

To reach as-Sukhna you need to drive to the nondescript village of al-Mansuriya, 44 km south-east of al-Hudayda (YR 20 to YR 40 by bus or taxi), then take local transport along the 20-km gravel road north-east to the spa village

BAYT AL-FAQIH
(bayt al-faqi:h; Bait, Beyt)
The Friday market of Bayt al-Faqih, established in the early 1700s as a trading point for coffee, is by far the most famous of Yemen's weekly markets. There was already a very small village here, founded in the 13th century by Sheikh Ahmad ibn Musa of the 'Akk tribe from Wadi Zabid. Sheikh Ahmad travelled a great deal and was famed as a very wise man – hence the name of the town: 'House of the Wise Man'

The system of weekly markets is well established in many countries and has operated for thousands of years. For obscure reasons, this system has developed to its extreme in the northern part of Yemen (it is not in use in the southern part of the country). In the early 1980s Western specialists and explorers doing fieldwork in the YAR catalogued more than 300 weekly markets. The

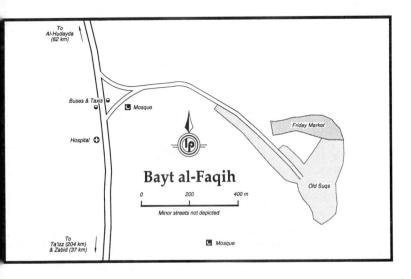

To
Al-Hudayda
(62 km)

Buses & Taxis

Mosque

Friday Market

Hospital

Bayt al-Faqih

0   200   400 m

Minor streets not depicted

Old Suqs

To
Ta'izz (204 km)
& Zabid (37 km)

Mosque

number is currently estimated at well over 500.

Contrary to expectation, the custom did not wane after the revolution and the resulting upheaval in the YAR's economy. The street markets you see in those towns or villages which have asphalted roads operate every weekday. These markets are a new element in the economy, having developed mainly in the 1970s, but they have not suffocated the weekly markets. Instead, the systems seem to complement each other and, when the economy is boosted, both types benefit. In fact, both the number of weekly market sites and the number of traders operating in existing markets have been steadily rising since the revolution.

The goods sold at the weekly markets have traditionally been agricultural and handcraft products, and this remains very much the case. In fact, the majority of traders at the weekly markets still belong to the subsistence sector of the economy. However, the relatively few traders who offer imported commodities already reap most of the riyals.

The town's location in central Tihama made it an ideal trading centre – it was easily accessible from the coffee-growing mountain areas and the ports were not far away. Trade in mocha coffee soon made Bayt al-Faqih famous among coffee-consuming Arabs all over the world. Carsten Niebuhr describes the place:

Traders from Hijaz, Persia, Egypt, Syria, Constantinople, Habash, Tunis, Fez and Morocco come to the market of Bayt al-Faqih to purchase the coffee beans, to send them from there via the ports of al-Makha and al-Hudayda further. Even buyers from India and sometimes from Europe meet here.

There are far fewer restrictions on photography in the Tihami culture and attitude than you'll find in the mountain villages, and the businesspeople of Bayt al-Faqih certainly understand the value of advertisement. Most people here are too busy to assume those horrible poses young Yemenis are so fond of, and they are not likely to get angry at your camera exploits.

The cuppers are an exception to this rule. They practise their ancient art in open houses in the middle of the market. You can see several customers lying on beds, their naked backs covered with half a dozen or more small horns. The cupper sucks blood up into these horns through small incisions in the skin. The idea is to free the patient from 'bad blood' (considered to be the source of various ailments). The process is somewhat intimate, and photographing it will definitely not be appreciated.

Orientation & Information

If you arrive by taxi, the driver will probably take you straight to the 'supermarket'. If you come by bus, you will be left at the crossroads and will have to walk a km or so from the main road. The taxi fare to the market area should not be more than a couple of riyals.

Modern facilities are found along the main road, though there aren't too many of them here, only a hospital for emergencies, a pharmacy and a petrol station – no post and no money exchange.

Apart from the market, there is little to see in Bayt al-Faqih. The town has rather modest Tihami brick houses; in the vicinity are hamlets of reed houses with mud walls. The Turkish-built fortress Husn Uthman, in the centre of town, can hardly be considered a sight.

The Market

The Friday market is the attraction of Bayt al-Faqih. The market area is huge, consisting of both open-air spaces and covered alleys, with different areas for each type of goods. You can easily walk around for more than an hour without passing the same place twice. There must be well over 1000 traders.

Today coffee no longer makes up the bulk of the trade in Bayt al-Faqih. Instead, you can buy whatever products the Tihami agriculture or handcraft industry has to offer. Here's your chance to find some Yemeni pottery, colourful Tihami clothes and baskets. How about a camel, cow, donkey, lamb or

Top: Shibam in the Wadi Hadhramawt Valley
Bottom: Mud brick houses in Shibam

BETHUNE CARMICHAEL

BETHUNE CARMICHAEL

BETHUNE CARMICHAEL

Top Left: Mosque in Shibam
Top Right: Interior of mosque in Tarim
Bottom: Sultan's Palace in Sayun

chicken? All are going cheap. Fruit, vegetables or cereal? Anything you can imagine.

Places to Stay

I would not recommend that you stay overnight in Bayt al-Faqih. There is little to see on Friday evening, and no reason to loiter around here after the market. On the other hand, if you are coming from Ta'izz, you might want to arrive in Bayt al-Faqih Thursday evening to get an early start for your adventures in the marketplace. You will not be the only one wanting accommodation then – the places to stay will be crowded.

There really is nothing more than bottom-end accommodation in Bayt al-Faqih. Basic dormitories near the suq offer no-sheet beds for YR 200.

Places to Eat

Most food in Bayt al-Faqih is be fresh and safe. Elsewhere in Tihama, eating is a greater risk than in the highlands – food is more likely to be contaminated because of the hotter and more humid climate. Choose anything that is boiled, eat snacks from the market stalls and order full meals indoors – there is an alley full of restaurants. Try the soups; you are unlikely to be disappointed. If it is not a market day, you may prefer dry biscuits.

Getting There & Away

The easiest way to get to Bayt al-Faqih is from al-Hudayda; buses (YR 60) depart from al-Hudayda at 7 am and taxis (YR 100) leave at any time. The 55-km trip along a good asphalted road takes only an hour. En route you will see typical Tihama scenes but no particular sights – even the bigger town of al-Mansuriya lies a little way off the road. Some people count the Tihami petrol stations as 'sights'; with their imaginative decorations and colourful neon lights, they certainly provide an impressive display at night.

Coming from the direction of Ta'izz is less practical because it means that you have to stay overnight in some small Tihami town (offering only very modest accommodation)

in order to get a glimpse of the market. The trading activities peak between 7 and 10 am, and even if you start from Ta'izz at 6 or 7 am (the first bus leaves at 7 am), it takes three or four hours to reach Bayt al-Faqih. By Friday afternoon the town is almost as quiet as it is during the rest of the week.

It is easy to leave Bayt al-Faqih at noon on Friday. There is no need to wait for a bus – just go to the taxi station and climb into a taxi that's headed in the right direction. It will start in a couple of minutes. Be sure to negotiate the price first; YR 60 should take you to Zabid, YR 100 to al-Hudayda and YR 240 to Ta'izz.

ZABID

(zabi:d; Zebid, Zebed)

About 37 km south of Bayt al-Faqih lies Zabid, a town with a remarkable past. Zabid is one of the oldest towns in Yemen. Although badly neglected and its splendour largely gone, the town is still well worth a visit. In 1994 UNESCO decided to include the town on its World Heritage list as the third choice from Yemen, after San'a and Shibam. The organisation also started an international fund-raising campaign for the restoration and preservation of the town, but the civil war of the same year has apparently hindered action.

History

Little is known of life in the Tihama before the arrival of Islam, though it is certain that Wadi Zabid has been under cultivation from time immemorial. The Asha'ir tribe, who lived in the Tihama south of Wadi Rima' (the next major wadi north of Wadi Zabid), and the 'Akk tribe, who occupied the central Tihama north of Wadi Rima', adopted Islam during the Prophet's lifetime. The leader of the Asha'ir tribe, Sheikh Abu Musa bin Ash'ari, even visited the Prophet Muhammad in Madina; after his return, the sheikh built one of Yemen's very first mosques, near a well in Wadi Zabid.

Adopting Islam did not mean being loyal to the central rulers, and three major uprisings of the Tihami tribes were recorded in the earliest centuries of Islam. The first was repressed in the days of Abu Bakr, the first of the Umayyad caliphs. In 819 AD the third revolt occurred. It was against the Abbasid caliphs and resulted in the appointment of Muhammad ibn 'Abdullah ibn Ziyad as governor of the region. It is to this man that the founding of Zabid town in 820 is credited. Eventually he made his rule independent of the caliphs who had given him power and, before long, he ruled 'the whole of Yemen' (which probably means at least the Tihama).

Muhammad ibn Ziyad not only founded a town – he also founded a dynasty that lasted 200 years (820-1012) and an Islamic university that still partly functions.

The Arabic words for mosque *(ja:mi')* and university *(ja:mi'a)* both derive from the same root verb *(jama'a* – to gather, collect, bring together), and the concepts are indeed intertwined. Within every mosque is a Koran school, its main function being to teach boys and girls to read and write. The final exam involves a recital of the Koran in its entirety – by heart! The students learn this easily, as it is the only task they practise, even if the secrets of the alphabet are not fully grasped. Before the revolution, this was the only kind of education in Yemen. The illiteracy rate is still high, from 70% to 80%, even after more than a decade of modern schooling.

The university of Zabid was not just a Koran school but an ever-growing compound of all the schools and mosques of the town, leading to higher and higher education. Muhammad ibn Ziyad did not found the university alone; he brought a prominent Mufti, at-Taghlabi, from Baghdad for this task. Zabid soon became a famed centre of learning, attracting scholars from abroad. Some stayed for a short while, others for their entire lives. Those who left spread Zabid's fame – and Sunni teaching – across the Muslim world.

Naturally it was mostly questions relating to the creed and interpretations of Islamic law that were studied and taught in the university of Zabid. However, other disciplines included grammar, poetry, history and mathematics. The word 'algebra' has been attributed to a Zabidi scholar named Ahmad abu Musa al-Jaladi, who created a mathematical system he called al-Jabr.

The Ziyadid dynasty eventually ended and was replaced by lesser ones like the Najahids (1012-1153) and Mahdi'ids (1153-1173). Although Zabid was no longer the capital of 'the whole of Yemen', the university prospered. Even when the Ayyubids ruled Yemen from Egypt (1173-1229), the university continued to expand, reaching its peak during the Rasulid era (1229-1454). I is said that during this period, some 5000 students occupied the more than 200 schools and mosques of Zabid; the town was the absolute centre of learning for the southern part of the Islamic Empire.

During the Tahirid rule (1454-1526) and the following decades of disorder, and especially during the first Ottoman occupation (1545-1636), the activities of the Zabid university began to diminish. The following centuries brought the Tihama several interregnums, when foreign conquerors landed in Yemen. Only the Zaydis of the mountains were finally able to successfully resist the outside forces, so the centre of Sunni teaching gradually lost its importance. Although there are still many mosques and Koran schools in Zabid today, they certainly don't form a university any more.

Orientation

The Zabid junction on the al-Hudayda to Ta'izz road used to attract the attention of a traveller because of its many trees. Unfortunately, during our last visit they were all cut down. Hopefully they will be replanted - Wadi Zabid has enough water to grow pleasant shade trees which provide some relief from the heat. The climate of Zabid is among the hottest in the country; indeed, when the Tihamese around Zabid heard we were heading for Zabid, they warned against it and recommended a visit to al-Khawkha instead.

The town itself lies on the western side of the road, leaving only a few newly built commercial buildings and shacks by the roadside (Zabid is one of the few Yemeni towns not having exploded after the 1970s).

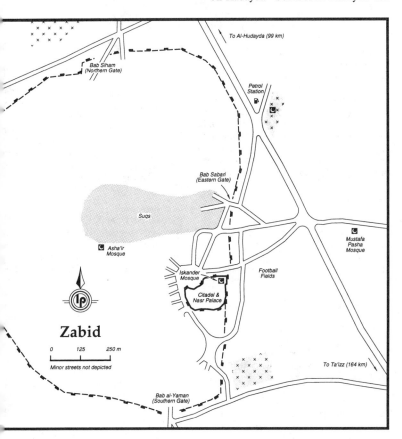

To Al-Hudayda (99 km)

Bab Siham
(Northern Gate)

Petrol
Station

Bab Sabari
(Eastern Gate)

Suqs

Mustafa
Pasha
Mosque

Asha'ir
Mosque

Iskander
Mosque

Football
Fields

Citadel &
Nasr Palace

Zabid

0   125   250 m

Minor streets not depicted

To Ta'izz (164 km)

Bab al-Yaman
(Southern Gate)

Walking along the alley that leads directly to the suq area of Zabid, you will notice a large square to your left, just before the town itself, with some imposing buildings behind it. This is the new government 'centre' of Zabid – the old centre is the suq.

Once you dive into the town, you'll find it easy to get lost. The alleys are winding and the blocks are closely built, with no visual axes or hills. Don't panic. Getting lost here is not a serious matter because the town is not that big; you will soon reach open fields, so it is not difficult to find your way back.

The city itself, inside its remaining walls, is quite a sight. Walking through the winding suq alleys, where small shops alternate with eating houses and tearooms, your sense of direction and dimension is soon distorted, making you very receptive to Zabid's atmosphere. The suq used to be covered but nowadays only a few side alleys offer you shade.

Houses

Once you're out of the suqs, the city appears reserved. This impression is created by the Zabid architects who developed a unique style while trying to hide the wealth of the house-owners from passers-by – the bigger the house and the more splendid its interior, the more modest the street facade. The outer walls of the one or two-storey brick houses show little decoration or paint.

If you catch a glimpse of the inner court-yards of the houses, the dazzling white, richly ornamented walls reveal the aesthetic preferences of the Zabid elite. Better still, if you get invited into a Zabid home (not very likely), you'll be struck by the great contrast between the inner grandeur and the outer simplicity of the construction and decoration.

Mosques

During the golden days of the Zabid university there were 236 mosques in Zabid. Over the centuries two out of every three mosques have vanished but Zabid, with its 86 mosques, is still extraordinary (San'a is famous for its 64 minarets but is a much larger city). The mosques still function as Koran schools, making Zabid an important centre of Shafa'i teaching.

The usual rule applies here – it is difficult, if not downright impossible, for a nonbeliever to enter places of worship. To the untrained eye, many remarkable mosques, including the vast al-Asha'ir Mosque, or Great Mosque, seem modest from the outside, since they don't raise their cupolas to great heights. Instead the mosques extend themselves over a wide area, but this feature is difficult to grasp when looking at a mosque from the nearby alleys; you're simply too close.

Perhaps the easiest mosques for a lay person to appreciate lie just outside the old city.

Iskandar Mosque With its 60-metre-high minaret, the Iskandar Mosque stands inside the citadel walls, near the square. It is said to have been built by the Turk Alexander Ramoz (hence the name) during the first Ottoman occupation. The mosque can be entered if you arrive at a suitable non-prayer

time and pay a few tens of riyals to th guards.

Mustafa Pasha Mosque Also known as th Baishiya Mosque, this is another mosque o Turkish origin, bearing the name of the firs Ottoman governor of the Tihama (1540 This imposing mosque with a dozen cupola stands on the eastern side of the Ta'izz t al-Hudayda highway, half a km out of towr It was one of the city mosques in earlier time but much of the city has since vanished leaving only the mosque standing solemnly

Nasr Palace

The palace by the citadel draws the attentio of travellers because of its central location o the site of a much older Turkish building The palace itself was built in the late 1800 and today serves as a government building though it is obviously perceived as a touris sight, with signs on the walls of the 1st floo bearing an account of Zabid's history. Ther is a good view over the town and environ from the tower. Entry is granted to visitors

Places to Stay

If you have no choice, it is possible to sta overnight in Zabid. However, it is always hc here, even at night. There are a few tradi tional hotels in the market area and aroun the square – no sheets, no tap water, n privacy, where you can stay overnight fo YR 200 per person.

In the small inn by the square we wer presented with a guest book to sign. Judgin from the mostly unprintable comment recorded by German travellers, the place wa not up to middle-European standards. Still this is the kind of hotel you will find nea Yemeni markets (if you find anything at all

Getting There & Away

Travel to and from Zabid is by bus or tax along the Tihama highway, either from the north (92 km and YR 160 to YR 20(from al-Hudayda; 37 km and YR 80 to YF 100 from Bayt al-Faqih) or from the south

(161 km and YR 280 to YR 300 from Ta'izz; 35 km and YR 80 to YR 100 from Hays).

HAYS
(Hays)

As you continue south from Zabid, you will pass a couple of towns with more examples of south Tihami brick architecture. Fourteen km from Zabid you reach Suq al-Jarrahi, a town with a Monday market, and 21 km further on is the town of Hays.

While neither of the towns possess a glorious past, Hays is well worth visiting if you have a couple of extra hours. Sunday, market day, brings even more people into this very densely built, busy little town. Keep an eye open for those yellow-and-green glazed clay pots common in the northern part of Yemen; plenty of them are manufactured here, using techniques introduced by the Mamelukes in the 14th century.

Although the houses of Hays are generally smaller than those in Zabid, they are plastered very white with gypsum, causing the whole city to glimmer brightly in the sun. As in Zabid, the houses have rich decoration only on the walls facing the inner courtyard.

AL-KHAWKHA
(al-khawkha; al-Khokha, Khokhah, Cocha)

Al-Khawkha is the biggest fishing village on the southern coast of the Red Sea. The Yemenis, especially the Tihamese, are very fond of the place and many will highly recommend a visit to al-Khawkha if you talk with them about your travel plans. (Guided tours that include the Tihama usually visit al-Khawkha.)

Palm groves decorate the shores, the climate is more pleasant than that of inland Tihama (not so hot, though still windy), the waters lend themselves to a nice swim (but don't risk swimming past the reefs because there are sharks) and grilled fish is fresh and cheap. When wading along the shores make sure not to go barefoot, otherwise you risk being bitten by a scorpion fish which can inflict a very painful wound. Camping is no problem here; the locals are used to it, and after a walk of a few km along the shores, you should be able to find a suitable place – if your tent is strong enough to withstand the wind.

On the other hand, this may not be what you came to see in Yemen. Al-Khawkha certainly is a sight to the Yemenis because it is very different from anything else in their country. Government tourist officials have seen how Europeans flock to places like the Seychelles or Maldives, so al-Khawkha seemed a way to make some bucks. However, they haven't invested a buck in the place themselves. If I were after this kind of holiday, I would choose the Seychelles instead.

Places to Stay

Although al-Khawkha is touted as a major holiday resort, the village itself offers accommodation that can only be described as primitive. Should you not feel inclined to stay in a filthy no-sheet YR 300 funduq in the market area, you can either sleep in the open, camp in your own tent or choose a place in either of the two 'tourist villages' a few km to the north of the village.

The *Sindibad Garden*, (or Sinibad's Tourist Village), is less than two km from the village. It has seven very basic clay huts and a few open bamboo huts in a beautiful palm grove right on the beach. Meals are also available. You pay YR 1550 for a clay hut per night; each hut contains four or five no-sheet beds. The bamboo huts are cheaper at YR 1050, with greater atmosphere but no privacy. The swimming here is good, and boats are available to rent for snorkelling on the coral reef, however, you will need to bring your own snorkel and mask. While some visitors have enjoyed their stay here, others report that they would rather have slept in the open, which you can actually do here for a fee of a few hundred riyals.

The *al-Khawkhah Tourist Village* is an older but more modern and bigger place, one and a half km further to the north. You pay YR 1400 for a two-sheet double with air-con and private bathrooms, and there is a small restaurant there too. However, you have to walk 150 metres to the beach which is shallow and not as good as the one at Sindibad's.

Getting There & Away

The easiest way to reach al-Khawkha is to take a taxi from Hays. A seat should cost no more than YR 80 but a whole taxi may be as much as YR 400. The trip is only 29 km and the road, while not asphalted, is rather good – though some may try to tell you otherwise.

Another road runs along the shore from al-Makha. This route is twice as long and carries virtually no regular traffic, so you would almost certainly have to hire a very expensive private car.

Ta'izz

The most populous province of all of Yemen, Ta'izz occupies the southernmost part of the former YAR, extending to the southern Tihama. Its port is al-Makha. A great part of the province is mountainous, with most towns and villages at an altitude of 1000 to 2000 metres. The mountains receive the first rains brought by the monsoon winds, so the climate is pleasant and the province is quite fertile, with great agricultural potential.

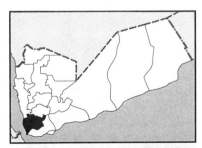

The region's inhabitants have long enjoyed a cosmopolitan status among the Yemenis because of the proximity of two main ports, al-Makha and Aden. For generations people from the Hujjariya district, to the south of Ta'izz city, have sailed to remote destinations, returning years, even decades, later. After the oil boom, they were among the first to join the mass migration of labour. Today the high mobility of the Hujjariya people also benefits domestic activities: plenty of shopkeepers and craftspeople in various northern towns and villages turn out to be of southern origin. The 2.2 million inhabitants of the province are among the most prosperous in the country.

Ta'izz stood to gain the most in the unity of Yemen – with the opening of the PDRY/YAR border, the city would become more centralised and would benefit from strengthened economic ties with the more populous Lahej and Aden governorates. The YSP gathered a higher percentage of votes in the elections of 1993 than in any other northern province.

For the traveller, the province includes several historical sites, from the al-Makha port to the al-Janad Mosque. Scenic drives around the Hujjariya or Jabal Sabir are another possibility, although they are not especially breathtaking – certainly there are more spectacular mountains and villages with older buildings in upper Yemen. However, if you have the time, you will find spending a couple of days in the Province of Ta'izz interesting.

Interior of the al-Janad Mosque

AL-MAKHA

(al-makha:; al-Mukha, Mocha, Mokka)
This old coffee port in the southernmost part of Tihama continues to attract visitors because of its fame from times long gone. Al-Makha today is a small village with few attractions. As one disappointed visitor put it, al-Makha is 'for name-addicted romantics

167

only'. A couple of hours should be enough to walk through all the streets and still leave you plenty of time to admire the waves of the Red Sea. But hopefully not the sunset, beautiful as it is, because there are no facilities for an overnight stay.

Al-Makha was the former YAR's second most important international port. Even so, the village's main claim to fame was as the Republic's main smuggling port, especially for booze from Djibouti. Plans to develop the port were scrapped after the unification in 1990, when Aden became the most important port of the new Republic of Yemen. The major power plant, built nearby in the mid-1980s, was never needed for the port – in the civil war of 1994 it was bombed to pieces by the separatist forces.

History

There was already a major port somewhere in this area in Himyarite times, before Islam reached Yemen. Little is known of al-Makha's early development, however, the first written documents date from the early 1400s. By the time Europeans appeared in these waters, al-Makha was already a prospering city.

In 1616 a Dutch visitor to al-Makha, Pieter van der Broecke, noted a caravan of 1000 camels carrying goods imported from as far away as Hungary and Venice. Exports through al-Makha included fruit, cloth, spices, dyes, pottery and, most importantly, coffee, the latest craze in Europe, grown in the Yemeni mountains.

Two years later the English and Dutch built al-Makha's first coffee factories. They were soon followed by other Europeans, even Americans. By the 1630s coffee houses were being opened in Venice, Amsterdam and elsewhere, and the demand for coffee rose to such heights that Yemen was no longer able, on its own, to meet the demand. Prices soared, bringing prosperity to the coffee merchants of al-Makha, who built gorgeous villas in the city.

During those years Yemen had a virtual world monopoly on the beans, to the extent that the trade name 'Mocha coffee' has sur-

vived to the present day. Eventually, however, the plant was smuggled out of the country, and new plantations were growing in Ceylon (now Sri Lanka) and Java by the early 1700s. The monopoly was broken and al-Makha fell into decline. The final blow to the town came in 1839, when the British captured Aden and started to develop it as the main port of southern Arabia, robbing al-Makha of the remaining trade.

Coffee is still grown in the mountains of Yemen, although farmers derive greater profits from qat. The restoration of the coffee trade is a much-argued issue among those foreigners working in development-aid projects and wanting to see coffee plants once again filling Yemeni mountain slopes instead of qat.

Things to See

The ash-Shadhli Mosque, with its beautiful Zabid-influenced architecture, is about 500 years old. Ruins of the coffee merchants' villas also bear interesting ornaments in the Tihami style. Most villas have already shrunk to sand-covered rubble – there are many such heaps around.

Places to Stay

There are a couple of teahouses in the centre of al-Makha but the village has no overnight accommodation.

Getting There & Away

Buses don't serve al-Makha. The easiest way to reach the village is by taxi from Ta'izz, a 105-km ride on a good asphalted road. A seat in a taxi should cost you no more than YR 220. However, traffic to al-Makha is not heavy, so you might have to wait an hour or more for the car to fill up – and just as long in al-Makha to get back! Leave for al-Makha early in the morning to be sure of getting back without any problems.

If you are travelling southwards along the Tihama highway, you might consider getting out at Mafraq al-Makha (the al-Makha junction), 70 km from Hays, to wait for a ride to al-Makha. The village is actually a couple of km north of the crossroads, so watch for the right place to get out of the car.

TA'IZZ

(ta'izz; Taiz, Tais)

Although it is another former capital of Yemen, Ta'izz is a relatively young city by Yemeni standards and has a mostly modern, almost European appearance. Most of the architecture in Ta'izz is postrevolutionary – concrete apartment buildings with painted walls. In recent years much of the city has been rebuilt, and comprises new living quarters and commercial centres more modern than any other city in the country.

However, the town does have very old quarters and many beautiful old mosques dating from the Rasulid era, so a walk in the old town is worthwhile. Ta'izz is dramatically located at an altitude of 1400 metres, in the northern foothills of Jabal Sabir, the province's highest mountain. The city has a definite charm – quite unlike al-Hudayda, for example.

History

Historians are not certain when and by whom Ta'izz was founded. Although Jabal Sabir was already inhabited in pre-Islamic times, the first written record of Ta'izz dates from 1175 AD. By then Ta'izz must have existed for 100 years or so, since the Ayyubid ruler Turan Shah, after conquering the Mahdi'ids in Zabid, decided to live in Ta'izz. Zabid remained the Ayyubid capital, but for a man of Egyptian origin, the climate of Ta'izz was much more pleasant, especially during the summer.

After the decline of the Ayyubids the southern parts of Yemen fell into the hands of the Rasulids (1229-1454), who ruled the southern mountains and the Tihama from Ta'izz. Occasionally their kingdom spread as far north as Mecca and as far east as Oman, so Ta'izz was unquestionably Yemen's capital during the Rasulid era. The city prospered greatly under the Rasulids; fortifications were built, mosques were constructed, water was brought to the city by means of an aqueduct from Jabal Sabir, and the city became a remarkable trade centre.

The period of Rasulid rule was followed by the 'dark centuries', during which Ta'izz fell to various foreign conquerors and local rulers. The Ottoman Turks often invaded the highlands via Ta'izz and, in the years of defeat, were sometimes able to hold the city even when the northern mountains, with their Zaydi population, were lost.

In the 20th century Ta'izz was again made the capital of Yemen, after a power struggle in 1948. The 'Free Yemenis', a group opposing imamic rule, was organised in Aden. The Free Yemenis consisted mainly of Shafa'i merchants of the south but also included a Zaydi leader, Muhammad Mahmud az-Zubayri. In early 1948 the group succeeded in assassinating Imam Yahya and proclaimed an imam of their own choosing, Abdullah al-Wazir, in San'a. However, with Saudi support, Yahya's son Ahmad soon defeated the rebels and became the imam of Yemen.

Imam Ahmad made Ta'izz his residence and the new capital of Yemen, never returning to San'a. Much of the current prosperity of Ta'izz thus derives from the period between 1948 and the 1962 revolution. Even during the civil war (fought mainly in the north) Ta'izz served as a 'second capital' of Yemen, and most of the foreign diplomatic missions moved to San'a only in the early 1970s.

Today Ta'izz is a booming commercial city, which sees much of the post-unity politics of Yemen as backward and contra-business. Mass demonstrations against corruption and against the government's inefficient economic policy have taken place here.

Orientation

Ta'izz is not the easiest city to find your way around. Because it is built in a hilly area, the streets of this vast city wind up and down, left and right. Without a map, you can easily get lost. Keep in mind that the huge and highly visible Jabal Sabir stands to the south.

Two long streets wind their way through the city in an east-west direction. Gamal Abdul Nasser St is the main thoroughfare,

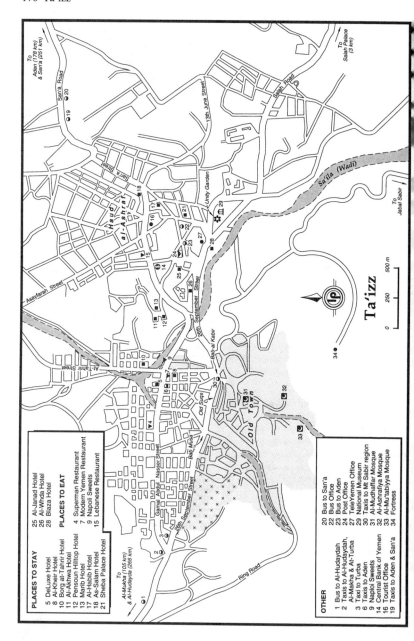

PLACES TO STAY

5 DeLuxe Hotel
8 Al-Kheir Hotel
10 Borg at-Tahrir Hotel
11 Al-Akhwa Hotel
12 Pensoun Hilltop Hotel
13 Marib Hotel
17 Al-Habib Hotel
18 As-Salam Hotel
21 Sheba Palace Hotel
25 Al-Janat Hotel
26 Al-Whda Hotel
28 Blaza Hotel

PLACES TO EAT

4 Superman Restaurant
7 Modern Yemen Restaurant
9 Napoli Sweets
15 Lebanese Restaurant

OTHER

1 Bus to Al-Hudaydah
2 Taxis to Al-Hudaydah,
   Al-Makha & Al-Turba
3 Taxi to Turba
6 Taxis to Aden
9 Napoli Sweets
14 Central Bank of Yemen
16 Tourist Office
19 Taxis to Aden & San'a
20 Bus to San'a
22 Bus Office
23 Bus to Aden
24 Post Office
27 TeleYemen Office
29 National Museum
30 Taxis to Mt Sabir region
31 Al-Mudhaffar Mosque
32 Al-Ashrafiya Mosque
33 Al-Mu'tabbiya Mosque
34 Fortress

Ta'izz

and buses leave you at either end of the street, depending on the direction you come from. The smaller 26th September St passes by the walls of the old city, further to the south. At one point, near the Haud al-Ashraf part of town, the streets run very close to each other. There are plenty of hotels and restaurants in this region.

Information

Tourist Office There is an office of the Public Corporation for Tourism on Gamal Abdul Nasser St, some 200 metres from its junction with San'a St, where the San'a bus leaves you. The staff here are very helpful; they have few customers and show genuine interest in solving any problems.

Visa Extensions Since it is presumably possible to enter Yemen through the al-Makha port or the Ta'izz 'international' airport, the city has an immigration office. This is useful if you need a visa extension. The office is inconveniently located out of the town centre, on the Ring Rd.

Money Moneychangers have offices throughout central Ta'izz. Their existence is, at any time, subject to the measures the government is imposing on the trade; if currently illegal, try the shops selling silver jewellery in the suq. There are plenty of banks in the main streets of the city.

Post The post office is in Haud al-Ashraf, opposite the al-Janad Hotel, near the main bus office.

Telephone The TeleYemen office, on 26th September St downhill from the Plaza Hotel, offers phonecard service for international calls from 7:30 to 8:30 pm – exceptional hours in Yemen, where people only work in the morning! The phones at the GPO are for domestic calls only.

Maps A map of Ta'izz was published by the General Tourist Corporation in 1982. It details the city at 1:10,000 and the centre at 1:5000. On the other side is a map of the province (1:250,000 scale). Although already quite outdated, this map is very handy and is available from the Public Corporation for Tourism office.

Central Market

The old town of Ta'izz was once walled, and parts of the city wall can still be seen on the mountain slopes south of the city. The liveliest part of the old town is definitely the market area comprising the old suqs, by the northern wall of the old city. The market is not big – just a couple of parallel alleys joining the wall's two main gates, Bab Musa (the Gate of Sheikh Musa) and Bab al-Kabir (the Great Gate) – but it is interesting. Most of the items sold in the San'a suqs can be bought here, some at slightly lower prices. If you are seriously considering the purchase of a pricey piece of Yemeni silver, check the Ta'izz suq before returning to San'a. Bargaining is the rule here, unlike most other suqs of Yemen, so don't close your deals at the first shop you visit!

The wide range of food on offer includes fish from the Red Sea and subtropical fruits from the nearby wadis and the Tihama. If you have already developed a taste for qat, you should appreciate the quality of the stuff here. It is advertised that the best qat in Yemen grows on the slopes of Jabal Sabir.

Unlike in most areas of the Yemeni highlands, you'll find female merchants at the market. Most Yemeni tour guides are eager to tell you about the women of Jabal Sabir, who are such tough bargainers that they, instead of the men, sell goods at the market. Enjoying such a 'liberated' status, the colourfully clothed women often wear no veils on their faces, so you can admire the tattoos typical of Yemeni women. They still cover their hair, though, as required by the Koran.

Al-Ashrafiya Mosque

Of exceptional design, al-Ashrafiya Mosque stands majestically on top of the old town. This Rasulid mosque, with its twin minarets, was built in the 13th and 14th centuries by two followers of Turan Shah, al-Ashraf I and al-Ashraf II. It is no longer in active ceremonial use but a Koran school still functions in the side building. Children may be willing to guide you around in the afternoon. If allowed in, women should cover their hair and arms before entering and all visitors should take their shoes off. From the minaret there are wonderful views over the old town and its many mosques.

Other Mosques

West of al-Ashrafiya is another remarkable mosque, al-Mu'tabiya, built in the 16th century. Although this mosque was built by the Turks, its style, with many cupolas but no minaret, is borrowed from Egypt.

Also visible is al-Mudhaffar Mosque, to the south of al-Ashrafiya, with one minaret and more than 20 cupolas. It was built during the 13th century.

The Fortress of Cairo

The fortress, or Qal'at al-Qahira (Unconquerable Fortress), stands on a cliff, high above the city. You will have to admire this much-advertised 'sight' from a distance because it is still in military use and is impossible to enter.

National Museum

The former palace of Imam Ahmad is now a museum. It can be found near the eastern end of 26th September St and is open from 8 am to noon. The entry fee is YR 20 per person.

'The monument of antirevolution', this must be one of the most impressive thematic museums anywhere in the world. According to the official legend, everything has been left just as it was on the night of 26 September 1962, when Imam Ahmad died – including the bedroom filled with the medical equipment he depended on daily. The rooms of the palace are crammed with an astonishing abundance of earthly wealth – wardrobes, perfumes, guns, radios, presents from contemporary rulers – obviously preserved on an 'as is' basis to demonstrate the social injustice of imamic rule.

Visitors born before the early 1950s will experience an eerie sense of déjà vu here, since many common Western household utensils from the 1940s and 1950s are on show as exotic parts of a rare collection.

Salah Palace

Salah Palace, another former palace of the imam since converted into a national museum, stands on the eastern outskirts of Ta'izz. A taxi will take you there from anywhere in the city for about YR 30. Minibuses shuttle continuously along Salah Rd; the fare is YR 20.

This museum is planned more traditionally than the National Museum; there are glass showcases with old silverware like jambiyas and dhumas, a collection of coins, manuscripts of the Koran, clothes, original government documents and photographs of Imam Ahmad. Note the bulging eyes; Ahmad was famed as a cruel ruler and it was generally believed that as a young man, he had practised throttling himself to cultivate this fierce appearance.

On the walls, aerial photographs from around the early 1960s show the former YAR's major towns: San'a, al-Mahwit, Hajja, Sa'da, Dhamar, Yarim, Ibb, al-Hudayda, Zabid, Ta'izz, even al-Makha. These very interesting photos give the layout of all the old Islamic cities. Unfortunately, snapping photos in the museums is *mamnu'*.

The only zoo in Yemen is part of the Salah Palace. The few small cages feature the lions of the imam (but are perhaps more likely their offspring), as well as a couple of other species, like jackals. Considering Yemen's lack of wildlife, it is not surprising the zoo is not bigger.

Both the museum and the zoo charge separate entry fees of YR 20 and are only open before noon.

Places to Stay

As the third largest city in Yemen and with well over 300,000 inhabitants, Ta'izz has plenty of hotels to choose from.

Places to Stay – bottom end

Between the San'a bus stop and the GPO, there are plenty of cheap, one-sheet hotels with double to quadruple rooms. *Sheba*

Palace Hotel, for example, offers beds in triple rooms for YR 300 each; the common bathrooms are filthy, with cold shower only. Around the corner the *al-Habib* offers doubles and triples with private bathrooms for YR 300 per bed; it's not very clean and has cold showers only.

On 26th September St the *al-Whda Hotel* (or al-Wahida Hotel) in a brand new building was already run down barely a year after opening; it offers modest doubles for YR 400. At the corner of San'a St and Gamal Abdul Nasser St is the *as-Salam Hotel*. In this basic but clean hotel a double is YR 400.

If you get into a taxi and ask for a hotel, you will probably be driven to the *DeLuxe Hotel* (☎ 22651) on Gamal Abdul Nasser St, north of Bab al-Kabir. This huge hotel with plenty of rooms is conveniently situated near the old town. While there is nothing terribly 'deluxe' here, this is an acceptable one-sheet hotel with private bathrooms. Prices are around YR 350 per person.

At the very bottom end, no-sheet dormitories are easy to find in the vicinity of the bus stops from both the San'a and al-Hudayda directions.

Places to Stay – middle

Some 100 metres north of the Gamal Abdul Nasser St intersection is the *Borg at-Tahrir Hotel* (☎ 221482). This two-sheet hotel has clean common bathrooms with hot showers and charges YR 350/500 for singles/doubles.

To the south of Gamal Abdul Nasser St, next to the central fruit market, the new *al-Kheir Tourist Hotel* (☎ 216642) charges YR 900 for a clean two-sheet double with hot shower and TV.

Other good hotels in the upper-middle range include the *Plaza Hotel* (☎ 220224) and the *al-Janad Hotel* (☎ 210529) close to the bus office, towards the centre of the city. These comfortable hotels are smaller, however, and tend to be fully booked in advance. In the al-Janad Hotel doubles cost YR 800, while the Plaza Hotel has introduced dollar pricing, rendering itself less competitive, with doubles costing US$20.

Places to Stay – top end

There is a concentration of more expensive hotels on the al-Dabwa mountain, a hill north of the Haud al-Ashraf, on the opposite side of Gamal Abdul Nasser St. The top-class *Marib Hotel* (☎ 210350) offers you Western-style accommodation for up to US$45 per person. The *al-Akhwa Hotel* (or *al Ekhoh*, as the Ta'izz map spells it, ☎ 210364) is cheaper, at YR 1200 to YR 2500 for a double, and at least as good renovated. Both hotels have singles and doubles available.

The *Pensoun Hiltop* (or *Hel Top Hotel*on the Ta'izz map, ☎ 210318) is on the same hill. This is a slowly decaying place, originally in the same category as the other two, but neglected ever since it was built. However, it's much better value for money – doubles with private bath cost YR 600.

An additional benefit here is a nice view over the city. Even if you stay elsewhere, it pays to visit this hill (bring your camera).

Places to Eat

Ta'izz has plenty of eateries evenly distributed around the modern city. There are several on Gamal Abdul Nasser St, ranging from the *Superman Restaurant* to simple shacks on the street selling grilled chicken and similar fare. Uphill from the DeLuxe Hotel, a place named *Restaurant* serves pretty good French-style food at prices only slightly higher than those of the Yemeni eateries.

The *Modern Yemen Restaurant* next to the al-Kheir Hotel is a basic eatery and quite popular with travellers.

A Ta'izzian phenomenon are the so-called 'park restaurants' which feature landscaped courtyards – there are a few within easy reach of the DeLuxe Hotel. The *Lebanese Restaurant* (formerly the *al-Boustan Restaurant*) at the eastern end of Gamal Abdul Nasser St is a neat tidy restaurant, with a large back room for families and wedding parties. You'll easily spend twice the money here than in the more basic restaurants; shih taouq costs YR 430 while shrimps are YR 1000. A pet eagle suffers in his all-too-small cage next to the family room.

Ta'izz has plenty of marvellous sweet shops, which also serve coffee and tea. Try the nameless one on 26th September St, in the commercial area a couple of blocks to the east of the central suqs, or *Napoli Sweets* on central Gamal Abdul Nasser St. The latter also has a small restaurant.

Getting There & Away

It's easy to get to Ta'izz from San'a or al-Hudayda. The Ta'izz airport is north of the city, 20 km along the San'a road.

Bus For bus connections, see the table of bus routes in the Getting Around chapter. Several buses leave daily for al-Hudayda, San'a and Aden. The stations to San'a and al-Hudayda are just outside the city on of the corresponding roads, while buses to Aden leave from near the GPO. Tickets can be bought on the bus or in advance from the bus office.

Taxi Taxis are also easy to find, with fares 10% to 15% above those of the buses. If you come from San'a, sit on the right-hand side of the vehicle. This makes it easier to watch the spectacular scenery of the mountain stretches, especially the Sumarra Pass.

There are separate taxi stations for taxis heading in different directions. Taxis to al-Hudayda (and to al-Makha and at-Turba) wait at the corner of 26th September and Gamal Abdul Nasser Sts, while taxis going in the San'a and Aden direction wait at the junction of the San'a and Aden roads.

When trying to get a city taxi to the station, be careful not to accept offers to drive you all the way to your destination (YR 8000 to San'a, for example); YR 20 should be enough to reach the station.

Getting Around

Unlike San'a, Ta'izz has no city buses. Instead, black-striped minibuses shuttle along Gamal Abdul Nasser St, 26th September St and other longish streets. The fare is YR 10 to YR 20 per person, according to the

length of the ride. If you don't fix the price beforehand, you may well pay YR 100.

AROUND TA'IZZ

You can make a couple of short excursions in the area around Ta'izz.

Jabal Sabir

The high mountain to the south of Ta'izz has been inhabited since time immemorial and, even today, it is under heavy cultivation, with terraces of qat and other crops stretching to the very top of the 3006-metre peak. Depending on the weather, the views of the Ta'izz area can be extraordinary or completely obscured by clouds. In the rainy seasons, however, the weather changes rapidly.

The 1600 metre change in altitude means a significant drop in temperature (between 8°C and 16°C), so be sure you have enough clothing before heading out for the windy mountaintop.

The road up the mountain is not asphalted; in fact it is very bumpy. The 4WD taxis start their 1½-hour climb from Bab al-Kabir, and a seat may cost you YR 160. This is reasonable given the circumstances, although the trip is only six km. Ask for a village called al-Ar'us – it is nearest to the summit. Army camps are often held somewhere near the top of the mountain, making it impossible for a tourist to ascend to the highest peaks.

Sitting in a taxi is not exactly enjoyable here, so you might consider walking back. This also gives you a better chance to admire the green terraced slopes covered in roses and other bushes. Remember that if it rains here, it will rain in the afternoon.

Hujjariya

(Hujjariya; Huggariyah)

A trip to the Hujjariya countryside can best be made by visiting at-Turba, the southernmost town in the area of the former YAR to which you can travel.

Taxis to at-Turba leave from the western taxi station in Ta'izz (see the Ta'izz map). A seat for the 1½-hour trip should not cost more than YR 160. Alongside the road you will see perhaps the biggest tree in Yemen, a baobab *(Adansonia digitata)* with a trunk circumference of 20½ metres. There are some other places of interest, too.

Suq adh-Dhabab

After the at-Turba junction the asphalted road soon descends into a very green wadi (one of the upper branches of the Wadi Bani Khawlan) between Jabal Sabir and Jabal Habashi. The Suq adh-Dhabab village has a lively Sunday market. Ask for directions from the locals since the place is five minute's walk from the main road. As you pass through this fertile valley, with its palms and philodendrons, the origins of the subtropical fruits in the Ta'izz market become obvious. Many families from around Ta'izz like to come here to wash clothes as water is plentiful, but the place is also popular simply for recreation.

Yifrus

(yifrus; Yufrus, Yafrus)

A few km further on, the road again descends to cross the Wadi Bani Khawlan. Twenty-two km from the at-Turba crossroads, a small dirt road crosses to the right. This road leads to a village named Yifrus, famed for its 500-year-old mosque. The white mosque is spectacular, visible long before you reach the village, even from the at-Turba road.

According to the scriptures, this mosque was built by the last Tahirid ruler 'Amir bin 'Abd al-Wahab, to honour a learned man and scholar, Ahmad ibn Alwan. Ahmad lived in Yifrus during the Rasulid era and wrote many books on Sufism and Sunni law.

The mosque is still in full operation, and the original three-km aqueduct brings water to it. You will probably not be allowed in, but the structure is a sight in itself, with its beautifully balanced cupola and minaret.

At-Turba

(at-turba; al-Turbah)

Beyond the Yifrus junction, the at-Turba road rises through Naqil Hasus (the Hasus Pass), at about 1400 metres, to the very stony Hujjariya plateau. The name Hujjariya literally means 'stony'; the appropriateness of the region's name becomes clear along the next 50 km to at-Turba. The vegetation of the region is perhaps more reminiscent of African savanna than that of any other area in Yemen.

The at-Turba village is not very big. Its modest stone houses, few more than three storeys high, have few decorations, the most notable being the clearly protruding waste shafts on many of them.

More spectacular than the village is its location on a steep cliff. The huge Wadi al-Maqatira, which flows towards the Indian Ocean, has eaten its way some 800 metres into the base rock, and many houses have been built on the very edge of the cliff. Perhaps here more than anywhere else in the country, the Yemeni fondness for dramatic locations has dictated the site. In clear weather you can see deep into the Lahej Governorate in southern Yemen.

Al-Janad

(al-janad; Ganad)

Al-Janad, near the Ta'izz airport, is a poor village with only a few clusters of modest, one-storey houses. It attracts a steady flow of travellers, both Muslim and non-Muslim, because it is the site of Yemen's oldest mosque – or a mosque at least as old as the Grand Mosque of San'a. Both were originally built before the Prophet's death in 632 AD and, since then, have been renovated and enlarged many times.

The mosque has a 70-metre-high minaret. Inside, a tranquil atmosphere prevails, encouraged by a certain asceticism of construction. An open rectangular square is surrounded by halls with white stone arches and pillars. There is almost no decoration – just the solemn feel of a holy place.

Many tourist groups are shown this mosque, so the imam of al-Janad has grown used to visitors. If it is not prayer time, you will probably be allowed to enter, as long as you are properly clothed. Take your shoes off first, and give the imam some baksheesh as you leave.

Getting There & Away It is fairly easy to reach al-Janad from Ta'izz. From the San'a taxi station, get a seat in a short-haul taxi up to Mafraq al-Janad. (In this region, to the south of the Sumarra Pass, 'j' is pronounced like the 'g' in 'girl'.) A typical price is YR 50 to YR 60 (six km). No taxis go to al-Janad, but for a few YR (or even for free), virtually any passer-by will take you on the five-km ride. Coming back, you can return to Ta'izz or go on in the direction of Ibb. The taxis will probably take you from Mafraq al-Janad to al-Qa'ida for YR 40 to YR 60 (12 km). From there you can continue to Ibb (YR 45 for the 36-km trip is typical).

Ibb

The Province of Ibb stands to the north-east of Ta'izz and to the south of Dhamar Province. Most of it is at altitudes of over 1500 metres and parts of it are more than twice that high. The highest peaks are Jabal Ta'kar (3230 metres), south of the town of Jibla, and an unnamed 3350-metre mountain north-east of the town of Ibb.

Ibb is known as 'the fertile province' because it gathers most of the rains brought to Yemen by southern winds, receiving five to 10 times more than Ma'rib. Ibb receives 1500 mm of rainfall between late May and early September, when it rains almost every afternoon. There are also occasional showers during the winter months. On a typical summer afternoon, walking around is very impractical because torrents of water flood the streets and roads – something you'd hardly anticipate in Arabia!

Nicknames like 'the Green Land of Arabia' are no exaggeration – the slopes are terraced from the valley floors to the mountaintops. The terraces are very old and some have been here for thousands of years. With water available throughout the year, the fields are harvested three or four times annually. Every imaginable crop, from dates and grain to coffee and qat, can be cultivated somewhere in this province which is the granary of Yemen.

IBB

('ibb; Ebb)

The capital of the province, Ibb was built on a hilltop (altitude 1850 metres) near a valley that cuts through the mountain ridge from north-west to south-east. In recent years the town has spread all the way down to the valley, transforming arable land into streets and buildings – a common occurrence in growing Yemeni cities and towns, which originally served as settlements for farmers cultivating the surrounding land. From 35,000 inhabitants in 1981, this busy town's population has grown to well over 100,000.

The architecture of Ibb features the stone tower houses common in the Yemeni moun-

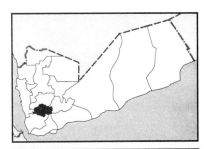

Stone tower house, Ibb

tains. Traditionally, buildings have been made from local grey or pink-toned stone but postrevolutionary construction has favoured the more easily cut orange lava rock which is transported 80 km from the north.

Orientation & Information

The asphalt road between San'a and Ta'izz

no longer passes through the modern centre of Ibb. When the Ibb to al-'Udayn asphalt road was built in the late 1980s, the highway was diverted to pass a couple of km west of Ibb. If you arrive by bus, you will get off at the junction of these roads. A black-striped taxi will take you to the centre for a few riyals.

Basic services (restaurants, hotels and petrol stations) can be found in the new centre, within 10 minute's walk of the al-'Udayn road's junction with the old highway. The new centre, just below and to the west of the old town, is rapidly expanding along the al-'Udayn road. Eventually the road may continue to Suq al-Jarrahi,

near Zabid, where a dirt road already leads from al-'Udayn.

Market day in Ibb is Saturday, when the province's great variety of agricultural products is displayed.

Things to See

Ibb is often neglected by tourists, even though many travellers stop here en route to nearby Jibla. However, the old town inside the almost intact city wall is certainly worth a walk. Take the uphill street from the central market area or from the taxi station.

The stone-paved streets that crisscross the

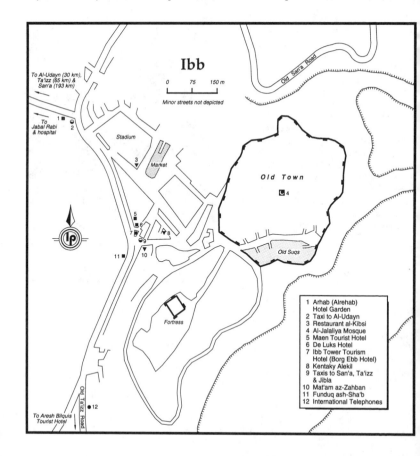

Ibb

To Al-Udayn (30 km),
Ta'izz (65 km) &
San'a (193 km)

Old San'a Road

0   75   150 m

Minor streets not depicted

To Jabal Rabi & hospital

Stadium

Market

Old Town

4

5
6
7
9
8
10
11
Old Suqs

Fortress

To Aresh Bilquis Tourist Hotel

Old Ta'izz Road

12

1 Arhab (Alrehab) Hotel Garden
2 Taxi to Al-Udayn
3 Restaurant al-Kibsi
4 Al-Jalaliya Mosque
5 Maen Tourist Hotel
6 De Luks Hotel
7 Ibb Tower Tourism Hotel (Borg Ebb Hotel)
8 Kentaky Alekil
9 Taxis to San'a, Ta'izz & Jibla
10 Mat'am az-Zahban
11 Funduq ash-Sha'b
12 International Telephones

hilltop are often so narrow that you can't pass around a donkey. The four or five-storey **stone houses** are unpainted, with occasional lime plastering in the footings and window openings. Decoration is sparse but effective – friezes and tiny, round, alabaster-paned windows grouped in twos, threes or fives in arched openings. Old Ibb is a very well-preserved example of the traditional rock architecture of the Yemeni highlands.

The **al-Jalaliya Mosque** in the centre of the old city dates back to the first Ottoman occupation and remains perhaps the most important mosque of the period in all of Yemen. It was built in 1773 AD by the Ottoman viceroy Jamal ad-Din Muhammad Ibn Muhammad an-Nidhari. Muslim visitors may admire the exceptionally beautiful decorations with Quranic scriptures on the mihrab, while non-Muslim visitors are restricted to viewing those on the 35-metre-high minaret. However, the mosque has suffered from neglect during the last couple of centuries, and is in urgent need of restoration.

The old fortress on top of the neighbouring hilltop is for government use and cannot be visited nor approached too closely. To get a better view of the whole town and the green landscape around it, go to the small mountain called **Jabal Rabi** (Mountain of God) halfway between the city centre and the San'a to Ta'izz highway. A taxi should take you to the summit for YR 100, or you can get out at the hospital (Mustashfa Jumhuriya) and walk the rest of the way via a track. On the summit there is an oval-shaped government resort with a restaurant and a swimming pool. There are plans to build a hotel.

Places to Stay

As a rapidly developing provincial capital, Ibb has a selection of hotels, though none are in the top-end category. Most are along the old San'a to Ta'izz road.

Places to Stay – bottom end

There are plenty of one-sheet and two-sheet hotels within 100 metres of the street junction which is used as a station by taxis to Jibla and San'a. These places offer beds in double or triple rooms for around YR 300 to YR 450.

The *De Luks*, near the taxi station, is entered from the upper street. One-sheet doubles go for YR 400, with common bathrooms. You're unlikely to get hot water. The two-sheet *Maen Tourist Hotel* (Ma'in), the next hotel along the San'a road, is essentially the same as De Luks, though it does offer private bathrooms (cold water only).

The *Ibb Tower Tourism Hotel*, also known as the Borg Ebb Hotel, offers filthy doubles with common bathrooms at YR 450. The hotel has a very noisy location – the middle of the taxi station.

Continuing in the Ta'izz direction, *Funduq ash-Sha'b* (winding stairs to the 2nd floor from the street) is what its name promises – a people's hotel. A bed in the dormitory costs YR 300, while in a four-bed room it's YR 500. There is no shower but a cold-water tap and bucket are provided.

Places to Stay – middle

The *Arhab Hotel Garden* (or Alrehab), was built in the late 1980s. Clean doubles with private hot showers cost YR 420. The 'garden' is probably the modern teahouse between the hotel and the junction of the old San'a to Ta'izz road with the new al-'Udayn road.

The *Aresh Bilquis Tourist Hotel* (☎ 402630), on the western side of the old Ta'izz road, is a few hundred metres south of the international telephone cubicles. Clean doubles go for YR 550.

Places to Eat

A good place is the *Mat'am az-Zahban* on the old Ta'izz road opposite the Funduq ash-Shab'. It has two signs; one in Arabic and the other in English. They have a family room upstairs and will guide you there if your group includes females. The small restaurant opposite is more basic but also OK.

The *Mat'am wa Bufiya ash-Shahid al-Kibsi* by the stadium has good views from large windows. Although its sign is in Arabic only, the 2nd-floor restaurant is easy to spot.

The *Kentaky Alekil*, up towards the old town from the central market, is also neat and tidy.

Getting There & Away

You will arrive in Ibb along the north-south highway. The bus fare from San'a (193 km) is YR 280, from Ta'izz (65 km) YR 120. Buses leave you at the new San'a to Ta'izz road and al-'Udayn road junction; take a black-striped taxi or minibus into the centre *(markaz)* of Ibb. Green-striped taxis also run frequently along this stretch and will often take you to the very centre. For a seat in a shared taxi, add YR 40from San'a and YR 20 from Ta'izz.

About 10 km before you reach Ibb, the views of the most dramatic mountains in all of Yemen are spectacular. Approaching Ibb from the north, the road ascends to 2800 metres at the Sumarra Pass, about 45 km before Ibb; 20 km to the south of Ibb there is the Sayyani Pass at 2400 metres. For photographs, it is best to sit on the western side (right-hand side from San'a).

For transport from Ibb to either Ta'izz or San'a, go to the new San'a to Ta'izz road and hail a bus there. The green-striped taxis are a more convenient alternative if you are leaving from the very centre of Ibb.

Getting Around

Ibb is small enough to easily walk around. Black-striped taxis also shuttle along the main roads.

JIBLA

(jibla; Jiblah, Giblah)

A small town with a big history, Jibla is only eight km from Ibb and three km from the Ta'izz road.

History

Jibla is another former capital of Yemen, or at least of the highlands. From 1064 to 1138 the region was ruled by the Sulayhids, a dynasty founded by 'Ali as-Sulayhi. He was a devout Muslim whose doctrine was called Fatimism, an Ismaili branch of the Shi'a sect of Islam. In 1064, after 15 years of preaching, he had attracted enough followers to proclaim his way the right one. Eventually, he founded an independent state, his immediate rivals being the Najahids of Zabid and the Zaydi imams of Sa'da. After starting his revolution on Jabal Masar he ruled the country from San'a.

In 1067 King 'Ali was killed while on pilgrimage to Mecca and his son Mukarram became the new king. However, when Mukarram became seriously ill soon after, his wife, Arwa bint Ahmad, took over the role of head of state. When Mukarram died a few years later, she became queen, ruling until her death, in 1138, at the age of 92. Although she died without issue and the Sulayhi state soon dissolved, her influence was profound.

Queen Arwa's first task was to move the capital of the Sulayhi state to Jibla. During her reign the town flourished and the foundations of the Mosque of Queen Arwa, enlarged many times since, were laid. The ancient terraces on the slopes of the neighbouring mountains were greatly developed in Queen Arwa's days. She was a learned and wise woman, spending the state budget for the common benefit of her people. After 850 years the region of Jibla still bears signs of prosperity and welfare.

Medical Services

The Jibla Baptist Hospital is staffed by US, Dutch and Filipino volunteers. This is the place to go in the region for medical assistance.

Things to See

Jibla is attractively located on a basalt hill between two wadis that join under the town. After crossing the bridge you come to a road leading into town. Take the first street to the left, just after the town funduq and before a small mosque. You will come to the suqs and, eventually, to the **Mosque of Queen Arwa**.

The mosque was built by Queen Arwa, who is buried by the northern wall of the prayer hall, next to the mihrab, which is decorated in Persian style. Her gravestone bears inscriptions in Qufic and old Naskhi calligraphic styles. Incredibly, this tomb was among those attacked by religious extremists in early 1995.

The mosque, a large one with two minarets, and the attached Koran school are still fully functioning. Since the place is frequented by tour groups, you may be allowed to enter the mosque if you are lucky and don't arrive at prayer time. The visit is certainly worthwhile – this is one of the most remarkable and beautiful mosques in Yemen. Even if you're not allowed to enter, you can see the mosque from the slopes of the hill.

If you continue through town, you'll pass the beautiful small mosque **Qubbat Bayt az-ZumQubbat Bayt az-Zum**, which many visitors mistake for the Mosque of Queen Arwa.

The houses of Jibla are stone towers built in the same style as those in Ibb, though many of those in Jibla are more richly ornamented. The road leads to the upper slopes of the hill. From here you can admire the aqueduct built in the days of Queen Arwa. It still brings water from the mountains past the graveyard to the town. On top of the hill you will also find the ruins of the Palace of Queen Arwa.

Places to Stay

There is a small one-sheet hotel as you enter the town. It has clean doubles for YR 350 and common cold-water bathrooms. It's worth considering as an alternative to the similarly priced hotels in Ibb – there is certainly less street noise.

Getting There & Away

From Ibb, you can get a seat in a shared taxi for YR 40; the taxis depart from the main taxi station. Coming from Ta'izz, you could get off at Mafraq Jibla and walk the unpaved road (three km).

AL-'UDAYN

(al-'udayn; Odein)

Thirty km west of Ibb, this very friendly small town by the almost tropical outskirts of Wadi Zabid is well worth visiting, even though it offers no special sights and is not a good place for an overnight stay. If you enjoy

travelling the less visited roads of Yemen, the journey to and from al-'Udayn certainly makes the trip worthwhile.

Getting There & Away

The easiest way to reach al-'Udayn is via the asphalt road built from Ibb in the late 1980s. The road quickly descends more than 1000 metres, meaning a rapid change of atmosphere. There are old stone watchtowers all along the hilltops. A seat in a shared taxi is only YR 80; taxis leave from the junction of the old San'a to Ta'izz road and al-'Udayn road.

Since the new Ibb to al-'Udayn road was built, fewer taxis use the alternative route from Ta'izz via the picturesque mountain town of Mudhaykhira. Taxis leave from in front of the central suqs and charge YR 400 per seat for the 60-km trip to al-'Udayn. However, you may have to use separate taxis to and from Mudhaykhira. The mountain roads make driving difficult. Allow one day for the trip.

The third route to al-'Udayn takes you from the Tihami towns of Hays or Suq al-Jarrahi (near Zabid) via al-Mabraz (59 km from al-'Udayn and 36 km from the Tihama highway). This route is not served by regular taxis at all, so you'll have to rely on walking and getting occasional rides between villages.

DHAFAR

(zafar; Dhofar, Zafar, Zofar)

The capital of the once mighty Himyarites is today a forgotten small village on the northern border of the Ibb Province. If you ask a Yemeni where Dhafar is, the most likely answer is Oman, meaning the western province of that country. Few Yemeni maps show Dhafar, yet it is an officially recognised site of antiquity, with one of the less than 10 museums in Yemen.

History

The Himyarite state was born in the 2nd century BC, when after a civil war in the state of Qataban, two provinces – Himyar and Radman – became independent. They occupied the region at the very south-western end of the Arabian Peninsula, controlling the Bab al-Mandab Strait. This strait soon became very strategic when new discoveries in the field of navigation made it possible for the Romans to send ships to India and back through the Red Sea.

Around 20 BC the Himyarites began to build a new capital, Dhafar, on the high plateau (3000 metres above sea level) near present-day Yarim. The flourishing state kept extending its power and, in 50 AD, there was a profound change in the southern Arabian balance of power – the Sabaean state collapsed. It had been weakened by continuing wars with its neighbours and internal power struggles, and faced diminishing income because the new sea routes stole traffic from the old caravan routes. The age-old Sabaean dynasty was replaced by rulers from the highlands.

Although the Sabaeans were able to successfully revolt against the Himyarites in 190 AD, the Himyarite hegemony was restored barely 100 years later. In the end, the Himyarite king Shammar Yuharish ruled an area that encompassed all of present-day Yemen. He called himself 'King of Saba, Dhi Raydan, Hadhramawt and Yamna'.

The Himyarites later moved their capital to Ma'rib; after all, Saba had been the spiritual centre of the region for centuries, lending its gods – the Moon, Sun and Venus – to its rivals. The holiest temples were also in Ma'rib. Dhafar took a step backwards in importance. The next centuries before the arrival of Islam saw the destruction of the Himyarite Kingdom in continuing wars between Ethiopian Aksumites and Persians on Yemeni soil.

Things to See & Do

Dhafar is a small village. Some guys make money by acting as guides (very rare in Yemen) but you hardly need a guide. Still, you may find it difficult to refuse one!

Dhafar is an impressive example of the spontaneous preservation of antique items – every other modest stone house seems to have a Himyarite **sculpture** (or a piece of

one) used as a building block, often above the main entrance. You can see bulls' heads, reliefs of other beasts, plants and human motifs. The small government-built **museum** in the centre of the village seems to open its doors whenever there are customers. Entry costs YR 20.

A walk through the village is also worthwhile; the cliffs around the village are full of **caves** that are used as houses or as donkey stables. The disparity between these rough dwellings and the fine sculptures used within them demonstrates the enormous timespan over which the hill has been used.

Getting There & Away

Visiting Dhafar is a problem if you are travelling on your own, even though the village is only a 30-minute ride from the San'a to Ta'izz road (4WD needed). The small village of Kitab is served by taxis that operate between Ibb, Yarim and Dhamar, some five km south of Yarim. The fare from Ibb is the same to either Kitab or Yarim – YR 120.

It is here that the problems begin. Dhafar is a very small village and very little traffic heads from Kitab to Dhafar in the morning or early afternoon. This makes it impossible to get a seat in a shared taxi. The drivers are aware of your predicament and will charge exaggerated sums like YR 2500 for the return trip to Dhafar. They simply don't offer a one-way ticket for the seven-km trip. If you are in a group of six, YR 1200 would be fair, with one hour in Dhafar, but you are unlikely to get a bargain like this.

We chose to hitchhike instead. After passing the first village in the midst of the fields, you'll see a conical mountain. It makes a good landmark, and behind it the mountains embracing Dhafar begin. Finding the village by the cave-dotted slope was the easy part – we got a ride on the platform of a Toyota van. You can then walk back down the mountain road between impressive volcanic formations, then along the desolate mud road running through the fields. Heavy rain in the Sumarra Pass can make this route considerably difficult, especially in the rainy season.

An alternative route is from Yarim. Take the road east to Qa'taba and get off at a village named Chaw. Then walk or drive south some 10 km to Dhafar. It might be interesting to combine these routes, using one to reach Dhafar and a different one to leave. The region is sparsely populated, however, so if you get lost, you may have to walk for hours before meeting anybody to ask for directions.

YARIM
(yari:m; Yerim)

Yarim, in the fertile Yarim basin, is the north-ernmost town in the Province of Ibb. At 2550 metres above sea level, it is the highest-standing town in Yemen. Although Yarim is a very old settlement, most of the structures were built after the civil war of the 1960s. When the famous Danish expedition's botanical expert, Finnish-born Peter Forsskal, died here in 1763, Yarim was just a tiny village.

The Yarim and Dhamar basins are in the most volcanically active area of northern Yemen. There are many hot springs, with bathhouses built around them. Look out for very low buildings with small cupolas on the roofs; the hammams are built partly below street level to preserve heat, while the openings on top of the cupolas let sunlight in.

Modern-day Yarim is another roadside-market town, with plenty of eateries and a few modest no-sheet hotels (about YR 300 per person) along the main road.

HAMMAM DAMT
(Hamma:m damt)

This bath resort is near an extinct volcano, 47 km to the east of Yarim. The asphalt road continues all the way to Aden.

Things to See

Your first impression of Hammam Damt will probably be the **volcano** on the north-eastern side of the main road. The original village of Hammam Damt is behind the volcano; in recent years it has grown into a sizeable town, with modern buildings all the way from the village around the volcano up to the main road.

It takes only a few minutes to climb the volcano; steel stairs on the volcano's village side help you up the steepest part. There is a police station at the bottom of the stairs – you may have to ask for permission to climb the volcano. There is no entrance fee.

The volcano is by far the freakiest 'sight' Yemeni nature has to offer. A very even pathway leads almost all the way around the crater, leaving only 20 metres impossible to walk on. Deep within the crater, a small lake with green water shimmers in the sun – magical!

Hot springs abound on the northern side of the volcano, many with bathhouses built around them. The big bathhouse by the creek is accessible to both men and women but at different times of the day. On the other side of the creek are more tiny craters.

The place is obviously frequented by Yemeni tourists, since there are more restaurants and hotels than you would normally find in such a small town. One day this site may become a major tourist attraction, but when we last visited we were the only foreigners in town.

Places to Stay & Eat

The *Damt Tourist Hotel* by the main road, at the start of the main street through the town, is a clean one-sheet hotel offering doubles for YR 700. Hot water is available in shared bathrooms. The first bathroom receives water from the hot springs.

By the main road a couple of hotels, with signs in Arabic only, offer more basic accommodation for YR 300. No-sheet hotels intended for Yemenis coming for a healing bath are to be found in the main village.

The Damt Tourist Hotel also has a restaurant, competing with the eateries by the main road. There are more restaurants in the new town by the main street.

Getting There & Away

Hammam Damt is served by buses and taxis. From San'a take the Qa'taba bus, which departs from Bab al-Yaman at 7 am. The fare is YR 300 for buses and YR 320 for taxis. Alternatively, you can get to Hammam Damt from Yarim by bus or pay about YR 120 for a seat in a taxi.

Beyond Yarim the road soon descends into a steep gorge, which subsequently opens into a densely populated and extensively cultivated wadi. This is one of the headwaters of Wadi Bana, a huge wadi that flows through the Abyan Governorate in the southern part of the country, reaching the Indian Ocean near the town of Zinjibar. About 34 km from Yarim there is a village named ar-Radhma. Hammam Damt is 13 km further on.

QA'TABA

(qa'taba; Qatabah)

Some 35 km beyond Hammam Damt, you will reach Qa'taba, an old border town by the former YAR-PDRY boundary. It lies on the Yarim to Aden highway, which continues to Qa'taba's South Yemeni sister town, adh Dhala', standing on a mountain slope on the other side of the former border (see adh Dhala' in the Lahej chapter).

The asphalt road up to Qa'taba was completed in the mid-1980s and continued to adh-Dhala' after the 1990 unification. It opened the shortcut to Aden, used by buses and taxis from San'a.

Dhamar

The Province of Dhamar lies in the central highlands; the important agricultural basins of Ma'bar and Dhamar are at an altitude of almost 2500 metres. Irrigation has been practised in this region from ancient times and wide areas are under intense cultivation. The surface is relatively flat, so the large terraces are well suited to the use of modern machinery, making the region ideal for grain production.

To the west the province descends all the way to the Tihama east of Bayt al-Faqih and Zabid. The province seems to serve mainly as a thoroughfare for both Yemeni business people and foreign tourists, whose activities tend to target the neighbouring regions.

Politically, Dhamar is a place of rivalry for the two ruling parties, the People's General Congress (PGC) and the Yemeni Congregation for Reform (Islah), both of which have strong support in the province. After the unification of Yemen in 1990 strong military units from the former PDRY were placed here in an unsuccessful attempt to achieve balance: it was in the city of Dhamar that the 1994 civil war finally broke out on 4 May between the supporters of the Yemeni Socialist Party and its northern opponents.

DHAMAR
(dhama:r)
The town of Dhamar, in the centre of the Dhamar basin, is of ancient origin. It was founded by the legendary Himyarite king Dhamar 'Ali, renowned for restoring the great dam of Ma'rib. Dhamar is the only town in northern Yemen which is not surrounded by a wall or natural defensive formations; it is just a settlement on the plains. Centrally situated with good connections to the nearby provinces, the town has prospered as a market and meeting place for tribes living nearby.

Architecturally the houses of Dhamar are a mixture of the stone tower houses and the mud houses of the eastern plains, combined

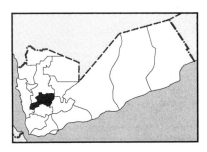

with the brick construction method common in bigger towns. The stone walls often have inlaid arches and fanlights of brick. To give a smoother appearance, brick walls may be plastered with mud, inside and out. The decorations are not as elaborate as those in San'a, though. The Ottoman-style al-Amir Sunbul Mosque in the centre of the old city was completed in 1622 AD. The square building is made of granite rock, with a 35-metre minaret of red brick with gypsum decorations.

Qa' al-Yahud is the former Jewish quarter of Dhamar. This closely-walled section of mud houses demonstrates the isolation in which the Yemeni Jews once lived, typical of the Yemeni Jews all over the country.

Orientation
The San'a to Ta'izz road passes through narrow 'modern Dhamar'; the old town is to the east. Although Dhamar would be a remarkable place seen in isolation, you would probably not rate it as a 'sight' after a week in Yemen because there's nothing particularly special about it.

Places to Stay
Dhamar has no nice hotels but you will find some one-sheet hotels on the San'a to Ta'izz road. These places have quadruple rooms (YR 300 a bed) and common bathrooms (cold showers only).

If you really have to stay overnight in this region, I recommend you take the one-hour ride to Rada' (see Rada' in the al-Baydha chapter), where there is much more choice.

Getting There & Away
Dhamar is on the San'a to Ta'izz highway, 99 km from San'a and 139 km from Ta'izz, so it is an easy place to reach by bus or taxi – and even easier to go straight past.

MA'BAR
(ma'bar; Mabar, Maabar)
Ma'bar is a small town 31 km north of Dhamar, on the San'a to Ta'izz road. Its main peculiarity is that the two-storey houses in the old town are built exclusively of mud. While this kind of architecture is common on the eastern plateaus, it is rare in this area where stone or mixed construction dominates.

The road to al-Hudayda, completed in the mid-1980s, branches to the west in Ma'bar.

DHAWRAN
(zawra:n; Dawran)
Dhawran, a small town some 15 km west of Ma'bar, once served as a royal town. The partly ruined old mosque here is built to the same plan as the mosque at ar-Rawdha, near San'a.

HAMMAM 'ALI
(Hamma:m 'ali; Hammam Ali)
This famous bath resort 35 km north-west of Dhamar owes its existence to the countless hot sulphurous springs on the southern slopes of Jabal Dhawran. The numerous bathhouses here are eagerly visited by Yemenis from near and far. They believe that the hot water is good for their health – it probably is. The high season is January to February, the coldest part of the winter, when a hot bath is a most welcome contrast to the raw mountain climate.

Apart from the bathhouses, which are scattered along the lower slopes of the valley, there is little to see in the small village of Hammam 'Ali. The tiny stone huts higher up on the slopes serve as temporary shelters for the customers. During the high season all the huts are occupied; at other times most of them stay empty.

The typical bathhouse here is a longish one-storey building divided into a row of small bathing chambers. The water runs through the building from one chamber to the next and small openings in the ceilings let in the sunlight.

If you decide to take a relaxing bath, it should not cost you more than a few riyals. There are separate bathhouses for men and women.

Market day in Hammam 'Ali is Monday.

Places to Stay
There are plenty of modest, traditional Yemeni hotels in the village. This is one place where you don't have to worry about the hotel washing facilities – just go to a bathhouse for a hot bath!

Getting There & Away
There are two ways to get to Hammam 'Ali: the old, interesting way and the new, easy way.

The interesting route starts from Dhamar, where 4WD taxis wait to transport bathers to Hammam 'Ali for YR 120 to YR 160 per person. This route takes you first along the highway; eight km north of Dhamar you branch west onto a dirt road and head towards a conical mountain far on the horizon. After a 30-minute ride, past a hilltop village that was badly damaged in the 1982 earthquake, the road descends to a steep wadi. From here it is a one-hour drive to Hammam 'Ali.

The easy route uses the new Ma'bar to Bajil road, which passes near Hammam 'Ali before reaching Madinat ash-Sharq further in the same wadi. If you continue beyond Hammam 'Ali you will end up on this road.

BAYNUN
(baynu:n)
For history freaks only, the ruins of still another Himyarite capital, Baynun, lie east of Dhamar. The town was completely destroyed in about 525 AD by Aksumites, or

Ethiopians. Baynun is one of the less-researched ancient sites in Yemen, and it is not clear when the town was founded or how big it eventually got.

The most impressive structures, easily appreciated even by a lay person, are the nearby irrigation channels and tunnels, hewn in the bedrock. These are at least 1500 years old but are well preserved, even though they do not carry water any more.

The famous Yemeni historian al-Hamdani, of the 10th century AD, described Jabal Baynun as a mountain completely drilled-through. It is still possible to walk through one tunnel that is 150 metres long. The rocks by the tunnels bear inscriptions stating that the channels were dug in order to help irrigate the plantations in Wadi an-Numara to the east of the mountain.

Getting There & Away

There are several dirt roads which reach Baynun from Dhamar, but none of these provide an easy way to find the place. No regular shared taxis are available. A 4WD vehicle and a local guide are strongly recommended, the latter because the villagers by Baynun are a bit suspicious of strangers.

The most direct route is along a dirt track north-east of Dhamar, which leads to the village of an-Numara. The 35 km to 40 km stretch to Baynun takes some two or three hours.

A longer but more interesting route goes via the spectacular volcanic region by Jabal Isbil. Take the al-Baydha road east from Dhamar for some 30 km, then turn left just before the roadside market village called Sanaban. The dirt road proceeds via the village of Hammar Sulayman towards the 3190-metre high Isbil mountain, where hot springs abound. The village of Jarf Isbil there is frequented by Yemenis because of its many hot baths, but fails to offer any facilities for Western travellers.

The road eventually continues between the Isbil and the nearby Dhi Rakam mountains to the north-west, and after another hour or two you will end up in Baynun.

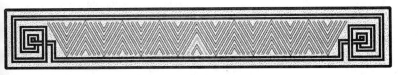

Al-Baydha

The relatively sparsely populated Province of al-Baydha is in the south-eastern part of the former YAR, east of Dhamar and Ibb and to the south of Ma'rib. The capital of the province, al-Baydha, lies at the very south-eastern tip of the province, next to the town of Mukayras, in the Abyan Governorate of the southern part of the country.

Before unification the province's southern and eastern borders with the PDRY were undemarcated, and tourism in the province was understandably restricted. Such obstacles no longer exist, though the infrastructure to support tourism will take some time to develop. An asphalted road leads through the province and links its two major towns, al-Baydha and Rada', with Dhamar.

In the towns, stone and mud architecture coexist, often within a single house – stone in the lower storeys and mud in the upper levels. Along the road there are a couple of larger villages between the towns but most of the settlements in the south-eastern mountains are small hilltop clusters of one and two-storey houses, built in stone and surfaced with mud. Here and there you will see towers built of schist stone, with their characteristic sharply raised corners.

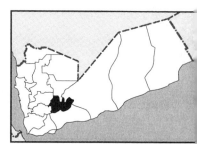

RADA'

(rada:'; Radaa, Rida)
Although Rada' does not have the status of a provincial capital, it is the more important of the province's two towns. In recent years the town has experienced explosive growth. It lies on a plain, and at one side of the old town there is a fortified rocky hill. Parts of the town wall, together with the western gate, still stand. Although the town is mainly built of mud, the wall is made of stone.

Orientation

Buses and taxis leave you by the Dhamar to al-Baydha road, with old Rada' to your left. The first stop will probably be in the midst

Houses in Rada'

of the new town, which materialised seemingly out of nowhere in the latter half of the 1980s. You'd do better to ask for the Brother's Hotel (Funduq al-Ikhwa). You will then be dropped off at a junction only a couple of hundred metres from the old town. The road leads you straight to the centre, where you'll find all the facilities you'll need, from hotels and restaurants to the police station and pharmacy.

Things to See

You'll find it rewarding to walk around the very large **old centre**, built of brick and mud. The **houses** present a striking contrast to the stone architecture of the midlands – compare Rada' with Ibb, for example. Although the ground floors may be of stone, the next floors are usually built of brick and finished with a beautiful, smooth mud surfacing that needs to be renewed every year. If you are lucky, you may even see this elaborate manual process. The local mud has an odd greyish tone, unique in Yemen.

Keep an eye open for the **windows** and **fanlights**. The double or triple-arched fanlights with huge alabaster panes and mud-and-brick framing are unique to Rada' and cannot be seen anywhere else in Yemen. A walk in the **old suq** next to the al-Amiriya Mosque is also rewarding.

The new town is a pleasing example of the Yemeni respect for local conditions and tradition in architecture. Compare the mud-covered houses along the Dhamar to al-Baydha road with the new houses in San'a or Ta'izz, for example.

Al-Amiriya Mosque This exceptional mosque with grooved cupolas at the corners stands in the centre of the old town. It was built, in a style unique in Yemen, by 'Amir bin 'Abd al-Wahab, the same Tahirid sultan who built the Yifrus Mosque in the Hujjariya. Almost 500 years old, the mosque is no longer in active ceremonial use and was even in severe danger of collapse in the late 1980s. Fortunately a restoration project finally commenced in 1990, and is still continuing.

Places to Stay

The *Brothers Hotel*, visible from the Dhamar to al-Baydha road, was built in 1986 in modern style and is obviously targeted at foreigners. With triples for YR 550, it is an economical one-sheet hotel. There is one bathroom (with warm shower) for every two rooms, and a dormitory on the ground floor caters for those travelling on a tight budget.

If you prefer an old Yemeni-style house, just look some 300 metres further – to the left is a tower house with the clear sign 'HOTEL' on the roof. This is the *'Arsh Bilqis Hotel*, with doubles, triples and quadruples for YR 350 a bed. Common bathrooms in the corridors have showers; boilers will be switched on upon demand. This place has a very amiable atmosphere but is not that clean.

Places to Eat

There are several restaurants along the main road, between the Brothers Hotel and the central market. When we visited, three of them were serving huge whole fish, grilled over a roaring fire.

Getting There & Away

Rada' is served by regular bus connections from San'a (see the table of bus routes in the Getting Around chapter). From Dhamar, the easiest way to get to Rada' is by shared taxi. The 55-km ride on the very good road across the plain costs YR 100 per person and takes less than one hour.

Just a few km before Rada' you can spot the youngest volcano in Yemen, al-Lisi, still fuming steam now and then. There is a telecommunications station on top of the mountain.

AL-BAYDHA

(al-Bayza:; al-Bayda, al-Beida)
Many tourists think that al-Baydha must be very exotic because of its remote location on the south-eastern outskirts of the former YAR. However, there's nothing special about it. The town is just a small, albeit fast-developing, provincial capital with plenty of stone buildings in postrevolutionary style, often painted in strikingly inappropriate colours.

Older houses are built either of stone or of

mud. Combinations also occur, with lower floors built of stone and perhaps the uppermost floor made of mud. Windows are small and waste shafts are replaced by protruding drainage pipes.

The road to al-Baydha does not offer many surprises, either. Apart from a couple of larger villages along the road and some hilltop hamlets here and there, you will mainly see desolate stony stretches with the occasional shrub. A few very small wadis cross the road in this watershed between the drainages of Wadi Bana, which flow towards the Indian Ocean, and those of Wadi Adhana, which flow to Ma'rib. Some very beautiful

mud villages can be found in the vicinity of al-Baydha.

Getting There & Away

You can get to al-Baydha easily from San'a on the twice-daily bus. From Rada' it's best to take a taxi to al-Baydha – YR 160 will buy you a seat for the 125-km ride. Traffic is not heavy on the asphalt road that passes through this sparsely populated province.

From al-Baydha you can continue to al-Mukayras and Lawdar in the Abyan Governorate and further to southern Shabwa and Hadhramawt.

Ma'rib

Ma'rib is the easternmost province of the former YAR. Only its western border is clearly defined; no boundary stones mark the sands of ar-Ruba' al-Khali desert, nor have the borders been drawn on a map. This is the land of Bedouin tribes. Only a few villages line the wadis that descend from the eastern mountains to spill their scanty waters in the sands.

Sparse vegetation and an equally sparse population make the province look like a developing area, a burden to the country. Yet it was here that Saba, the mightiest kingdom of ancient Arabia, flourished. Ma'rib is also the site of the oil discoveries of the 1980s that promise to save the Yemeni economy.

There are not many places you can visit in Ma'rib Province. While the province is no longer officially off limits, apart from Ma'rib itself and the road to Shabwa via Harib, most of the province is, in practice, off limits to tourists, most likely because local tribes hold more power than the central government. You also are not welcome to visit the oil production areas without an invitation and guidance from the company. Before the asphalt road from San'a to Ma'rib was built in 1980, visitors usually had to fly to Ma'rib. Today the airport is for military and industrial use only.

MA'RIB

(ma:'rib; Mareb, Maarib, Maareb)

Ma'rib is the most famous archaeological site in Yemen. Once the capital of the Kingdom of Saba, the city was reduced to a small village in the 6th century AD after the final collapse of the kingdom. For hundreds of years the village remained basically the same; the earliest European expeditions to reach it depicted 19th-century Ma'rib very much as it appeared in the mid-1980s.

Ma'rib is often a destination for foreign tourists. Yemenis expect every traveller to see Ma'rib, though many have not been there themselves. Because it is easily reached

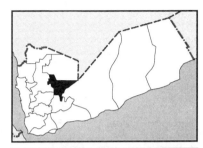

The five pillars of the Temple of the Moon

from San'a, you can hurry through the sights of Ma'rib and Baraqish (in al-Jawf) in a single day, starting early (6 or 7 am) from San'a and being back by sunset. However, a lazier pace is certainly worthwhile – if you've got a car of your own, it also gives your driver some time to recuperate before the drive back.

Another possibility is not to return to San'a but to continue on to Shabwa and/or Hadhramawt from Ma'rib.

History

Ma'rib was probably inhabited much earlier than the oldest written accounts testify. Human survival on the eastern escarpment, where annual rainfall is scanty (below 300 mm), is based on the existence of wadis that collect their waters from the rainfall over large areas of arid land. One of the greatest of these wadis, Wadi Adhana (or Wadi Dhana), by which Ma'rib lies, has a catchment area of 10,000 sq km, reaching from the Dhamar basin in the south-west.

In the 8th century BC a great dam was built in Ma'rib, which was at that time called Maryab. The wadi flowed through a gorge between two mountains, Jabal Balaq al-Qibli and Jabal Balaq al-Awsat. Between these mountains a 680-metre wall of sand, mud and gravel was built, strengthened by rocks of lava and limestone. Over the centuries the wall was gradually enlarged and strengthened until, finally, its height reached 16 metres in the middle of the wadi. This remarkable feat of ancient engineering was so dominant a feature that it gave the entire wadi a new name: Wadi as-Sudd, or the Wadi of the Dam.

Sluice gates were constructed at the northern and southern ends of the dam to divert

Sabaean Script

The development of many alphabetic scripts in use today has been traced down to ancient Phoenician, a script which developed around the year 1000 BC on the eastern shores of the Mediterranean Sea. Alphabetic script was a significant step forward from the pictorial script used in Pharaonic Egypt, as the system greatly reduced the number of different characters to be mastered. Scholars debate the details, and the exact dates of each phase are not known, but the evolution of the scripts can be outlined.

Between 800 BC and 600 BC the use of alphabetic script spread among Mediterranean cultures, and the scripts of old Greek, Aramaic and Hebrew each evolved from the Phoenician. Simultaneously, or soon after that, use of the script spread south along the Arabian Peninsula, producing two variants by the year 500 BC or so: the North and South Arabian scripts.

The latter is often called the Sabaean script after the most famous kingdom to have used the script, although 'Sabaean' inscriptions have been found all around Southern Arabia when archaeologists have excavated ruins and sites of many capitals dating from the thousand-year era around the beginning of our calendar. To date, some 4000 Sabaean texts have been discovered.

Eventually, the Sabaean script fell into disuse, as the cultures that based their literature on it declined. New scripts originating from the North emerged. The present script of Arabic originally developed from the Nabatean script, itself a successor of Aramaic. Nabatean script spread with Christianity, while Arabic is, of course, the script of Islam. While Christianity and Judaism both made brief appearances in Southern Arabia before the advent of Islam, very few traces of the use of Nabatean or Hebrew are left in the region.

The South Arabian script didn't vanish, however. It accompanied Axumite conquerors across the Red Sea to the present-day Ethiopia, where it was preserved after the withdrawal of the Axumites from Saba. Ancient Ethiopic was a worthy successor of the Sabaean script – by the time Christianity reached Ethiopia in the fourth century AD, the script had developed into that of Ge'ez, the language in which the Ethiopian translation of the Bible was written and which is still in clerical use in the country. The common scripts of Amharic and Tigrinya, languages spoken in Ethiopia and Tigrinya today, are very similar to the script of Ge'ez.

Phoenician, Sabaean, Hebrew and Arabic share a common feature: they are all consonant scripts. Vowels are not generally indicated in writing, although diphthongs can be written down and some characters may be pronounced as vowels in certain contexts. Hence the scripts have a conveniently limited number of characters – 28 in Arabic, for example. The Greek script developed into a familiar Western-style one with vowels as independent characters. On the other hand, the Ethiopian script is a syllabaric script, with each consonant-vowel pair having a character of its own, hence the number of distinct characters is as high as 276.

water to the fields that were cultivated on both banks of the wadi, known as the North and South oases. In fact, the dam was not for collecting water in a huge reservoir, but was designed to steer water to the terraces and fields higher up on the wadi banks. Even so, silting was a major problem (the water carried heavy sediment that caused the fields of the oases to rise more than one cm a year), so the dam eventually had to be raised and constant maintenance was needed to guarantee proper irrigation of all fields.

The system was nonetheless effective; for more than a thousand years it provided irrigation to 96 sq km of fields, sustaining a population of between 30,000 and 50,000 people. Excess water was no doubt used by smaller settlements along the wadi. Cereals such as teff, millet, barley and oat were grown, as well as broomcorn, grape, cumin, flax, garden sorrel and sesame.

There were even palm plantations in the capital of Saba, providing travellers along the incense route with welcome shade on the long desert road. By virtue of this strategic location on the incense road, Saba's fame spread across the civilised world, from Rome to India. The opportunity to collect taxes from the caravans that passed by with their precious loads gave Saba a prosperity that would not have been possible for a purely agricultural settlement.

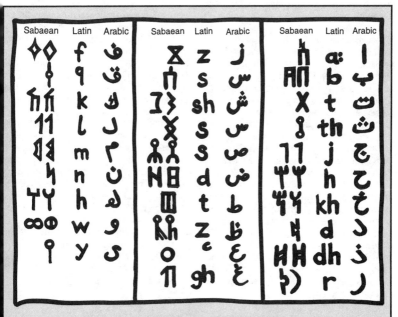

This illustration compares the scripts of Arabic, Latin and Sabaean, in Arabic alphabetic order, showing some but not all variants of the Sabaean characters. The Arabic and Sabaean scripts are written from right to left. But don't expect to be able to read the columns in Ma'rib or in the museums of Yemen, as vowels can only be speculated. Scholars still haven't agreed on, for example, whether the ancient Sabaeans pronounced the name of their moon god, *L-M-Q-H*, as Almaqah or Ilumquh. ■

Over the centuries the Kingdom of Saba waged several wars against neighbouring rival states. In about 500 BC Ma'rib was fortified with a wall. Then around 400 BC the northern tribes freed themselves from Sabaean rule, founding the state of Ma'in. To the east, the Hadhramawt also gained independence. Although Saba was meanwhile able to destroy the Kingdom of Awsan, Qa'taban (to the south) simultaneously gained strength. Wars against Qa'taban, Ma'in and Hadhramawt continued through the 5th century BC.

During the following centuries peaceful periods alternated with wars. New enemies appeared; in 25-24 BC even the Romans, led by Aegius Gallius, carried out a military expedition in southern Arabia. They reached the walls of Ma'rib but were unable to conquer the city. By around 50 AD the rise of the Himyarites and the subsequent wars against them greatly weakened the Kingdom of Saba. In the 2nd century AD the traditional dynasty of Saba was brought to an end and was replaced by rulers from the highlands. Later on, when the Himyarite state was at its largest and during the Ethiopian occupation in the 5th and 6th centuries, Ma'rib was ruled from distant capitals in the mountains.

Maintaining a structure as sophisticated as the Great Dam of Ma'rib called for a strong central authority. The decline of the Kingdom of Saba and the subsequent failure to maintain the dam led to several disasters in which the dam was greatly damaged, even partly washed away by floods after exceptionally heavy rains. The earliest such occasion was recorded in 319 AD. In 542 the dam broke completely but the Ethiopian ruler of Yemen, Abraha, ordered 20,000 workers to do repairs and they succeeded in restoring the dam.

The final catastrophe occurred in 570, when the dam was irrevocably washed away. Most of the inhabitants of Ma'rib fled to various parts of the Arabian Peninsula. Many Arabians today carry the surname 'Yamani', indicating that they are descended from ancient Sabaeans.

After the dam's collapse only a few families stayed in Ma'rib and nearby villages. The incense trade had long since vanished, and the region became 'far from everywhere'. Little is known about the apparently scanty developments of the next 1400 years.

During the civil war of the 1960s, Egyptian forces made Ma'rib a base for their operations. The village was heavily bombed in the intense battles and its future looked grimmer than ever. However, in the 1970s pump irrigation revived agriculture in the region – even in the absence of the dam, ground water was accumulated. By the mid-1980s, the population of the region had grown to about 13,000, far too many for the area to support. The level of ground water sank, drying up the wells.

Ma'rib's future nevertheless seems prosperous for two main reasons. First, in the early 1980s Hunt Oil Corporation found oil east of Ma'rib. Yemen's first oil well went into production in 1986 and a pipeline was built from Ma'rib to as-Salif, north of al-Hudayda. (The YAR was already an oil-exporting country before the unification of the Yemens, though the exports were modest in scale.)

Second, the government of the YAR, conscious of tradition, had an ambitious plan to revive agriculture in the region by means of a new Ma'rib dam, to be built a few km upstream from the site of the ancient dam. Although the economic rationality of the plan was much disputed, the project went ahead and Ma'rib is now a much greener place than it was in the mid-1980s.

The Ma'rib of today is a bustling town; heavy trucks raising dust in the windy air is a common sight. One wonders what will remain of the ancient relics which probably lie buried in the sands.

Orientation & Information

If you have hired a car and a driver you will not have to worry about orientation. If, however, you arrive by bus or shared taxi, you will be left at what is called 'New Ma'rib', a collection of shops, petrol stations, government offices and other houses

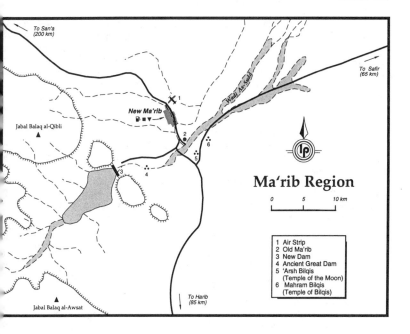

Ma'rib Region

0   5   10 km

1 Air Strip
2 Old Ma'rib
3 New Dam
4 Ancient Great Dam
5 'Arsh Bilqis
   (Temple of the Moon)
6 Mahram Bilqis
   (Temple of Bilqis)

ust past the Ma'rib airport. Here you can have something to eat and buy bottles of fresh water for the visit to old Ma'rib. Buy plenty of water; the air is extremely hot in Ma'rib and you will sweat a lot more here than in San'a. If you plan to do a lot of walking, take some salt tablets with you to replenish your salt levels.

The road continues to the old village of Ma'rib, a couple of km away on the bank of Wadi as-Sudd. Just before the village a new road branches to the right, leading to the sites of the old and new dams a little way upstream. The archaeological sites are widely scattered around the wadi, so you will need a car to see everything. This involves a 30-km round trip along the asphalted roads built through the sands in the late 1980s.

If you are travelling on your own, you should be able to get lifts with the Toyotas passing by. Another possibility is to hire a car locally; around YR 1000 should be enough.

Things to See

The usual schedule for tourists includes the old village of Ma'rib, three archaeological sites and the new dam, though the banks of the wadi probably conceal many other sites worth excavating. If you take a walk around here you will see many small heaps of rubble and sand – closer inspection shows them to be the ruins of ancient houses.

In addition you will probably see several sand-carrying whirlwinds. I have seen more of them here than anywhere else in Yemen.

Old Ma'rib The village stands on a tiny hill and can be seen from the new Ma'rib. Old Ma'rib is an impressive place, with its small-windowed mud skyscrapers, their stone basements often sporting stones from ancient monuments. You will see Sabaean inscriptions, ornaments and figurative motifs such as ibex heads on these stones.

Many of the houses lie in ruins following the bombings of the civil war in the 1960s, while many more have been damaged through lack of care and maintenance that these mud buildings require. Only a couple of families still live in old Ma'rib, and you might think it was deserted were it not for the goats and children greeting you. Perhaps it won't be long before the place is totally abandoned.

'Arsh Bilqis On the other side of the wadi, just a couple of km south-southwest of old Ma'rib, you will find the remnants of remarkable Sabaean temples, now half-buried in a sand dune and surrounded by a wire fence. Before the building of the new dam it was possible to walk the distance during the dry season. Nowadays water flows all year, making walking impractical.

A longer but easier route takes you along asphalt roads. As you head along the road from new Ma'rib to the dam, turn left to Jaw al-Ubar, over the wadi. Turn left again at the Safir-Harib junction, eight km from new Ma'rib, and you will soon see a sign pointing left to the 'Balqis Palace'.

A few hundred metres to the west stand the five pillars of the Temple of the Moon. The sixth pillar is broken in the middle, as if to remind you of the five undisputed pillars and the one disputed pillar of the faith of Islam (see Religion in Facts about the Country). Local people call this 'Arsh Bilqis, or the Throne of Bilqis. Bilqis is the Yemeni name for the legendary queen of Saba, who visited King Solomon in the 10th century BC.

Archaeologists disagree with this view, holding instead that the pillars once belonged to a temple consecrated to the moon god Almaqah (Ilumquh). Further research on the question is needed, and excavations are under way.

Mahram Bilqis An even more imposing site can be reached by continuing further in the direction of Safir and turning right at the sign reading 'Sun Temple'.

Yemenis call this temple Mahram Bilqis, which translates as 'Temple of Bilqis'. Again, this attribution is probably wrong, since archaeological studies indicate that the temple was actually built around 400 BC and was originally known as the Temple of Awwam. The word *maHram* means 'Temple of Refuge', indicating that it was not an ordinary temple but one which enjoyed so-called *haram* (taboo, forbidden) status. Persecuted people could take refuge inside, and even the worst criminal could obtain temporary shelter.

American archaeologists performed excavations here between the years 1950 and 1952, exposing most of the temple from the sands. Their work was, however, interrupted by local tribespeople whose suspicions of the oddly behaving strangers finally turned to open hostility. Today the desert has reclaimed much of the temple, leaving only pillars rising from the sands. The temple's oval form is not easily perceived; it is surrounded by a wall nine metres high and four metres thick. Visiting this place makes you wonder what other surprises Yemen's dunes might hide.

The Great Dam of Ma'rib Back on the road that leads to the dams, you come to the ancient Great Dam of Ma'rib, some eight km upstream. Little of it remains; there is no trace of the dam in the bottom of the wadi, just the ruins of the sluice gates on each bank. Looking across from one sluice to the other gives you an idea of the immense scale of the ancient construction.

The northern sluice was originally the bigger of the two, although less remains of it today. A police checkpoint by the roadside marks the site today, and the site is well worth a close study. If you wander around it you can clearly see the canal system that distributed water to fields at different heights. Nearby are the so-called 'Stones of King', with Himyarite inscriptions from the 4th century AD describing dam repairs. The site also contains carefully cut stones that carry Sabaean inscriptions.

The New Dam Continuing just a couple of km along the green wadi from the old dam you will come to the vast new dam, which connects the two mountains like a giant ruler.

Walking on top of the huge structure, 40 metres high and 760 metres long, gives you ample time to contemplate this incredible combination of respect for ancient history and confidence in modern technology.

In the first place, the whole thing is a gift from Sheikh Zayed bin Sultan al Nahyan, the ruler of Abu Dhabi, whose ancestors lived in Wadi Nahayan, near Ma'rib, and migrated to the shores of the Persian Gulf after the great disaster of 570 AD. In the 1980s Sheikh Zayed donated US$75 million to the government of the YAR to develop the Ma'rib region. A couple of hundred metres before the dam, a memorial stone stands erected on a hill on your right-hand side, with inscriptions in both Sabaean and Arabic script describing the history of the new dam. It is guarded by the pictures of President Salah and Sheikh Zayed.

The dam was built by 400 Turkish workers to plans drawn up by a Swiss company. It is capable of storing 400 million cubic metres of water in the artificial lake. After years of work, the dam itself was finished in 1986, although construction of an elaborate system of irrigation channels and some 20 smaller dams in the region is still taking place.

Whether the money could have been used more reasonably is not a question you should raise with the Yemenis. Today's problem is where to find families who are willing to move to Ma'rib and start taking advantage of the agricultural opportunity created by the dam. Quite a few new farms, including sizable orange plantations, already flourish here and there, and the Ma'rib region is today surprisingly green compared to the desert of the mid-1980s.

Places to Stay – bottom end
The tour operators will want to book your accommodation in one of the top-end hotels, and a look at the cheaper alternative tells you why. The *Brothers Hotel*, by the gasoline station in the main street of new Ma'rib, advertises 'Family Rooms and Suites'. What they have to offer is filthy one-sheet quadruples (YR 300 per bed) with shared

bathrooms. The place also has a dormitory filled with pipe smoke.

Places to Stay – top end
Perhaps partly as a result of recent oil finds and partly in appreciation of the tourism potential of the archaeological sites, there are a couple of higher standard hotels in the rapidly expanding new Ma'rib. A 1st-class hotel opened on the south-western side in 1986. Head towards old Ma'rib until you reach the *Hotel al-Jannattyn* sign by the roadside. The hotel even has a swimming pool in the garden – a most unexpected sight in the middle of the desert, even if it is seldom filled with water. The full name of the place is *Funduq Urdh al-Jannattayn*, or 'Land of Two Paradise Hotel', reflecting the Koran's description of ancient Saba. Prices range from YR 700 to YR 1400; air-conditioning is available.

Another holiday resort hotel, the even more gorgeous *Bilqish Mareb Hotel* (☎ 2666, telex 4033 BQSHT YE), offers doubles for YR 2000. As you arrive from San'a beyond the bus and taxi stations, turn right just after the Brothers Hotel – after a couple of km, well outside the town, the hotel approach is marked by a double gateway.

Places to Eat
For simple eating, there are quite a few Yemeni-style restaurants by the market near the taxi station in new Ma'rib. Take a look at your choices at the street parallel to the main street (they are all about the same) choose whichever is the busiest. The Brothers Hotel also runs a restaurant, popular for lunch.

Getting There & Away
Visiting Ma'rib can either be done within one day, or you can spend the night there in order to continue to Hadhramawt or Shabwa.

Getting to Ma'rib from San'a is easy. There is only one daily bus, leaving from Bab ash-Sha'ub at 2 pm. The 158-km trip takes 2¾ hours and costs YR 300. If you want an early start, yellow-striped taxis start at 6 or 7 am; they charge YR 360 a seat.

However, traffic to Ma'rib is not very heavy, the buses run half-empty and I would not recommend that you rely on getting a taxi later than at 9 or 10 am.

The road first heads north-east, leaving ar-Rawdha and its grape gardens to the west. Then it gradually ascends from the San'a basin to a pass, Naqil bin Ghaylan (altitude 2300 metres), 35 km from San'a. Soon thereafter the road crosses the upper parts of Wadi al-Jawf, then winds through the eastern mountains, turning east. About 70 km from San'a you reach another pass, Naqil al-Farda. The final descent to the eastern deserts now begins, very steeply at first and offering spectacular views to the north. Shortly after Naqil al-Farda an asphalt road branches to the north, leading to Baraqish (see Baraqish in the al-Jawf chapter).

The rest of the road is rather straight, descending to an altitude of 1100 metres and passing through dry lands where rocky hamada-type semidesert alternates with deserts of sand dunes and protruding black lava rocks. Small wadis cross the road here and there. Vegetation consists of small shrubs and grasses, with acacia and tamarisk trees growing where there is enough moisture in the ground. Local tribes practise goat-herding here; you can witness their influence from the many checkpoints en route.

From the south-eastern part of the province, you can reach Ma'rib by taking the road to Harib and continue on to Bayhan (see Bayhan in the Shabwa chapter). This route, however, is subject to restrictions due to security; enquire about current conditions at the tour operators' office in San'a or locally at the taxi station of Ma'rib. During times when peace prevails, it is possible to hitch your way first to Harib and then to Bayhan, although you have to prepare to spend the night in the very small town of Harib, where there are no hotels.

Bedouin Taxis To continue east from Ma'rib, you can contact the Bedouins who organise 4WD vehicles to cross the desert to Hadhramawt; they can also arrange private cars to Bayhan. However, this is outrageously expensive. They use Toyota Land Cruisers which accommodate up to six passengers, and from Ma'rib to Say'un in the Hadhramawt valley the fare is US$300. Whether or not this is feasible depends on the size of your group and your budget. The desert is not difficult to negotiate and the trip only takes five to seven hours – the explanation for the high price is that it also includes security against car hijackers, something that oil companies or tour operators alone cannot guarantee.

Negotiations between travellers and the Bedouins are handled by a tour company called al-Sharef. They operate in the al-Jannattyn Hotel; just ask at reception. The schedule is always the same: you will start punctually at dawn, since the driver has to return the car the same day. You have to provide your own food and drink for the day. (In addition to plain desert-crossing, they also rent camels.)

To further justify the cost, you can choose to visit Shabwa en route (this will add only a couple of hours to your trip). The scenery is much more varied than that along the direct route, and you have a good chance of meeting some Bedouins tending their herds in the desert. If you choose this option, they'll try hard to persuade you to rent a tent for overnighting in the desert, but this will cost another US$100 and is absolutely not necessary. Watch your belongings if you choose this option; the Bedouins are not bound by strict laws against stealing from strangers, and some travellers have lost nearly everything while sleeping.

No similar arrangement exists for travel in the direction of Hadhramawt to Ma'rib, but you may coincidentally come across a Bedouin driver in Say'un, Shibam or al-Qatn, starting his return to Ma'rib in the early afternoon. Here you should be able to negotiate the cost to around US$100 – still expensive but more reasonable. As the memories of the civil war of 1994 fade and tourists return to Yemen, more choices will certainly become available.

SIRWAH
(**s**irwa:H)

The asphalt road from San'a to Ma'rib takes the northern route around the mountains to the east of San'a. The old road to Ma'rib took a more southerly course, past the ancient town of Sirwah.

Sirwah lies by Wadi Ghada, south-west of Jabal al-Barra and 37 km west of Ma'rib, surrounded by mountains. It was the capital of the Sabaean Kingdom before the construction of Ma'rib's irrigation system in the 8th century BC. Exactly when the city was established and when the capital was transferred to Ma'rib is still to be determined by archaeological research, which has been hampered by the suspiciousness of local tribes. However, the reason for the transfer of the capital is clear – the tiny Wadi Ghada was not able to sustain as large a population as the bigger Wadi Adhana.

Modern-day Sirwah, like old Ma'rib, is only a shadow of its past self, a mere village near the ruins of the ancient capital. Sirwah does still have sizable ruins but it is likely only archaeology buffs will appreciate them.

Getting There & Away
There is no regular public transport to Sirwah, so you will need to arrange your own transport and a local guide. Consult the travel agencies in San'a. After a break of many years some tour operators are again willing to organise tours to Sirwah, but security might again pose a problem. In late 1994, however, visits were only arranged in convoys of a minimum of three cars.

Al-Jawf

The Province of al-Jawf encompasses the north-eastern region of semidesert and total desert formerly inhabited only by the nomadic Bedouins. Tourists are usually neither allowed nor wanted in the province. This was the stronghold of Royalists during the civil war of the 1960s; the local sheikhs still consider themselves to be in charge and are hostile to strangers.

Oil explorers of the 1980s and the subsequent flow of government and foreign oil workers did not help the situation. The Bedouins' share of the wealth brought by oil is nil, yet their way of life is being destroyed. They see every 4WD vehicle as a potential threat, bringing disorder and disturbance to their world. Whether it carries oil workers or tourists makes little difference. Some have even dealt with the situation by forcing the car to stop at gunpoint and taking it over.

However, should the province open up to foreign travellers, there are a couple of places of interest.

The province gets its name from Wadi al-Jawf, a giant wadi originating in the mountains north-east of San'a and south-east of Sa'da. The region may not always have been as arid as it is today; in antiquity an important kingdom called Ma'in flourished here, with Saba and Hadhramawt as its foes. Also known as Minaeans, the people of Ma'in were originally subordinate to Ma'rib but, in the course of centuries, gained strength and independence.

Ma'in is the least researched of the ancient kingdoms of southern Arabia. What is known is that it was at its strongest between the years 410 BC (when it started to cause severe trouble for the Sabaean rulers) and 120 BC (when it was conquered by the Kingdom of Saba). In its heyday Ma'in controlled a large stretch of the incense route between Ma'rib and Najran.

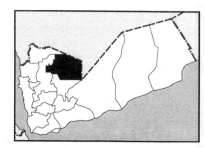

BARAQISH
(bara:qish)

The original capital of the Kingdom of Ma'in and also known as Yathil, Baraqish stands on the eastern bank of Wadi Farda, a tributary of Wadi al-Jawf. Even today the ruins are most impressive, though the centuries have not been kind to the place. It is the only historic site in al-Jawf Province that can occasionally be reached by travellers.

Baraqish was the capital for just a few decades around the year 400 BC. It was a very tightly built urban settlement. The 14-metre-high city walls are still mostly intact; the dozens of impressive watchtowers were once visible from a distance of many km. The wall certainly had a defensive function but was even more important as a demonstration of wealth.

Little is known about developments in Baraqish after the capital was moved to Ma'in. However, the city remained inhabited for centuries, with new houses built on the ruins of old ones.

Old stones that bear Minaean inscriptions have been used to repair the city wall here and there. The top layer of the now deserted city almost reaches the top of the surrounding walls, with the remaining few houses built in the Islamic architectural style. In the centre of the area are the ruins of a mosque, with a deep well in the middle. Excavations have partially exposed ruins of what is thought to be a temple of the main god, Attar.

The city is surrounded by a wire fence with a gate on the northern side. Make sure you stay on friendly terms with the Bedouins guarding the site; the only payment they get is from tourists.

Getting There & Away

Visiting Baraqish can be conveniently combined with a visit to Ma'rib, since it only adds about an hour to the driving time. In the late 1980s an asphalt road to al-Hazm was built from the San'a to Ma'rib highway, 35 km south of Baraqish. The new road passes through Baraqish and Ma'in. There is no public transport to Baraqish, so you'll have to either make a deal with a tour operator in San'a or hire a private taxi in Ma'rib.

MA'IN
(ma'i:n)

The much less intact ruins of the subsequent capital of the Kingdom of Ma'in, also known as Qarnawu, are only some 20 km north of Baraqish.

The place has never been included on the list of tourist destinations, and tour operators are not including the site in their programmes. Instead, you can persuade a taxi driver from Ma'rib to take you there in a combined visit to Baraqish, if the current security situation allows it.

AL-HAZM AL-JAWF
(al-Hazm)

The modern capital of the Province of al-Jawf, al-Hazm al-Jawf is today served by domestic Yemen Airways flights. The town, only a few km north-west of the ruins of Ma'in, is the base for the oil drillers and explorers in the region and is of no particular interest. To the west, along the wadi, the ruins of two ancient towns, as-Sawda and al-Bayda, are not currently accessible to travellers.

Aden

The Aden Governorate has the smallest area of the southern governorates, comprising just Aden, its immediate surroundings and the island of Suqutra.

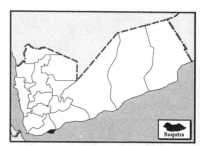

ADEN
('adan)

The most important sea port and the winter capital of Yemen, the city of Aden is built on a site of past volcanic activity. The huge lava mountains by the shore shelter a natural deep port that is capable of harbouring even the largest of vessels.

History

Considering the geography of Aden, it is not surprising that the site has been inhabited from time immemorial. The similarity of the words Aden and Eden has given rise to some wildly improbable myths, and the graves of Cain and Abel are said to lie here. Another popular Yemeni legend claims Aden was the site where Noah's ark was built, making the town nearly the oldest port in the world.

More recently, it is known that Aden served as the port of the ancient Kingdom of Awsan between the 7th and 5th centuries BC. The site of this kingdom's capital has yet to be discovered. In 410 BC Awsan was defeated by Saba, starting a long sequence of changes in the sovereignty of Aden. Ancient kings, local sheikhs and sultans of the Islamic era as well as distant colonists from Ethiopia, Egypt and Europe all ruled over or enjoyed the benefits of this natural port's convenient location on the major sea route between India and Europe.

After 1497 AD, when Vasco da Gama discovered the alternative route around Africa, the importance of Aden began to diminish, only to be revived when the Suez Canal was completed in 1869. The British, who had held Aden for 30 years at that time, remained in control until 1967 when the independent South Yemeni state was born. During the later years of the British rule

Entrance of al-'Aydarus Mosque, Aden

Aden was one of the largest ports in the world, serving as an important stop for passenger ships from Europe to India.

Throughout its independence the PDRY was plagued with political instability, repeatedly manifested in the worst imaginable way – violent unrest either within the country or along its borders. The last such event took

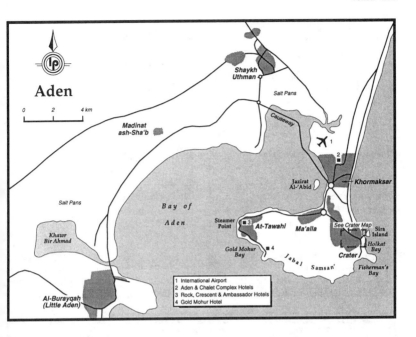

Aden

0 2 4 km

Shaykh Uthman

Salt Pans

Madinat ash-Sha'b

Causeway

Jazirat Al-'Abid

Khormaksar

Salt Pans

Bay of Aden

Khawr Bir Ahmad

Steamer Point

At-Tawahi

Ma'alla

See Crater Map

Sira Island

Holkat Bay

Gold Mohur Bay

Crater

Jabal Samsan'

Fisherman's Bay

Al-Burayqah (Little Aden)

1 International Airport
2 Aden & Chalet Complex Hotels
3 Rock, Crescent & Ambassador Hotels
4 Gold Mohur Hotel

place in January 1986, when an 11-day civil war devastated Aden. Several thousands of people were killed and the country was practically closed to foreigners for six months.

When the two Yemens finally united on 22 May 1990, Aden was declared the 'economic capital of the country', though the new country was to be governed from San'a. The decision to make Aden the trade capital was obviously because of its superior port.

However, the plans for the role of Aden in the unified country were not realised during the four years between unification and the civil war of 1994. While Yemeni politicians were occupied in power struggles in San'a, Aden was all but neglected, along with other southern governorates. Moreover, it lost its former status as the hub for all transport between the northern and southern part of the country. New road connections from al-Baydha to Lawdar and from Ma'rib to Wadi Hadhramawt bypassed the southern capital, where previously travellers would often stop

overnight. The same applied to air traffic, with direct flights from San'a to al-Mukalla and Say'un reducing the need to visit Aden.

The civil war of 1994 was particularly brutal for the Adenis. For most of the two months, the city was under siege. Towards the end of the war most of the water pumping facilities were destroyed, with afternoon temperatures hovering around 45°C. The lack of drinkable water gave rise to cholera outbreaks, threatening those who survived the actual fights. When the northern troops finally marched on to the centre of the besieged city, Adenis cheered at the enemy tanks arriving with soldiers waving plastic cans of water.

Aden was not bombed heavily, but in the aftermath of the war the city suffered significant intentional damage. The most visible legacy of British influence, the Seera brewery (which had continued to supply the country with beer) was finally bombed to pieces. Hotels and restaurants that had been serving alcoholic drinks were damaged. Moreover, all government buildings and shops in Aden were looted, and the city's prospects seemed grim.

However, President Salah decided to restore order by declaring the city as the 'winter capital of Yemen'. Few people believed these were anything more than empty words, but in November 1994 Salah did indeed move the government from San'a to Aden for three months.

Today, Aden is a much different city than it was before the war. Chewing qat as well as carrying jambiyas is now legal, as in elsewhere in the southern governorates. Regrettably, strict rulings against littering were abandoned too, and today the formerly clean southern towns are as cluttered with debris as the northern ones have always been.

Aden used to be the most secular city in all of Yemen, with the socialist legislature emphasising education and equality of the sexes. Since the war, religion has been used

extensively as a means for power by the northerners in the south. Women now wear veils in Aden; at our last visit we were left unserved in one of Aden's cafes while the all-male staff were literally chasing one of the last ladies of Aden, refusing to veil herself and demanding service against all odds, out of the establishment.

Orientation

Despite the long history and cosmopolitan flavour of this very old seaport, (the population consists of Arabs, Bedouins, Somalis and other Africans, Pakistanis, Indians and Chinese), Aden is not exactly the place to go in search of *l'exotique*.

Aden actually consists of several towns: the classical port city of Aden on the cape, the industrial Little Aden with its huge oil refinery on the western shores of the Bay of Aden and the new government centre, Madinat ash-Sha'b (also spelt al-Shaab). This centre, the 'people's city', was some-

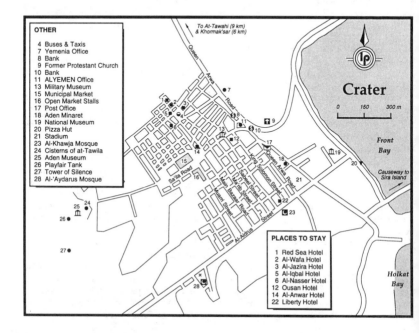

OTHER

4 Buses & Taxis
7 Yemenia Office
8 Bank
9 Former Protestant Church
10 Bank
11 ALYEMEN Office
13 Military Museum
15 Municipal Market
16 Open Market Stalls
17 Post Office
18 Aden Minaret
19 National Museum
20 Pizza Hut
21 Stadium
23 Al-Khawja Mosque
24 Cisterns of at-Tawila
25 Aden Museum
26 Playfair Tank
27 Tower of Silence
28 Al-'Aydarus Mosque

To At-Tawahi (9 km)
& Khormak'sar (6 km)

Queen Arwa Road

Crater

0   150   300 m

Front Bay

Causeway to Sira Island

Holkat Bay

Sa'ila Road
Miani Street
Main Bazaar Road
Gabriel Street
Ali Abdu Street
Queen Arwa Road
Solomon Street
Al-Adrus Street

PLACES TO STAY

1 Red Sea Hotel
2 Al-Wafa Hotel
3 Al-Jazira Hotel
5 Al-Iqbal Hotel
6 Al-Nasser Hotel
12 Ousan Hotel
14 Al-Anwar Hotel
22 Liberty Hotel

times referred to as the actual capital of the PDRY during the years of communist rule, and is marked in some Western atlases from the period, too. To the north of the old city are the suburbs of Khormaksar, in the neck of Cape Aden, and Sheikh Othman (named after the founder of Aden), a few km inland. Between them is Aden's international airport. Salt works can be seen on the plains between the towns.

The old city is scattered around the almost 600-metre-high volcano that forms Cape Aden. The oldest and biggest subcentre is the Crater (also spelt Critir or Critire) area, on the eastern part of the cape, surrounded by majestic lava rocks. To the east, Crater opens to the sea at Holkat Bay, with the mountainous Sira Island topped by an old Turkish fort on the left.

To the west of Crater is the central Ma'alla, facing the harbour to the north, and around the western tip (the colonial Steamer Point) of the cape is at-Tawahi, where you'll find the oldest of the city's hotels. Here you may also come across some tax-free shops. Although an oddity today, these shops have a remarkable past: during the last years of British rule in the 1960s, more than 200,000 transit passengers and tourists visited Aden each year, and the city's duty-free trade was the fourth largest in the world (after London, Liverpool and New York). In an effort to regain its former status, Aden was declared a free port again in May 1991.

Continuing along the coast you finally arrive at Gold Mohur Bay, a fine beach frequented by residents of Aden. The rest of the southern coast is rocky and undeveloped.

In spite of the city's age, Aden has relatively few old buildings. The strong British influence in architecture was replaced by an even stronger Russian influence during the existence of the PDRY. As an official leaflet from the early 1980s proudly puts it, 'Aden is a clean, well-organised city with many modern buildings'. There are dozens of blocks of these modern buildings in the Ma'alla district. Although many books state that the extraordinarily grim-looking buildings by the Ma'alla Main St are a showcase

of Socialist Realism in architecture, they were actually built during British rule to house the families of the British forces stationed in Aden.

Information

Banks in Aden are open from 7.30 am to 12.30 pm; market rates for your greenbacks are available at the Ma'in Bazaar Rd in Crater. The ALYEMEN office for domestic flights is on Main Ma'alla St in eastern Ma'alla; for international flights go to the Queen Arwa Rd office in central Crater.

Cisterns of At-Tawila

The Cisterns of at-Tawila are among the very oldest sights in Aden. These huge cisterns are high on the slopes of Jabal Shamsan, with excellent views over Crater to the north-east. The 18 cisterns can store a total of 42 million litres of water. It takes extraordinary heavy rains to fill all the cisterns, an occurrence which takes place only a few times in a century.

The cisterns were probably built by the Himyarites in the 1st century AD. The official brochures from the days of the PDRY give 427 BC as the date of construction, but any project of this magnitude must have taken decades, and the 'BC' is likely to mean 'Before Hijra' rather than 'Before Christ'. Little more is known of the cisterns; in the memoirs of the Maghrebian traveller Ibn Battuta from the 14th century, cisterns of Aden are mentioned. In any case, over time the cisterns fell into disuse, filling with debris and laying forgotten for centuries. In 1854 a British lieutenant named Lambert rediscovered the cisterns. The present appearance of the cisterns is the result of renovations carried out by the British led by the then lieutenant, later Sir Lambert, in the mid-1800s. The cisterns carry the name Playfair Tanks in British literature.

They are no longer used for their original purposes: to store drinking water and to regulate excess water during heavy rains. This is regrettable as the channels leading to the sea from the cisterns have been filled and are now used as streets. The torrential rains of

1993 caused the cisterns to overflow, which resulted in serious floodings and heavy damage in Crater.

The few lower, larger cisterns can be admired on a leisurely stroll, but to see the cisterns higher up the mountain, you need perseverance and must not be susceptible to vertigo. A barely recognisable stone path leads up from one of the lower cisterns – ask the local keepers of the cisterns for guidance. You need half a day and several litres of water per person to visit. Leave early in the morning to avoid the heat.

Aden Museum

This tiny museum, in a garden just by the cisterns, displays photos and illustrations as well as some technical drawings from the 1930s, when the site was last refurbished. The museum is presently open on demand only. During the British reign this was a dance restaurant for the Westerners, a tradition continued by the PDRY – an extremely unlikely possibility in unified Yemen!

Tower of Silence

This holy site of the Zoroastrian community of Aden is today totally abandoned. From the 7th century BC Zoroastrianism was the religion in Persia, named after the founder, Zoroaster. The followers of the religion fled to India after the advent of Islam, where they were called Parsees after their Persian origin. Today there are some one hundred thousand Parsees left, mostly living in the region of Bombay.

In late 1800s a group of Parsees from Bombay arrived in Aden along with the British. They built this tower, enclosed in circular concrete walls, according to their tradition. The tower was used in their burial ceremonies and as a place of pilgrimage. In the tower an eternal holy fire used to burn; in the 1970s, when the Adeni Parsees re-emigrated to India, the fire was transferred to the temple of Lonavala in India.

To get to the tower, head along the road which leads from the Cisterns of Tawila towards Sa'ila Road, and turn right at the car

repair shop. In the backyard, behind the huge unbuilt block, a gate shows the way up on the left hand side of the mountain. You can get to the gate by going round the block also taking the first street to the right after the car repair shop, but the climb is steeper here. The road is well laid but unkept, and it takes some twenty minutes to half an hour to reach the tower.

Al-'Aydarus Mosque

Al-'Aydarus (al-'idaru:s) Mosque, on al-Aidrus St, is one of the oldest mosques in Aden. First built in the 14th century AD, it was rebuilt after being destroyed in 1859. Today, however, it is one of the few buildings in Aden constructed before 1900.

In September 1994, two months after the 1994 civil war ended, the tomb and shrine of al-'Aydarus next to the mosque were bombed to pieces by religious extremists from northern Yemen. Also destroyed was the shrine at the al-Hashimi Mosque in Sheikh Othman, the northern suburb of Aden. The explanation for the destruction lies in the Zaydi interpretation of a passage in the Koran, where building a mosque on top of a grave is prohibited. Because many mosques in the Shafa'i areas in southern Yemen have tombs and shrines attached, they have been religious targets for political ends.

The al-'Aydarus Mosque should not be mistaken for the nearby **al-Khawja Mosque**, a blazing-white mosque with Indian Mogul influence evident in the cupolas and minarets.

Aden Minaret

Although the 8th century mosque to which it belonged is long gone, this blazing white minaret still stands among the modern houses of the central Crater area, not far from the central post office.

Rimbaud House

During the British rule, Aden was visited by many famous people. One of the most cele-

Rimbaud

In his short and tragic life, the French poet Arthur Rimbaud (1854-1891) wrote some of the greatest and most influential poetry of the modern era. Rimbaud was a child prodigy who began writing as a form of rebellion against his repressive upbringing and the depravity of his times. He repeatedly ran away from his mother's provincial home, roaming the streets and countryside during the terrible Franco-Prussian war and rise of the Paris Commune.

In his later teens, the impoverished poet tried to win the respect of the Paris literary set, but they were appalled by his ragged clothes, lice-infested hair and obvious use of hashish and opium. His scandalous homosexual affair with the married poet Verlaine sealed his fate as an outcast. During a quarrel, Verlaine shot and wounded Rimbaud.

After completing *Ma Bohème* (My Bohemian Life), and the extraordinary prose poems *Les Illuminations* and *Une Saison en Enfer* (A Season in Hell), Rimbaud, at the age of 19, abandoned writing forever. He took to the open road, travelling for many years across Europe and as far east as Java.

In 1880 Rimbaud arrived in Aden and gained employment as a clerk in the shop of a coffee exporter named Bardey. He wrote to his family: 'Aden is a frightful rock without a single blade of grass or a drop of fresh water...I am like a prisoner here.' For the next 11 years Rimbaud moved between Aden and Bardey's other store in Harar, Abyssinia (Ethiopia), and made disastrous attempts at selling guns to warring tribes. For four years Rimbaud lived in the walled Muslim city of Harar. While there, he explored the surrounding country and wrote a report on his findings that was published by the Société de Géographie in Paris.

In 1884 Rimbaud returned to Aden with a slave girl with whom he lived. In the greatest misadventure of his gunrunning career, Rimbaud used his savings to buy a large arsenal of weapons, and spent the next four years trying to sell them. His search for a buyer eventually led him on a perilous four-month journey into Abyssinia during which his caravan was repeatedly attacked by Danakil tribespeople. In the end, he was forced to sell his guns for a pittance. Rimbaud persisted in his trading endeavours until 1891, when he developed a severe knee tumour that eventually forced him to sail from Aden back to France. In Marseilles he had his right leg amputated and died soon after, at the age of 37.

Arthur Rimbaud

Bethune Carmichael

brated was the French romantic poet and arms trader Arthur Rimbaud, who spent time in Aden during his travels to Harar in Ethiopia from 1880 to 1891. The house he lived in still stands in Crater, one hundred metres east of the GPO. The French have renovated the house and in November 1991 a high-ranking French delegation inaugurated the *maison Rimbaud* (also known as the *Espace culturel et poétique franco-yéménite, dit maison Rimbaud*), which is now the French Cultural Centre and consulate.

Sira Island

You can glimpse Sira Island near the National Museum from many parts of Crater. It is easily distinguishable by the Turkish fort on top of the mountainous island; the Britons continued fortifying the island in the mid-1800s. The island would no doubt offer fantastic views over the Crater, but unfortunately, you can't climb the mountain as the fort is still in military use.

In the post-unification bliss of 1990 a decision was made to develop the island into a first-class international recreation centre. But apparently in response to military influence, it was Crater's adjacent shores that were partitioned for various companies interested in joining the project rather than the island. During our visit several building projects were still in their early stages.

At-Tawahi

The international port and passenger terminal of Aden during the British rule was in the western part of the city. At-Tawahi was called Steamer Point by the Britons, and the region still offers glimpses of the colonial past. The historical Rock and Crescent hotels are mere shadows of their former grandeur and the Aden Gardens in the centre of at-Tawahi are comparatively unkempt. Even the Monument of the Unknown Soldier, erected in the 1980s in pompous Socialist style next to the Crescent Hotel, was destroyed in the aftermath of the 1994 civil war.

But continue to the west and you soon come to the Prince of Wales Pier with the passenger terminal waiting for better times, still housing a small souvenir shop even though there has been practically no passenger traffic for years. Halfway between the Aden Gardens and the pier is an antiquarian shop with items from the colonial times for sale. It is at Steamer Point where you are most likely to come across old chaps fluent in English and with vivid memories, who may tell you stories of the Aden of the 1960s, and how the city has changed.

Half a km or so further towards Gold Mohur Bay on the left is the only functioning Christian church in Yemen – St France's Catholic Church. Just before the church, on top of the mountain, is Little Ben, a copy of London's Big Ben. This monument has also faced destruction in the upheavals since the departure of the British.

Places to Stay

Finding accommodation in Aden is a real problem because the hotels are always overbooked, and the good old ones have been mismanaged during and after the communist era. Furthermore, since unification many hotels serving alcohol were damaged in terrorist attacks or wars. Trying to confirm your reservation beforehand is not reliable, and you might end up phoning other hotels from the reception area of the one you had booked!

The *Aden Hotel* near the airport has been completely renovated since its restaurant was bombed in early 1991.

The *26 September Hotel* (☎ 322266), in at-Tawahi, was known in the colonial era as the *Rock Hotel at Steamer Point* and is still better known by this name. Foreign journalists used to frequent this place, and it's a tempting choice for those with a sense of nostalgia. However, the hotel is still badly damaged from the wars of 1986 and 1994, and the few functioning rooms seem to be occupied by permanent residents. The nearby *Ambassador Hotel* has reopened and charges from YR 1200 to YR 1800 per room.

Places to Stay – bottom end

The *Red Sea Hotel*, *Iqbal Hotel*, *al-Jazira Hotel* (☎ 321234) and *al-Nasser Hotel* are one-sheet hotels in the central Crater, within one block from the bus/taxi station. In the same category are *al-Hurriya*, also known as the *Liberty Hotel* (☎ 3252217) and *Ousan Hotel*, near the Military Museum. They are all modest establishments with more or less filthy common bathrooms. Pricing is per bed, usually varying from YR 300 to 450, less in rooms with no air-conditioning. The smallest rooms are usually doubles, but if you arrive later in the afternoon only quadruples may be left, which is not cost-effective for solo travellers or couples.

Places to Stay – middle

Continuing in the one-sheet category but in newer and cleaner buildings, the *al-Wafa Hotel*, near the central taxi and bus stations of Crater, offers doubles with air-conditioning and common bathrooms for YR 750. Of similar standard is the *al-Anwar Hotel* near the Cisterns of at-Tawila; doubles with air-conditioning cost YR 850 while a room with a fan is only YR 420.

More expensive in the two-sheet category

is the completely renovated *Sailors' Club*
(☎ 203209/203559) in western at-Tawahi.
Doubles cost YR 1450.

The *Chalet Complex Hotel* (☎ 341301) at
Khormaksar is expensive but cheaper than
the luxury Aden Hotel Moevenpick (see
below), if you like listening to aircraft during
the night.

The *Funduq al-Hilal* (☎ 323471) (better
known as the Crescent Hotel) is the biggest
hotel in at-Tawahi, comprising two separate
buildings. It offers doubles for US$60, a
price which is on par with the fame and
tradition of this historic hotel but definitely
not with the present condition of the place.
The establishment has not been renovated
since the Britons were expelled in 1967, and
the building is rapidly deteriorating.

Places to Stay – top end
Aden Hotel Moevenpick (☎ 32947) in
Khormaksar, near the airport, was extensively renovated in the late 1980s. Doubles
in this luxury hotel cost US$210.

Places to Eat
The bigger hotels in Aden have restaurants,
though the food is usually average. At the
time of writing, the *Sailors' Club* was about
to open a restaurant with an open-air area on
the waterfront.

In at-Tawahi, between the hotels and the
bus station, you can't miss the *Cafeteria
Broast Roasting*, in the Aden Gardens. The
very popular open-air cafe next to it is highly
recommended. Here you can sip coffee or
tea and, in the evenings, admire the incredibly colourfully lit fountain nearby. On the
northern side of the park the *Osan Broast &
Restaurant Tourist*, boasting a 'part for
familis' (separate dining-room), offers high-
quality low-spice meals at inflated prices.
This very clean place is recommended if
you need a change from the basic Yemeni
eateries.

In Crater, the best teahouses and traditional restaurants are in the suq area around
the Ma'in Bazaar Rd, to the east from the
central bus and taxi stations. Several confec-
tionery shops here sell traditional Arabic

sweets. Next to Sira Island is the *Pizza Hut*
outlet.

Getting There & Away
Aden is served by buses and taxis from the
north and east. Alternatively you could fly to
Aden from San'a or from other southern
governorates. Flying directly to Aden
(instead of San'a) from other countries is
also possible. Aden used to be served by
numerous cargo ship lines, but after the 1994
civil war most of them have redirected their
routes and now go via al-Hudayda or
Djibouti.

Aden's main bus station is in Sheikh
Othman, which is connected with central
Aden by blue city buses and taxis (both cost
YR 20). A private taxi should not cost more
than YR 200. Buses leave at 6 am for al-
Mukalla (YR 800 per person), at 6.30 am for
Ataq (YR 300) and Azal (YR 300), and at 7
am for Ta'izz (YR 400). You have to show
up at the station early in the morning to book
a ticket (at least 30 minutes before the bus
leaves).

Near to the bus station there are the taxi
stations of Sheikh Othman, serving more
spontaneous travellers and those who have
just missed the bus. Shared taxis travel to the
places listed above at fares from 20% to
100% higher than bus fares. Taxis to nearby
places leave from a different station than
those which cover long-distance trips; ask
the minibus driver to drop you off by the
right station for your destination.

More conveniently, a few taxis also leave
from the city bus station in Crater. However,
it is advisable to be here early in the morning,
no later than 7 am, to be sure of getting a seat.

Getting Around
Aden used to have a functional public transport system, with large and small blue buses
shuttling between the subcentres. However,
this state-run system now seems to be on the
verge of collapse. The private white
minibuses, introduced after unification cost
YR 10 to 20 per person depending on distance. You pay the driver after the ride.

Using private taxis is also affordable in

Aden but, unlike in the north, you have to bargain hard. The yellow taxis are old, the white ones are post-unification competitors. They should take you between any two points on the cape of Aden for YR 100 and to Sheikh Othman for YR 200 but you will often be asked for a few times this amount.

SUQUTRA
(suqutra; Socotra)

The Horn of Africa points towards Suqutra, in the Arabian Sea. Yemen's largest island, Suqutra is 350 km off the southern coast of the Arabian Peninsula and almost 1000 km from Aden. It is part of the Governorate of Aden and is of significant strategic interest because it is the only island of any considerable size in this area and one which many ships pass through. It was the entry point to the area for European colonialism in the 16th century, when the Portuguese first occupied it, and was under British rule from 1876 to 1967. During the Cold War era the importance of a Soviet naval base here was much disputed although today we are left to wonder if one ever existed.

Suqutra has been inhabited for at least a few thousand years but written accounts are scanty. It is known that the Sabaeans occupied the island in the 6th century BC. The population was converted to Christianity around 600 AD and in 900 AD Christian missions were launched to mainland Yemen by the Suqutran bishop. Even today, many of the island's 30,000 inhabitants are Christian, though the form of Christianity they practise is greatly influenced by Islam.

The island, with its many rare plant (including giant dragon blood trees and bottle trees) and bird species, was dutifully listed as one of the 'tourist sites' of the former PDRY. No doubt its sandy beaches and the many fish in its waters offer considerable potential for a tourist resort. No steps, however, have been taken to develop the island, and today it is all but inaccessible for sightseeing purposes. (Research carried out by UNESCO in 1993 suggested the establishment of a nature and bio-diversity conservation programme on the island instead.)

The only way to reach Suqutra is to book a seat on the weekly flight from al-Mukalla. However, there is only one guesthouse in Hadibu, the capital of the island, and getting around the island is difficult – if not impossible – due to the poor condition or lack of roads. For a group of nature-enthusiasts fluent in Arabic (or Suqutric, the local language!) and with their own tent and time to spare, a trip to Suqutra could be worthwhile.

Lahej

The westernmost two of the southern governorates, Lahej and Abyan occupy the area between the former YAR and the Gulf of Aden. These are the most fertile governorates in the southern part of the country and the only ones with mountains high enough for qat cultivation. Several wadis flow into the region from the mountains of the north; the most important of these, Wadi Bana, forms the border between Lahej and Abyan.

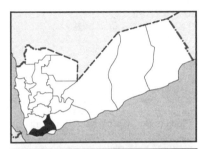

Lahej, however, as a governorate sandwiched between the powerful cities of Ta'izz and Aden, has suffered from years of neglect. While unification in 1990 placed local officials under the governance of San'a, the situation remained unchanged. During the civil war of 1994, northern armies rolled over Lahej on their march to Aden, failing to clear thousands of landmines sown by the separatist forces.

If you travel from Tai'zz to Aden by road, you will descend from the mountains and travel along the beautiful Wadi Tuban, and through the central part of the Lahej Governorate. Alternatively, the road from San'a passes through the towns of Qa'taba, adh-Dhala' and al-Habilayn before joining the Ta'izz to Aden highway.

LAHEJ
(laHij; Lahij, Lahaj)

Lahej, the capital of the governorate, is some 45 km north of Aden. The new, official name of the town is al-Hawta (al-Hu:ta). Lahej has some 25,000 inhabitants, and is located in the midst of a very productive agricultural region. The roadside market in the centre of the town is at its most lively in the morning.

Before the 1967 revolution, the Sultan of Lahej, one of the mightiest sultans in the southern part of Yemen, lived here. His palace, in the centre of the town, on the eastern side of the taxi station, having since been a school of agriculture as well as a bank office, is still worth seeing

Mosque ash-Sha'b

despite almost 30 years of neglect. Black marble columns guarding the main door are about the only remains of the past splendour of the house, along with the front garden where you can barely see the pattern of paths lined by white marble columns, and a fountain that is sadly broken.

A couple of hundred metres to the east

211

of the taxi station, past the palace, is the Mosque ash-Sha'b, the most notable of the town's mosques.

Getting There & Away

Shared taxis from the Sheikh Othman short-haul taxi station in Aden will take you to Lahej for YR 40. When asking around for the right taxi, note that in the south Lahej is pronounced as Laheg, with the 'g' as in 'go', otherwise you will not be understood. If you are still not understood, try asking for al-Hawta.

If you are coming from the north and heading for Aden by bus or taxi, you could get off in Lahej, spend an hour or two here, and then continue on in one of the frequently departing share taxis.

ADH-DHALA'

(a**z**-**za**:la:'; Dhala, Talla, ad-Dali)
Adh-Dhala' is 96 km from Aden at the northernmost tip of the governorate, very close to the town of Qa'taba in the Province of Ibb. Due to its high altitude and mountainous scenery, Adh-Dhala' was listed as one of the most touristy destinations in the low-lying former PDRY. However, the town pales in comparison with the average northern Yemeni mountain village, so is hardly worth a visit. If you do visit adh-Dhala', try to do so on a Thursday, which is market day.

On the central mountaintop in the middle of the town, are the three tower houses which once belonged to Emir Amir Sha'fal who resided in adh-Dhala' before the 1967 revolution. After the revolution of 1967 one of the palaces was converted into a museum which featured ancient relics as well as monuments to the 1967 revolution. Along with most of the museums in the southern governorates, this one was closed after the 1994 civil war.

The European-looking houses in the northern part of the town were built as summer residences for the families of British officers stationed in Aden. The relatively high altitude, and therefore cool climate of adh-Dhala', provided relief from the heat of the coast.

Abyan

The Abyan Governorate is to the north-east of Aden, bounded by the al-Baydha Province to the north, the Lahej and Aden Governorates to the west and the Shabwa Governorate to the east, with the Gulf of Aden to the south. This governorate, rich in culture, has been very important in the history of Yemen as many revolutionaries of both the former YAR and PDRY were born here. Dances and music from Abyan are often performed throughout the country.

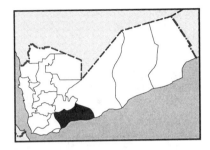

However, Abyan has relatively few sites of interest to the average tourist. Much of the 1994 civil war was fought on the soil of Abyan, which left the infrastructure of the Governorate and the few facilities for travellers in a state of decline.

If you travel to the east from Aden, you are bound to visit the capital of the governorate, Zinjibar, which was also known as Abyan. It is a surprisingly dull town. Further to the east you'll arrive at the fishing village of Shuqra – the whole south Yemeni coast is excellent for fishing. Beyond Shuqra the road turns inland to the north-east, entering the green town of Lawdar. Although it is a few km off the Aden to al-Mukalla asphalt road, Lawdar is nevertheless a stop for the buses and taxis passing through.

Mukayras

(mukayra:s; Mukairas, Mukeiras)
From Lawdar you might visit Mukayras, which stands on the slopes of Jabal Thira (also called az-za:hir), 33 km from Lawdar and only 21 km from the town of al-Baydha. This genuine Yemeni mountain town has a very pleasant climate because of its altitude of more than 2000 metres (the highest town in the southern governorates). Its orchards produce peaches that are famous in the region.

During the days before unification this town was listed as a major sight of the Marxist PDRY and even boasts a small tourist hotel. Today it is just one more mountain town in Yemen, but the road from Lawdar over the 2250-metre Thira Pass offers some wonderful views.

Umm 'Adi

(umm 'adi; Am Adiya, Amadi)
Only ten or so km to the north-east of Mukayras are the ruins of Umm 'Adi, once an important town of the Awsan Kingdom. Although interesting, the ruins are not among the major sights in Yemen, and you will need a local guide to find the site. Try asking for one at the hotel or in the taxi station. The road is very bad and hiring a private car is relatively expensive at about YR 2000.

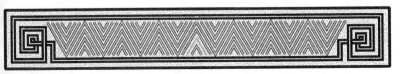

Shabwa

The Governorate of Shabwa stretches inland from the southern coast of the republic to the undrawn border with Saudi Arabia and the deserts of ar-Ruba' al-Khali (the Empty Quarter) in the north. To the east of Shabwa lie Abyan, al-Baydha and Ma'rib, while to the west lies Hadhramawt.

There is plenty to see in Shabwa – if you have enough time and determination. In the northern part of the governorate lie the upper stretches of Wadi Hadhramawt, where major kingdoms once flourished along various incense routes. The ruins of the ancient capitals Shabwa and Timna' are significant archaeological sites.

The ancient town of Qana, on the southern coast near the present-day fishing village of Bir 'Ali, was at one end of these caravan routes.

The problem with visiting Shabwa is that the northern part of the governorate is one of the most restless areas in the country. Local tribes engaged in skirmishes throughout the 1980s and early 1990s, and during the 1994 civil war there were major tank battles in the region. Other kinds of heavy armaments were also in use, according to Western oil-company workers. For this reason it may be very difficult to visit certain sites.

The road from Aden to al-Mukalla, built by the Chinese in the 1970s, runs some distance from the coast for most of its course through the Shabwa Governorate, crossing the foothills of the coastal mountains at altitudes below 1000 metres. The road passes many villages and small towns built on wadi banks.

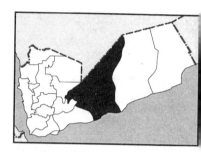

HABBAN

(Habba:n)

Some 340 km from Aden, just beyond the 'Ataq junction, is the smallish town of Habban. It was once noted for its Jewish inhabitants who, along with their silversmithing traditions, are now mostly gone.

Habban, like many nearby villages built in the same style, has a most impressive appearance. The town is built low on the banks of Wadi Habban, framed on all sides by majestic table mountains. Over millions of years, the wadi has eaten its course deep into the chalk stone. The setting is reminiscent of the landscapes of Wadi Hadhramawt.

A distinctive feature of houses in the Wadi Habban region and parts of south-west Hadhramawt are the highly protruding corner peaks on the roofs. These are often painted white with chalk and are of age-old design. The houses are made from mud brick even though there is ample stone available in the area.

Newer mud-brick houses of four to five storeys are larger than those in most other Yemeni towns. You can also see houses with grey plaster *(qatat)* instead of the usual browner substance. The grey variant is more expensive and prestigious. Note also the imaginatively coloured roof-top decorations on the newest houses; this style can be seen all the way from al-Mahfidh in Abyan to 'Azan.

'AZAN

('aza:n; Azzan)

'Azan is the next town to the east of Habban and some 390 km from Aden. Although the modern centre of the town is not too attractive, the wadi is fine with impressive escarpments and beautiful villages built in the traditional style.

'Azan is the closest town to the ruins of Mayfa'a, the ancient capital of lower Hadhramawt. Mayfa'a had its heyday in the last three centuries BC and is not to be mixed up with the present-day village of Mayfa'a, established by the British as a district capital in the late 1950s, some 15 km east of 'Azan.

The ruins of Mayfa'a, well worth seeing, can be found in the vicinity of the present-day village of Naqb al-Hajar, only two km from the main road; turn right approximately four km after leaving 'Azan from the south-east.

BIR 'ALI
(bir 'ali; Bir Ali)

This fishing village on the coast of the Gulf of Aden is the last one along the Aden to al-Mukalla highway before the road enters the Hadhramawt Governorate. The new oil pipe from the Shabwa oil fields terminates at the small tanker port here. Bir 'Ali is easily visited en route between Aden and Mukalla – the road passes right by it. There is a rest house in Bir 'Ali and it is possible to stop here for a meal. Although there are no facilities for overnighting, you can camp by the shore.

There is a strong sense of history in this village, which stands near the site of ancient Qana, the principal southern point of the incense route. The ruins of Qana are by the volcanic hill called Husn al-Ghurab (Crow Fortress), to the west of the present village. The remains of a 1st century temple are one of the best preserved sights. The Husn al-Ghurab makes a rewarding climb – on your way up you'll find some Himyaritic inscriptions.

The geology around Bir 'Ali is as impressive as the ancient ruins. Black volcanic rock extends to the horizon in all directions, providing a strong contrast with the white sands of Bir 'Ali – sheer magic.

'ATAQ
('ataq)

The scenery around 'Ataq, the capital of the Shabwa Governorate, is actually much more impressive than the smallish and rather uninteresting town itself. The mud-brick Palace of Ba Jammal is among the few noteworthy buildings.

The 'Ataq Museum suffered most extensive damage during the 1994 civil war. It is uncertain when it will open again.

Places to Stay

The *Hotel ar-Raka* is some 200 metres from the central roundabout in the direction of Habban. Rooms are overpriced at YR 1000 for an acceptable double. More modest accommodation is available at the taxi station in small four-bed rooms, at YR 300 per bed.

Getting There & Away

To get to 'Ataq, turn off the Aden to al-Mukalla road at a junction just west of Habban. 'Ataq can be reached directly from Aden or al-Mukalla, either by bus (YR 400) or by taxi (YR 600). The stations in 'Ataq are by the central market place. You should be there early to catch a ride either away or to the town. From Habban shared taxis take you to 'Ataq for YR 100 a seat, but the service is infrequent.

BAYHAN
(bayHa:n; Beihan, Bihan)

Before the unification of the two Yemens, Bayhan, the westernmost part of the Shabwa Governorate, was a cartographic anomaly: in a region where no borders between the YAR and the PDRY had been drawn, Bayhan belonged to the PDRY as indisputably as al-Baydha, to the south of it, belonged to the YAR. The nearby oil finds of the late 1980s would finally have forced the countries to define the border, had they not decided in 1990 to kick away the empty oil barrels that marked the temporary dividing line.

There are several ancient sites worth visiting around Bayhan. In 1950 and 1951, large-scale excavations were conducted near Bayhan by the US archaeologist Wendell Phillips. Russian archaeologists continued the explorations in the 1980s. Unfortunately, the Bayhan Museum – which housed finds from the excavation sites – was plundered during the 1994 civil war.

Things to See

Ancient **Timna'** (also spelt 'Tamnou' or referred to as Hajjar Kuhlan), once the capital of the Kingdom of Qa'taban (not to be confused with the present-day town of Qa'taba), is the best known ancient capital in southern Arabia. It is thought that Timna' was originally founded by the Sabaeans in around 400 BC and that it later grew in power by exploiting periods of weakness in the Kingdom of Saba. Some accounts give even earlier foundation dates – official brochures claim the ruins are 4000 years old! The Kingdom of Qa'taban existed for 500 years until it was defeated by Hadhramawt in the year 100 AD. Timna' lay on the incense road halfway between Shabwa and Ma'rib; the three towns were surprisingly close given that they were rival kingdoms. The site consists of 21 hectares of ruins, including 10-metre pillars and the stone remnants of temples, houses and fortifications. A wealth of Qa'tabanian inscriptions is to be found on the stones.

On Jabal Aqil, 1½ km to the north of Timna', is the **cemetery** of Timna'. On Jabal an-Nasr, to the west of Timna', there is a large **water cistern**.

The ruins of **Hajr bin Hamid** (Hajr bin Humayd, Hajr bin Humayd), another historical site, are halfway between Bayhan and Timna'.

Places to Stay

Lokandah Beyhan offers beds for YR 300 in a no-sheet dormitory with no washing facilities. No women are allowed, and Western guys may also be turned away. A new hotel was planned before the war, but it is not yet open.

Getting There & Away

Bayhan is 214 km north-west of 'Ataq. If you are coming from 'Ataq by service taxi and you wish to get to Timna', you should drop off at the small town of Nuqub, 188 km from 'Ataq and 26 km before Bayhan. From Nuqub you should hire a car or guide at a negotiable price (YR 2000 is a good start) to get to Timna' 5 km to the north.

A seat in a taxi from Nuqub to Bayhan should cost YR 100 , but there may not be any other passengers, so you might end up paying for the whole car. An alternative is to hitchhike. Service taxis from 'Ataq to both Bayhan and Nuqub cost around YR 300 for the 200-km stretch along a good asphalt road (completed in 1993).

You can also get to Bayhan from Ma'rib on a road which follows the ancient incense route and crosses several remarkable passes. The 70 km between Harib and Bayhan are rough and a 4WD taxi is needed, but the 75 km between Ma'rib and Harib is asphalt. The fare is YR 700. The service is not frequent, but occasionally there are taxis driving all the way from San'a. You can also try to hitchhike.

If you don't plan to overnight in Bayhan, you should start early and be prepared to leave the town by early afternoon at the latest.

SHABWA

(shabwa; Shabwah, Shabwat)

Shabwa, also known as Shawa Attarikhiyya, was the ancient capital of the Kingdom of Hadhramawt. The early history of the kingdom is poorly recorded, so it is not known when Shabwa was founded, let alone when it became the capital.

A kingdom named Hadhramawt was first mentioned in scriptures dating from 750 BC. Greek historians recorded their knowledge of the place in the 4th century BC. Shabwa is first described by the Greek Eratosthenes, in the 3rd century BC, under the name 'Sabota'. According to the Roman historian Pliny, in the 1st century BC, the flourishing city had 60 temples inside its walls. At its largest, the irrigated and cultivated area

The Arts of Ancient Yemen

Although most is known about the art of Saba, with its capital in Ma'rib, those kingdoms situated in the region of the present Governorate of Shabwa have recently passed their treasures on to scientific research, greatly enriching the picture of the pre-Islamic Arab culture of Southern Arabia.

Archaeological studies of Yemeni art have concluded that two parallel lines of tradition coexisted for thousands of years – one indigenous, the other a mixture of imported styles and motifs. The existence of these two lines is demonstrated in two of the best-preserved forms of artistic expression – coins and sculpture.

The indigenous art is inspired by religion, and has produced countless pieces of sculpted works. Religious artists based their motifs and styles on domestic tradition. The sculptures of South Arabian gods illustrate that the people of the kingdoms of the area worshipped their own unique gods which were different to those worshipped by the people further to the north. For example, Shams, the deity of Sun, was a goddess in South Arabia, while northern Semitic people invariably depicted Sun as a male. On the other hand, Athtar, the deity of love, was masculine in South Arabia while female in most other cultures of the time.

According to the inscriptions, statues of gods were crafted in gold and silver. However, only very few small examples of works in the precious metals have been preserved. With the demise of the kingdoms and the arrival of Islam, most of these statues were melted and the valuable materials used for other purposes. Bronze and alabaster statues have been found in larger numbers and sculptures in stone are numerous. Ibex friezes are one of the most pervasive themes in temple decoration in the area, and bulls (symbolising the moon god Sin), bears, eagles and snakes are common.

Secular art was linked with commerce, with its earliest example being coins. The earliest contacts with Mediterranean cultures are estimated to have taken place around 1200 BC, but the oldest coins of the antique world stem from the 7th century BC. The Athenian silver tetradrachmas served as the hard currency of the world for several centuries BC and AD, and from the 5th century BC they also found their way into South Arabia. Imitations of the tetradrachma were soon minted, with equal material and weight but increasingly domestic decorations and texts. Over the centuries quite a few foreign currencies entered Yemen and were applied to local use.

Along with the trade came clothes, weapons and jewellery. Some South Arabian kings wore Greek or Persian-style clothing. Egyptian, Greek and Mesopotamian forms of expression were adopted and varied by the South Arabian artists, mixing them with Yemeni elements. It is also evident that foreign artisans moved or were brought in for employment in South Arabia, as some relics in Yemeni style carry Greek inscriptions.

Plenty of ancient statues and statuettes have been found by farmers plowing their fields or construction workers digging the foundations for new buildings. Traditionally, such articles have been kept as family treasures or objects of trade. The Adeni merchant family of Muncherjee accumulated a remarkable collection of works of ancient art during the British rule in the city. The Aden Museum was founded in 1960, its collection donated, and included, among other things, three statues of Awsan kings, with inscriptions that have greatly contributed to knowledge about the ancient kingdom. After the advent of the PDRY, several state-run museums were founded to collect and preserve the Yemeni heritage in the governorate capitals. During the civil war of 1994 most of these museums were looted and plundered, but some of the treasures have since been returned under a 'no-questions-asked' arrangement. ■

Statues of Awsan kings

around the city is said to have covered 15,000 hectares.

During the 220s AD, Shabwa was defeated by the Sabaeans. The final blow was the emergence of a central-Arabian nomadic tribe, the Kinda, 30,000 of whom arrived in the Shabwa region. The original population eventually fled east to the town of Say'un. During modern times only a few families have inhabited the site, earning a living from salt mining.

Even today the central government has no firm control over the local nomads in northern parts of the Shabwa Governorate. This is cited as one of the main reasons for the authorities' extreme reluctance to let tourists visit Shabwa. French archaeologists conducted excavations here between 1975 and 1985, exposing much of the western part of the ancient city. The other parts lie beneath the present-day villages of Matha and al-Hajar.

The ruins of Shabwa are buried beneath sand and salt. What there is to see is mostly broken walls that have been partially exposed by excavators. For the lay person, Shabwa is perhaps too much in ruins to be appreciated, but the dramatic location on a hill in the midst of large wadis with their dramatic bedrock is memorable.

Getting There & Away

Shabwa is in the westernmost part of Wadi Hadhramawt, some 500 km north-east of Aden. Although it once derived its wealth from its strategic location on the incense route, Shabwa today is not well connected to anywhere, and nothing but tracks and paths lead to the ruins.

The rough road to Shabwa crosses 100 km of semidesert from 'Ataq in the south. There is no public transport, and taking this route presents a risk even tour operators are not often willing to take.

A better connection is across the desert of Ramlat as-Sab'atayn in the north. If you don't want to take an organised tour, you can hire either a Bedouin taxi from Ma'rib for the most scenic route, or a 4WD for the drive across western Wadi Hadhramawt. Both options are expensive, since only drivers with the right connections to the Bedouin tribes living in the area are able to make the crossing. Expect to spend up to YR 20,000 if you start from Say'un, three times as much if you start from Ma'rib.

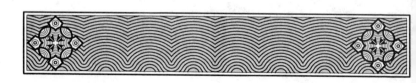

Hadhramawt

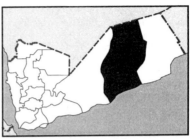

Extending from the coast of the Arabian Sea to the southern deserts of ar-Ruba' al-Khali, Hadhramawt is the largest governorate in Yemen. It has a population of around 500,000. But apart from the port of al-Mukalla and the historic towns of Wadi Hadhramawt, there is little to see.

The Hadhramawt Governorate, like most of the southern governorates, is very hot. Summer is definitely not the time to visit, with afternoon temperatures approaching 50°C and night temperatures hovering above 30°C; coastal areas are very humid as well. Winter is the most suitable time to visit – during the cooler months the dry climate of Wadi Hadhramawt inland is quite pleasant.

Getting There & Away

There are several routes to Hadhramawt, depending on what you want to see both in the governorate (Wadi Hadhramawt, the coast, or both) and in the rest of the country (Aden, Ma'rib etc).

The asphalt road which covers the 620 km from Aden to the coastal town of al-Mukalla was built by the Chinese as a development aid project for the former PDRY, as the Chinese grave monuments at both ends of the road testify. This stretch takes nine hours by taxi or 12 hours by bus, with just one obligatory meal stop (at the Restaurant of the Sons of Hadhramawt). If you wish to make sightseeing stops you will have to allocate more days, or else hire a private taxi by paying for all nine seats.

Another possibility is to skip Aden altogether and use one of the newer road connections opened since unification. Coming south from San'a you can turn east by Dhamar and continue all the way past al-Baydha, reaching the Aden to al-Mukalla road at Lawdar. However, apart from the town of Rada', this route offers relatively little to see.

The northern route from San'a goes via

Al-Muhdar Mosque in Tarim

Ma'rib, Harib and 'Ataq, reaching the Aden to al-Mukalla road at the an-Nuqba junction, a few km south-west of Habban. This route is quite scenic and offers you the chance to visit the historic sites around Bayhan. However, this region is sparsely populated so traffic is quiet and accommodation is scarce: you'll have to hop from one town to the next in shared taxis (few and far between) and overnight in small towns with limited (if any) budget accommodation.

Continuing another 300 km from al-Mukalla over the mountains, you finally reach the Hadhramawt valley and the towns of Shibam, Say'un and Tarim. The asphalt road, built in 1982, runs straight across the table mountains. The trip takes five hours in a bus or taxi.

If money is not a concern, you can even skip al-Mukalla and travel in a Bedouin taxi from Ma'rib to Wadi Hadhramawt straight over the Ramlat as-Sab'atayn desert. (See the Ma'rib chapter for details.)

It is also possible to fly to Hadhramawt. Both al-Mukalla and Say'un, one of the remarkable historical towns of Wadi Hadhramawt, can be reached either from San'a or Aden. While Yemenia only serves these destinations from San'a, ALYEMEN flies both from San'a and Aden.

AL-MUKALLA
(al-mukalla; Mukallah, Makallah)

The capital of the governorate, al-Mukalla is a prosperous seaport and an important centre for fishing, one of the main export industries of the southern part of the country. With 100,000 inhabitants, al-Mukalla is the second largest city in the southern governorates.

Al-Mukalla is a very old town, and has been the port of Hadhramawt for hundreds of years. It was founded as a fishing village in 1035 AD but only acquired town status in 1625. In the 18th and 19th centuries al-Mukalla's importance grew as the economy of the Wadi Hadhramawt area strengthened and in 1866 al-Mukalla became the capital of the Qu'aiti Sultanate, ruling all of the coast and much of the interior of Hadhramawt, excluding the Kathiri Sultanate which had its capital in Say'un. The growth in al-Mukalla's population has continued since the 1967 revolution as new

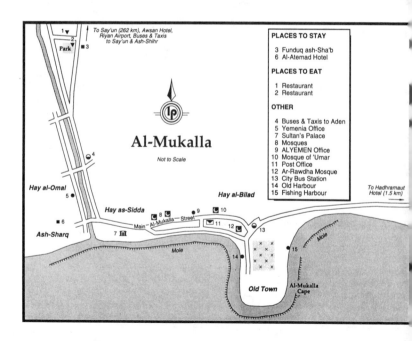

To Say'un (262 km), Awsan Hotel, Riyan Airport, Buses & Taxis to Say'un & Ash-Shihr

Park

Al-Mukalla

Not to Scale

Hay al-Omal

Hay al-Bilad

Hay as-Sidda

Ash-Sharq

Main — Al-Mukalla — Street

Mole

Mole

Old Town

Al-Mukalla Cape

To Hadhramaut Hotel (1.5 km)

PLACES TO STAY

3 Funduq ash-Sha'b
6 Al-Atemad Hotel

PLACES TO EAT

1 Restaurant
2 Restaurant

OTHER

4 Buses & Taxis to Aden
5 Yemenia Office
7 Sultan's Palace
8 Mosques
9 ALYEMEN Office
10 Mosque of 'Umar
11 Post Office
12 Ar-Rawdha Mosque
13 City Bus Station
14 Old Harbour
15 Fishing Harbour

suburbs have been built. After the unification, the growth rate accelerated, and the town lost much of its charm in the process.

Things to See

The most impressive sight in al-Mukalla used to be the coastline of the old town, squeezed between the sea and huge volcanic mountains. The chain of white houses, built next to the waterfront, seemed to rise straight out of the water. Unfortunately the scene was effectively demolished in the late 1980s by the construction of a gigantic **mole**. This now embraces all of al-Mukalla, from the new western suburbs to the harbour east of the town.

The destruction was further completed in the early 1990s when the western part of the old town, Hay as-Sidda, was torn down and replaced with new concrete houses, leaving only the **Sultan's Palace** and the **Mosque of 'Umar** intact.

While the 'shining white port' of southern Yemen no longer shines, many **houses** in the eastern and oldest part of the town, or **Hay al-Bilad**, are still worth seeing. Take a walk and look for the finely engraved wooden window blinds and balconies. Much of the al-Mukalla Cape is occupied by the town **cemetery**, which is surrounded by a high wall so that all you can see is a beautiful white dome over the eastern wall. A walk around the cape is rewarding, though. The style of the remaining old houses with their turquoise window decorations is a fascinating mix of Yemeni, Arabic and Indian influence, as you might expect from an old port town on the south coast of the peninsula.

Mosques Al-Mukalla has some beautiful mosques. Most notable of these are ar-Rawdha Mosque, in the centre of the old town, next to the al-Mukalla Hotel, and the Mosque of 'Umar, on Main al-Mukalla St. At night both these mosques are illuminated in a most bizarre way. An evening stroll along the eastern part of the main street is pleasantly accompanied by the scent of dhoop and incense burned by the merchants.

Al-Mukalla Museum By the bay of al-Mukalla stands the former palace of the sultans. The last of the sultans, Sultan Umar bin Ghalib, emigrated to Jedda in 1967. The Qu'ayti sultans had moved their capital from ash-Shihr to al-Mukalla in 1915, and built this marvellous house which has a combination of Indian and colonial neoclassical influences.

In the days of the PDRY the building was renamed as the 14th October Palace, serving as a 'folklore and antiquities' museum, and exhibited some finds from the old town of Shabwa. The museum was closed in late 1994, apparently because most of its exhibits were stolen during the civil war of that year. It is uncertain when it will reopen.

Husn al-Ghuwayzi Topping an imposing cliff just out of the town on the Riyan road, this tiny fortress is a perfect example of the bizarre imagination of the Yemeni architect. It was built in 1884 and is irresistible to any visitor with a camera, even if you can't visit the military museum it houses.

Places to Stay – middle

There are a couple of simple hotels in al-Mukalla: *Funduq ash-Sha'b* near the bus and taxi stations and *Funduq al-Mukalla* in the old town, by the seashore. At the time of our visit the al-Mukalla hotel was closed for renovation. The two-sheet ash-Sha'b hotel has doubles for YR 900, with private bathrooms in the corridor, fans and (mostly dysfunctional) air-conditioning. This hotel also needs renovating.

The *Awsan Hotel*, in a newer building beyond the Say'un taxi station, is cleaner. Doubles with private bath and air-conditioning cost YR 1000 but you may be asked for as much as YR 1500. Should we have stayed, service and taxes would probably have been added in the morning.

Al-Atemad (Alatmad) Hotel (☎ 52493/ 9551199), is the cleanest and the most expensive of the mid-range hotels. It's in ash-Sharq, the western part of the town, and offers singles/doubles/triples for YR 1100/1550/1750, plus service (10%) and tax

(2%). The hotel also has a fairly good restaurant.

Places to Stay – top end
The *Hadhramaut Hotel* is expensive. It can be found on a desolate rocky shore about two km to the east from the city, past the Bay of Khalf with the new harbour and its oil tanks. The hotel has several small bungalows; doubles cost US$75 each. The hotel was still partially under construction at the time of our visit, but apparently it will sport a tennis court, swimming pool and a bar with a view of the sea. Judging from their restaurant, already in operation, they still have a long way to go to get their services on par with the prices.

Places to Eat
Try the numerous small restaurants both in the old town and the new suburbs; they serve excellent fish as well as the ubiquitous grilled chicken. Tuna, pilchard and lobster are common here but the real winner in al-Mukalla is dried shark.

In front of the ash-Sha'b Hotel there is a park restaurant with friendly service. Another restaurant along the street opposite the hotel serves delicious spicy grilled chicken.

Getting There & Away
Buses and taxis arriving from the direction of Aden enter the town through ash-Sharq and Hai al-Omal (Hay al-'uma:l) and cross the bridge spanning what was once a wadi but is now a huge open gutter. Taxis and buses to Aden leave from here. Be there early – the first bus arrives at the station at 5.45 am, gets full immediately and may be the only one for the day, leaving at 6.30 am. Taxis continue to collect passengers for a few more hours. A seat in a shared taxi costs YR 1300 while a bus ticket is only YR 800.

Buses for Say'un (in Wadi Hadhramawt) also leave daily at 6.30 am. Again, arrive at the station at least 30 minutes before the bus leaves. A ticket to Say'un costs YR 700. The station for Say'un is in the northern suburb of Hai Uktubr, ten minutes' walk from

Funduq ash-Sha'b. Here you can get a shared taxi to Aden or Wadi Hadhramawt any time in the morning; there are hardly any taxis in the afternoon. The trip to Say'un costs YR 1000 and takes six hours.

Flying to or from al-Mukalla means using the desert airport of Riyan, some 25 km north-east of al-Mukalla. No buses seem to serve the airport; try to find somebody to share your taxi, since the fare for the 30-minute ride is YR 800. The Yemen Airways (ALYEMEN) office is on Main al-Mukalla St, near the Mosque of 'Umar, while the Yemenia office is in Hai al-Omal, on the bank of the wadi.

Getting Around
The old town of al-Mukalla is squeezed between the mountains and the Bay of al-Mukalla and is easily covered on foot. The suburbs and the nearby towns and villages are served by an extensive bus network. There are schematic line maps at the main bus stops with captions in Arabic only. The station at the eastern end of Main al-Mukalla St is conveniently in the centre of what remains of the old town.

AROUND AL-MUKALLA
Around al-Mukalla are some interesting old towns and villages that you can visit by bus or taxi. Unless you rent a private vehicle, start early to guarantee return the same day.

Ghayl Ba Wazir
Some 40 km to the north-east of al-Mukalla is Ghayl Ba Wazir where the former sultan's summer palace has been converted into a tiny rest house. This fine building has five simple rooms and one swimming pool, and is warmly recommended by those who have spent a night there. However, the place is often fully booked by tour groups, and you'd be wise to make a reservation through a tour agency.

You have to negotiate your own transport here since there are no shared taxis. The rest house is just 10 km to the north of Riyan airport, so it's a good idea to visit here first if you arrive in Al-Mukalla by air.

Ash-Shihr

(ash-shiHr)

This small fishing port, 54 km east of al-Mukalla, is a very old settlement. An established port in the days of antiquity, ash-Shihr is also mentioned in the writings of Marco Polo. Still in existence are parts of the own wall and a couple of its gates, Bab al-'Aydarus and Bab al-Khur, originally built in the 13th century. The present structures date from 1887; Bab al-'Aydarus, was renovated in 1985.

Ash-Shihr was for many years the principal port of Hadhramawt. Its importance declined with the development of al-Mukalla in the late 1800s. The old dirt road to Wadi Hadhramawt starts from ash-Shihr and winds its way along Wadi 'Adim to al-Ghurfa, east of Say'un. It has been all but abandoned since 1982, when the western asphalt road from Riyan was finished, cutting some 10 hours off a 16-hour drive. Until Toyotas replaced camels as the beasts of burden, the trip used to take seven to nine days.

Around ash-Shihr, you might appreciate bathing in the hot-spring pools by the road to al-Hami, 25 km to the east. You can also watch local beekeepers at work.

Halfway between Riyan and ash-Shihr there is the CanOxy petroleum export terminal, feeding tankers with oil from the Masila block 120 km inland.

Burum

(buru:m)

Some 20 km west of al-Mukalla, this small old village is easily spotted from the main road. A km or so towards al-Mukalla, pillars of smoke rise from the ovens where gypsum is burned. Between Burum and the gypsum ovens a dramatic crack in the rocks reveals the alignment of the old al-Mukalla road.

Wadi Hadhramawt

Wadi Hadhramawt (wa:di: HaZramawt), the biggest wadi in the Arabian Peninsula, is one of the major attractions of southern Yemen. This famous valley runs for 160 km, west to east, amidst arid, stony desert plateaus (called *ju:l*) about 160 km from the coast. At the western end is the sandy desert of Ramlat as-Sab'atayn. Downstream, the wadi joins the dry and inhospitable Wadi Masila, which connects the system to the sea.

Wadi Hadhramawt with its numerous tributaries, however, is very fertile, making it possible for a population of 200,000 to live on agriculture and goat-herding. Formed by erosion of the sandstone bedrock over millions of years, the main wadi is today some 300 metres deep and two-km wide on average, with the wadi bottom at an altitude of 700 metres. Ground water is available throughout the year; the rainy seasons bring abundant floods to replenish it, creating this most unexpectedly green valley between the desolate tablelands.

History

The abundance of archaeological sites in the Wadi Hadhramawt area reveal that the region has been settled throughout human history and that it prospered greatly in ancient times. Indeed, some historians argue that the place was mentioned in the Book of Genesis, with its name spelt 'Hazarmaveth'. According to local tradition the earliest inhabitants of the wadi were descendants of the prophet Hud, who was descendant of Joktan, a grandson of Noah.

Wadi Hadhramawt is located on the ancient incense route. The oldest archaeological finds here date from the 9th century BC, and Hadhramawt was known to Greek historians of the 3rd century BC. Shabwa, at the far western end of the wadi, was halfway between Qana and Ma'rib, and Wadi Hadhramawt was ruled from this city for centuries before the 3rd century AD. Elaborate irrigation systems were developed and maintained throughout the centuries of the frankincense trade. Even frankincense itself was grown in Wadi Hadhramawt, as well as on the southern coast (the bush still grows wild in some of the side wadis).

The history of Hadhramawt between the

demise of Shabwa and the entry of Islam is obscure. Certainly the Persian Sassanids, who were invited by Yemeni kings to fight against the Ethiopians in the 6th century AD, also presided in Hadhramawt. Evidence of their presence can be seen in the Persian style of the ruins in Husn al-'Urr, in the eastern part of the wadi.

Records of early Islam's influence here are fragmentary and very few original documents remain. Although Hadhrami soldiers were among the Muslim troops who conquered Egypt, there was also resistance to Islam in the wadi. Only the holy town of Tarim is said to have followed the Islamic faith continuously through the centuries.

In 746 AD a man called 'Abd Allah ibn Yahya, from Basra, Iraq, introduced the Ibadi school of thinking to Hadhramawt. The Ibadi sect survived in the wadi for at least 450 years, although Yemeni caliphs tried to conquer Hadhramawt on several occasions. Most importantly, in 951 Sayyid Ahmad ibn 'Isa al-Muhajir, a descendant of the Prophet Muhammad, came here with 80 families and settled in Hajrayn, in the eastern part of Wadi Hadhramawt, establishing Shafa'ism in the region. The tomb of al-Muhajir is still an important place of pilgrimage, and the town of Tarim has remained the centre of Shafa'i teaching in Hadhramawt.

In the 10th century a Ziyadid ruler of Yemen, Husayn ibn Salama, allowed the building of many mosques and wells along the caravan route between Hadhramawt and Mecca, including the ar-Rashid Mosque in al-Huraydha, in the western part of the wadi. The first centuries of the 2nd millennium saw the conquest of Hadhramawt by rival Yemeni dynasties. Following the demise of the Ayyubids in the 13th century, the wadi was ruled by the Rasulids who presided in an era of great stability and prosperity for the region.

The year 1488 was an important one for Wadi Hadhramawt. The Kathiris of Hamdanis, a San'a tribe, conquered Hadhramawt and eventually settled permanently in the wadi. The Kathiri Sultanate was founded in the eastern part of the wadi, first with Tarim and subsequently with Say'un as its capital.

In the 16th century the western part of the wadi fell under the rule of the Qu'aitis, a Yafi'i tribe originally brought to the region by the Kathiris as paid soldiers. The Qu'aiti Sultanate made the town of al-Qatn their capital. The constant warring between the rival tribes had, by now, greatly reduced the wadi's agricultural output, resulting in famines.

While the subsequent centuries brought increasingly long periods of peace, a severe setback occurred in 1809, when the Sa'udi Wahhabis (the dominant tribe of Saudi Arabia) looted the wadi and destroyed all the tombs and prestigious buildings (including mosques) they could find. Innumerable manuscripts were burned or dumped into wells during this ghastly episode.

A century-long period of hostilities started in 1830, when the Qu'aitis and the Kathiris again fell into dispute. The confrontation was over who would rule the town of Shibam, located between al-Qatn and Say'un, the capitals of the sultanates. Twenty-seven years of war left the impoverished city, previously under the joint rule of the two sultans, in the hands of the Qu'aitis.

Wadi Hadhramawt remained thus divided, with the border between the Qu'aiti and Kathiri sultanates drawn to the east of Shibam, for almost a century. The colonial power of Great Britain was slow to extend its rule this far in the hinterlands. Hadhramawt and al-Mahra formed the so-called Eastern Aden Protectorate, and the British ruled through protection treaties with the local sultans. In 1888 one such treaty was signed with the Qu'aiti Sultan in al-Mukalla, but the Kathiris did not follow suit until 1918. It was only in 1934 that the British finally extended their control to Wadi Hadhramawt, mediating between the warring tribes and signing hundreds of treaties with them, as well as half a dozen or so with the most important sultans.

Thus the isolation between the sultanates of al-Qatn and Say'un was lifted by the 1940s. The 1967 revolution brought a final resolution to the dispute: with the sultans fleeing to Saudi Arabia, the central govern-

Mud-Brick Architecture of Wadi Hadhramawt

Tower houses are an invention of Hadhramis, original in style and unchanged by the centuries. The buildings are made exclusively of mud bricks. This applies not only to old tower houses but to virtually all constructions, even today – mosques, tombs, wells and walls are all made of mud bricks. It was only after the unification of the two Yemens in 1990 that concrete was introduced in the Hadhrami towns, and it is still used in only a very small proportion of all new buildings.

If you spend a few days in Wadi Hadhramawt during the dry season you can hardly avoid witnessing the making of mud bricks. Wet mud is mixed with some straw to give it strength. The mixture is spread out on the bare earth and shaped into bricks using wooden frames that mould two thin rectangular bricks at once. The width of the bricks varies from 25 cm to 50 cm. Thicker bricks are used for the ground floor and thinner bricks are used for the top floor.

After the walls have been built from bricks, they are plastered smooth. Two main types of plaster are used: brown earth (for most walls) and light lime plaster (for top floors). For decorative purposes an even whiter plaster is used, made with egg shells. The parapets on the roof terraces of many houses are often whitewashed, and shine magnificently at sunset. ■

Making mud bricks

Shibam houses

ment of the new republic was able to completely replace the age-old ruling institutions. From here on, Wadi Hadhramawt has been able to develop peacefully, with the later turmoils of the country, including the 1994 civil war, barely touching this distant community.

Still, Wadi Hadhramawt has changed considerably in the unified Yemen, and not only for the better. Jambiyas and qat were once rare sights here during the PDRY era, and the towns were remarkably tidy compared with those of the YAR. One hopes the Hadhrami spirit will endure in the grip of the inevitable change.

Orientation & Information

The unofficial capital of Wadi Hadhramawt is Say'un, in the middle of the wadi, with an airport and other central traffic facilities. If you arrive by car, you travel through much of the wadi before entering Say'un.

The asphalt road from al-Mukalla descends to the wadi through one of its western tributaries, Wadi al-Qasr, by the town of Haura (or Hawra). A little beyond Haura is a junction – dirt roads to the left lead to other side wadis where important historic sites can be found: al-Huraydha in Wadi 'Amd and al-Hajjarayn and Raybun in Wadi Daw'an (or Wadi Hajjarayn).

From Haura the main road continues to the wadi proper, passing the towns of Haynin, al-Qatn, Shibam and al-Hawta before reaching Say'un. From there the road continues to Tarim. Beyond Tarim there are still sites of historical interest along the road to Wadi Masila, including Husn al-'Urr and Qabr Nabi Hud.

Getting Around

Service taxis shuttle all day along the asphalt road that links the towns of Wadi Hadhramawt. Fares vary from 35 riyals per person from Say'un to Shibam and 50 riyals from Say'un to Tarim. Blue buses also cover this

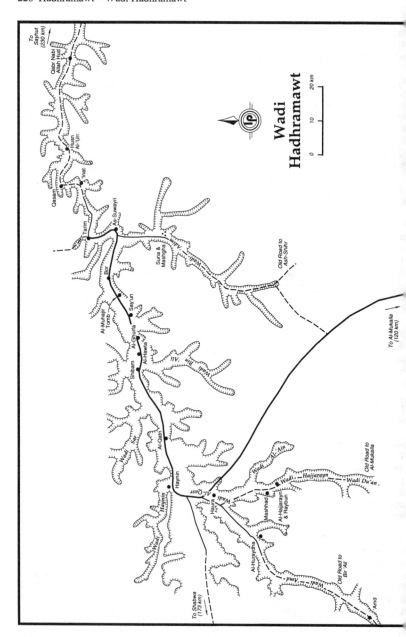

route for slightly less, but only operate from morning to early afternoon; you buy tickets on board.

You can hire a private taxi for excursions for a negotiable fare of a few thousands of riyals. If you are travelling on your own and usually rely on buses and service taxis, this is the place to burn your money on private transport. You can visit many of the historical sites and interesting villages within one day, with the opportunity for photo stops anywhere you wish.

AL-QATN
(al-qatn)
Although not celebrated for any ancient monuments, al-Qatn is a fine example of a traditional town in the Wadi Hadhramawt style. Should you arrive in a private car from the direction of al-Mukalla, this place is well worth a stop. If you arrive late it could be a good idea to start early the next day for Shibam and Say'un instead of heading straight to Say'un.

Places to Stay
In addition to a couple of cheap traditional hotels, the *ar-Rawdha Tourist Hotel* by the main road, in the eastern part of the town, is new to al-Qatn, and offers doubles for YR 1100.

SHIBAM
(shiba:m)
Shibam is to the south what old San'a is to the north – the most celebrated Arabic Islamic city built in traditional style. Shibam is a tight collection of some 500 skyscrapers, five to seven-storeys high, crammed into an area of perhaps only half a sq km. Aptly dubbed 'the Manhattan of the desert', the town rises straight from a slight elevation in the central part of the valley; it is not on the wadi bank, like Say'un for example. Shibam is a sight you will never forget – entering the town for the first time is guaranteed to make you forget the trouble you may have had getting here. Although you may have seen pictures of Shibam, the reality is likely to exceed your expectations.

Shibam is a very old city. It was already the capital of the Hadhramawt area in the 3rd century AD, after the fall of Shabwa, and served as the capital several times until the 16th century. Today it has a population of around 7000.

Shibam, with its extremely compact layout, is a remarkable example of ancient town planning. It has an earth wall and the houses are built with mud bricks and wooden superstructures on stone foundations. The highest house has eight storeys, with a height of almost 30 metres above street level and 39 metres from the wadi bottom. Most of the houses have four to seven storeys, depending on the height of the elevation on which they stand, so that the roofs of the buildings are all at the same level. Because the town is built so low, at the bottom of the wadi, it is vulnerable to floods and was, indeed, partly destroyed by floods in 1532-33 AD.

In the 1980s Shibam, like San'a, was the target of a US$40-million UNESCO programme to safeguard the cultural heritage of the human race. There was plenty of work to do. Many of the houses had been badly damaged by heavy floods in 1975 and 1982 (and again in 1989). Building costs have been steadily rising, so the owners cannot afford the necessary repairs after such damage. Outside help is still badly needed. Projects include restoring the dams that protect the city, building drainage and sewerage systems, restoring individual houses, and so on. There were plans to spend another US$40 million on other sites in Wadi Hadhramawt, however, the 1994 civil war has delayed progress.

Things to See
You can explore Shibam's narrow streets or admire the town from a distance, from the sandy wadi bottom to the south or from the palm groves in other directions. If you fly to the Hadhramawt you'll also get a great view of the town.

Seen from the wadi bottom in front of the town, Shibam's appearance is somewhat nondescript because of the white-chalked newer houses built in the mid-1900s between

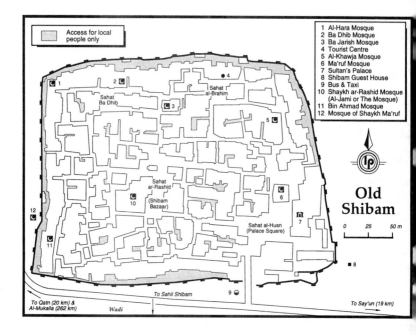

Old Shibam

1 Al-Hara Mosque
2 Ba Dhib Mosque
3 Ba Jarish Mosque
4 Tourist Centre
5 Al-Khawja Mosque
6 Ma'ruf Mosque
7 Sultan's Palace
8 Shibam Guest House
9 Bus & Taxi
10 Shaykh ar-Rashid Mosque (Al-Jami or The Mosque)
11 Bin Ahmad Mosque
12 Mosque of Shaykh Ma'ruf

the road and the town wall. It's a traditional tourist practice to photograph the town at sunset from the cliffs above the new suburb of Sahil Shibam, or Sihayl, on the southern side of the wadi.

Entering the walled city you first arrive at the main square known as **Sahat al-Husn**, the Palace Square. The **citadel** by the main square is quite old, dating from the 13th century AD. It is not to be confused with the neighbouring **Sultan's Palace**, which was not built until the 1920s.

A walk among the streets of the town is recommended. Most of the present **houses** date from the 16th century AD, many having been rebuilt about 100 years ago. Look for the finely engraved wooden doors; the locks are also made from wood. The elaborately carved wooden lattice screens for windows (known as *khalfa*) are made locally by master craftspeople who have shops in Sahil Shibam. See if you can spot two identical screens!

Mosques The biggest of the seven mosques in the walled city is Shaykh ar-Rashid Mosque, near Sahat ar-Rashid, the second largest square of the walled city. It was built in 133 AH (904 AD) by Caliph Harun ar-Rashid on the site of an earlier mosque. Since then it has been rebuilt several times, most recently in the 1960s.

The mosque you see first as you enter the city through the main gate is the Ma'ruf Mosque, also more than 1000 years old. It was last rebuilt in the 1940s.

In the western palm grove stands the splendid white Mosque of Shaykh Ma'ruf, more than 400 years old.

Places to Stay & Eat

The *Shibam Guest House* outside the eastern wall of the old city is a creation of the tourist boom in 1992 to 1993. Complete with its own small garden, the only hotel of Shibam is clearly overpriced when compared to the many hotels in Say'un. For YR 1400 you get a clean double with air-conditioning, private bathroom, balcony and breakfast; a 12% service tax will be added to your bill. The hotel also has a fairly good but pricey restaurant, the only alternative to the very basic eateries along the main road.

SAY'UN
(say'un; Saiwun, Seiyun, Siun, Sayaun)
This town of 30,000 people is the largest in the Hadhramawt valley and was the capital of the northern Hadhramawt Protectorate during the final years of British rule. It is the entry point for tourists visiting the area by plane or by car. Say'un is 320 km north of al-Mukalla, in the middle of Wadi Hadhramawt, and is called 'the town of a million palm trees'.

Say'un, an age-old marketplace, is on a major caravan route. Its economy was greatly boosted in 1490 AD, when some 10,000 members of a North Yemeni tribe, the Kathiris of Hamdanis, immigrated to the town and made it their capital, ruling it until the 1967 revolution. The imposing buildings of the town are excellent examples of the clay brick architecture of Wadi Hadhramawt. Some of the most beautiful mosques and minarets in all of Yemen can be found in Say'un.

Orientation & Information
Say'un is an easy town to find your way around. Most of the activity is within a couple of hundred metres of the taxi and bus stations by the splendid Sultan's Palace. The main road passes through Say'un from west to east, making some turns in the centre, leaving most of the town on the southern side of the road.

The Say'un airport is to the north, only 10 minutes from the town (YR 100 by private taxi); the road forks from the western main road, in the direction of Shibam. The Yemen Airways (ALYEMEN) office is within walking distance of the town centre; go east

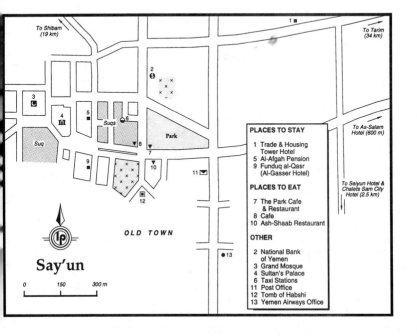

PLACES TO STAY

1 Trade & Housing
   Tower Hotel
5 Al-Afgah Pension
9 Funduq al-Qasr
   (Al-Gasser Hotel)

PLACES TO EAT

7 The Park Cafe
   & Restaurant
8 Cafe
10 Ash-Shaab Restaurant

OTHER

2 National Bank
   of Yemen
3 Grand Mosque
4 Sultan's Palace
6 Taxi Stations
11 Post Office
12 Tomb of Habshi
13 Yemen Airways Office

To Shibam
(19 km)

To Tarim
(34 km)

To As-Salam
Hotel (600 m)

To Seiyun Hotel &
Chalets Sam City
Hotel (2.5 km)

OLD TOWN

Suqs

Suq

Park

Say'un

0   150   300 m

along the main road until you come to the first junction. Turn right along the boulevard, go past the main post office and you will find the airline office in the 3rd block, on the opposite side of the street.

Sultan's Palace

The Sultan's Palace in Say'un is perhaps the most pompous of all South Yemeni palaces, a multistorey, white-plastered colossus with light-blue window decorations. It stands on an elevation next to the town's central suqs. The present shape of the building stems from the 1920s and 1930s when the Kathiri sultans Mansur bin Ghalib and his son 'Ali rebuilt the earlier palace. The mud-brick wall around the palace is from 1987 when the building was last renovated.

The palace is now mostly empty, having been converted into a museum after the 1967 revolution. The museum, open daily from 7.30 am to noon, occupies several halls and rooms on various floors but leaves plenty of space unused. The permanent archaeological show includes several maps and aerial photographs that illustrate the sites of the finds. Raybun appears to have been a very productive site, and there are Semitic and Himyarite writings and artefacts from the Raybun excavations on display in this very interesting show.

On the top floor you will find various departments dedicated to folklore, such as handcraft, marriage and birth, coffee and tea customs, and Arabic medicine. Of special interest is the Customs room with coins and banknotes from the days of the sultanates; a passport from Say'un, Kathiri State, Aden Protectorate vividly illustrates the nearness of the period of British occupation.

In addition to the museum, the palace houses the Say'un Library. There is also a small souvenir shop by the outer wall, to the left of the main entrance, selling, among other things, Hadhrami and Omani wedding belts made of silver.

Things to See

The turquoise **Tomb of Habshi** is in the centre of Say'un. It dates from 1910. The nearby **Mosque of al-Haddad** is much older, dating from the 16th century AD. Non-muslims are forbidden to enter the site of the tombs as well as the nearby graveyards; the same applies to all graveyards in the Hadhramawt valley.

On the southern side of the palace you will find the old **suq** of Say'un. The shopping malls of the new suqs, to the east of the palace, by the bus and taxi stations, clearly owe their design to the old suq.

On the far southern edge of the old suq, next to the residential area and the graveyard, you can find what is probably the best cassette shop in Wadi Hadhramawt. Here you can buy the works of singers born in various Hadhrami towns, some of them now famous all over the Arabian Peninsula.

Places to Stay – bottom end

In the centre of Say'un there are a couple of very basic hotels in traditional tower houses. *Funduq al-Qasr* (al-Gasser Hotel) offers two sheets on mattresses on the floor, cold showers in communal bathrooms and a splendid view of Say'un's central market to the Sultan's Palace, all for YR 560 per double. The one-sheet *al-Afgah Pension* offers one-sheet mattresses for YR 300.

Places to Stay – middle

The *Trade & Housing Tower Hotel* (☎ 3575) derives its curious name from the large two-storey building with shops on the ground floor and hotel rooms on the first floor. Apparently there are plans to expand the hotel by building more storeys. This new two-sheet hotel is clean with private bathrooms and fans and is good value at YR 1000 for a double, including breakfast. The hotel is an easy walk from Say'un centre towards Tarim.

The pleasant *as-Salam Hotel* (☎ 2341/ 2401), 1½ km from the town centre in the direction of Tarim, has singles/doubles with air-conditioning for YR 1200/1800, including breakfast. The hotel complex also has a swimming pool and a souvenir shop.

The huge *Seiyun Hotel* is inconveniently located some three km from the centre. The place stands high on the mountain east of Say'un, offering splendid views over the entire town. Doubles cost YR 1100 with breakfast, but the prices are sure to rise considerably once tourists again flock to the Hadhramawt. Another choice in the same direction and price range is the *Chalets Sam City Hotel*, also far from the centre.

Places to Eat
In the very centre of Say'un, next to the new suq and the taxi station, a pleasant cafe serves both tea and cold drinks. From here you can see the town's only noteworthy restaurants: the *ash-Shaab Restaurant*, on the 1st floor of the building opposite, and the *Park Cafe & Restaurant*, in the south-western corner of the central park. You'll also find a few no-name places nearby.

All the middle-range hotels also have restaurants of their own.

TARIM
(tari:m; Terim, Trim)
Tarim is the last of the three important towns in Wadi Hadhramawt. This town of 15,000 inhabitants is some 35 km to the east of Say'un. It is overshadowed by vast rock cliffs on one side and surrounded by palm groves on the other.

Tarim has long been an important centre for the Shafa'i school of Sunni Islamic teaching. From the 17th to 19th centuries the several hundred mosques of Tarim (the official count today is 365, one for each day of the year!) were as important in spreading the Shafa'i teachings in and from Hadhramawt as those of Zabid were in the Tihama.

Orientation & Information
The places of interest in Tarim are all within walking distance from the central square, where you will be dropped by buses and taxis from Say'un. The road approaches the centre of the city from the south, passing a small park on your right (to the east). The GPO of Tarim is on the road that connects the square with the small park.

Things to See
Tarim is a beautiful town marked by the high minarets of its many mosques. The most famous, **al-Muhdar Mosque**, is named after the religious leader Omar al-Muhdar, who lived in Tarim in the 15th century AD. Rebuilt in 1914, this mosque is the symbol of the town. Its 50-metre-high square minaret, built of mud brick, is the highest minaret in Southern Arabia and appears in every pictorial description of Wadi Hadhramawt. The mosque is just a couple of blocks to the north-east of the central square.

The finest palace in Tarim is **Sayyid 'Umar bin Shaykh al-Kaf**, also known as 'Ishsha Palace. It belongs to a whole area of mud-brick mansions originally built by the

---

Tarim's Architecture – a touch of South-East Asia
A striking feature of Tarim's architecture is its distinctively South-East Asian flavour, introduced in the 19th century by Hadhrami emigrants to the region, particularly those from Java. By the 1930s the Hadhrami community of Indonesia and Singapore had grown to 300,000. Many worked as traders, owning significant properties there, before deciding to return to their home country after spending their working years abroad.

The huge palaces they built in this 'Javanese Baroque' style are now in various stages of decay. Even so, a leisurely stroll through the streets of the town is still worthwhile. After the demise of the communist rule in southern Yemen, much of the property is being returned to the original owners; some of the palaces have already been renovated. ∎

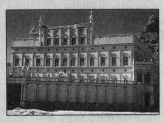

Al-Mansura Palace

Hadhrami Emigration

Yemen has always been a great source of emigrants, but Wadi Hadhramawt exceeds all other regions in this respect. Throughout its history, Wadi Hadhramawt has sent waves of emigrants to other parts of the world. The Hadhramis were certainly numerous among the Arabs who spread Islam in its early centuries, but this was just one episode in an exodus that has lasted for thousands of years.

Geography largely explains this phenomenon: the resources of a fertile valley surrounded by inhospitable deserts can support only a limited number of people. The region's proximity to the sea has meant that emigrants have flocked to shores all over the Indian Ocean. While the nearby Arabic countries along the Red Sea and the Persian Gulf have certainly received their share of emigrants, Hadhramis have settled in East Africa, India, Malaysia and Indonesia in great numbers.

The Hadhrami Yemenis have left their mark in the societies they have lived in by remaining true to the culture of their homeland. Because the number of returnees has also been high, Wadi Hadhramawt has been more susceptible to outside influences than most other regions in the mountains of western Yemen. One of the very first cars in Yemen outside Aden was imported by Sultan al-Kaf in Tarim in 1933. Wadi Hadhramawt has also prospered economically from emigrants who have sent part of their earnings home, and returnees who have brought their successes back with them. ■

---

al-Kafs. From the al-Muhdar Mosque, follow the signs of Shabib Antiques & Services and you will walk past the giant palace which is mostly empty since the sultan resides in Saudi Arabia. The keepers of the Shabib store have the keys to the palace and they can let you in for a small fee.

If you enjoy perfection in Arabic calligraphy, the place to visit is the **Al-Ahqaf Library** (named after the Quranic name *al-aHqa:f*). The library was founded in 1972 to preserve the spiritual heritage of the region's Islamic teachers, and books were gathered from all over Wadi Hadhramawt. Among its 14,000 volumes are some 3000 antique manuscripts, and several brilliant works of art are on show. Unfortunately the books are locked behind glass doors. You can find the library in the small park; the library is closed on Fridays.

Although it is not appropriate for a non-Muslim to actually enter, the graveyards of Tarim, to the south of the town centre, are worth a glimpse or two through the gates. The uniformly designed sandstone monuments with their deft calligraphy represent a style unique in Yemen.

Places to Stay – bottom end

The *Brothers Pension Tourist* has a convenient location on the central street of Tarim, next to the place where buses from Say'un drop you. Room prices in this simple one-sheet place range from YR 450 for singles to YR 900 for doubles, some of which have additional beds. YR 100 buys you a bed for six hours in the common room, useful to escape the afternoon heat.

Places to Stay – middle

The Rest House Qasr al-Qubba is an interesting alternative. This tiny hotel is attractively built in a very green grove of palms and other trees, and has two swimming pools. The rest house was the first one in Wadi Hadhramawt, built in 1955 by a man returning from Indonesia, where he had been introduced to the concept of tourism. The rooms have recently been renovated but stay true to the old style, and the place is quite clean. Each room is different, ranging from YR 550 for singles to YR 1000 for doubles with air-conditioning and bathroom.

Qasr al-Qubba is less than two km from the centre of Tarim. From the street where the Say'un bus drops you, head west by the park, over an open square near which taxis wait for customers, and go between the graveyards. After two-thirds of a km there is a fork in the road– take the road to the left and, after another few hundred metres, you will find the hotel on your left-hand side.

Getting There & Away

To get to Tarim from Say'un, take the eastbound bus or taxi from the Say'un centre past the as-Salam Hotel. A shared taxi is the only choice later in the afternoon because the buses no longer operate then. A seat in a taxi costs YR 100, less than that in the bus.

AROUND WADI HADHRAMAWT

Outside the central towns there are plenty of things to see in Wadi Hadhramawt. Historical villages and archaeological sites abound along the tributaries of the main wadi, and innumerable tombs and mosques have been erected in honour of holy men. The abundance of small mosques in the area is explained by the fact that wealthy emigrants each built a mosque upon returning to their homeland. A similar explanation applies to the numerous covered wells (called *siqa:ya*) that dot the landscape.

Some remarkable sites (from west to east) are listed below:

Al-Huraydha

Al-Huraydha, by Wadi 'Amd, is some 80 km south-west of Shibam. This village has a peculiar reputation: the best mediators in tribal disputes come from al-Huraydha, and the quarrelling parties take their judgements as final. The first vice president of the unified Yemen, Haidar abu Bakr al-Attas, traces his origins to this village.

The ruins of the town of Madubum, dating from the 5th century BC, lie some three km north-west of al-Huraydha. The site was excavated in the late 1930s by a British archaeological team which found a large temple dedicated to the moon god. Several tomb caves from the same period were also discovered. Today the drifting sands have reclaimed much of the structures.

Al-Hajjarayn

Also called Hagrayn, this is a remarkable stone village atop a rocky slope of Wadi Daw'an. This is one of those ancient villages (it is more than 1000 years old) that Yemenis like foreigners to see, so it is rather easy to arrange a visit here. It is the remarkable

harmony which the village creates together with its dramatic surroundings that sets al-Hajjarayn apart from many similar villages of stone houses in the northern part of the country.

Raybun

Raybun is one of the most important archaeological sites in Wadi Hadhramawt. Close to al-Hajjarayn, this ancient town was demonstrably settled by the 10th century BC. Not much of it remains today but finds from Raybun abound in the Say'un museum.

Mashhad

Next to Raybun, Mashhad is a village with some fine tombs. The Tomb of Hasan ibn Hasan dates to 1591, while the complex of the five Tombs of 'Ali ibn Hasan (and his family) was reputedly rebuilt in the 1830s. The domed buildings are most imposing.

Wadi Daw'an
(Wadi Du'an, Wadi Doan)

In the past there were two roads from Wadi Hadhramawt – the eastern one through Wadi Masila and the western one through Wadi Daw'an (also known as Wadi Hajjarayn). If you have your own transport (4WD required) it pays to drive along this wadi which has plenty of beautiful old villages. The road is laid with rocks and is actually in better condition than the modern asphalt road which is neglected and full of holes.

Al-Ghurfa

Six km to the west of Say'un, al-Ghurfa is the site of the important 16th-century Mosque of Ba'bath. Inside the mosque are well-preserved original ornaments and other remarkable decorations in the Tahirid style. A huge, impressive tomb stands out in the cemetery.

Tomb of Ahmad ibn 'Isa al-Muhajir

This tomb is about five km east of Say'un, on the southern bank of the wadi bottom. Clearly visible from the main road, this tomb of the 10th-century Shafa'i spiritual leader is, even today, an important place of pilgrimage. It has been well maintained and its beauty is obvious, even to the untrained eye. In the nearby village of Bor, on the other side of the road, a mosque built by the saint's son 'Abd Allah Ahmad ibn 'Isa has been recently restored.

A visit to this tomb can be combined with a visit to Tarim without too much hassle – on your return from Tarim just hop out of the taxi at the site and walk the couple hundred of metres to the site. You should not have to wait too long for the next taxi to pass by.

Suna & Mashgha

These two pre-Islamic settlements on opposite banks of Wadi 'Adim are some 20 km to the south of Tarim. They are still waiting for further research.

'Inat

The graveyard of this town 19 km east of Tarim has a remarkable collection of impressive tombs, known as the Seven Domes, warranting a stop even if you are not allowed to enter the cemetery area.

Husn al-'Urr

This fort is about 35 km east of Tarim, on a hill in the middle of the main wadi. Probably dating from around the 1st century BC or 2nd century AD, it has reportedly been used for over 1000 years, abandoned in 1258 AD. There is enough left of the fortification and the cistern next to it for even a lay person to appreciate.

Qabr Nabi Allah Hud

This tomb, another 35 km to the east of Husn al-'Urr, is one of the most important places of pilgrimage in Wadi Hadhramawt. The town has been built next to the tomb housing the shrine of the pre-Islamic prophet, Hud. Next to the tomb a prayer hall has been built extraordinarily around a giant rock.

The amazing thing is that this finely kept town is actually inhabited for only three days a year, during the Ziyara pilgrimage which takes place between the 9th and 12th days of the Sa'ban month of the Muslim calendar.

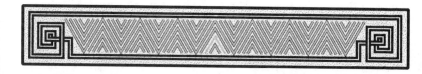

Al-Mahra

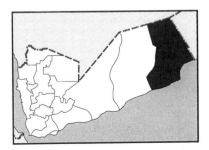

With only 110,000 inhabitants, most of whom are Bedouins, the distant region of al-Mahra is the least populated governorate in Yemen. It has no remarkable towns or major roads – just its small capital, al-Ghayda, and a couple of fishing ports. Al-Mahra is Yemen's most underdeveloped area. During the period of British colonial rule the region was formally under the power of the Sultan of Suqutra, although there was little to rule. Before and after the 1967 revolution the region was the scene of some military action when the Leftist movement tried (in vain) to expand its influence to the Dhofar area of western Oman.

With almost no agriculture, limited livestock herding and some fishing, living conditions here are hard. For decades the major source of income for the families of al-Mahra was remittances from relatives who had emigrated to Kuwait. The Gulf crisis of 1990/91 therefore hit this governorate particularly hard, forcing those emigrants to return home in their thousands, leaving their property behind.

You might be able to arrange a trip to al-Mahra if you are an anthropologist or a linguist who specialises in South Arabian people and dialects, otherwise it is unlikely you will visit the area. The original inhabitants of al-Mahra belong to the oldest tribes of South Arabia – you may still meet people speaking one of the three local dialects: *Mahric*, *Shahric* and *Suqutric*. All are Semitic dialects but they are so different from Arabic that they are considered to constitute a linguistic group of their own.

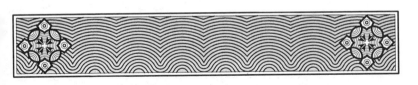

Glossary

'ayla – nuclear family

baksheesh – alms
bani – the sons of
bayt – house; extended family
bint al sahn – sweet bread (dessert)
bunn – coffee

dhabar – minibus
dhuma – nobleman's dagger

FLOSY – Front for the Liberation of Occupied South Yemen
funduq rakhi:s – cheap hotel
funduq/u:ti:l – hotel
futa – loincloth

hammam – bathroom, toilet, bathhouse

ingiz – private taxi

jambiya – tribesman's dagger

khubz – bread
khubz tawwa – ordinary fried bread

lahuh – festive pancake-like bread

mada'a – water pipe
madiff – rhythmical instrument
mafra – rhythmical instrument
mafraj – room with a view; top room of a tower house
maktab al-jawa:za:t – passport office
mamnu' – forbidden
manzar – attic, on top of a tower house
medina – old walled centre of any Islamic city
mihrab – decorated wall in mosque indicating direction of Mecca
mizmar – Yemeni wind instrument, reed pipes

muezzin – call for prayers

NLF – National Liberation Front

PDRY – People's Democratic Republic of Yemen
PGC – People's General Congress

qahwa – coffee
qat – mildly narcotic leaves commonly chewed in Yemen
qatat – plaster/rendering
qirsh – coffee-bean shells

rakats – cycles of prayer
rubta – small bundle of qat
ruti – bread bought from stores

salta – stew (national dish)
samsara – storehouse/inn of suq
sarwis – shared taxi
sawaqi – method of irrigation
shaykh – sheikh
shaykh as-suq – controller of the suq
shurba – cross between soup and stew

tabla – rhythmical instrument
takhrim – window decoration
tasri:h – tour permit

'ud – Yemeni instrument similar to a lute

wadi – seasonal river

YAR – Yemen Arab Republic
YSP – Yemen Socialist Party

Zabur architecture – technique of laying clay courses on top of each other, common in Sa'da

Index

TEXT

PLANET TALK
Lonely Planet's FREE quarterly newsletter

We love hearing from you and think you'd like to hear from us.

When...is the right time to see reindeer in Finland?
Where...can you hear the best palm-wine music in Ghana?
How...do you get from Asunción to Areguá by steam train?
What...is the best way to see India?

For the answer to these and many other questions read PLANET TALK.

Every issue is packed with up-to-date travel news and advice including:

- a letter from Lonely Planet founders Tony and Maureen Wheeler
- travel diary from a Lonely Planet author - find out what it's really like out on the road
- feature article on an important and topical travel issue
- a selection of recent letters from our readers
- the latest travel news from all over the world
- details on Lonely Planet's new and forthcoming releases

To join our mailing list contact any Lonely Planet office.

Also available: Lonely Planet T-shirts. 100% heavyweight cotton (S, M, L, XL)

LONELY PLANET PUBLICATIONS
Australia: PO Box 617, Hawthorn 3122, Victoria
tel: (03) 9819 1877 fax: (03) 9819 6459 e-mail: talk2us@lonelyplanet.com.au

USA: Embarcadero West, 155 Filbert St, Suite 251, Oakland, CA 94607
tel: (510) 893 8555 TOLL FREE: 800 275-8555 fax: (510) 893 8563
e-mail: info@lonelyplanet.com

UK: 10 Barley Mow Passage, Chiswick, London W4 4PH
tel: (0181) 742 3161 fax: (0181) 742 2772 e-mail: 100413.3551@compuserve.com

France: 71 bis rue du Cardinal Lemoine – 75005 Paris
tel: 1 46 34 00 58 fax: 1 46 34 72 55 e-mail: 100560.415@compuserve.com

World Wide Web: http://www.lonelyplanet.com/

LONELY PLANET TV SERIES & VIDEOS

Lonely Planet travel guides have been brought to life on television screens around the world. Like our guides, the programmes are based on the joy of independent travel, and look honestly at some of the most exciting, picturesque and frustrating places in the world. Each show is presented by one of three travellers from Australia, England or the USA and combines an innovative mixture of video, super-8 film, atmospheric soundscapes and original music.

Videos of each episode – containing additional footage not shown on television – are available from good book and video shops, but the availability of individual videos varies with regional screening schedules.

Video destinations include:
Alaska; the Arctic (Norway & Finland); Australia (Southeast); Baja California; Brazil; Chile & Easter Island; China (Southeast); Costa Rica; East Africa (Tanzania & Zanzibar); Ecuador & the Galapagos Islands; Great Barrier Reef (Australia); Indonesia; Israel & the Sinai Desert; Jamaica; Japan; La Ruta Maya (Yucatan, Guatemala & Belize); Morocco; North India (Varanasi to the Himalaya); Pacific Islands; Papua New Guinea; the Rockies (USA); Syria & Jordan; Turkey; Vietnam; Zimbabwe, Botswana & Namibia.

The Lonely Planet television series is produced by:
Pilot Productions
Duke of Sussex Studios
44 Uxbridge St
London W8 7TG
United Kingdom

Lonely Planet videos are distributed by:
IVN Communications Inc
2246 Camino Ramon
California 94583, USA

For further information on both the television series and the availability of individual videos please contact Lonely Planet.

Guides to Africa

Africa on a shoestring
From Marrakesh to Kampala, Mozambique to Mauritania, Johannesburg to Cairo – this guidebook ha
all the facts on travelling in Africa. Comprehensive information on more than 50 countries.

Central Africa - a travel survival kit
This guide tells where to go to meet gorillas in the jungle, how to catch a steamer down the Congo...eve
the best beer to wash down grilled boa constrictor! Covers Cameroun, the Central African Republi
Chad, the Congo, Equatorial Guinea, Gabon, São Tomé & Principe, and Zaïre.

East Africa - a travel survival kit
Detailed information on Kenya, Uganda, Rwanda, Burundi, eastern Zaïre and Tanzania. The latest editio
includes a 32-page full-colour Safari Guide.

Egypt & the Sudan - a travel survival kit
This guide takes you into and beyond the spectacular and mysterious pyramids, temples, tombs
monasteries, mosques and bustling main streets of Egypt and the Sudan.

Kenya - a travel survival kit
This superb guide features a 32-page 'Safari Guide' with colour photographs, illustrations and informa
tion on East Africa's famous wildlife.

Morocco - a travel survival kit
This thoroughly revised and expanded guide is full of down-to-earth information and reliable advice fo
every budget. It includes a 20-page colour section on Moroccan arts and crafts and information o
trekking routes in the High Atlas and Rif Mountains.

North Africa - a travel survival kit
A most detailed and comprehensive guide to the Maghreb – Morocco, Algeria, Tunisia and Libya. I
points the way to fascinating bazaars, superb beaches and the vast Sahara, and is packed with reliabl
advice for every budget. This new guide includes a 20-page full colour section on Moroccan arts an
crafts.

South Africa, Lesotho & Swaziland - a travel survival kit
Travel to southern Africa and you'll be surprised by its cultural diversity and incredible beauty. There'
no better place to see Africa's amazing wildlife. All the essential travel details are included in this guid
as well as information about wildlife reserves, and a 32-page full colour Safari Guide.

Trekking in East Africa
Practical, first-hand information for trekkers for a region renowned for its spectacular national parks an
rewarding trekking trails. Covers treks in Kenya, Tanzania, Uganda, Malawi and Zambia.

West Africa - a travel survival kit
All the necessary information for independent travel in Benin, Burkino Faso, Cape Verde, Côte d'Ivoire
The Gambia, Ghana, Guinea, Guinea-Bissau, Liberia, Mali, Mauritania, Niger, Nigeria, Senegal, Sierr
Leone and Togo. Includes a comprehensive section on traditional and contemporary music.

Zimbabwe, Botswana & Namibia - a travel survival kit
Exotic wildlife, breathtaking scenery and fascinating people...this comprehensive guide shows a wilde
older side of Africa for the adventurous traveller. Includes a 32-page colour Safari Guide.

Also available:
Swahili phrasebook, **Arabic (Egyptian)** phrasebook & **Arabic (Moroccan)** phrasebook

Guides to the Middle East

Arab Gulf States - a travel survival kit

The Arab Gulf States are surprisingly accessible and affordable with an astounding range of things to see and do – camel markets, desert safaris, ancient forts and modern cities to list just a few. Includes a comprehensive Arabic language section for the area. Covers travel in Bahrain, Kuwait, Oman, Qatar, Saudi Arabia and the United Arab Emirates.

Egypt & the Sudan - a travel survival kit

This guide takes you into and beyond the spectacular pyramids, temples, tombs, monasteries and mosques, and the bustling main streets of these fascinating countries to discover their incredible beauty, unusual sights and friendly people.

Iran - a travel survival kit

The first English-language guide to this enigmatic and surprisingly hospitable country written since the Islamic Revolution. As well as practical travel details the author provides background information that will fascinate adventurers and armchair travellers alike.

Israel - a travel survival kit

Detailed practical travel information is combined with authoritative historical references in this comprehensive guide. Complete coverage of both the modern state of Israel and the ancient biblical country.

Jordan & Syria - a travel survival kit

Two countries with a wealth of natural and historical attractions for the adventurous traveller...12th century Crusader castles, ruined cities, the ancient Nabatean capital of Petra and haunting desert landscapes.

Middle East on a shoestring

All the travel advice and essential information for travel in Afghanistan, Bahrain, Egypt, Iran, Iraq, Israel, Jordan, Kuwait, Lebanon, Oman, Qatar, Saudi Arabia, Syria, Turkey, United Arab Emirates and Yemen.

Turkey - a travel survival kit

This acclaimed guide takes you from Istanbul bazaars to Mediterranean beaches, from historic battlegrounds to the stamping grounds of St Paul, Alexander the Great, the Emperor Constantine and King Croesus.

Trekking in Turkey

Explore beyond Turkey's coastline and you will be surprised to discover that Turkey's variety of terrain makes for walks and hikes to suit every taste.

Also available:

Arabic (Egyptian) phrasebook and *Turkish* phrasebook.

Lonely Planet Guidebooks

Lonely Planet guidebooks cover every accessible part of Asia as well as Australia, the Pacific, South Americ
Africa, the Middle East, Europe and parts of North America. There are five series: *travel survival kits*, coverir
a country for a range of budgets; *shoestring guides* with compact information for low-budget travel in a maj
region; *walking guides*; *city guides* and *phrasebooks*.

Australia & the Pacific
Australia
Australian phrasebook
Bushwalking in Australia
Islands of Australia's Great Barrier Reef
Outback Australia
Fiji
Fijian phrasebook
Melbourne city guide
Micronesia
New Caledonia
New South Wales
New Zealand
Tramping in New Zealand
Papua New Guinea
Bushwalking in Papua New Guinea
Papua New Guinea phrasebook
Rarotonga & the Cook Islands
Samoa
Solomon Islands
Sydney city guide
Tahiti & French Polynesia
Tonga
Vanuatu
Victoria
Western Australia

North-East Asia
Beijing city guide
China
Cantonese phrasebook
Mandarin Chinese phrasebook
Hong Kong, Macau & Canton
Japan
Japanese phrasebook
Korea
Korean phrasebook
Mongolia
Mongolian phrasebook
North-East Asia on a shoestring
Seoul city guide
Taiwan
Tibet
Tibet phrasebook
Tokyo city guide

South-East Asi
Bali & Lombc
Bangkok city guid
Cambod
Indones
Ho Chi Minh City city guid
Indonesian phraseboc
Jakarta city guid
Jav
Lac
Lao phraseboc
Malaysia, Singapore & Brun
Myanmar (Burma
Burmese phraseboo
Philippine
Pilipino phraseboc
Singapore city guid
South-East Asia on a shoestrin
Thailar
Thailand travel atla
Thai phraseboc
Thai Hill Tribes phraseboc
Vietna
Vietnamese phraseboc

Middle East
Arab Gulf States
Egypt & the Sudan
Arabic (Egyptian) phrasebook
Iran
Israel
Jordan & Syria
Middle East
Turkey
Turkish phrasebook
Trekking in Turkey
Yemen

Afric
Africa on a shoestri
Central Afri
East Afri
Trekking in East Afric
Keny
Swahili phraseboc
Morocc
Arabic (Moroccan) phraseboc
North Afri
South Africa, Lesotho & Swazilar
West Afri
Zimbabwe, Botswana & Namit